CONTENTS

THE LIFE COURSE AND FAMILY PATTERNS

THE CRAFT OF FAMILY HISTORY

FAMILY HISTORY AND SOCIAL CHANGE

Preface

The *Journal of Family History* celebrated its tenth anniversary in 1986. Because the career of the *Journal* overlaps significantly with the development of the new field of family history and the *Journal* had had a major role in this development, we felt it would be appropriate to use the anniversary occasion to assess the current state of research and to consider new directions.

With the support of a grant from the National Endowment for the Humanities and Clark University, we convened an international conference at Clark University on November 14–17, 1985. Earlier versions of the essays in the present collection were first presented at the Clark conference. In addition to specific discussion sessions on each essay, the conference also included extensive consideration of future directions in the field, and a keynote lecture by Peter Laslett titled "The Historical Development of the Family In England and Western Europe."

While we were fortunate to have at the conference excellent representation for European, American, and Japanese family history, we acknowledge that we were not able to extend coverage to several areas of the world—such as other Asian countries, Africa, and South America—where family history research is now also being conducted. Similarly, in the original plan for the conference, we had also hoped to include essays on family law, the family economy, and the family's social space. The absence of more inclusive coverage in the present collection reflects, in part, the problem of schedule conflicts and workloads of potential contributors, and, in part, the slower pace of emerging research in the areas and on the topics not represented. Yet despite the fact that this collection is not exhaustive, we hope it will stimulate new directions of research, as well as new approaches in the areas already well developed.

We would like to thank the National Endowment for the Humanities for its support of the anniversary conference; Robert Wheaton, who served as associate editor of the *Journal* during its first nine years, for his collaboration in planning the conference; and the conference participants for their valuable contributions to the discussions and the present collection, and for complying with the rigorous editorial schedules.

Tamara K. Hareven
Editor

Andrejs Plakans
Associate Editor

FAMILY HISTORY AT THE CROSSROADS

Tamara K. Hareven

Since its emergence as a new field of research, the history of the family has excited the imagination of historians as well as scholars in other disciplines, especially in sociology, anthropology, psychology and economics. It has sparked new questions, and has driven scholars to search for new source materials and appropriate methodologies for their analysis. As part of the new social history, the history of the family has introduced the lives of ordinary people into historical research, and has opened windows to levels of historical experience long overshadowed by political and institutional history.

During the past twenty years, historians of the family have pursued a wide variety of topics, ranging from medieval peasants to industrial workers, and from courtship in pre-modern France to the life course in modern America (cf. Mitterauer and Sieder, 1982; Houlbrooke, 1984; Flandrin, 1979; Elder, 1974; Hareven, 1982). In all these areas, they have exploited not only traditional sources such as letters, diaries, government documents, and newspapers; but also previously unexplored sources, ranging from demographic records to wills and paintings, and from factory and hospital case records to photographs and material artifacts. These sources have all been woven into new tapestries of family life in the past. The patterns, however, are by no means complete yet, and the challenge of integrating them with the larger processes of social change is still before us.

The time has come, therefore, to assess twenty years of research in this field, and to identify the main goals of future research. In Charles Tilly's formulation (p. 325, this collection) the goal of family history is "to relate the concrete experience of living in families at various points in space and time to the larger social structures and processes." This in turn, is part of the larger goal of social history—"to connect small-scale life with great structures and transformations." In working toward this goal, historians of the family have reconstructed past patterns and experiences, have interpreted them in the context of their actual meaning to the people living through them, and have related them to the cultural values and constraints shaping people's attitudes and choices in different time periods.

The contributions of historical research on the family have thus consisted not only of providing a perspective of change over time in family behavior, but also in examining family behavior *within* specific time periods, in various social and cultural contexts. Family history research has thus contributed to examinations of diachronic changes, as well as to investigations of synchronic patterns with discrete time periods (Hareven, 1977).

As the field developed, family history succeeded not only in providing the missing link for understanding the relationship between individuals and social change. Findings in the field have actually led to the revision of some of the interpretations of the pace and meanings of the "grand" processes. Most notably, the historical evidence about family behavior has revised prevailing interpretations of industrialization and urbanization, and has challenged the premises of modernization theory (Anderson, 1971; Hareven, 1975, 1977a, 1978b, 1982). By denying a simple cause-and-effect relationship between industrialization and social change, research on the family has led to the questioning of the standard periodization in European and American history, and has opened up new questions about the "phasing" of historical change in various areas of social life (Wrigley and Schofield, 1981). It has led, in a word, to the rejection of simplistic linear interpretations of the process of social change.

Since its emergence two decades ago, the historical study of the family has undergone several important transformations. From a narrow focus on the family as a household unit at one or several points in time, research has moved to a consideration of the family as a process over the entire lives of its members. Similarly, there has occurred a move from the study of discrete domestic family or household structures to the nuclear family's interaction with the wider kinship group; and from the study of the family as a separate domestic unit to an examination of its interaction with the worlds of work, education, and correctional welfare institutions (Hareven, 1985).

More recently, the life-course approach has influenced historical research on the family greatly by introducing a dynamic, developmental dimension. It has led researchers to shift from a static cross-sectional examination of the family and the household to one which captures the complexity of individual and family change in the context of historical time. This developmental dimension has in turn required a focus on age and cohort comparisons in ways that link individual and family development to historical events (Elder, 1978a, 1978b; Hareven, 1978c; Vinovskis, 1977).

Assessing this rich harvest of the past twenty years poses the challenge of identifying the directions we should pursue in the future, in order to realize the original goals and promises of the field. In the following collection of essays, we raise methodological and substantive questions about the current state of research and about the nature of inquiry. The essays report on the state of the art in the authors' respective areas, and suggest future directions. In addition, Charles Tilly proposes new overall directions and reconsiderations of the craft, and Peter Laslett raises serious questions about the very nature and identity of family history.

I will examine the opportunities for future development and new directions in those areas where the most promising work has been undertaken recently—kinship, the life course, family strategies, and the grand themes of social change. The list is by no means exhaustive, but it does identify important current directions. In assessing these areas I will be guided by Charles Tilly's concepts of "reconstitution" and "linkages" (explained in his essay) as the two major underlying processes of research in family history.

KINSHIP

While initial research in family history focused almost exclusively on the household and on demographic processes, kinship has received increasing attention during the second decade. Initially, most studies of kinship were limited to rural communities, as in the work of Wrightson (1981) and Netting (1982), especially in the pre-industrial period and particularly in relation to inheritance. By contrast, Robert Wheaton's reconstruction of kinship patterns in seventeenth-century Bordeaux provides an exemplary model of one of the few studies of urban kinship in the early modern period (Wheaton, 1980).

For nineteenth- and twentieth-century urban populations, Anderson (1971) and Hareven (1978b, 1982) have demonstrated the central role of kin in organizing migration from rural areas to industrial cities, in facilitating settlement in the urban community, and in adaptation to new conditions. In my study of the textile workers in Rochester, New Hampshire, for example, I found that the workers' kinship networks effectively interacted with the modern, industrial system in the late nineteenth and early twentieth centuries and cushioned the adaptation of immigrant workers to new settings without excessively restricting their mobility. Relatives often acted as major brokers between the workers and the industrial corporations. They initiated the young and the new immigrants into the work process, technology, and industrial discipline and provided protection on the job (Hareven, 1975, 1978a, 1982). At the same time they socialized newly arrived immigrant workers to collective working-class behavior. Kinship networks were instrumental in serving the industrial employer as well as in advancing relatives' interests.

The salient role of kin also extended beyond the immediate community to encompass long-distance functions. To be sure, kinship ties were most effective in interaction with local institutions and in meeting immediate crises. Yet networks typically stretched over a region and were most useful when conditions failed in the local community during migration. The strength of locally based kinship networks lay in stability; the strength of extended networks was in their fluidity and continuous reorganization (Hareven, 1978a, 1982).

The important roles that kin fulfilled in their interactions with the workplace and modern corporations exemplify both the continuity in the functions of kin as mediators between the nuclear family and public institutions and their assuming new functions in response to the requirements of the industrial system. The behavior of kin as brokers between individuals, or between the nuclear family and institutions of industrial capitalism, needs further research in contexts other than the textile industry, such as educational and welfare agencies. While most studies of kinship are directed inwardly toward the nuclear family or the kinship network itself, research on kinship should also move outwardly from the nuclear family to environments such as the workplace, in order to understand the multiplicity of functions served by brokers.

As Andrejs Plakans and Robert Wheaton point out in their respective essays, research on kinship awaits development in several other directions. First, one needs to examine systematically the interaction between the household and the kin group, not only in Eastern Europe, as Plakans demonstrates, but also in other geographical settings. The very challenge of pursuing this effort requires a systematic definition of what the unit of analysis is—a process which family historians have had trouble with so far. Earlier studies of the household (Laslett and Wall, 1972) inadvertently caused a confusion between the residential family unit and the wider kinship group. In more recent studies, an imprecise or inconsistent use of the term "kinship" has led to a confusion as to who is included in this category. Sometimes the term is used to encompass only the nuclear family; other times, it includes the extended kinship group as well. A concerted effort among historians studying kinship is needed, therefore, in order to define categories more specifically and to achieve greater uniformity in terminology (Plakans, 1984).

In formulating such categories, it will be necessary to entertain two different approaches in the analysis of kinship and to achieve some clarity as to which one is being followed. As Charles Tilly observes in his essay, one approach, exemplified in Martine Segalen's essay, reconstructs the processes inherent in the society studied and develops the analytical categories from the inside; the other, as exemplified by Andrejs Plakans's work, applies social scientists' definitions of categories to the population patterns studied. Ideally, historians should follow both approaches simultaneously. The juxtaposition of processes internal to the community with structurally defined categories, should itself become an important empirical and conceptual challenge.

The application of the life-course approach also provides a new and yet unexplored dimension to the study of kinship, namely, the changing configurations of kin that individuals relate to over their lives. These configurations are formed and re-formed as individuals move over their life course. Their composition, their relationship to the nuclear family, and to each other change over time, as do their functions at different points in time. These configurations of kin, which resemble schools of fish in their movement, are referred to by sociologists of the life course as "convoys" or "conso-ciates" and are an important yet neglected topic of study. A systematic examination of these changing networks and their function over the life course would capture a more dynamic pattern of kin interaction.

The area of mutual assistance and obligation among kin, especially as they have changed over time, also requires further study. The question of how kin organized their reciprocal relations, and how individuals negotiated obligations and various exchange relations with kin over their life course has not been pursued since the opening up of this question by Anderson (1971) and its subsequent examination in another setting by Hareven (1982). The question of how and when the strong obligation of individual members to the kinship group has eroded, as increasing individualism in family relations emerged, has not yet been addressed. This question is fundamental, however, not only to the understanding of kin, but also to the whole issue of change in family relations over time.

Finally, in the study of kinship, as in other areas of research in the history of the family, we need to find a comfortable equilibrium between quantitative analysis and "thick description" (discussed in Robert Wheaton's essay), which assembles varieties of disparate qualitative evidence. Too often, the uses of quantitative and qualitative meth-odologies have been presented as mutually exclusive (Stone, 1981). Analysis of kinship would be served best, however, by merging the two into a coherent interpretation, contingent on the combination of quantifiable, behavioral patterns and qualitative data. We need to integrate structural patterns of kinship networks and quantitative data on kin relations with data deriving from the subjects' own perceptions of their kinship ties and relations.

THE LIFE COURSE

The life-course approach has introduced a dynamic dimension into the historical study of the family, and has moved analysis and interpretation from simplistic stages of the family cycle to an examination of individuals' and families' life transitions. Life transitions are determined by changes in family status and in accompanying roles, as well as by age. The influence of the life-course approach on family history has been most powerful in understanding three areas of family behavior: the synchronization of individual life transitions with collective family changes; the interaction of individual and collective family transitions with historical conditions; and the effect of earlier life transitions on later ones.

The emphasis on timing especially has led to an examination of the synchronization of individual with collective family transitions in the context of changing historical time. "Timing" takes into account the historical context defining the social circumstances and cultural conditions that affect the scheduling of life events, on both an individual and familial level (Elder, 1978b; Hareven, 1978c; Neugarten and Hagestadt, 1976; Riley, 1978; Vinovskis, 1977). Timing involves life transitions on both the nonfamilial and the familial levels in areas such as entering and leaving school, joining or leaving the labor force, migration, leaving or returning home, marriage and setting up an independent household, and, in the later years of life, movement out of active parenting into the "empty nest" and retirement.

Even though historians started to apply a life-course approach to the family about ten years ago, its use by family historians is still limited and subject to misunderstandings. "Life course" (Elder, 1978b) is still occasionally confused with "family cycle" (Cuisenier, 1977), and sometimes these terms are used interchangeably. The life course, however, differs considerably from the family cycle. While the family cycle is limited to stages of parenthood, the life course encompasses individual *and* family development in relation to each other. The family cycle uses a priori stages that are not always relevant to historical conditions; the life course is concerned with transitions from one stage to the next, or from one role to another, both on the individual and the familial level.

The life-course approach is, therefore, more dynamic than the family cycle, and examines a diversity of family patterns and modes of interaction. It has enabled historians of the family to capture the complexity of interaction between individual transitions and collective family goals, as both change over the individual's and the family's life. Thus the difference between the life course and the family cycle is not merely a difference in semantics, but also one in the interpretation of the interaction of individuals and the collective patterns of both their families of orientation and families of procreation over the course of their lives. That interaction between individuals and the family unit over time, and under changing historical conditions, is the very essence of the life-course approach.

Some scholars have also misunderstood the life-course approach to fit strictly individual career patterns, and have therefore questioned its utility in societies where there is a strong emphasis on family collectivity. In her essay, Martine Segalen, for example, disclaims the utility of the life-course approach for the study of peasants in nineteenth-century France, because of the collective character of peasant families during this time period. The dichotomy which Segalen creates here, however, does not fit the life-course approach because even under conditions of increasing individualism, such as the ones which Segalen describes in the later period of her communities, transitions of individuals do not become entirely individualistic—the problems of synchronizing individual and collective family moves continue to be present. Life-course analysis does not merely encompass individual transitions. Because of its emphasis on interaction and synchronization between individual and family, it helps us identify analytically the varying degrees of synchronization of individual members and family collectivity.

Segalen observes that the life-course approach is ill suited for the analysis of French peasant families because the "individual's choices are made by the older generation and careers are embedded within the household and controlled by the community" (p. 223). For that very reason, however, the life-course approach would be very effective for Segalen's communities, because it would reveal to us how life transitions are accomplished and timed under conditions of tight collective controls, and how individuals diverge from these controls. Segalen also claims that the life-course approach does not seem helpful for the investigation of kin in relation to marriage and inheritance. Both marriage and inheritance, however, are central to the life course and are the type of variables that the life-course measures. Even though the basic unit in life-course analysis is the individual, the analysis itself covers the temporal interdependence of that individual with other family members, both in the nuclear family and the kin group; the interdependence of the individual life course and the collective one of the family; and, finally, the interdependence of all these and the process of social change. As Morioka points out, even in Japanese society, which is still characterized by high collectivity in family ideology, the life-course approach helps identify the tension between the individual and the collective family, in a society in which family life is rapidly modernizing. As Elder suggests in his essay, one of the most promising future directions in life-course research is to link change over the life course with kinship and generational relations.

Application of the life-course approach to historical research on the family can also illuminate the relationship between *behavior* and *perception (mentalité)* over the life-course. While the actual timing of life transitions can be reconstructed from demographic records, perceptions of patterns of timing and their meaning to the individual undergoing them hinges upon an understanding of *mentalité*. How individuals perceived their timing in relation to family goals, how they negotiated family obligations, and how they interpreted the constraints and opportunities inherent in their timing in relation to those of other family members is an important, unexplored area of family life, and yet one central to the understanding of changing family dynamics in the context of social and economic conditions and cultural values. In the present collection, the first steps in these directions, taken for Canadian and Japanese family history in the essays by Morioka and by Landry and Legaré respectively, demonstrate the great potential in linking demographic patterns and cultural variables.

An effective application of the life-course approach to family history requires, however, the development of methodology that can capture the complexity of timing on all three levels: individual, familial, and historical. In utilizing the life-course approach, one needs to remember that the life course is in itself not an explanatory theory, nor a methodology. Rather it is a framework that draws attention to the complexity of these interactions. We need to develop, therefore, a methodology for the analysis of family life-course patterns, which is sensitive both to historical change and individual and family development.

In crafting such a methodology, we will have to grapple with the dearth of sources, especially with limited availability of longitudinal data. As Plakans has warned us, this problem is not unique to life-course analysis: when longitudinal data are not available, it is difficult if not impossible for historians to assess the duration and change of patterns identified as existing at one point in time. Despite the scarcity of longitudinal data, however, we have not yet even come close to exhausting the potential of life-course research, even when using cross-sectional data. Even where longitudinal data are absent, longitudinal patterns can be inferred from cross-sectional data if the questions are formulated with precision (Hareven, 1978c; Wall, Robin, and Laslett, 1983).

FAMILY STRATEGIES

Even though strategies and choices are implicit in the decision-making process of various family groups, there has been to date little systematic work on the strategies that families and individual members chart in relation to other institutions and changing social and economic conditions. A study of family strategies enables us to examine the interaction between, on the one hand, the social and economic constructions and external cultural values in the society which dictate these choices; and, on the other hand, the family members' values, to the extent that those values diverge from the external ones.

As several essays in the present collection suggest, an examination of strategies provides a key to the linkage and interaction between family patterns and larger social and economic processes such as migration (see Kertzer and Brettell, and also Brettell, 1986), the inheritance and management of family resources (see Gaunt, Segalen, Bouchard, and Cornell in this collection), and the world of work (Hareven, 1982; Scott and Tilly, 1975; Kertzer, 1984).

An understanding of strategies also illuminates the family's interaction with other social institutions. Family strategies guide the extent of cooperation or conflict between the family and institutions such as the church or schools. For example, David Herlihy in his essay comments on the emergence of the couple-centered family in medieval Europe as a result of a "fit" between the Catholic Church's introduction of codes of monogamy, and families' strategies to exercise closer control over inheritance through agnatic lineages. In an effort to maximize control over family resources and inheritance through a more strictly defined lineage, families cooperated with the Church, and accepted monogamy laws and prohibitions of incest (cf. also Goody, 1983).

On the other hand, in the case of the family's interaction with the emergent school system in Massachusetts, as described in the essay by Maris Vinovskis, family strategies and those of the school were less harmonious. In documenting the uneasy relationship between the family and the school in the transfer of educational functions from the former to the latter, Vinovskis juxtaposes the family's strategies with those of the school and illuminates the areas of conflict. In the case of the Massachusetts school system, as in the case of the family's interaction with the industrial system, the family did not respond blindly to these external institutional changes. Rather, its relationships with these institutions was guided by its own strategies.

Research on strategies, however, still remains wide open for systematic research and definitions. One important issue is: whose strategies are we actually observing? Historians of the family have often erred in the direction of treating the family as a monolithic unit, rather than distinguishing among the roles and positions of the various individual members within it. We need, therefore, to be concerned with the actual family decision-making process and with the imposition of such decisions on individual members.

Collective family strategies were not always in harmony with the strategies of individual members. For example, in areas such as inheritance, the timing of marriage, leaving home, and leaving school in order to start work, individual preferences and priorities may have differed considerably from those of the family. An examination of strategies also requires an understanding of tensions and conflicts within the family, behind the front of uniform strategies which the family might be projecting to the outside world.

In the case of industrialization, for example, historians have followed William Goode's (1963) challenge to revise the stereotype of the family as a passive agent in the process of industrialization. Yet, the reversal of the stereotype, and the conceptualization of the family as an active agent, can result in another simplistic stereotype. A study of family strategies in their interaction with the institutions of industrial capitalism, on the other hand, would help differentiate between those circumstances when the family is an active agent and those when it is on the receiving end of the grand changes (for example, under the impact of business cycles, depressions, and changing employment policies). In either case, the family charts its strategies in response to the structures, constraints, and opportunities which are dictated by these outside processes. The nature of the family's response to these circumstances, how it adjusts to change, and how it initiates change— in short, how it translates the import of these larger structural changes and demands to its own sphere, can be identified through an examination of strategies.

The implementation of this agenda hinges, as always, on the availability of adequate sources. Initially, historians have inferred strategies from quantitative, behavioral sources. For example, individual household census schedules were used to infer family strategies concerning women's labor force participation, or school attendance versus child labor (Modell and Hareven, 1978). Similarly migration strategies were inferred from quantitative data and family economic strategies were extrapolated from expenditure patterns in family budget data (Modell, 1978). As Laslett warns us, however, inferences about choices from behavioral statistical data can be misleading. In the absence of the type of rich ethnographic records available from certain societies, such as those used by Gaunt and Segalen in their essays, we are challenged to search more systematically for relevant data, and to integrate it with behavioral patterns.

THE FAMILY AND THE PROCESS OF SOCIAL CHANGE

The most important consensus in recent historical study of the family has formed around the effect of industrialization on the family. Historians now agree that industrialization did not bring about the characteristics of demographic behavior and family and household patterns previously attributed to it (Wrigley and Schofield, 1981; Wrigley, 1987). Some of the patterns associated with "modern" family behavior—family limitation, the spacing of children, a later age at marriage, a nuclear household structure—were actually evident before industrialization. As Laslett has pointed out and Herlihy has shown in his recent book (Herlihy, 1985), simple household structures can be traced back to the Middle Ages, thus defying any use of the "old reliable" grand processes as explanations for long-term changes in the family. Alternative explanations to the "old reliables" attribute the emergence of "new" family patterns to the commercial revolution in the sixteenth and seventeenth centuries. But such explanations still fall short of addressing comprehensively the origins of "modern" family behavior, as Laslett and Gaunt point out in their respective essays in the present collection.

On the basis of his analysis of the ethnographic literature in Nordic countries, David Gaunt postulates that major changes in family life which are usually associated with the impact of industrializations had emerged already in the eighteenth century: privacy in generational relations, a shift to the father-son dyad as the preferred system of land transfer, the separation of land ownership and household authority, and the use of the courts to solve family disputes. Gaunt does not offer, however, an explanation of what may have caused these changes.

The discovery of such patterns in earlier time periods and the increasing emphasis on continuity in family household patterns reaching back to the twelfth century, raise serious questions not only about the causes of change but about what the continuity actually was. While the emphasis on continuity—particularly in nuclear household structures in the preindustrial period—has challenged simplistic explanatory categories of industrialization, urbanization, and modernization, it has also tended to obscure important historical differences under the surface of similarities. For example, nuclear households in the preindustrial period were considerably different from contemporary ones in their membership and life-course configurations (Demos, 1970; Greven, 1970). Preindustrial households were larger in size both because of the number of children and the inclusion of boarders, servants, and other unrelated individuals. They also had very different configurations of membership over their life course because of later marriage, later child bearing, higher fertility, and lower life expectancy. Similarly, one could suspect that patterns of family life in the medieval period differed from those of the seventeenth- and eighteenth-century bourgeois family described by Philippe Ariès (and by Andrè Burguière in the present collection), and from our contemporary families. Thus the notion of the "emergence of modern family patterns" in the past challenges us to look underneath the external surfaces of form and organization in order to capture the substantive differences.

Historians and sociologists now agree that industrialization in itself did not cause the breakdown of traditional family patterns and that migration to urban industrial areas did not destroy traditional kinship ties. Following William Goode's (1963) assertion that the family was an active, rather than a passive agent in the process of industrialization, historical studies have provided documentation for the family's and kin group's active role in the process. This research, however, has called into question the idea that the family type most "fit" to interact with industrial capitalism was the nuclear family. Rather, recent historical research has shown that nuclear families embedded in extended reciprocal relations with those kin are most adaptable to the industrial system (And son, 1971; Hareven, 1978, 1982).

While rejecting the assumption that industrialization generated a new ty structure, historians agree that industrialization affected family function and the timing of family transitions. Many of these changes were no directly to industrialization but emerged as consequences of the restructuring of the economy and of increased urbanization following industrialization. There is general agreement that the most crucial change wrought by industrialization was the transfer of functions previously held by the family to other social institutions. As has often been pointed out, the preindustrial family served as a workshop, church, reformatory, school, and asylum (Demos, 1970). Over the past century and a half, these functions have become in large part the responsibility of other institutions. The household has been transformed from a place of production to a place of consumption, and the family's major purpose has become the nurturing of children. The family has withdrawn from the world of work, and the workplace has generally become nonfamilial and bureaucratic (Degler, 1980).

The family has turned inward, assuming domesticity, intimacy, and privacy as its major characteristics as well as ideals, and the home is viewed as a retreat from the outside world (Cott, 1977; Degler, 1980; Welter, 1966). The commitment to the domesticity of the family by itself is the outcome of a long historical process that commenced in the early modern period in Western Europe, a process characterized by Philippe Ariès as follows: "The modern family ... cuts itself off from the world and opposes to society the isolated groups of parents and children. All the energy of the group is expended in helping the children to rise in the world, individually and without any collective ambition, the children rather than the family" (1962:404).

By contrast, writes Ariès, the premodern family "was distinguished ... by the enormous mass of sociability which it retained" (1962:404). Both family and the household were the foundation of the community. Reacting to economic growth and industrialization, the family became a specialized unit, its tasks limited primarily to consumption, procreation, and child-rearing. The contracting of family functions and the resulting privatization of family life marked the emergence of the modern family; the family became nuclear, intensive, inward-turning, and child-centered at the expense of sociability and greater integration with the community.

The question is still open, however, as to what effect the transfer of many of the family's former functions, combined with shrinking household membership, has had on the internal dynamics and the quality of family relationships. Ariès claims that these developments weakened the family's adaptability and deprived children of the opportunity to grow up in a flexible environment with a variety of role models to follow. To date, however, historians have done little to document and to explore closely the effect of these changes on internal relations within the family.

One must remember that Ariès wrote about bourgeois families, and that his followers tended to generalize to the entire society on the basis of the middle class (a common problem especially in American family history). The absence of consensus in this area quite naturally raised the problem of a typology of change. Since the family changes more slowly than other social institutions do, and since, as has been shown, the family does not passively respond to change but also generates it, it has been difficult for historians to develop a typology of change in the family over time. Historians attempting to date the emergence of the "modern family" in the West place it somewhere between 1680 and 1850. Ariès and Lawrence Stone have singled out the late seventeenth and early early eighteenth centuries, while Edward Shorter dates its emergence in the late eighteenth and early nineteenth centuries. Stone holds that the "closed domestic nuclear \mily" emerged sometime between 1640 and 1800. American historians generally date its emergence in the late eighteenth or early nineteenth century (Ariès, 1962; Degler, 1980; Shorter, 1976; Stone, 1977).

Following in Ariès's footsteps, Stone and Shorter have focused on the rise of affective individualism as the major criterion of the modern family. They generally agree that the modern family is privatized, nuclear, domestic, and child-centered and that its crucial base is the sentimental bond between husband and wife and between parents and children. They have all pointed to the weakening influence of extended kin, friends, and neighbors on family ties and to an isolation of the family from interaction with the community. Marriages are based on "emotional bonding" between husband and wife and are a result of personal and sexual attraction rather than of alliances between sets of parents or lineages. Stone, as to some some extent does Degler, sees the weakening of bonds with kin as an inevitable consequence of this type of family.

While there has been general agreement on these characteristics of modern family life, there is some disagreement and, at times, lack of clarity as to which class first initiated these changes. The scholars discussed above follow basically a "trickle down" theory. Ariès, Stone, and, more implicitly, Degler view the bourgeoisie and the gentry as the vanguard, while Shorter has assigned a crucial role to peasants and workers. For American society, Degler places the origins of the "modern family" in the middle class, although he generalizes from the experience of the middle class to the entire society. The most important aspect still absent from historical studies of long-term changes in the family over time is more systematic distinctions between social classes and a more detailed understanding of the historical process by which modes of family behavior were adopted by other classes, if indeed that was the case, and, conversely, of what class differences have survived (Ariès, 1962; Degler, 1980; Shorter, 1976; Stone, 1977). These studies of broad change over time also hold in common their acceptance of ideological and cultural factors as the major explanations of change in family behavior rather than social and economic ones. Shorter is the only one among them to cite "market capitalism" as the major cause for the emergence of family sentiment, but, as his critics have pointed out, he does not identify an explicit connection between these economic forces and the transformations of family relations (Tilly and Cohen, 1982).

Stone offers a "multicausal" explanation rather than one single factor, but he tends to favor the predominance of cultural and ideological explanations over social and economic ones, as does Degler (Degler, 1980; Stone, 1981). This is precisely where the most fundamental disagreements about social change and the family are likely to emerge among historians. Not only is there a lack of consensus over the relative importance of ideological or socioeconomic causes in long-term changes in the family, but there is also a greater need to know how the changes took place and what the nature of interaction among these different factors was. The "grand" explanations of change are vulnerable particularly in some of these studies' claims for linear change over time.

The characterization of what was typical behavior for the middle class modern family does not necessarily hold true for other classes. In the United States, for example, there has not been sufficient research over time to identify specific differences between middle class, working class, black and immigrant families. There is, however, sufficient evidence to suggest that privacy, child-centeredness, affective individualism, and isolation from extended kin, which emerged as characteristic traits of urban middle class families—carries of the modern family type—were not necessarily typical of other classes and ethnic and racial groups. Among working class and ethnic families, some preindustrial family characteristics have persisted, although in modified form (Hareven, 1982; Scott and Tilly, 1975).

The realization that historical changes in the family have not taken place uniformly throughout society has led historians to react against a simplistic, linear interpretation of change and to focus instead on research that is carried out on a synchronic level, examining family interaction with societal processes and institutions within discrete historical contents ("reconstruction," to use Charles Tilly's term). While such work has already helped us to revise earlier generalizations, it must still be integrated into a more systematic pattern ranging over a longer historical period ("linkage": Tilly).

ASSESSMENT

As we stand at the crossroads of research in family history we need not lose sight of the original goals. Charles Tilly's formulation of the characteristics of social history also fits family history: "the means of detecting ordinary people's experiences and describing large structural changes; the actual assessment of that experience; the identity and character and causal priority of the relevant structural changes" (see pp. 322, this collection). While much has been achieved in the first two areas, a formidable agenda is still awaiting us in the third. The challenges before us include thematic, methodological, and conceptual directions. One direction, expressed in most of the essays of this collection and by Stone (1981), is to pursue topics which have not received sufficient attention, and to carry existing ones in new directions. In the former category one could list numerous examples, such as the family's relationship to social space; and a more systematic study of the family in relation to religion, the state, and the legal system. As suggested above, further expansion is needed in the areas of kinship, the life course and family strategies, especially where the family's interaction with other institutions is concerned.

A second direction is that of achieving more systematic linkages between various aspects of family patterns and processes: for example, a closer integration of the study of demographic patterns with household structure and internal family dynamics, as both Laurel Cornell and Akira Hayami suggest in their essays on Japan; a closer integration of the study of the household with kin outside the household, as Plakans suggests for Eastern Europe; and a more careful linkage of household patterns with migration, as Kertzer and Brettell suggest.

From a methodological and conceptual point of view also, the agenda before us is rich in its diversity and challenge. The recurring issues running through all historical research on the family concern linking quantitative behavioral data with qualitative analysis of perceptions (*mentalité*), and constructing longitudinal patterns from cross-sectional data. Initially, some critics of the new social history and of family history posed false dychotomies between quantitative behavioral and qualitative data. These are not mutually exclusive or conflicting approaches. Ideally, family history should integrate the two. There is also, as Louise Tilly suggests in her essay, a mediating role for family history: as historians of women analyze the interactions between women's lives and work and larger socioeconomic processes, the steps of that analysis are likely to lead through the institution of the family.

The methodological agenda includes as well rigorous definitions of concepts and terms used. For example, the reoccurring reference to "cultural values" in many writings on family history, including some of the essays in this collection, challenges us to define what is meant by "values" more precisely and to understand how these general values in the society interact with specific family values among different subgroups. The anthropologically oriented essays in this collection (Kertzer and Brettell, and Segalen) emphasize the importance of cultural values in shaping and dictating family behavior. Kertzer and Brettell provide a specific list of values in Iberian society, such as male honor, which they use as an explanation for family structure and inheritance patterns; and Burguière draws effectively on cultural values to explain the emergence of the couple in France. But we still lack definitions of "cultural values" for other historical studies of the family, where the term is used without defining what it entails.

Similarly, there is a need to define what Charles Tilly calls "coherent social units" for the study of the history of family and kinship. Both Daniel Scott Smith and Tilly urge us to depart from some of the traditional analytical categories. Smith proposed to explain the early decline in fertility in the United States by studying the principal "action-groups"—religious, ethnic and economic—instead of the usual categories of class, ethnicity, and religion. He suggests that the use of action groups would avoid the circular reasoning that allows Yankees to have low fertility because they are "modern" and for their modernity to be illustrated by their practice of "family limitation."

Where analysis of timing is concerned, Charles Tilly proposes that we substitute time sequences for age categories. If we follow this strategy we would escape the pitfalls of the reification of age as an explanatory variable. As Tilly suggests, timing and synchronization could be best captured by examining sequences and time gaps in statuses and roles of family members, rather than strictly through mechanical age categories. Proposals such as those by Smith and Tilly can potentially lead us not only to new types of analysis, but to a reformulation of the questions we ask. The danger of following these recommendations exclusively is, however, in replacing one approach by another, when, in fact, as Glen Elder suggests in his essay, we should expand our methodology by using both approaches: calendar time (as expressed in age variables) and event sequence. The same would hold true for Smith's proposal. If we strictly replace ethnic group, religious and class explanations for fertility and family behavior by "action group" organization, we would be losing an important explanatory variable, particularly for the behavior of people who are not included in "action groups."

Another area to consider at the crossroads is that of regional or national comparison. Many of the generalizations about family behavior in the past were hammered out at the expense of cross-national and regional differences. The question of uniqueness of family patterns in the West, or of American versus European patterns, still remains a pressing and open one. The great internal diversity of family patterns within each country defies any comparison with national units. As the essays in this volume suggest, internal differences even within regions (Iberia, Eastern Europe), defy any simple generalizations. The problem remains, therefore, how to achieve such comparisons given the great disparities within regions. In this respect, Laurel Cornell's attempt in the present collection to test John Hajnal's model of marriage in Japan, suggests an imaginative way of examining conceptual model derived from one society in another.

The question of the family's relationship to social change still remains wide open. When the historical study of the family first emerged, it drew its vitality and motivation from the need to link family patterns to the community and to larger social processes in order to explain social change. That original impetus to understand the role of the family in the process of social change was shared by the pioneer generation of family historians and endowed the historical study of the family with its initial depth and energy.

The major challenge still is one of doing justice to this goal by achieving the proper equilibrium between the constitution of time-specific family patterns and their linkage to larger social processes. The manner in which most of these linkages were carried out to date can be compared to strings of pearls. What we need to do now is to integrate each string into the interpretative tapestry of social change. The string-of-pearls model is one of a linear sequence of change over time; the integrated tapestry model is one of intertwining of time- and locality-specific family patterns with larger social structures and processes. This model implies the acceptance of complexity both in the family patterns and in the larger processes into which they are integrated. It also represents a rejection of simple linear models of change, whether in family history or social history in general. It advocates, instead, an interaction between many layers of social activity inside the family and in the larger society.

REFERENCES

Anderson, Michael. 1971. *Family Structure in Nineteenth-Century Lancashire.* Cambridge: Cambridge University Press.

Ariès, Philippe. 1962. *Centuries of Childhood: A Social History of Family Life.* New York: Vintage.

Brettell, Caroline B. 1986. *Men Who Migrate, Women Who Wait: Population and History in a Portuguese Parish.* Princeton: Princeton University Press.

Cott, Nancy F. 1977. *The Bonds of Womanhood: Woman's Sphere in New England 1780-1835.* New Haven, CT.: Yale University Press.

Cuisenier, Jean, ed. 1977. *The Family Life Cycle in European Societies.* The Hague.

Degler, Carl N. 1980. *At Odds: Women and the Family in America From the Revolution to the Present.* New York: Oxford University Press.

Demos, John. 1970. *A Little Commonwealth: Family Life in Plymouth Colony.* New York: Oxford University Press.

Elder, Glen H., Jr. 1974. *Children of the Great Depression: Social Change In Life Experience.* Chicago: University of Chicago Press.

_____ 1978a. "Approaches to Social Change and the Family." Pp. 1-38 in John Demos and S.S. Boocock, eds., *Turning Points: Historical and Sociological Essays On the Family.* Chicago: Chicago University Press.

_____. 1978b. "Family History and the Life Course." Pp. 17-64 in Tamara Hareven, ed., *Transitions: The Family and the Life Course in Historical Perspective.* New York: Academic Press.

Flandrin, Jean-Louis. 1979. *Families in Former Times: Kinship, Household, and Sexuality.* Cambridge: Cambridge University Press.

Goode, William J. 1963. *World Revolution and Family Patterns.* New York: Oxford University Press.

Goody, Jack. 1983. *The Development of the Family and Marriage in Europe.* Cambridge: Cambridge University Press.

Greven, P. 1970. *Four Generations: Population, Land, and Family in Colonial Andover, Massachusetts.* Ithaca, NY: Cornell University Press.

Hareven, Tamara K. 1975. "Family Time and Industrial Time: Family and Work in a Planned Corporation Town, 1900-1924." *Journal of Urban History* 1:365-389.

_____. 1977. "Family Time and Industrial Time." *Daedalus* 106: 57-70.

_____. ed. 1977. *Family and Kin in Urban Communities, 1700-1930.* New York: New Viewpoints.

_____. 1978a. "Cycles, Courses, and Cohorts: Reflections on the Theoretical and Methodological Approaches to the Historical Study of Family Development." *Journal of Social History* 12(1):97-109.

_____. 1978b. "The Dynamics of Kin in an Industrial Community." Pp. 151-182 in John Demos and S.S. Boocock, eds., *Turning Points: Historical and Sociological Essays On the Family.* Chicago: Chicago University Press.

_____. 1978c. *Transitions: The Family and the Life Course in Historical Perspective*. New York: Academic Press.

_____. 1982. *Family Time and Industrial Time*. New York Cambridge University Press.

_____. 1985. "Historical Change in the Family and the Life Course: Implications For Child Development." Pp. 8–23 in A.B. Smuts and J.W. Hagen, eds., *History and Research In Child Development*. Chicago: University of Chicago Press.

Hareven, Tamara K., and John Modell. 1980. "Family Patterns." Pp. 345–354 in S. Thernstrom, ed., *Harvard Encyclopedia of American Ethnic Groups*. Cambridge, MA: Harvard University Press.

Herlihy, David. 1985. *Medieval Households*. Cambridge, MA: Harvard University Press.

Houlbrooke, Ralph A. 1984. *The English Family 1450–1700*. London and New York: Longman.

Kertzer, David. 1984. *Family Life in Central Italy 1880–1910: Sharecropping, Wage Labor, and Coresidence*. New Brunswick, NJ: Rutgers University Press.

Laslett, Peter, and Richard Wall, eds. 1972. *Household and Family in Past Time*. Cambridge: Cambridge University Press.

Mitterauer, Michael, and Reinhard Sieder. 1982. *The European Family*. Oxford: Basil Blackwell.

Modell, John. 1978. "Patterns of Consumption, Acculturation, and Family Income Strategy in Late Nineteenth-Century America." Pp. 206–244 in Tamara Hareven and Maris A. Vinovskis, eds., *Family and Population In Nineteenth Century America*. Princeton: Princeton University Press.

Modell, John, and Tamara K. Hareven. 1978. "Transitions: Patterns of Timing." Pp. 245–260 in Tamara K. Hareven, ed., *Transitions: The Family and Life Course in Historical Perspective*. New York: Academic Press.

Netting, Robert McC. 1982. *Balancing On an Alp: Ecological Change and Continuity In a Swiss Mountain Community*. Cambridge: Cambridge University Press.

Neugarten, B., and G.O. Hagestad. 1976. "Age and the Life Course." Pp. 35–65 in R.H. Binstock and E. Shanas, eds., *Handbook of Aging and the Social Sciences*. New York: Van Nostrand.

Plakans, Andrejs. 1984. *Kinship In the Past: An Anthropology of European Family Life 1500–1900*. Oxford: Basil Blackwell.

Riley, M.W. 1978. "Aging, Social Change, and the Power of Idea." *Daedalus* 108: 35–52.

Scott, Joan W., and Louise A. Tilly. 1975. "Women's Work and Family in Nineteenth-Century Europe." *Comparative Studies In Society and History* 17:319–323.

Shorter, Edward. 1976. *The Making of the Modern Family*. New York: Basic Books.

Stone, Lawrence. 1981. "Family History in the 1980s." *Journal of Interdisciplinary History* 12: 51–57.

_____. 1977. *The Family, Sex, and Marriage In England 1500–1800*. New York: Harper & Row.

Tilly, Louise A., and M. Cohen. 1982. "Does the Family have a History?" *Social Science History* 6: 181–199.

Vinovskis, Maris A. 1977. "From Household Size to the Life Course: Some Observations on Recent Trends in Family History." *American Behavioral Scientist* 21: 265–267.

Wall Richard, Jean Robin, and Peter Laslett, eds., 1983. *Family Forms in Historical Europe*. Cambridge: Cambridge University Press.

Welter, B. 1966. "The Cult of True Womanhood, 1820–1860." *American Quarterly* 18: 151–174.

Wheaton, Robert. 1980. "Affinity and Descent in Seventeenth-Century Bordeaux." Pp. 111–134 in Robert Wheaton and Tamara K. Hareven, eds., *Family and Sexuality in French History*. Philadelphia: University of Pennsylvania Press.

Wrightson, Keith. 1981. "Household and Kinship in Sixteenth Century England." *History Workshop Journal* 12.

Wrigley, E.A. 1987. *People, Cities, and Wealth: The Transformation of Traditional Society*. Oxford: Basil Blackwell.

Wrigley, E.A., and R.S. Schofield. 1981. *The Population History of England, 1541–1871: A Reconstruction*. Cambridge, MA: Harvard University Press.

Families, Ideas, and Institutions

THE FAMILY AND RELIGIOUS IDEOLOGIES IN MEDIEVAL EUROPE

David Herlihy

ABSTRACT: *The medieval Christian Church was slow in developing a comprehensive theology or canon law of marriage, but it did establish certain principles of great significance in social life. Sexual morality was the same for both sexes, all classes and all nations. Marriage was monogamous, and close or incestuous marriages were forbidden. A uniform sexual morality worked to create uniform or commensurable household units. The requirement of monogamy and the incest prohibition prevented powerful males from monopolizing women. And monogamy and a stricter sexual morality were preconditions for the formation, from the eleventh century, of agnatic lineages. Finally, religious writers of the period, particularly the authors of saints' lives, made frequent use of familial images. The article contends that these images can be used in investigating the emotional life of medieval families.*

The histories of medieval religion and of the family intersect at so many points that we need a clear analytical framework with which to guide our discussion. To begin with, the objects of our inquiry are the medieval Christian religion and the Christian family. Space and the author's competence preclude an examination of family and religion in Byzantium, in Islam, or in medieval Jewry, in spite of the interest of recent work in these areas.[1] Nor can I consider in any depth the currently de-

bated issue of what was the true domain of Christianity in medieval society.[2] Was it limited to a tiny elite of clergy and literate laymen, while the unlettered masses followed a folk religion with its origins lost in Indo-European antiquity? We assume

David Herlihy is Barnaby Conrad and Mary Critchfield Keeney Professor and Professor of History at Brown University. His most recent book is Medieval Households, *published in 1985 by Harvard University Press.*

here that the Christian religion, and its variants in the form of heresies, governed marriage and family life in the Middle Ages. There is no evidence, as far as I can judge, that folk religion ever challenged the precepts regarding marriage proposed by the established Church, or ever reached the status of recognition and fear as a formal heresy.

As our analytical framework, I shall use the distinction common in the social sciences between performance and structure. Performance is action and event, or, in a historical context, the record of events. Structure is everything that makes possible, supports or affects action and event. It includes a community's natural surroundings, from stable lands to unstable weather. The characteristics of the community itself—its size; distribution of members across space, and by sex and age; their health—are similarly parts of structure. So also are its laws, customs, attitudes, values and ideologies. Structures of course are themselves changing constructs, and occasionally they echo and reinforce events, sometimes absorbing and transforming them into laws, customs and rituals. But they alter only slowly, and their relative immobility gives them high visibility in the historical record. The analysis of structure does not allow us to organize our observations into causes and effects; but it does make more understandable the complex happenings of history.

In this article, I seek to filter out one element of the structure of the medieval world, religion, and to examine how it interacted with performance, specifically marriages and domestic organization. Are there discernible some reciprocal influences between religious life and domestic life in the Middle Ages?

We look first at medieval religion, and then at the medieval family.

RELIGION

What did the fathers and doctors of the ancient and medieval Church think about the family?[3] The answer must be, not a great deal, in both meanings of the phrase. Not really until the twelfth century did the Church develop a comprehensive canon law, and an accompanying theology, of marriage. Before then, secular law, Roman legislation or the barbarian codes, had directed the behavior even of Christians in regard to marital and domestic issues. It is striking to observe that the sixth-century *Corpus Iuris Civilis* of the Emperor Justinian still permits divorce, as Roman law had always done; this Christian emperor was governing a Christian state, and yet he did not feel compelled to revise the traditional law of marriage.[4] The Church limited its interventions in marital matters to questions of sin and of penitence. Its appeal did not reach beyond the private consciences of Christians.

ATTITUDES AND ETHICS

This long-standing indifference to most questions of marital and family life surely reflects the dominant ascetic temperament of the patristic and early medieval Church. Questions of contract, of dowry and bridewealth, of inheritance—these were secular issues, and the true kingdom of God was not of this world. Then too, the Christian fathers looked upon the state of matrimony as distinctly inferior to virginity and even to widowhood. St. Jerome scores the relative value of these three states: virginity rates 100 points, widowhood 60, and wedlock only 30. "I praise weddings, I praise marriage," he writes, "but because for me they produce virgins."[5] The fathers saw little value in those two traditional functions of households—production and reproduction.

Production implied involvement in material things. Reproduction, in the patristic view of the world, was, strictly speaking, not needed.

In lauding virginity over marriage, the fathers had to face an embarrassing rebuttal. If all Christians adopted the preferred state of virginity, would not the Church quickly disappear? Augustine, for one, feigns indifference. This would be altogether a good thing; it would indicate that the roster of predestined saints had been filled, and the number of fallen angels replaced; like stars falling from the heavens, it would portend that history was nearing its term. "The coming of Christ," he affirms, "is not served by the begetting of children."[6]

The fathers saw no need for the further expansion of the human race, but they still insisted that every act of sexual intercourse between married persons be open to procreation. Here again, Augustine was the chief formulator of what would become the official norm. John T. Noonan, in his valuable history of contraception in Catholic thought and discipline, believes that Augustine was here reacting against the Manicheanism of his youth (Noonan, 1965). The Manichees, opposed to the multiplication of material bodies, minions of the god of darkness, allegedly considered contraception a meritorious act. Whatever the accuracy of this view, the Catholic Church has retained to this day an essentially Augustinian view of the uses of sex within marriage.

In giving low prestige to procreation, the Christian fathers reflect a cultural attitude which was common among pagans too. This was the sense that the world was already excessively crowded with people, and could contain no more.[7] Christians too need rear few children, but they must train them conscientiously. Parents and teachers must suppress the promptings of concupiscence within the growing child through harsh discipline. The patristic (and especially Augustinian) theory of concupiscence assured the survival under Christian auspices of that cruel principle of ancient schooling: "no progress without pain."[8]

Moreover, there is within the Christian tradition a strain of suspicion concerning family ties. The claims of kin might compete with the claims of God. "He who loves father or mother more than me," Jesus warns, "is not worthy of me; and he who loves son or daughter more than me is not worthy of me" (Matthew 11.37–38). Numerous medieval saints enter the religious life over the adamant opposition of their families. St. Francis defies his father before the bishop of Assisi, strips off his clothes, and hands them back. He will no longer address Pietro Bernardone as father; only God in heaven deserves that title (Englebert, 1965:36). The mother and brothers of Thomas Aquinas kidnap him, hold him prisoner in a castle for two years, and send a "lusty girl" to tempt him, so that he will lay aside the habit of the Dominican Order (Foster, 1959:28). Catherine of Siena warns her correspondents, particularly women, against excessive attachment to husband and children.[9] These are the things of this life, not the things of God.

UNIFORMITY AND PERMANENCE

And yet, in spite of indifference and even wariness toward the family, its needs and its claims, the patristic and early medieval Church did develop some general principles of great significance in the future. The fathers affirmed that sexual morality had to be the same for both sexes, and for all nationalities and social classes, "because," as Paul says, "with God there is no respect of person" (Romans 2.11). "Una lex de mulieribus et viris," says Jerome, "there is one law for women and for men."[10] Moreover, the union of husband and wife was both privileged and permanent. Jesus himself cites with approval the text from Genesis: "Wherefore a man shall leave father and mother, and shall cleave to his wife: and they shall be two in one flesh" (Matthew 19.5). Paul develops an extended analogy between the conjugal union and the relationship of Christ to the Church (Ephesians 5.21–33). Drawing inspiration from all these texts, Augustine attributes three "goods" to marriage, *fides*, *proles*, *sacramentum*, fidelity, offspring, and permanent union.[11] Marriage had to be indissoluble, even as the union of Christ and the Church. This Augustinian analogy—husband is to wife as Christ is to Church—becomes the basis for the Church's rejection of divorce. The union of Christ and the Church, and its earthly analogue, the marriage of husband and wife, were perforce dissoluble.[12] Consistent with his view of marriage, Paul advocates a kind of ethical reciprocity among all household members. Roman law, by its famous doctrine of the *patria potestas*, had made the father a despot over the family. Paul rather emphasizes the father's obligations. He is ethically bound to love his wife as his own body, and he ought not nag his children. Paul draws domestic relations between husband and wife, parents and children, masters and slaves, fully into the domain of Christian consciousness and conscience. The household becomes a domain of intense moral relationships.

INCEST

A final area in which Christian teachings exerted a profound influence was eligibility for marriage. The Church accepted the requirements of Roman law concerning age of marriage (twelve completed years

for girls and fourteen for boys) and sexual maturity and potency. But it greatly expanded the incest prohibitions characteristic not only of Roman but also of ancient Jewish law. Roman law had allowed first cousins to marry, who were related by four degrees of kinship in Roman count. The early medieval western Church extends the prohibition to the full seven degrees. Already the Council of Toledo in 527 and later the Council of Rome in 721 declared that if a man and a woman even suspected that they were related by blood, they could not marry.[13] The Church was comparably rigorous in prohibiting the marriage of affines. Finally, the spiritual relationship assumed by the sponsor toward the recipient at baptism or confirmation also precluded their marriage.

Jack Goody's recent study of family and marriage in medieval Europe examines as one of its principal themes the incest prohibition of the western Church (Goody, 1983). The great service of this book is that Goody, from his knowledge of many cultures, is able to show historians that the medieval western incest prohibition is extraordinarily broad, perhaps unique in human experience. He also tries to explain why the Church was so opposed to close marriages. In his view, great lay property owners sought to pursue an "heirship strategy" based on close marriages to prevent the dispersion of their landed holdings. The incest prohibition obstructed this strategy. Prohibited from marrying blood relatives, great property owners would often not marry at all. Childless and heirless persons were more likely than others to bequeath their properties to the Church. The incest prohibition is thus linked with the Church's desire to increase its landed endowment.

The argument is ingenious, but not in the final analysis convincing. It would be difficult to show from the thousands of surviving donations to churches that the donors were childless in any significant number. No contemporary hints at or alludes to this rather devious strategy. The Church needed personnel as well as property, and its leaders were drawn from the same class of wealthy property owners from whom donations might be expected. Would the Church have wished them childless, and its own pool of potential leaders reduced? Moreover, when an offspring entered the religious life, he or she almost always brought property to the Church, as a kind of spiritual dowry. It is not at all certain that the strategy Goody describes would have had the results he attributes to it. I shall make further comments on the incest prohibition (and suggest a reason why the Church may have favored it) later in this essay.

MODELS

The body of ecclesiastical teachings concerning marriage formed the legal and religious model of marriage during the Middle Ages. The word "model" has been much used in the recent literature, at times, in my mind, inappropriately. Georges Duby, for example, identifies two models of marriage in twelfth-century France (Duby, 1978, 1979, 1981, 1983a, 1983b). One was based on the Church's rule of monogamy and its prohibition of divorce and remarriage, bigamy and incest. The second, associated with the lay aristocracy, allowed divorce and remarriage, and incestuous unions, whenever the good of the lineage required such actions. The "modern marriage" which Duby believes took shape in northern France by the thirteenth century was a fusion of and compromise between these two formerly competitive models.

Duby's studies provide a vivid and valuable picture of marriages within the northern French aristocracy in the twelfth century, but his analysis seems to confuse two quite different kinds of models. These can be either prescriptive or descriptive. A prescriptive model is a set of rules or recommendations, which may or may not be respected. The apostolic exhortation, *Familiaris consortio*, which Pope John Paul II issued in 1980, presents a model of this sort, but it could hardly be called a description of modern marriage. A descriptive model, on the other hand, is a generalized portrayal of actual behavior, and is commonly utilized in the social sciences. Now, the ecclesiastical model of medieval marriage, described by Duby, is incontrovertibly prescriptive. But the lay model is just as surely descriptive, as it is constructed out of chronicle accounts of elite behavior. Nowhere is it suggested that the French lay aristocracy was bent on establishing norms for others to follow. Duby treats the two types of model as the same, and this clouds his analysis. To say that the two fused seems only to mean that behavior eventually influenced the norms that governed it, as it often does.

FAMILIES

How did these teachings affect this history of the medieval family? We must first, as best we can, recapitulate that history. There are three areas of domestic life in which changes across the Middle Ages seem especially pronounced (Herlihy, 1985). The first touches upon the internal structure of families and households. In the slave-holding societies of antiquity, households differed so greatly across society that they were never treated, whether by policy makers or by social theorists, as commensurable units. From about the year 700, medieval households display much greater uniformity. The domestic living arrangements of the medieval rich, in other words, show more similarities with than differences from the homes of the poor. The second major innovation in the history of the western medieval family is the emergence, from about the year 1000, of a new type of kin organization. The dominant kin group of early medieval society, often called in the literature by its German name *Sippe*, had been cognate or bilineal, which is to say, blood relationships were traced equally through men and through women. From approximately the eleventh century, initially on elite social levels, a new type of kin grouping, the agnate lineage or the patrilineage, achieves visibility. In the patrilineage, blood relationships are traced exclusively through males. The curiosity here is that the new agnate lineage does not really replace, but is superimposed upon, the older, cognate group. The competition between these two rival definitions of kin and family is a marked characteristic of domestic life in the central and late Middle Ages. The third area of change involves the distinctive roles which medieval culture comes to assign to family members—to wives, children, and husbands—and also the set of emotional rewards by which the culture encouraged good performance.

COMMENSURABILITY OF HOUSEHOLDS

Many factors doubtlessly contributed to the emergence in the early Middle Ages of commensurable households. Chief among them was the decline of ancient slavery. By about 700, in place of the great villas worked by gangs of slaves, the small peasant property, worked by families, overlay the European countryside. The emergence of commensurable households is thus intimately connected with the crisis of ancient slavery, and the rise of the new peasant economy of the Middle Ages.

But religion contributed too, particu-larly in its insistence that rich and poor, the free and the unfree, follow the same sexual morality. To be sure, the patristic assumption that in sexual matters there was but one law for all triumphed only slowly. Apparently not until the twelfth century did Pope Hadrian IV (1152–1159) explicitly declare that the marriages of serfs were as valid as any other. So also, the Church's insistence on monogamy encountered tenacious opposition among the European elites, as several scholars have shown (Wemple, 1981:38–40). But unquestionably, the Church's teachings acted as a powerful levelling, standardizing and stabilizing influence (Bishop, 1985).

The success, even if limited, of this rule of monogamy, and the associated opposition to other forms of sexual liaison, had this subtle, but I think profound social repercussion. Women came to be distributed more evenly across society. Males who controlled wealth and power could not use these resources to accumulate women as well. Males of the lower social order now had improved chances of attracting a mate. The incest prohibition should have had a comparable effect. It prevented privileged households from claiming or retaining more than their fair share of women. Gregory of Tours tells of a Merovingian queen named Aregund, who asked her husband Chlothar to find a rich and powerful husband for her sister Ingund (Gregorius turonensis, 1951:136–37). Upon viewing the beautiful young woman, Chlothar decided that the most suitable husband was himself; he therefore married her, bigamously. The Church's rule of monogamy, if effective, would have prevented this union; the incest prohibition would have blocked him from ever marrying Ingund, even after Aregund's death. He cannot have his pick of women.

The incest prohibition meant that after the death of her husband, the widow cannot marry any male already in her household—not her father-in-law, not a brother-in-law, not a step-father, or step-brother. If she wishes to marry again, she must move out of her former household. The incest prohibition thus forced a circulation of women through society, and made them accessible to a larger group of males. The households of the great and powerful cannot monopolize women.

Would not this enhanced accessibility of women have reduced incidents of rape and abduction, commonplace events in the social history of the early Middle Ages? And would this not act as a pacifying, stabilizing influence in society? The result too was an assimilation of family forms at all social levels.

LINEAGES

The second major change we have identified is the coming of the agnate lineage.[14] It differs in several crucial ways from the older cognatic kin group, the *genus* or *cognatio* in contemporary terms, the *Sippe* in much modern scholarship. The *cognatio* was ego-focused, as anthropologists would say, in the sense that lines of relationship were viewed as radiating forth from the living individual. The boundaries of the *cognatio* changed with every generation, as its center came to rest on a new ego. The lineage was, in contrast, ancestor-focused, as it characteristically traced its descent in the male line back to a historic, or sometimes mythical, founder. It was a solidarity of males linking the living and the dead. It displayed that solidarity through the use of a family name, which sometimes recalled the revered ancestor himself, sometimes the castle or estate associated with him. It showed it also through the adoption of a coat of arms, a written genealogy, and sometimes even a mythology. The daughter passed out of the lineage at marriage, and all her

descendants after her; they became members of their father's line.

The role of religion in the appearance of the agnatic lineage is again secondary but still significant. The chief motivation for this redefinition of the kin group seems to have been the desire of elite families to limit claims upon their resources, particularly their landed patrimonies. The chief losers in this effort were daughters and, in lesser measure, younger sons. The claims of daughters were limited to the dowries they now needed to contract an honorable marriage; those without suitable dowries had little choice but to enter the religious life. Younger sons were often forced to delay marriages; rather than remain inactive at home, many chose to wander widely over Europe in search of fortune. The common strategy was that the family's resources should be mobilized primarily in support of a single heir, usually the eldest son, who could best maintain the prestige and power of the lineage.

However, no agnatic or patrilineal identification of principal kin can operate under conditions of sexual promiscuity. And the reasons for this seem clear. The promiscuity of males tends to invite promiscuity among females. The legal wife might resent the entry of another wife or concubine into her home, and seek revenge through infidelity. And extramarital liaisons will inevitably obscure the line of descent through males. Instances of uncertain paternity are common in early medieval sources. According to Gregory of Tours, the Merovingian king Gunthram refuses to believe that the son of Fredegundis, who was married to his deceased brother Chilperic, was truly his brother's (Gregorius turonensis, 1951: 376). "I think," he broods, "that he is the son of one of our retinue [leudi]." To prove the child's paternity, Fredegundis must summon the great persons of the Frankish realm—three bishops and 300 *optimati*—and before this august assembly she swears that Chilperic really was the boy's father. "And thus," Gregory tells us, "the suspicion of the king was removed." But could he be absolutely certain?

In the tenth century King Hugh of Italy allegedly ignored his queen and consorted with three concubines, who were popularly nicknamed after pagan goddesses, Venus, Juno and Semele (Liutprand of Cremona, 1930:199). He sired children on all of them. Or did he? "As the king was not the only man who enjoyed their favors," our source Liutprand of Cremona, relates, "the children of all three are of uncertain parentage." He writes parentage, but he means paternity.

In sum, prerequisite to the appearance of the patrilineage was the Church's success in imposing the rule of monogamy and in repressing sexual promiscuity, among both men and women. At the same time, the Church did not allow the patrilineage to overwhelm and replace the old *cognatio*. As Duby again has illustrated, the great laymen wanted to arrange the marriages of their offspring in the interest of the lineage, and their designs often ran up against the incest prohibition (Duby, 1983a). And the old rules continued to determine degrees of kinship and eligibility for marriage. The Church liberalized the rules a little when, at the Fourth Lateran Council in 1215, it reduced the degrees in which marriage was prohibited from an unrealistic seven to four. But it still maintained that relationships through women were no less important than those through men, in determining who might marry.

The Church also restricted the authority of the chiefs of lineages over their own offspring. Pope Alexander III in the twelfth century is credited—or criticized —with establishing in the canon law the principle that only the mutual consent of bride and groom, expressed through words of present tense, *verba de presenti*, was required in a valid marriage. To contract a valid marriage, serfs did not need the permission of their masters. Serfs who married without that permission contracted, in the technical language, an illicit, but not an invalid marriage. They could be punished; even so, they remained validly married. Curiously, even the blessing of the Church was not a prerequisite to a valid marriage. But most important, the principle precluded even parents from exerting control over the marriages of their children. The necessary and sufficient condition for a valid marriage was the consent of otherwise eligible partners: nothing less and nothing more. This principle prevented an unrestricted patriarchy from dominating medieval society. Religion made possible the emergence of the patrilineage, but also limited its triumph.

The exclusion of daughters and younger sons from a full share in the family's resources inevitably induced tensions within the medieval household. Medieval heresies, which were waxing strong even as the patrilineage took form, perhaps reflect those tensions in the antagonism they often manifest toward marriage. Most notorious though not alone in their opposition toward marriage were the Albigensians or *Cathari*, who in the twelfth century mounted a powerful challenge to orthodoxy in southern France and northern Spain. "For the common opinion of all *Cathari*," a former heretic declared, "is that physical marriage has always been a mortal sin, and that in the future no one will be punished more severely because of adultery or incest than for legitimate matrimony. So also among them no one is more gravely punished than for this" (cited in Herlihy, 1971:134). For many of the heresies, the principle held: *In matrimonio non est salus*. And the heresies had particular appeal to women. St. Dominic, for example, established his order's first convent for women at Prouille, where the *Cathari* were many. He wished to counter the success of the heretics, who had been rearing and teaching poor and probably unmarriageable noble girls, and teaching them how to read (Jordanus, 1935:39). Presumably, the heretics told the girls that the marriages they could not have were sinful anyway, and that the parents who treated them so shabbily were the devil's minions. Ironically, proof of the parents' sinful ways was the girls themselves. The system of medieval marriages was not without its committed enemies.

FEELINGS

We enter now into the emotional life of the medieval family, indisputably the most elusive of subjects. According to various early modern or modern historians, medieval people were wanting in an appreciation of childhood, and medieval families were not "affective" (Ozment, 1983; Stone, 1977; deMause, 1974:1–74). Supposedly, sensitivity to childhood and familial affection first appear either in Reformation Europe or in the seventeenth century, or in comparatively recent times. But these views seem based on false assumptions concerning the emotional life, or lack thereof, of the medieval family. As Barbara Hanawalt (1986:xvii) has recently argued, the families with which these authors people the Middle Ages are made of straw. Weinstein and Bell's study of the life course of 864 medieval and early modern saints draws the same conclusion: "The widely held modern view that a concept of childhood did not emerge until the early modern period is emphatically contradicted by our reading of the evidence on saints, where we find a clear sense of what it was to be a child" (Weinstein and Bell, 1982:19). Their study also shows the exceptional value of saints' lives in assessing the domestic emotions of the Middle Ages.

In the history of emotions, medieval religion serves both as a mirror and a model. In other words, medieval spiritual writers, particularly the authors of saints' lives, make constant appeal, by analogy, to domestic acts and emotions. These familial images, I argue, must respond to the emotional climate of real medieval households. Doubtlessly, too, the familial images they employ were meant to influence domestic conduct. The faithful should both empathize with, and imitate, the behavior of the saints. Structure, in this case religious structure, directs behavior.

We look first at marriage itself. Mystical marriages are commonplace in the pious literature, and they usually unite a female saint with Christ (Herlihy, 1985: 118). Some of them, such as the life of Angela of Foligno in Italy, who died in 1309, go beyond formalities of marriage to unabashedly sexual allusions to embraces and kisses.[15] One of the most revealing images of marriage comes from the life of St. Hermann of Steinfeld near Cologne, who died about 1240; his biography is written by a contemporary who knew his subject well.[16] Hermann marries the Virgin Mary. One day, two angels escort Mary to him; she is described as a young girl of ineffable beauty and royal bearing. "It is fitting," says one of her angelic sponsors, "that this brilliant virgin be married to you." The angel took his right hand and joined it to the hand of the virgin, and with these words he married them. "Behold," the angel said, "I give you as wife this virgin, even as she had been married to Joseph. And you shall take the name of the husband even as you take the bride." Hermann thus replaces Joseph as Mary's spouse, and assumes his name as well.

The domestic life of this mystically married pair was blissful. In fact, even before the formal wedding, they cultivated a supportive relationship. "We often heard that it happened to him," his biographer writes, "that in a recess of the monastery, as he was occupied in prayer and meditation, he would hear the voice of his holy and dearest friend standing across from him ... he would go to her, and sitting together in some place, Blessed Mary would ask him in detail upon his affairs and he would answer; and he in turn would ask of her, whatever he wanted. In such conversations he passed in contentment the nighttime hours. With such a consoler, he bore defeats of any kind; he was warmed by the consoling breasts of such a mother; by such a teacher, through her instruction, he learned of many doubtful and uncertain things." Encouragement, advice, consolation, instruction, and dearest friendship—this is what Hermann Joseph gained from Mary, his *amica* and his bride. Surely this spiritual marriage celebrates and idealizes earthly marriage too.

The image of the mother is as common as that of the bride or wife in the religious literature. She is the intercessor *par exellence*; she aids, whenever summoned, her poor banished children. As Bynum (1982) shows, medieval religious writers applied the figure of mother even to the person of Jesus. I have argued elsewhere that within the real world of the Middle Ages women often fulfilled that function, intervening between aged fathers and their often alienated sons (Herlihy, 1985:120–23). The strategies adopted by the lineage imposed late marriages on men, if they were allowed to marry at all, and early marriages on women. The young wife thus typically found herself set between conflicting male generations. She was ideally placed to soothe the tensions and quarrels that divided them. The mother of Francis of Assisi frees him from the chains, with which his angered father

has bound him in the dungeon of their home (Engelbert, 1965:35).

But perhaps a more instructive role, which women saints assume, is that of teacher. From the thirteenth century, as several scholars have observed, women saints multiply to the point of dominating the ranks of the blessed (Vauchez, 1981: 243; Weinstein and Bell, 1982:220; Kieckhefer, 1984). Often they attract a following, a spiritual family, whom they instruct in matters of holy wisdom. The best known of these spiritual families is the "joyous brigade" that accompanied Catherine of Siena. But many holy women exercise a similar spiritual leadership. "Who can count," writes the biographer of Margaret of Cortona, who died in 1297, "the number of Spaniards, Apulians, Romans and others, who came to her, that they might be instructed by salutary admonitions" (Herlihy, 1985:122, 210). Christ himself confers on her the office and title of *mater peccatorum*, the mother of sinners, in recognition of her achievements. Does this role assumed by numerous women saints of the late Middle Ages find no parallel within real families? Here too, the comparative youth of mothers, which allowed them longer and closer contact with their children than aged fathers could enjoy, may have equipped them to serve as prime conveyors of religious and cultural values. Anthropologists tell us that one avenue to prestige and power in any society is the possession of knowledge, including and perhaps especially sacred knowledge. If this analogy has any value, women may not have been repressed and passive persons within the late-medieval household. They had more functions, and more important functions, than we have recognized.

The cult of the child Jesus enjoys great popularity, at least from the twelfth century. Did it not conceal beneath it a cult of childhood? The infant or child Jesus visits many saints, both men and women. One of the most charming of these visitations involves St. Ida of Louvain in modern Belgium, who died in 1300. Mary, and her cousin St. Elizabeth, bring the blessed infant to Ida, and Ida is honored with the chore of giving the infant a bath.[17]

> Taking him, she squeezes him hard with hugs and kisses, as his mother blessed above all things stands by . . . On the other side was the mother of [John] the Lord's precursor, Elizabeth. She drew a bath to wash the child, with tubs already prepared. Together with the venerable Ida, she lowered the child ever so carefully into the warm water. When he was sitting, this the most chosen of all children, after the manner of playing infants, clapped with both hands in the water, and in childlike fashion stirred and splashed the waters. He thus soaked his surroundings, and as the waters splashed here and there, he made all parts of his little body wet, before the ladies could wash him . . . After the bath, she again lifted the baby from the water, wrapped him again in his swaddling cloths, enfolded him on her breast, playing intently with him as mothers do. How she wonderfully exalted in her saving God, cannot be described or imagined.

The male author of this life had clearly observed babies in the bath, and noted the delight which real mothers took in washing their infants.

These familial images would have been totally ineffective, had they not reflected authentic domestic experiences and emotions. But in one particular area the medieval Church apparently did not make a conscious effort not only to reflect but to shape a particular domestic role. It is strange that after the thirteenth century— the age of Francis, Dominic and Louis of France—there are virtually no prominent male saints, and none who might serve as an example to married men and heads of households. Patriarchy did not rule the ranks of the blessed, at least not in the late Middle Ages. In what seems a reaction to the dearth of saints, several prominent

churchmen set about promoting the cult of St. Joseph.

Joseph had been nearly a forgotten saint in the early medieval world (Seitz, 1908; Hengge, 1980). The *Patrologia Latinae* of J. P. Migne, containing over 200 volumes of religious tracts antedating 1216, provides an index of saints mentioned in the prolix writings. Joseph appears not at all. And he rarely figures in the visions recorded in saints' lives. When he makes a showing, he is usually presented as old and ineffectual. In the life of St. Hermann of Steinfeld, previously quoted, he loses his wife and even his name to Hermann. He seems unable or unwilling to preserve his rights.

But from the late fourteenth century, figures such as Jean Gerson, chancellor of the University of Paris, and Bernardine of Siena in Italy, undertake an active campaign in favor of Joseph, demanding for him a major feastday, urging Josephine devotions upon the faithful.[18] They systematically rework his image. Joseph, they argue, could not have been, as traditionally presented, an ineffectual old man. He had to be young and vigorous when he married Mary. How else could he have protected and supported the Holy Family during their seven years of exile in Egypt? He was the *seculus administrator*, the attentive head of the holy household and promoter of its fortunes. These doctors claim that Joseph, like Mary, was assumed bodily into heaven. It was appropriate that the Holy Family, which endured so much together on earth, should be reunited in body as well as spirit, in their heavenly home. Joseph is the head of the Holy Family, and as such holds under his loving authority Jesus himself and his immaculate mother. Ruling the rulers, Joseph, the doctors claim, deserves recognition as lord of the world.

Evidence, such as the choice of proper names, indicates that the cult of Joseph was slow to evoke a spontaneous response from the faithful, and not until the sixteenth and seventeenth century did he achieve the stature which Gerson and Bernardine sought to attain for him. In Florence, for example, the name Giuseppe, commonly borne today in Italy, was absolutely rare before 1500.[19]

Why were these ecclesiastical leaders so interested in promoting the cult of Joseph? It is tempting to argue that they were seeking to counter certain trends in late-medieval piety. In his massive study of sanctity in the medieval West, the French scholar André Vauchez speaks of a "feminization" of sainthood and of sanctity across the late Middle Ages (Vauchez, 1981:243). Now, the Church was traditionally uneasy about women assuming the functions of prophets and priests. St. Paul instructed women to be silent in the churches, and some early Christian sects, which accepted women prophets, became branded as heresies. Perhaps there was a fear, as there seems to be today, that the admission of women would eventually compromise the prestige of such offices and provoke a flight of males. At all events, the late-medieval doctors seem intent on developing Joseph as a counterpoise to Mary and a correction to the lack of contemporary male saints.

The promotion of Joseph thus seems connected with the history of piety, and doubtlessly also with the history of the family. This age of plague, famine, war and death placed many households in jeopardy and required of their chiefs the sedulous administration which Bernardine admires in Joseph. As Gerson affirmed, this world is Egypt.[20] Harrassed fathers needed a patron, a powerful figure in heaven who knew and understood the difficulties they confronted, and, as lord of the world, could come to their assistance. If nothing more, the image of Joseph, the conscientious, wise and loving father, shows us what great churchmen thought to be appropriate deportment, for real fathers in a troubled world.

The history of medieval religion is thus intimately connected with the history of the family. The rule of monogamy and the prohibition of incest fostered the spread of commensurable household units within society, achieved a more even distribution of women across social levels, and helped pacify and stabilize social relations. The same ethic made possible the emergence of the patrilineage in the central Middle Ages, but also restricted the power of fathers within it. And religious cults both mirrored and modeled domestic roles and emotions. The connections between religious history and domestic history are thus many, even if they cannot be entirely untwined from the web of social interactions. Perhaps no other motives so powerfully affected the behavior of medieval people than family interests and religious commitments. And in affecting people, the medieval Church, and the medieval family, inevitably affected each other.

NOTES

1. Goitein, (1967-). Initial orientation into the Byzantine family can be gained from Evelyne Patlagean (1981). Not recent, but recently reprinted, is W. Robertson Smith (1979). The book was originally published in 1903.

2. The argument that official Christianity did not penetrate beyond the clerical and a tiny lay elite has been most vigorously advanced by Delumeau (1977) and Delumeau et al. (1981), to cite only two of Delumeau's many publications. Jacques Le Goff and Jean-Claude Schmitt have also maintained that the unlettered masses of medieval society followed a kind of folk religion, with roots stretching far back into the European past. For the latter, see Schmitt (1983).

3. For orientation in the literature, particularly in regard to the development of canon law, see Jean Gaudemet (1980:454–77), "Bibliographie internationale d'histoire du mariage" (prepared with the collaboration of Marie Zimmermann). On the formation of the early Christian ideas on marriage, see

among recent publications Cottiaux (1982); and Fuchs (1983).

4. On the slow and late extension of the Church's jurisdiction over marriage, see Esmein (1968, I, 3 ff). As late as the ninth century, Hincmar of Rheims apologizes for speaking out on a marriage issue, "concerning a civil judgment, of which we bishops are not supposed to be experts." Hincmar (1975:90): "In quibus nihil de civili iudicio, cuius cognitores non debemus esse episcopi, ponere, sed quae ecclesiasticae diffinitioni noscuntur competere, quantum occurrit memorare, breviter studui adnotare." On the issue of divorce, see Delpini (1979).

5. "Laudo nuptias, laudo coniugium, sed quia mihi virgines generant." Cited in Humbert (1972: 321). On the origins of the Christian valuation of virginity, see Deschner (1974:48–61), "Die Heraufkunft der Askese." McNamara (1983), analyzes the particular appeal of this attitude for women. Bugge (1975) traces the later history of this ideal.

6. From the tract *Contra Jovinianum*. See Augustine (1955:159). On Augustine's theology of marriage, see Schmitt (1983). On patristic attitudes on procreation and the rearing of children, see my further comments in Herlihy (1978).

7. See, for example, the words of the North-African writer Tertullian (1954:827): "Everywhere there are buildings, everywhere people, everywhere communities, everywhere life."

8. See, for example, in Augustine (1963:45) the story how he and some friends stole pears for which they had no need. "... I became evil for nothing, with no reason for wrongdoing except the wrongdoing itself. The evil was foul, and I loved it; I loved destroying myself; I loved my sin—not the thing for which I had committed the sin, but the sin itself." See also 1963:26, for his views on pedogogy: "O God, my God, what misery did I experience in my boyhood ... if I failed to work hard at my studies, I was beaten. This kind of discipline was considered very good by our ancestors, and many people before us, who had gone through this way of life, had already organized wearisome courses of study along which we were compelled to go; the trouble was multiplied and so was the sorrow upon the sons of Adam." Marrou (1956, 1958:158–59) comments on this "brutality of discipline."

9. Caterina da Siena (1913–21, II, 102), to madonna Laudomia donna di Carlo degli Strozzi da Firenze. Catherine warns against excessive attachment to "o figliuoli o marito o alcuna creatura." Laudomia should regard them as "cose prestate."

10. Cited and discussed in Gaudemet (1952:62). See also Esmein (1968, I, 91).

11. Augustine (1894:275): "hoc autem tripartitum est: fides, proles, sacramentum."

12. Esmein (1968, I, 5), stresses this analogy as the basis for the Church's opposition to divorce. See also Torti (1979).

13. For the council of Toledo, see *Concilios visigóticos* (1963, II, cap. 5). "Nam et haec salubriter praecavanda sancimus, ne quis fidelium propinquam sanguinis sui, usquequo adfinitatis liniamenta generis successione cognoscit, in matrimonio sibi desideret copulari..." For the Roman provision, see MGH, Epistolae (1957, III, 485). "Nos... iuxta praedecessorum et antecessorum pontificum decreta... dicimus, ut, cum usque sese generatio cognoverit, iuxta ritum et normam christianitatis Romanorum non copulentur coniugiis."

14. The change in the structure of noble families from the early to the central Middle Ages was emphasized for Germany by Karl Schmid in the late 1950s. His most important studies have been reprinted in Schmid (1983). An English translation of a summary of his principal thesis is available in Reuter (1979:38–42).

15. The life of Catherine of Alexandria provides the apparent model for these mystical marriages, but many medieval women saints imitate her, including Catherine of Siena.

16. ASS (1863- , I Aprilis:692); cited in Herlihy (1985:119, 209).

17. ASS (1863-, II Aprilis:166); Herlihy (1985: 127, 211). On the linkage between representations of the Christ child and sentiments toward childhood, see Bonney (1980:1–23).

18. See especially the collection of devotional poems called the "Josephina," in Gerson (1960–73, IV).

19. Among 30,000 names of Florentine office holders I have collected from the middle fourteenth century to 1530, Joseph does not appear at all before 1500.

20. Gerson (1960–73, V, 97): "... nos heu retinet tenebrosa/ Torquet et Aegyptus."

REFERENCES

ASS. 1863–1910. *Acta Sanctorum quotquot toto orbe coluntur*. Paris.

Augustine. 1894. *De genesi ad litteram libri xii*. Edited by J. Zycha. Corpus scriptorum ecclesiasticorum latinorum, 28. Vienna: Tempsky.

———. 1955. *Treatises on Marriage and Other Subjects*. Trans. Charles T. Wilcox and others. The Fathers of the Church, A New Translation, 27. New York: Fathers of the Church.

———. 1963. *The Confessions of St. Augustine*. A New Translation by Rex Warner. New York: New American Library.

Bishop. Jane. 1985. "Bishops as Marital Advisors in the Ninth Century." Pp. 54–84 in *Women of the*

Medieval World: Essays in Honor of John H. Mundy. Oxford: Oxford University Press.

Bonney, Françoise. 1980. "Enfance Divine et Enfance Humaine." In *L'enfant au Moyen-Age* (Littérature et Civilisation). Colloque organisé en 1979 per le CUERMA. Aix-en-Provence: Edition CUERMA. Paris: diffusion H. Champion.

Bugge, John. 1975. Virginitas: *An Essay in the History of a Medieval Ideal*. The Hague: M. Nijhoff.

Bynum, Caroline. 1982. *Jesus as Mother: Studies in the Spirituality of the High Middle Ages*. Berkeley: University of California Press.

Caterina da Siena. 1913–21. *Le lettere di S. Caterina da Siena ridotte a miglior lezione*, 6 vols., edited by Piero Misciatelli. Siena: Giuntini and Bentivoglio.

Concilios visigóticos. 1963. *Concilios Visigóticos e hispano-romanos*, edited by Jose Vives. España cristiana, Textos, 1. Barcelona: Consejo Superior de Investigaciones Cientificas, Instituto Enrique Flórez.

Cottiaux, Jean. 1982. *La sacralisation du marriage de le Genèse aux incises Matthéennes*. Paris: Editions du Cerf.

Delpini, Francesco. 1979. *Indissolubilità matrimoniale e divorzio dal I al XII secolo*. Milan: Nuove Edizioni Duomo.

Delumeau, Jean. 1977. *Catholicism between Luther and Voltaire: A New View of the Counter Reformation*. Philadelphia: Westminster Press.

Delumeau, Jean, Geneviève Gaudet-Drillat, Stephanie Jannssen-Peigné, and Cathérine Tragnan. 1981. *Un chemin d'histoire: chrétienté et christianisation*. Paris: Fayard.

deMause, Lloyd, ed. 1974. *The History of Childhood*. New York: Psychohistory Press.

Deschner, Karlheinz. 1974. *Das Kreuz mit der Kirche: Eine Sexualgeschichte des Christentums*. 2d ed. Düsseldorf: Econ Verlag.

Duby, Georges. 1978. *Medieval Marriage: Two Models from Twelfth Century France*. Translated by Elborg Forster. Baltimore: Johns Hopkins University Press.

————. 1979. *The Chivalrous Society*. Translated by Cynthia Postan. Berkeley: University of California Press.

————. 1981. *Le chévalier, la femme e le prêtre: le mariage dans la France féodale*. Paris: Hachette.

————. 1983a. *The Knight, the Lady and the Priest: The Making of Modern Marriage in Medieval France*. Translated by Barbara Bray. New York: Pantheon Books.

————. 1983b. *Que sait-on de l'amour en France aux XIIe siècle?* Oxford: The Zaharoff Lecture.

Englebert, Omer. 1965. *St. Francis of Assisi: A Biography*. Translated by Eve Marie Cooper. 2d ed. Ann Arbor: University of Michigan Press.

Esmein, Adhémar. 1968. *Le mariage en droit canonique. Essays in History, Economics and Social Science, 7*. 2 vols. New York: B. Franklin.

Foster, Kenelm. 1959. *The Life of Saint Thomas Aquinas: Biographical Documents*. Baltimore: Helicon Press.

Fuchs, Eric. 1983. *Sexual Desire and Love: Origins and History of the Christian Ethic of Sexuality and Marriage*. Translated by Marsha Daigle. Cambridge: J. Clarke. New York: Seabury Press.

Gaudemet, Jean. 1952. "Les transformations de la vie familiale au Bas Empire e l'influence du Christianisme." Pp. 58–85 in *Romanitas: Revista de Cultura Romana, 5*.

————. 1980. *Sociétés et Mariage. Recherches institutionelles, 4*. Strasbourg: Cerdic Publications.

Gerson, Jean. 1960–73. *Oevres complètes. Introduction texte et notes*, 10 vols., edited by Mgr. Glorieux. Paris: Desclée.

Goitein, S. D. 1967– . *A Mediterranean Society: The Jewish Communities of the Arab World as Portrayed by the Documents of the Cairo Geniza*. 4 Vols. Vol. 3: *The Family*. Berkeley: University of California Press.

Goody, Jack. 1983. *The Development of the Family and Marriage in Europe*. Cambridge and New York: Cambridge University Press.

Gregorius turonensis. 1951. *Historiarum libri X*, edited by B. Krusch and W. Levison. Monumenta Germaniae Historica. Scriptores rerum merovincigarum. Hannover: Hahn.

Hanawalt, Barbara. 1986. *The Ties That Bound: Peasant Families in Medieval England*. New York and Oxford: Oxford University Press.

Hengge, Paul. 1980. *Der Vater Joseph von Nazareth: Untersuchungen zur Geschichte der Familie des Zimmermanns*. Vienna: Orac.

Herilhy, David. 1971. "Alienation in Medieval Culture and Society." Pp. 125–140 in *Alienation: Concept, Term and Meanings*, edited by Frank Johnson. New York: Seminar Press.

————. 1978. "Medieval Children." Pp. 109–142 in *The Walter Prescott Webb Memorial Lectures. Essays on Medieval Civilization*. Austin and London: University of Texas Press.

————. 1985. *Medieval Households*. Cambridge: Harvard University Press.

Hincmar. 1975. *Hincmari archiepiscopi remensis epistolae. Die Briefe des Erzbishops Hinkmar von Reims*. Monumenta Germaniae Historica, Epistolae 8, Teil 1. Munich: Monumenta Germaniae Historica.

Humbert, Michel. 1905. Le remariage à Rome: étude d'histoire juridique et sociale. Milan: A. Giuffre.

Jordanus. 1935. "Libellus de principiis Ordinis Praedicatorum." In *Monumenta Historica sancti patris nostri Dominici fasc. 11*. Monumenta Ordinis fratrum praedicatorum historica, 16. Rome: Institutum historicum Ff. Praedicatorum.

Kieckhefer, Richard. 1984. *Unquiet Souls: Fourteenth Century Saints and Their Religious Milieu*. Chicago: University of Chicago Press.

Liutprand. 1930. "Antapodis." In *The Works of Liudprand of Cremona*. Translated by F. A. Wright. London: C. Routledge and Sons.

Marrou, Henri I. (1956) 1981. *A History of Education in Antiquity*. Translated by George Lamb. New York: Sheed and Ward.

McNamara, Jo Ann. 1983. *A New Song: Celibate Women in the First Three Christian Centuries*. *Women and History*. 6-7. New York: Haworth Press.

MGH, Epistolae. 1957. *Monumenta Germaniae Historica. Epistolarum Tomus II: Merowingici et Karolini Aevi, I*. 2nd ed. Berlin: apud Weidmannos.

Noonan, John T. 1965. *Contraception: A History of Its Treatment by the Catholic Theologians and Canonists*. Cambridge: Harvard University Press.

Ozment, Steven. 1983. *When Fathers Ruled: Family Life in Reformation Europe*. Cambridge: Harvard University Press.

Patlagean, Evelyne. 1981. *Structure sociale, famille, Chrétienté à Byzance*. London: Variorum Reprints.

Reuter, Timothy (ed.). 1979. *The Medieval Nobility: Studies on the Ruling Classes of France and Germany from the Sixth to the Twelfth Century. Europe in the Middle Ages, Selected Studies, 14*. Amsterdam: North Holland Publishing Co.

Schmid, Karl. 1983. *Gebetsgedenken und adliges Selbstverständnis im Mittelalter; Ausgewählte Beiträge; Festgabe zu seinem sechzigsten Geburtstag*. Sigmaringen: Thorbecke.

Schmidt, Jean-Claude. 1983. *The Holy Greyhound: Guinefort Healer of Children Since the Thirteenth Century*. Translated by Martin Thom. Cambridge and New York: Cambridge University Press.

Schmitt, Emile. 1983. *Le mariage chrétien dans l'oeuvre de saint Augustine: Une théologie baptismale de la vie conjugale*. Paris: Etudes augustiniennes.

Seitz, Joseph. 1908. *Die Verehrung des h. Joseph in ihrer geschichtliche Entwicklung bis zum Konzil von Trent dargestellt*. Freiburg-im-Breisgau: Herder.

Smith, W. Robertson. 1979. *Kinship and Marriage in Early Arabia*. New York: AMS Press.

Stone, Lawrence. 1977. *The Family, Sex and Marriage in England*. New York: Harper & Row.

Tertullian. 1954. *Opera, II: Opera monastica. Corpus christianorum, series latina, 2*. Turnholt: Brepols.

Torti, Giovanni. 1979. *La stabilità del vincolo nuziale in Sant' Agostino e in San Tommaso*. Parma: Università degli Studi, Istituto di Lingua e Letteratura Romana.

Vauchez, André. 1981. *La sainteté en Occident aux derniers siècles du Moyen Ages d'après les procès de canonisation et les documents hagiographiques. Bibliothèque des Ecoles françaises d'Athènes et de Rome, fasc. 241*. Rome: Ecole française de Rome. Paris: diffusion de Boccard.

Weinstein, Donald, and Rudolf M. Bell. 1982. *Saints and Society: The Two Worlds of Western Christendom, 1000-1700*. Chicago and London: University of Chicago Press.

Wemple, Suzanne Fonay. 1981. *Women in Frankish Society: Marriage and the Cloister, 500-900*. Philadelphia: University of Pennsylvania Press.

FAMILY AND SCHOOLING IN COLONIAL AND NINETEENTH-CENTURY AMERICA

Maris A. Vinovskis

ABSTRACT: *Throughout the seventeenth, eighteenth, and nineteenth centuries, both parents and schools played an important part in the education of young Americans. While historians of the family and of education have frequently acknowledged these complementary, if not sometimes conflicting, institutions in the training of the young, very little effort has been made to examine the interactions between them. The family was an important source of education for children in colonial and nineteenth-century America. But from the very beginning churches and schools were directed to assist parents in the socialization of the young. Indeed, by the mid-nineteenth century, the role of the schools had expanded to such an extent that many of the educational tasks initially assigned to parents, such as teaching children the alphabet and how to read, became the responsibility of the schools.*

Twenty-five years ago Bailyn (1960) called for a new and broader interepretation of American colonial educational development—one that recognized the important historical role of the family in the transmission of culture from one generation to the next. While many of the specific elements of his analysis need to be reconsidered and revised in light of subsequent scholarship, Bailyn's challenge to historians to study the interactions between the family and schooling in the socialization of the young continues to inspire and guide researchers.

Maris A. Vinovskis, Professor in the Department of History at the University of Michigan, Ann Arbor, Mich., 48109, has just published The Origins of Public High Schools: A Reexamination of the Beverly High School Controversy *(University of Wisconsin Press, 1985), and is now completing* An Epidemic of Adolescent Pregnancy? Some Historical and Policy Considerations *(Oxford University Press, forthcoming).*

Despite the wide circulation and acceptance of Bailyn's essays on education in early America, few scholars have written directly on the relationship between the family and schooling—especially for the nineteenth century. Instead, most historians have analyzed particular facets of colonial and nineteenth-century family life or educational development without much explicit attention to the interactions between them.[1] This article will attempt to briefly survey some of the more recent findings in the fields of American family and educational history from the perspective of the changing relationship between the family and schools in the seventeenth, eighteenth, and nineteenth centuries. Rather than providing a detailed review or a comprehensive synthesis of the large number of studies in each field, this article hopes to create a stimulus for further research by exploring some of the more salient points raised in those studies. Furthermore, while some references will be made to educational developments throughout all of the United States, most of the attention will be focused on New England because of the greater availability of secondary analyses relating to family and education in that region.

FAMILY AND SCHOOLING IN COLONIAL AMERICA

Bailyn's (1960) seminal book on early American educational development is based upon several assumptions about the nature of English society on the eve of colonization and the transformation of the American family in the inhospitable environment of the New World. English families were seen as patriarchal and extended:

> The family familiar to the early colonists was a patrilineal group of extended kinship gathered in a single household. By modern standards it was large. Besides children, who

often remained in the home well into maturity, it included a wide range of other dependents: nieces and nephews, cousins, and, except for families of the lowest rung of society, servants in filial discipline. In the Elizabethan family the conjugal was only the nucleus of a broad kinship community whose outer edges merged almost imperceptibly into the society at large (Bailyn, 1960: 15–16).

These patriarchal families and the larger communities were the central agencies for the socialization and education of children. Formal schools were not readily available or particularly important, but the church played a key role in educating the young. "Family, community, and church together accounted for the greater part of the mechanism by which English culture transferred itself across the generations. The instruments of deliberate pedagogy, of explicit, literate education, accounted for a smaller, though indispensable, portion of the process" (Bailyn, 1960: 18–19).

Settlers coming to the New World did not anticipate any major changes in the way children were raised and educated. Yet within a few decades the colonists, particularly in Puritan New England, had to reconceptualize and reorder their system of educating the young. Central to this change was the unexpected destruction of the stable, extended English family:

> In many ways the most important changes, and certainly the most dramatic, were those that overtook the family in colonial America. In the course of these changes the family's traditional role as the primary agency of cultural transfer was jeopardized, reduced, and partly superseded.
> Disruption and transplantation in alien soil transformed the character of the traditional English family life. Severe pressures were felt from the first. Normal procedures were upset by the long and acute discomforts of travel; the ancient discipline slackened. But once re-established in permanent settlements the colonists moved toward re-

creating the essential institution in its usual form. In this, despite heroic efforts, they failed. At first they laid their failure to moral disorder; but in time they came to recognize its true source in the intractable circumstances of material life (Bailyn, 1960: 22).

In reasoning reminiscent of Handlin's (1951) analysis of nineteenth-century immigration, Bailyn argued that the role of children in the new environment was greatly enhanced at the expense of parental authority.[2] As a result, the civil authorities intervened to try to prop up the weakened and endangered family and required communities in Massachusetts to maintain local schools to educate children who were no longer being properly trained within the family. Thus, for Bailyn the demise of the stable, extended English family in the New World led to the establishment of elementary schools—an unexpected but crucial step in the long-term development of schooling in America.

In the two decades since the publication of Bailyn's interpretation of family life and education, much more has been learned about English society in the sixteenth and seventeenth centuries. Contrary to Bailyn's assumption that most English families were extended and geographically immobile, it appears that English families were much smaller and predominantly nuclear (Houlbrooke, 1984; Laslett, 1969, 1972, 1977). While there is still controversy over the exact extent of extended families as seen from a more dynamic view of family life (Berkner, 1972; Vinovskis, forthcoming [a]), there is general agreement that most English families in the sixteenth and seventeenth centuries were nuclear with fewer than five members present at any given time. In addition, although a few families remained in the same community over several generations, there was much more geographic mobility than Bailyn had assumed (Prest, 1976).

Similarly, in the area of education, the availability of formal schooling in England in the sixteenth and seventeenth centuries appears to have been greater than Bailyn portrayed. In the mid-1960s Stone (1964) argued that the extent of schooling and literacy in England in the seventeenth century was considerably higher than scholars had previously acknowledged. More recent work on English education (O'Day, 1982) suggests that the improvements in education and literacy were more gradual than suggested by Stone, but accepts his notion of the relatively high rates of schooling and literacy in England on the eve of North American colonization.

If Bailyn exaggerated the stability, size, and complexity of English families and underestimated the extent of formal schooling, he also overestimated the disruption of family life in the New World— especially in New England which was the pioneer in establishing local schools. Studies of the migration of settlers to Massachusetts (Allen, 1981; Powell, 1963), for example, emphasize either the continuation of many English customs and practices or a more orderly process of adjustment to the new environment than the more cataclysmic picture portrayed by Bailyn. Indeed, Greven (1970), one of Bailyn's own students, found that parental authority in seventeenth-century Andover, Massachusetts was stronger and family life more stable than in England.

The remarkable success with which Andover's first generation rerooted themselves in the soil of the New England and maintained their families for generations to come reflects the opportunities for the establishment of orderly and cohesive families and communities in the midst of the American wilderness. In no significant sense were the lives of the first and second generations in disorder, once their permanent roots had been firmly established in early Andover (Greven, 1970: 271).[3]

As a result, Bailyn's claim that the sudden and unexpected disintegration and transformation of the family in the New World led to the creation of schools no longer seems as convincing and compelling as when it was first proposed twenty-five years ago.

Yet if Bailyn's specific explanations for the development of colonial education no longer appear as satisfactory, his emphasis on the importance of the family and the church for the education of the young in England was well-founded. Protestants in England generally promoted household religion and the Puritans emphasized it more than other religious groups (Axtell, 1974; Morgan, 1966). The Puritans assumed that the family had the primary responsibility for education and that the state would only intervene when the family failed to instruct its members in reading and religion. Hence, the late Renaissance in England was a time of expanding familial responsibility for education while also a period of school expansion. Rather than the establishment of schools being a substitute for household education (Ariès, 1962), the two processes were complementary (Cremin, 1970).

In the New World, the role of the family in educating the young was even more important than in England—partly out of necessity since other institutions such as the school and the church were not readily available.

> The family, then, was the principal unit of social organization in the colonies and the most important agency of popular education; and it assumed an educational significance that went considerably beyond that of its English counterpart. Whereas England had by the 1640s and 1650s placed churches within reach of virtually every household, schools within the reach of most, and universities within the reach of at least the more ambitious and able, the colonies were only beginning in those directions. Hence, while metropolitan families could take for granted

> the ready availability of other institutions to assist in the educational task, colonial families could not. As a result, the colonial household simply took unto itself, by force of circumstance, educational responsibilities that the English family commonly shared with other agencies (Cremin, 1970: 135).

Indeed, even when local churches were available nearby, the New England Puritans before the 1660s continued to emphasize the role of the family over that of the church in the catechizing of children and servants (Axtell, 1974).[4]

For the New England Puritans, the primary educator in the family was the father who as the head of the household was expected to catechize his own children and servants. While the mother might assist the father in this task, it was his primary responsibility (Moran and Vinovskis, forthcoming).[5] After the Anne Hutchinson turmoil in the 1630s, the Puritan leaders were reluctant to entrust religious instruction to females.[6] In addition, the appropriateness of the father as the principal educator was reinforced by the fact that husbands usually were more literate than wives—an estimated sixty percent of men among the early settlers could sign their wills while only about thirty percent of women were able to do so (Lockridge, 1974). Indeed, Auwers (1980) found that female literacy in seventeenth-century Windsor, Connecticut was associated with the literacy of the father but not that of the mother.

While parents were expected to teach their own children how to read and to catechize them, Massachusetts also passed legislation in 1647 requiring communities of one hundred or more households to maintain a grammar school and those of fifty or more households to establish schools to teach reading and writing. As in England, this legislation was intended to complement rather than to replace parental efforts in the home (Cohen, 1974;

Cremin, 1970). Interestingly, Murphy (1960) found that in the first decade after the enactment of this law, only a third of the eligible towns complied with the requirement to establish petty or dame schools to teach elementary reading and writing while all eight of the towns required to maintain a grammar school did so. Thus, by the mid-seventeenth century, many of the larger Massachusetts communities provided some formal schooling for their inhabitants even though the emphasis was still on having parents educate and catechize their own household members.[7]

Bailyn was correct to point to a crisis in Puritan society in the seventeenth century. The exact nature of that crisis, however, may have been slightly different than he had envisioned. As Bailyn observed, church membership declined in the seventeenth century and this led many Puritans to conclude that there was a serious decline in religious commitment in their society. While more recent scholarship (Hall, 1972; Moran, 1979, 1980; Pope, 1969) on Puritan church membership portrays a more complex picture of declension than the one suggested by Miller (1953), there is little doubt that many Massachusetts residents in the seventeenth century were deeply concerned about this trend.

Rather than seeing the enactment of these early school laws as evidence of the disintegration of the stable family in New England, it is probably more accurate to see it as a reflection of the attempts to promulgate correct religious views and to overcome the growing indifference of many families toward religion and home education. In the aftermath of the Antinomian crisis, Puritan ministers and magistrates were very anxious about threats to their religion and wanted to make sure that correct doctrine was being taught in schools and at home (Foster, 1984; Hall, 1968). They also were reacting to the ap-parent growing indifference or unwillingness among many parents to catechize their own children (Axtell, 1974). As a result, the Puritans not only required the establishment of schools in towns and the use of approved catechisms in the home, they were even willing sometimes to remove children from households which failed to educate and catechize them properly (Morgan, 1966).

In addition to the apparent overall decline in church membership, there was simultaneously a growing unwillingness of adult males to join the church in the mid-seventeenth century. Church membership became increasingly feminized, although control of the congregation still rested in the hands of male elders and deacons (Moran, 1979, 1980; Moran and Vinovskis, 1982). As a result, many of the male heads of the households were unwilling or no longer could be entrusted to educate and catechize their children and servants as they were not church members. This led to a variety of experiments to provide alternative sources of education, including more emphasis on catechism within the churches and an increasing reliance on schoolteachers (Axtell, 1974; Hall, 1972). It also led in the long-run to a greater reliance on the mothers, who continued to join the church in larger proportions than their husbands, to educate and catechize their children—thus increasing the need for educating women beyond the simple ability to read the Bible by themselves. Not surprisingly, the literacy rate for women increased substantially during the colonial period from about 30% in the early seventeenth century to 60% at the end of the eighteenth century (Lockridge, 1974).

If there is general agreement that the rates of literacy for both males and females in colonial New England increased, there is considerable disagreement over how this was achieved. Lockridge (1974),

Daniels (1979), Auwers (1980), and Soltow and Stevens (1981) argue that the expansion in the number of schools in New England as the population density increased led to the rise in literacy. Lockridge (1974: 58) specifically dismisses home education as a possible explanation for the rise in literacy.

Some scholars (Moran and Vinovskis, forthcoming) have questioned the rejection of household education as a possible factor in increased literacy by pointing out that since the emphasis in Puritan religion was on being able to read the Bible, it is not surprising that many girls might be taught to read but not to write whereas the boys were more likely to be educated in both skills as part of their career preparation. In addition, Auwers' (1980) study of literacy suggests an increase in female literacy even in those sections of Windsor which were far removed from any schools. Furthermore, some educational historians (Cohen, 1974) have argued that opportunities for formal education may have declined for many children in the eighteenth century even though literacy was increasing during these years.[8] Thus, the relative role of the household or the schools in the education of colonial Americans in the late seventeenth and eighteenth centuries still awaits further research.

The manner of maintaining and running schools in colonial New England varied considerably. As Bailyn (1960) pointed out, the expectation that rents from lands granted for educational purposes would produce sufficient income for schooling did not materialize. Therefore several other sources of income were used, such as tuition, subscription, and increasingly annual grants from the town treasury (Cohen, 1974; Cremin, 1970; Murphy, 1960). The direct costs to parents of educating children also differed among Massachusetts communities. In some

towns all pupils attended school without any additional expense while in others all students except the children of the poor paid tuition.

Taxpayers were reluctant to assume the costs of elementary education and town meetings frequently reaffirmed the responsibility of parents for educating their own children. Yet once schools were established, especially at the expense of all taxpayers, parents were quite willing to send their children to these schools rather than teaching them to read and write at home (May and Vinovskis, 1977). Thus, even though the general increase in literacy in colonial America made parents more capable of training their children at home, most parents preferred, whenever possible, to send their offspring to public or private schools.

The Puritans emphasized education more than most other colonists (Cohen, 1974; Cremin, 1970, 1976; Morgan, 1966). New England led the rest of the colonies in literacy and schooling (Cremin, 1970; Lockridge, 1974). Although efforts were made to establish schools in the South, they failed due to the greater dispersion of population and the lack of sustained financial support locally (Cohen, 1974). Educating children was more difficult in the South because very high rates of mortality in the early decades of settlement made family life very unstable (Beales, 1985; Earle, 1979; Rutman and Rutman, 1979). Nevertheless, southern parents frequently tried to provide for the education of their children by setting aside funds for schooling in their wills (Carr and Walsh, 1977).

As southern society became more settled and family life more stable after mortality rates declined in the second half of the seventeenth century, it became easier to plan and provide for education. Yet southern parents did not seem to value education as much as their northern counterparts. Indeed, some planter sons were educated more as a sign of family respectability and achievement than as reflection of their commitment to learning (Smith, 1980).

Rather than trying to establish schools, most planters were content to hire tutors to educate their sons in the home and then send them abroad or North for a university education. While planters also provided for the training of their daughters, they usually did not encourage education much beyond reading and writing (Smith, 1980). Since the South did not develop an extensive system of schools, most children of less wealthy parents received only a rudimentary education and many did not even acquire literacy (Cohen, 1974; Cremin, 1970, 1976).

NINETEENTH-CENTURY PATTERNS AND PRACTICES

Analyzing the relationship between family and schooling has been a central concern for students of American colonial history but not for investigators of nineteenth-century educational or family development. One explanation for the lack of scholarly attention to families and schooling in the nineteenth century is that children did receive most of their education in schools. New England colonists stressed the importance of educating and catechizing children in the home; nineteenth-century parents assumed that learning to read and write would occur in a classroom. The role of parents, especially the mother, was not ignored in the socialization of the child in the nineteenth century, but they were not seen as an alternative to sending children to school. Therefore, it is not surprising that most analysts of antebellum education have devoted relatively little attention to the family.

Interpretations of family-school inter-

actions are influenced by how one explains increases in public schooling during the nineteenth century. Since the late 1960s, a group of revisionist scholars have argued that capitalists, in order to minimize labor unrest during industrialization, imposed education upon largely unwilling and uninterested working-class families. The revisionists tend to emphasize the tension between the interests of working-class families and the schools established by the capitalists; they also locate the rise of mass education in the decades prior to the Civil War and associate that increase with the industrializing Northeast (Bowles and Gintis, 1976).[9]

While the revisionist perspective has contributed to our understanding of antebellum education, especially by challenging many of the more traditional explanations and stimulating further research, it has not provided a satisfactory account either of educational developments or the reactions of families to schooling. The terms educational "expansion" and "reform" are often used interchangeably by the revisionists—even though they often refer to separate developments and which may have occurred in different time-periods (Vinovskis, 1985a). For example, contrary to the revisionist argument that mass education emerged in Massachusetts in the middle third of the nineteenth century, widespread schooling in that state originated much earlier and was influenced by Puritan religion as well as the establishment of a new republic which required a more educated citizenry (Kaestle and Vinovskis, 1980; Kerber, 1980; Norton, 1980).

We also need to recognize that there were large regional differences in schooling and literacy in nineteenth-century America (Kaestle, 1983). The South continued to trail the North in schooling and literacy—indeed in some Southern states on the eve of the Civil War, nearly 20% of white adult females were illiterate whereas almost all native-born Northern white adult females were literate (Vinovskis and Bernard, 1978).[10] Furthermore, the largest gains in education in the decades before the Civil War occurred in the Midwest even though that area was still mainly agricultural and had not experienced extensive industrialization as suggested by the revisionist model of educational development (Fishlow, 1966; Soltow and Stevens, 1981).

Rather than seeing common school education simply imposed upon working-class families, it is more accurate to acknowledge the strong, if not sometimes excessive and misguided, faith in public schooling among all segments of nineteenth-century New England society (Fuller, 1982; Kaestle, 1983; Katznelson and Weir, 1985; Mirel, 1981). While the leadership of educational reforms undoubtedly came from a smaller and more elite segment of the population, including not only capitalists but especially others like the clergy, there was widespread public support for common schools—even though the shift from private to public education meant that taxpayers had to shoulder a heavier burden (Vinovskis, 1985a).

While some infer an inevitable conflict between the family and schools as the latter multiplied in number and scope during the nineteenth century and seemingly competed with parents for the attention of children, the process was actually more complementary. The role of women in the raising of their children, for example, expanded considerably during the antebellum period (Kuhn, 1947; Ryan, 1981). Mothers were now seen as the natural and logical caretakers of their young children since fathers continued to reduce their active involvement in the socialization of the child (Demos, 1982; Vinovskis, forthcoming [b]). The doctrine of separate spheres rationalized and reinforced the growing

expectations and obligations of the mother to her children even though schools were playing a larger role in the formal instruction of the child than in the colonial period (Cott, 1977; Norton, 1980). Furthermore, as women replaced men as the school teachers for young children, any apparent separation between the home and the school was minimized as women continued their primary role of educating the young (Bernard and Vinovskis, 1977; Fitts, 1979; Boylan, 1985; Hoffman, 1981; Morain, 1980).

Parents did not oppose the expansion of schools in principle although in practice they often voted against any increases in their taxes for public education. According to the Massachusetts State Law of 1789, children enrolling in grammar schools were expected already to be able to read and write. Some of the citizens of Boston complained that since the community did not provide public primary schools, children of poor parents could not afford to go to private schools to learn to read and write and therefore were in effect excluded from the grammar schools (Schultz, 1973). The Boston School Committee appointed a subcommittee in 1817 to investigate the issue. The subcommittee reaffirmed the traditional, colonial view that parents could and should educate their own children in the home rather than in a public school (Wightman, 1860).

Although the Boston School Committee emphasized the role of parents in teaching children how to read and write, it acknowledged that most parents who could afford to send their children to private schools were already doing so. After some heated discussions, the Committee relented and established in 1818 a few free primary schools for children ages four to six. The demand for these public primary schools was much greater than had been anticipated. Not only did the children from poor families enroll in the new public schools, but also many whose parents were more affluent and had been sending their children to private schools (Wightman, 1860). Thus, while parents as taxpayers sometimes opposed an expansion of public schools, as individuals charged with the primary responsibility for the education of their young children they were quite willing in the nineteenth century to send their children to public schools to learn how to read and write.

The schools did not always try to expand their influence over young children. Indeed, it was often the parents who insisted that schools open their doors to very young children when many school teachers and administrators preferred to have them remain at home. During the 1820s the idea of schools for infants was imported from Europe as a means of helping children of poor or broken families to overcome their lack of adequate training in the home. Infant schools received favorable notices in Boston newspapers as a way of helping poor children (*Boston Recorder and Scriptual Transcript*, 1829). When middle-class parents realized that the children of the poor might derive an advantage over others by going to infant schools, they were quick to take advantage of these new institutions for their own children (*Ladies Magazine*, 1829: 89–90).

Despite the growing interest in early education, public schools were reluctant to accept children ages two or three in their classrooms. The considerable influence that parents had on local school boards, however, meant that educators often could not exclude young children— especially since there was strong pedagogical support for the infant schools among some experts in the late 1820s and early 1830s. As a result, it is estimated that nearly 40% of three-year-olds in Massachusetts may have been enrolled in public and private schools (May and Vinovskis, 1977).

The enthusiasm for infant schools among experts did not last long. Medical opinion, based upon the increasingly popular idea that mental and physical development in the early stages of childhood must be carefully balanced, turned sharply against early education and the infant schools. Amariah Brigham, a noted nineteenth-century physician, attacked early childhood education:

> Many physicians of great experience are of the opinion, that efforts to develope [*sic*] the minds of the young children are very frequently injurious; and from instances of disease in children which I have witnessed, I am forced to believe that the danger is indeed great, and that very often in attempting to call forth and cultivate the intellectual faculties of children before they are six or seven years of age, serious and lasting injury has been done both to the body and the mind....
>
> I beseech parents, therefore, to pause before they attempt to make prodigies of their own children. Though they may not destroy them by the measures they adopt to effect this purpose, yet they will surely enfeeble their bodies, and greatly dispose them to nervous affections. Early mental excitement will serve only to bring forth beautiful, but premature flowers, which are destined soon to wither away, without producing fruit (Brigham, 1833: 15, 55).

Brigham's strong admonitions against early education were received favorably in popular magazines and repeated in many childrearing manuals (Kaestle and Vinovskis, 1980). Simultaneously, schoolteachers and administrators who had opposed the presence of such young children in the classroom earlier as an unnecessary and unwarranted disruption to the rest of the class, now joined forces with those anxious to keep young children out of the schools. Nevertheless, many parents who had been brought up believing that children could and should be taught to read at a very young age refused to keep their young children at home. Since many local school committees, especially in the smaller communities, were still reluctant to refuse admission to children whose parents continued to insist that early education was beneficial, the process of eliminating young children from classrooms took more than a decade to complete (Kaestle and Vinovskis, 1980).[11]

The establishment and demise of infant education illustrates several points about the relationship between families and schools in the nineteenth century. Parents in the early nineteenth century were eager to enroll very young children in school because they thought children had the mental capacity to learn to read at ages three or four. As long as parents felt that schools could teach their children to learn to read at an early age, they were willing to relinquish them to the care of teachers rather than educating them at home. Although schoolteachers and administrators often opposed sending young children into the classroom, antebellum local school committees were reluctant to establish and enforce minimum ages for school attendance in the face of strong parental objections. In addition, there was a considerable time-lag between when prominent physicians and educators declared early childhood education dangerous and when most parents agreed by keeping their young children at home. Finally, the gradual expulsion of young children from the classrooms meant that mothers played a larger and longer role in the socialization of their young children in the home.

If many early nineteenth-century parents were eager to send their children to school, they were more reluctant to have them stay in school beyond the time necessary to obtain a basic common school education. Unfortunately, there is very little analysis of the relative role of the student or their parents in the decision to leave school. Most scholars seem to simply assume that the parents exercised

the most influence in deciding when their children would end their schooling; some recent work on high school attendance in the late nineteenth century, however, suggests that the experiences of the students themselves in school may have influenced that decision. Perlmann (1985b) has found that the grades students received in high school were a better predictor of whether or not they decided to stay in school than the occupation of their father.[12]

Historians of colonial education have found it difficult to analyze the characteristics of students and their families because of the lack of readily available information. Scholars of nineteenth-century education, however, have been more successful because they can ascertain the characteristics of school attendance in the decennial federal manuscript censuses from 1850–1880 and 1900–1910 which asked each person under twenty if they had attended any school during the past year.

The classic work by Thernstrom (1964) on school attendance in Newburyport, Massachusetts found that Irish Catholics were much less likely to keep their children in school than native-born Protestants. Thernstrom argued that Irish parents, eager to purchase their own home, sacrificed the future social mobility of their children by sending them into the labor force. Thernstrom's emphasis on the ethnicity and religion of the Irish as the explanation for the differential school attendance rates has been challenged by revisionists such as Katz (1975) who interpret variations in school attendance as class differences.[13] More recent studies (Kaestle and Vinovskis, 1980; Katz and Davey, 1978), using more sophisticated statistical techniques such as multiple classification analysis, have found that both ethnicity and occupation influence the likelihood of remaining in school. Furthermore, the argument that Irish families prematurely sent their children into the labor force in order to purchase a home has not been substantiated. In fact, several investigators (Katz, 1982; Perlmann, 1985a) have found a positive rather than negative relationship between home ownership and school attendance.[14]

Most studies of the influence of family characteristics on school attendance focus on the attributes of the head of household (i.e., ethnicity or occupation). Yet this provides only a limited sense of the needs and resources of the family as a whole. Some scholars (Kaestle and Vinovskis, 1980) have tried to develop a work/consumption index which takes into account the number of workers and consumers in each family according to information from the federal manuscript censuses. Yet the results from these investigations do not show a strong relationship between school attendance and the economic well-being of the family as a whole—perhaps suggesting that the particular work/consumption indices may not be an accurate reflection of the overall economic circumstances of the family.[15]

While studies of school attendance using census data are useful, they do not have the type of detailed financial information one would like to have in order to study the impact of the economic circumstances of the family on the school attendance of its children. Therefore, historians are now turning to the more detailed industrial household budget data from the late nineteenth century. Using the household budgets of textile workers in 1890, Angus and Mirel (1985) did find that the economic situation of the family played an important part in predicting whether or not a child stayed in school.

The frustration of school reformers in getting some children, especially those of immigrant parents, to go to school led to the passage of compulsory school attendance laws in the nineteenth century. Massachusetts led the nation in the enactment of legislation in the mid-nineteenth century which required children under fifteen years of age working in manufacturing establishments to attend school at least three months each year. Despite repeated exhortations by these reformers to the parents and manufacturers to comply with the laws as well as the attempt to hire truant officers in several communities, there was such widespread evasion of the compulsory school attendance laws in the nineteenth century that most contemporaries doubted that they had much of an impact upon school going (Kaestle and Vinovskis, 1980).

Many nineteenth-century Americans were convinced that cities were destroying the traditional family (Boyer, 1978). Conservatives also bemoaned the disestablishment of the state church and the rise of less orthodox religious groups such as the Unitarians (Howe, 1970; Turner, 1985). As a result, many educational reformers saw urban public schools replacing the family and the church as the primary means of educating children. Thus, while nineteenth-century educational reformers continued to speak of the complimentary roles of the family, the church, and the school in the proper upbringing of children, many of them openly or secretly feared that in fact the school was the last bastion for civilizing youths growing up in the cities (Schultz, 1973).[16]

While considerable research has been done on trends in nineteenth-century schooling as well as on the individual family characteristics of students, much less work is available on parent-school relationships. Many of the studies which do look at parent-school interactions focus on the tension between school reformers who wanted to professionalize teaching and advocated giving town school committees more control, and parents who favored having local school district committees making decisions since they were more responsive to the particular needs of that area (Katz, 1971). Gradually the proponents of centralization in Massachusetts, for example, won control of the public schools in the second half of the nineteenth century.

In the rural Midwest, however, parents exercised more control over their public schools longer since state governments gave local districts corporate powers with only minimal restrictions on how they were to be administered. The governance of these small school districts involved a high proportion of local families and provided them with an important sense of participation and power (Fuller, 1982).

Professional educators objected to the decentralization of education in the rural Midwest, but farmers welcomed it and resisted efforts to change it. While nineteenth-century educators pointed to the inefficiencies and ineffectiveness of that decentralized system, at least one researcher (Fuller, 1982) argues that the centralization of schooling at the township level in the Midwest hurt education overall by reducing local interest and support for it.

If town school committees and administrators clashed with parents over the control of hiring teachers and running local schools, they were also anxious to involve the parents in the classroom. Nineteenth-century educators frequently complained about parental apathy or indifference to schooling which permitted or even encouraged their children to be absent or tardy from school. In addition, teachers recognized the need for parental involvement in order to stimulate better performances by students and therefore encouraged parents to attend classes and special examinations. Most nineteenth-century teaching manuals advised teachers to encourage parents to visit classrooms regularly:

> The teacher should encourage parents frequently to visit his school. There is almost everywhere too great backwardness on the part of parents to do this duty. The teacher should early invite them to come in. It is not enough that he do this in general terms. He may fix the time, and arrange the party, so that those who would assimilate, should be brought together. It will frequently be wise to begin with the mothers, where visitation has been unusual. They will soon bring in the fathers. As often as they come they will be benefited. When such visits are made, the teacher should not depart from his usual course of instruction on their account... (Page, 1859: 251–252).

If educators sought parental cooperation and participation in the classroom, they were also aware of the conflicts which arose. Immigrant parents, especially those who were Catholic, often complained bitterly that their children were being indoctrinated in Protestantism in the public schools (Angus, 1980a; Ravitch, 1974). This often led to the removal of foreign-born children from the public schools and the establishment of parochial schools at great additional expense to the parents. Yet in some cities such as St. Louis, school reformers allowed students to be taught in German in order to attract more support for the public schools (Troen, 1975).

Parents also often objected to the type and extent of discipline imposed upon their children in the classroom as well as how and what they were taught. During the course of the nineteenth century parents reluctantly and often unhappily relinquished much of their involvement and influence over activities within the classroom.

In general, parents in nineteenth-century America wanted schools to take custody of their children, and they wanted schools to train their children in basic skills and attitudes. The eventual price that they paid was the loss of authority and control over their children's education. The trade-off was made. The state successfully exerted its right to discipline all children in values that served, first and foremost, the operational necessities of the school, but that also served the social leaders' image of appropriate adult behavior and the parents' image of appropriate childhood behavior. Despite the apparent grounds for consensus, this differentiation of function and shift of authority to the school ultimately produced not just different, but substantially contrary goals.

Elements of antagonism between school and family did not end with a new nineteenth-century equilibrium; they persist today. Clearer boundaries did not necessarily eliminate conflict, but in some ways merely prevented its expression. Compulsory attendance laws, the professionalization of teaching and administration, the development of pedagogical expertise, and the construction of fortress-like urban schools—these helped to insure that parents would interfere less: they did not insure that parents would feel happier or be better served (Kaestle, 1978: 15).

Thus, parents during the nineteenth century increasingly turned their children over to the schools even though it sometimes meant that they had to accept educational and disciplinary practices which they did not favor. Nevertheless, the interactions between parents and schooling continued to influence the nature of the nineteenth-century educational system since schoolteachers and administrators in most communities still were not sufficiently powerful simply to ignore the demands of parents.

CONCLUSION

Throughout human history, the family has played an important role in the socialization of its young. As civilizations developed, there was an increasing tendency to supplement the efforts of the family in the education of its young through other institutions such as churches and schools. The growth of these additional and alternative institutions of education reflect in large measure the recognition that the task of training the young is so vital to the interests of society that it cannot be entrusted exclusively to the family.

The family was an important source of education for children in colonial and nineteenth-century America. But from the very beginning churches and schools were directed to assist parents in the socialization of the young. Indeed, by the mid-nineteenth century, the role of the schools had expanded to such an extent that many of the educational tasks initially assigned to parents, such as teaching children the alphabet and how to read, became the responsibility of the schools.

Throughout the seventeenth, eighteenth, and nineteenth centuries, both parents and schools played an important part in the education of young Americans. While historians of the family and of education have frequently acknowledged these complementary, if not sometimes conflicting, institutions in the training of the young, very little effort has been made to examine the interactions between them. Despite Bailyn's call twenty-five years ago for a more comprehensive approach to the study of education, few historians have responded directly to that challenge. Nevertheless, as this article suggests, many of the particular components of a broader interpretation of the role of parents and schools in the education of the young now have been completed and prepare the way for a more dynamic and family-oriented analysis of the education of children in early America.

ACKNOWLEDGMENTS

I want to thank David Angus, Raymond Grew, Carl Kaestle, Jeffrey Mirel, Gerald

Moran, and James Turner for very useful comments on an earlier version of this essay.

NOTES

1. For an introduction to recent work on family history, see Degler (1980), Gordon (1978), Ryan (1982), and Vinovskis (forthcoming[a]). For developments in educational history, see Angus (1983), Cremin (1970, 1980), Graff (1977), and Vinovskis (1983, 1985a). There are two earlier essays (Angus, 1980b; Cremin, 1978) on the relationship between the family and education that are quite useful.

2. Although there are no specific references in Bailyn (1960) to the Handlin volume (1951), Bailyn probably drew upon some of the general ideas espoused by Handlin—especially the chapters which dealt with the reactions of parents and children to the New World.

3. While critics (Vinovskis, 1971) quarrel with some of Greven's methodology and findings, no one has contested his assertion that family life in New England was relatively stable. Similar results have been reported (Demos, 1970; Lockridge, 1970) for other communities in seventeenth-century Massachusetts.

4. The most detailed and comprehensive treatment of the role of education and the family among the New England Puritans is still Morgan (1966). While his account discusses the difficulties that Puritans experienced in trying to get families to fulfill their responsibilities, it does not convey the sense of disintegration and instability present in Bailyn's (1960) account.

5. Hiner (1973: 12) points out that "hardly any attention was devoted to mothers in seventeenth-century recitations of parental duties." Indeed, "if the Puritan father had a relatively equal teaching partner, it was not his wife, but his minister" (Hiner, 1973: 13).

6. On the changing role of women and religion during the seventeenth century, see Dunn (1980), Koehler (1980), Moran (1979, 1980), Moran and Vinovskis (1982, forthcoming), and Ulrich (1980, 1982).

7. According to Hiner (1973), seventeenth-century Puritans did not emphasize the importance of the lower schools. Beginning in the 1690s, however, Cotton Mather and others began to stress the need for these lower schools as a way of cultivating civility among unregenerate children.

8. Whether or not educational facilities increased or decreased proportionate to the population in eighteenth-century New England is not clear.

Part of the confusion stems from the fact that much of the evidence of school decline comes from data on grammar schools. Yet Teaford (1970) argues that although classical grammar schools did decline in the late seventeenth and eighteenth centuries, they were replaced by other secondary schools which taught English. According to Teaford, there is a transformation of the nature of secondary education in Massachusetts prior to the American Revolution rather than a decrease in interest in education. Thus, the entire issue of the relative availability of elementary schools to teach basic skills to children in the eighteenth century still awaits further research.

9. There is considerable debate over the exact meaning of the term "revisionist" since it encompasses a group of scholars who often disagree among themselves on important aspects of educational development. For a discussion of the term, see Ravitch (1978) and Katz (1976).

10. Relatively little has been written about education in the nineteenth-century South. For an introduction to some recent studies, see Burton (1985), Kett (1985), and Stowe (1985). On the educational experiences of slaves and freedmen, see Jones (1980), Webber (1978), and Wyatt-Brown (1985).

11. When kindergartens were established later, often very young children were excluded from attending them. In addition, kindergartens deliberately did not try to teach young children how to read (Finkelstein, 1985).

12. In general, there is very little concern among historians with the experiences of students in the classroom. For a good introduction to this issue, see Boylan (1985) and Finkelstein (1979). As an example of how nineteenth-century children learned to draw at home and in school, see Korzenik (1985).

13. Thernstrom's study of Newburyport education is now being revised by Vinovskis (1985b) who is analyzing the educational experiences of all children in that community rather than of just those who were the offspring of common laborers. Preliminary findings suggest that Thernstrom underestimated the extent of school attendance in Newburyport—even among the children of the common laborers he investigated.

14. Hogan (1985) maintains that home ownership and early school leaving are related in his study of Chicago, but he does not have any individual-level data which would either support or refute that proposition.

15. The work/consumption index seems to predict the likelihood of women going into the labor force (Mason, Vinovskis, and Hareven, 1978), but does not explain school attendance. Since many

nineteenth-century girls who dropped out of school stayed at home rather than entering the labor force, it may be that the processes of school leaving and entry into the paid labor force are not identical for females.

16. Public elementary and secondary schools were not the only institutions devised by nineteenth-century Americans to cope with their perceived crisis of raising children in the cities. Child-reform advocates also established orphan asylums (Hawes, 1971), Sunday schools (Boylan, 1979), and reform schools (Brenzel, 1983; Schlossman, 1977) for helping children. For an interesting introduction and interpretation of these and other institutions for the care of children, see Finkelstein (1985).

REFERENCES

Allen, David Grayson. 1981. *In English Ways: The Movement of Societies and the Transferral of English Local Law and Custom to Massachusetts Bay in the Seventeenth Century*. Chapel Hill: University of North Carolina Press.

Angus, David L. 1980a. "Detroit's Great School Wars: Religion and Politics in a Frontier City, 1842–1853." *Michigan Academician* 12: 261–280.

———. 1980b. "Families Against the System: Fifty Years of Survival, 1880–1930." *Educational Considerations*: 9–14.

———. 1983. "The Empirical Mode: Quantitative History." Pp. 75–93 in John Hardin Best (ed.), *Historical Inquiry in Education: A Research Agenda*. Washington, D.C.: American Educational Research Association.

Angus, David L. and Jeffrey E. Mirel. 1985. "From Spellers to Spindles: Work-Force Entry by the Children of Textile Workers, 1888–1890." *Social Science History* 9:123–143.

Ariès, Phillippe. 1962. *Centuries of Childhood: A Social History of Family Life*. Trans. Robert Baldick. New York: Vintage.

Auwers, Linda. 1980. "Reading the Marks of the Past: Exploring Female Literacy in Colonial Windsor, Connecticut." *Historical Methods* 4: 204–214.

Axtell, James. 1974. *The School Upon a Hill: Education and Society in Colonial New England*. New Haven, CT: Yale University Press.

Bailyn, Bernard. 1960. *Education in the Forming of American Society*. Chapel Hill: University of North Carolina Press.

Beales, Ross W., Jr. 1985. "The Child in Seventeenth-Century America." Pp. 3–56 in Joseph M. Hawes and N. Ray Hiner (eds.), *American Childhood: A Research Guide and Historical Handbook*. Westport, CT: Greenwood Press.

Berkner, Lutz. 1972. "The Stem Family and the Developmental Cycle of the Peasant Household: An Eighteenth-Century Austrian Example." *American Historical Review* 77: 398–418.

Bernard, Richard M. and Maris A. Vinovskis. 1977. "The Female School Teacher in Antebellum America." *Journal of Social History* 3: 332–345.

Boston Recorder and Scriptural Transcript. July 9, 1829.

Bowles, Samuel and Herbert Gintis. 1976. *Schooling in Capitalist America: Educational Reform and the Contradictions of Economic Life*. New York: Basic Books.

Boyer, Paul. 1978. *Urban Masses and Moral Order in America, 1820-1920*. Cambridge, MA: Harvard University Press.

Boylan, Anne M. 1979. "The Role of Conversion in Nineteenth-Century Sunday Schools." *American Studies* 20: 35–48.

———. 1985. "Growing Up Female in Young America, 1800–1860." Pp. 153–184 in Joseph M. Hawes and N. Ray Hiner (eds.), *American Childhood: A Research Guide and Historical Handbook*. Westport, CT: Greenwood Press.

Brenzel, Barbara. 1983. *Daughters of the State: A Social Portrait of the First Reform School for Girls in North America, 1856-1905*. Cambridge, MA: M.I.T. Press.

Brigham, Amariah. 1833. *Remarks on the Influence of Mental Cultivation and Mental Excitement Upon Health*. 2nd ed. Boston.

Burton, Orville B. 1985. *In My Father's House Are Many Mansions: Family and Community in Edgefield, South Carolina*. Chapel Hill: University of North Carolina Press.

Carr, Lois Green and Lorena S. Walsh. 1977. "The Planter's Wife: The Experience of White Women in Seventeenth Century Maryland." *William and Mary Quarterly*, 3rd Series 34: 542–571.

Cohen, Sheldon S. 1974. *A History of Colonial Education, 1607-1776*. New York: Wiley.

Cott, Nancy F. 1977. *The Bonds of Womanhood: "Women's Sphere" in New England, 1780-1835*. New Haven, CT: Yale University Press.

Cremin, Lawrence A. 1970. *American Education: The Colonial Experience, 1607-1783*. New York: Harper & Row.

———. 1976. *Traditions of American Education*. New York: Basic Books.

———. 1978. "Family-Community Linkages in American Education: Some Comments on the Recent Historiography." *Teachers College Record* 79: 683–704.

———. *American Education: The National Ex-*

perience, 1783-1876. New York: Harper & Row.

Daniels, Bruce C. 1979. *The Connecticut Town: Growth and Development, 1635-1790*. Middletown, CT: Wesleyan University Press.

Degler, Carl N. 1980. "Women and the Family." Pp. 308–326 in Michael Kammer (ed.), *The Past Before Us: Contemporary Historical Writings in the United States*. Ithaca, NY: Cornell University Press.

Demos, John. 1970. *A Little Commonwealth: Family Life in Plymouth Colony*. New York: Oxford University Press.

————. "The Changing Faces of Fatherhood: A New Exploration of American Family History." Pp. 425–445 in Stanley H. Cath, Alan R. Gurwitt, and John Munder Ross (eds.), *Father and Child: Developmental and Clinical Perspectives*. Boston: Little, Brown.

Dunn, Mary Maples. 1980. "Saints and Sinners: Congregational and Quaker Women in the Early Colonial Period." Pp. 27–46 in Janet Wilson James (ed.), *Women in American Religion*. Philadelphia: University of Pennsylvania Press.

Earle, Carville V. 1979. "Environment, Disease, and Mortality in Early Virginia." Pp. 96–125 in Thad W. Tate and David L. Ammerman (eds.), *The Chesapeake in the Seventeenth Century: Essays on Anglo-American Society and Politics*. New York: Norton.

Finkelstein, Barbara. 1979. "Reading, Writing, and the Acquisition of Identity in the United States: 1790–1860." Pp. 114–139 in *Regulated Children, Liberated Children: Education in Psychohistorical Perspective*. New York: Psychohistory Press.

————. 1985. "Casting Networks of Good Influence: The Reconstruction of Childhood in the United States, 1790–1870." Pp. 111–152 in Joseph M. Hawes and N. Ray Hiner (eds.), *American Childhood: A Research Guide and Historical Handbook*. Westport, CT: Greenwood Press.

Fishlow, Albert. 1966. "The American Common School Revival: Fact or Fancy?" Pp. 40–67 in Henry Rosovsky (ed.), *Industrialization in Two Systems: Essays in Honor of Alexander Gershenkron*. New York: Wiley.

Fitts, Deborah. 1979. "Una and the Lion: The Feminization of District School-Teaching and its Effects on the Roles of Students and Teachers in Nineteenth-Century Massachusetts. Pp. 140–157 in Barbara Finkelstein (ed.), *Regulated Children, Liberated Children: Education in Psychohistorical Perspective*. New York: Psychohistory Press.

Foster, Stephen. 1984. "English Puritanism and the Progress of New England Institutions, 1630–1660." Pp. 3–37 in David Hall, John M. Murrin, and Thad N. Tate (eds.), *Saints and Revolutionaries: Essays on Early American History*. New York: Norton.

Fuller, Wayne E. 1982. *The Old Country School*. Chicago: University of Chicago Press.

Gordon, Michael. 1978. *The American Family: Past, Present, and Future*. New York: Random House.

Graff, Harvey J. 1977. "The 'New Math': Quantification, the 'New' History, and the History of Education." *Urban Education* 11: 403–440.

Greven, Philip J. Jr. 1970. *Four Generations: Population, Land, and Family in Colonial Andover, Massachusetts*. Ithaca, NY: Cornell University Press.

Hall, David D. (ed.). 1968. *The Antinomian Controversy, 1636-1638: A Documentary History*. Middletown, CT: Wesleyan University Press.

————. 1972. *The Faithful Shepherd: A History of the New England Ministry in the Seventeenth Century*. Chapel Hill: University of North Carolina Press.

Handlin, Oscar. 1951. *The Uprooted: The Epic Story of the Great Migrations that Made the American People*. New York: Grosset and Dunlap.

Hawes, Joseph M. 1971. *Children in Urban Society: Juvenile Delinquency in Nineteenth-Century America*. New York: Oxford University Press.

Hiner, N. Ray. 1973. "The Cry of Sodom Enquired Into: Educational Analysis in Seventeenth-Century New England." *History of Education Quarterly* 13: 3–22.

Hoffman, Nancy. 1981. *Woman's "True" Profession: Voices from the History of Teaching*. New York: Feminist Press.

Hogan, David J. 1985. *Class and Reform: School and Society in Chicago, 1880-1930*. Philadelphia: University of Pennsylvania Press.

Houlbrooke, Ralph A. 1984. *The English Family, 1450-1700*. London: Longman.

Howe, Daniel Walker. 1970. *The Unitarian Conscience: Harvard Moral Philosophy, 1805-1861*. Cambridge, MA: Harvard University Press.

Jones, Jacqueline. 1980. *Soldiers of Light and Love: Northern Teachers and Georgia Blacks, 1865-1873*. Chapel Hill: University of North Carolina Press.

Kaestle, Carl F. 1978. "Social Change, Discipline, and the Common School in Early Nineteenth-Century America." *Journal of Interdisciplinary History* 9:1–17.

————. 1983. *Pillars of the Republic: Common Schools and American Society, 1780-1860.* New York: Hill and Wang.

Kaestle, Carl F. and Maris A. Vinovskis. 1980. *Education and Social Change in Nineteenth-Century Massachusetts.* Cambridge: Cambridge University Press.

Katz, Michael B. 1971. *Class, Bureaucracy, and Schools.* New York: Praeger.

————. 1975. *The People of Hamilton, Canada West: Family and Class in a Mid-Nineteenth Century City.* Cambridge, MA: Harvard University Press.

————. 1976. "The Origins of Public Education: A Reassessment." *History of Education Quarterly* 16: 381–407.

————. 1982. "School Attendance in Philadelphia, 1850–1900." Working Paper, Organization of School, Work and Family Life in Philadelphia, 1838–1920 Project, University of Pennsylvania.

Katz, Michael B. and Ian E. Davey. 1978. "School Attendance and Early Industrialization in a Canadian City: A Multivariate Analysis." *History of Education Quarterly* 18: 271–293.

Katznelson, Ira and Margaret Weir. 1985. *Schooling for All: Class, Race, and the Decline of the Democratic Ideal.* New York: Basic Books.

Kerber, Linda K. 1980. *Women of the Republic: Intellect and Ideology in Revolutionary America.* Chapel Hill: University of North Carolina Press.

Kett, Joseph F. 1985. "Women and the Progressive Impulse in Southern Education." Pp. 166–180 in Walter J. Fraser, Jr., R. Frank Saunders, Jr., and Jon L. Wakelyn (eds.), *The Web of Southern Social Relations: Women, Family, and Education.* Athens: University of Georgia Press.

Koehler, Lyle. 1980. *A Search for Power: The "Weaker Sex" in Seventeenth-Century New England.* Urbana: University of Illinois Press.

Korzenik, Diana. 1985. *Drawn to Art: A Nineteenth-Century American Dream.* Hanover, NH: University of New England.

Kuhn, Ann L. 1947. *The Mother's Role in Childhood Education.* New Haven, CT: Yale University Press.

Ladies' Magazine 2. February 1829.

Laslett, Peter. 1969. "Size and Structure of the Household in England Over Three Centuries." *Population Studies* 23: 199–223.

————. 1972. *Household and Family in Past Time,* Cambridge: Cambridge University Press.

————. 1977. *Family Life and Illicit Love in Earlier Generations: Essays in Historical Sociology.* Cambridge: Cambridge University Press.

Lockridge, Kenneth A. 1970. *A New England Town; The First Hundred Years: Dedham, Massachusetts, 1636-1736.* New York: Norton.

————. 1974. *Literacy in Colonial New England: An Enquiry into the Social Context of Literacy in the Early Modern West.* New York: Norton.

Mason, Karen, Maris A. Vinovskis, and Tamara K. Hareven. 1978. "Women's Work and the Life Course in Essex County, Massachusetts, 1880." Pp. 187–216 in Tamara K. Hareven (ed.), *Transitions: The Family and the Life Course in Historical Perspective.* New York: Academic Press.

May, Dean and Maris A. Vinovskis. 1977. "A Ray of Millenial Light: Early Education and Social Reform in the Infant School Movement in Massachusetts, 1826–1840." Pp. 62–99 in Tamara K. Hareven (ed.), *Family and Kin in American Urban Communities, 1800-1940.* New York: Watts.

Miller, Perry. 1953. *The New England Mind: From Colony to Province.* Cambridge, MA: Harvard University Press.

Mirel, Jeffrey. 1981. "The Matter of Means: The Campaign and Election for the New York Free Academy, 1846–1847." *Journal of Midwest History* 9: 134–155.

Morain, Thomas. 1980. "The Departure of Males from the Teaching Profession in Nineteenth-Century Iowa." *Civil War History* 26: 161–170.

Moran, Gerald F. 1979. "Religious Renewal, Puritan Tribalism, and the Family in Seventeenth-Century Milford Connecticut." *William and Mary Quarterly*, 3rd Series 36: 236–254.

————. 1980. "'Sisters' in Christ: Women and the Church in Seventeenth-Century New England." Pp. 47–65 in Janet Wilson James (ed.), *Women in American Religion.* Philadelphia: University of Pennsylvania Press.

Moran, Gerald F. and Maris A. Vinovskis. 1982. "The Puritan Family and Religion: A Critical Reappraisal." *William and Mary Quarterly*, 3rd Series 39: 29–63.

————. Forthcoming. "The Great Care of Godly Parents: Early Childhood in Puritan New England." In John Hagen and Alice Smuts (eds.), *History and Research in Child Development: In Celebration of the Fiftieth Anniversary of the Society.* Chicago: University of Chicago Press.

Morgan, Edmund S. 1966. *The Puritan Family: Religion and Domestic Relations in Seventeenth-Century New England.* New York: Harper & Row.

Murphy, Joanne Geraldine. 1960. "Massachusetts Bay Colony: The Role of Government in Education." Unpublished Ph.D. dissertation, Radcliffe College.

Norton, Mary Beth. 1980. *Liberty's Daughters: The Revolutionary Experience of American Women, 1750-1800*. Boston: Little, Brown.

O'Day, Rosemary. 1982. *Education and Society, 1500-1800: The Social Foundations of Education in Early Modern Britain*. London: Longman.

Page, David P. 1859. *Theory and Practice of Teaching: Or, The Motives and Methods of Good School-Keeping*. 25th ed. New York: A.S. Barnes and Burr.

Perlmann, Joel. 1985a. "Curriculum and Tracking in the Transformation of the American High School: Providence, R.I., 1880–1930." *Journal of Social History* 19: 29–55.

———. 1985b. "Who Stayed in School? Social Structure and Academic Achievement in the Determination of Enrollment Patterns, Providence, Rhode Island, 1880–1925." *Journal of American History* 72: 588–614.

Pope, Robert G. 1969. *The Half-Way Covenant: Church Membership in Puritan New England*. Princeton: Princeton University Press.

Powell, Sumner Chilton. 1963. *Puritan Village: The Formation of a New England Town*. Middletown, CT: Wesleyan University Press.

Prest, W.R. 1976. "Stability and Change in Old and New England: Clayworth and Dedham." *Journal of Interdisciplinary History* 6: 359–574.

Ravitch, Diane. 1974. *The Great School Wars: New York City, 1805-1973*. New York: Basic Books.

———. 1978. *The Revisionists Revised: A Critique of the Radical Attack on the Schools*. New York: Basic Books.

Rutman, Darret B. and Anita H. Rutman. 1979. "'Now-Wives and Sons-in Law': Parental Death in a Seventeenth-Century Virginia County." Pp. 153–182 in Thad W. Tate and David Ammerman (eds.), *The Chesapeake in the Seventeenth Century: Essays on Anglo American Society and Politics*. New York: Norton.

Ryan, Mary P. 1981. *Cradle of the Middle Class: The Family in Oneida County, New York, 1790-1865*. Cambridge: Cambridge University Press.

———. 1982. "The Explosion of Family History." *Reviews in American History* 10: 181–195.

Schlossman, Steven L. 1977. *Love and the American Delinquent: The Theory and Practice of Progressive Juvenile Justice, 1825-1920*. Chicago: University of Chicago Press.

Schultz, Stanley K. 1973. *The Culture Factory: Boston Public Schools, 1789-1860*. New York: Oxford University Press.

Smith, Daniel Blake. 1980. *Inside the Great House: Planter Family Life in Eighteenth-Century Chesapeake Society*. Ithaca, NY: Cornell University Press.

Soltow, Lee and Edward Stevens. 1981. *The Rise of Literacy and the Common School in the United States: A Socio-Economic Analysis to 1870*. Chicago: University of Chicago Press.

Stone, Lawrence. 1964. "The Educational Revolution in England, 1560–1640." *Past and Present* 28: 41–80.

Stowe, Steven M. 1985. "The Not-So-Cloistered Academy: Elite Women's Education and Family Feeling in the Old South." Pp. 90–106 in Walter J. Fraser, Jr., R. Frank Saunders, Jr., and Jon L. Wakelyn (eds.), *The Web of Southern Social Relations: Women, Family, and Education*. Athens: University of Georgia Press.

Teaford, Jon. 1970. "The Transformation of Massachusetts Education, 1670–1780." *History of Education Quarterly* 10: 287–307.

Thernstrom, Stephen. 1964. *Poverty and Progress: Social Mobility in a Nineteenth-Century City*. Cambridge, MA: Harvard University Press.

Troen, Selwyn K. 1975. *The Public and the Schools: Shaping the St. Louis System, 1838-1920*. Columbia: University of Missouri Press.

Turner, James. 1985. *Without God, Without Creed: The Origins of Unbelief in America*. Baltimore: Johns Hopkins University Press.

Ulrich, Laurel Thatcher. 1980. "Vertuous Women Found: New England Ministerial Literature, 1668–1735." Pp. 67-87 in Janet Wilson James (ed.), *Women in American Religion*. Philadelphia: University of Pennsylvania Press.

———. 1982. *Good Wives: Images and Reality in the Lives of Women in Northern New England, 1650-1750*. New York: Alfred A. Knopf.

Vinovskis, Maris A. 1971. "American Historical Demography: A Review Essay." *Historical Methods Newsletter* 4: 141–148.

———. 1983. "Community Studies in Urban Educational History: Some Methodological and Conceptual Observations." Pp. 287–304 in Ronald W. Goodenow and Diane Ravitch (eds.), *Schools in Cities: Consensus and Conflict in American Educational History*. New York: Holmes and Krier.

———. 1985a. *The Origins of Public High Schools: A Reexamination of the Beverly High School Controversy*. Madison: University of Wisconsin Press.

———. 1985b. "Patterns of High School Attendance in Newburyport, Massachusetts in 1860." Unpublished paper presented at the American Historical Association Annual Meeting, New York City.

_____. Forthcoming*(a)*. "The Historian and the Life Course: Reflections on Recent Approaches to the Study of American Family Life in the Past." In David Featherman and Richard Lerner (eds.), *Life-Span Development and Behavior*, vol. 8.

_____. Forthcoming*(b)*. "Young Fathers and Their Children: Some Historical and Policy Perspectives." In Arthur Elster and Michael Lamb (eds.), *Teenage Fathers*.

Vinovskis, Maris A. and Richard M. Bernard. 1978. "Beyond Catherine Beecher: Female Education in the Antebellum Period." *Signs* 3: 856–869.

Webber, Thomas L. 1978. *Deep Like the Rivers: Education in the Slave Quarter Community, 1831-1865*. New York: Norton.

Wightman, Joseph M. 1860. *Annals of the Boston Primary School Committee From Its First Establishment in 1818 to Its Dissolution in 1855*. Boston.

Wyatt-Brown, Bertram. 1985. "Black Schooling During Reconstruction." Pp. 146–165 in Walter J. Fraser, Jr., R. Frank Saunders, Jr., and Jon L. Wakelyn (eds.), *The Web of Southern Social Relations: Women, Family, and Education*. Athens: University of Georgia Press.

THE FORMATION OF
THE COUPLE

André Burguière

ABSTRACT: *Several interpretations have been proposed of the changes that transformed conjugal life in preindustrial Europe and brought about the emergence of the couple. Some focus on economics, others on the intellectual elites, and still others on the role of the state. In the period from 1500 to 1800, one can accept the idea of a permissive sixteenth, austere seventeenth, and liberated eighteenth century, but only in terms of non-linear evolution containing constraints, ruptures, and more than a simple loosening of control. It is during the long period of austere conjugal morality and surveillance of private life that a barrier between a public and private sphere become apparent, forming a space within which a couple was no longer a simple unit of reproduction but a focus of affection and solidarity.*

Was the couple, like happiness, a new idea in eighteenth-century Europe? Historians have proposed several interpretations of the changes that affected the formation of the couple and the atmosphere of conjugal life in preindustrial Europe.

Was economic change the force which caused the community constraints of traditional society to burst apart, thereby liberating the individual and inspiring in him the need to choose freely? Was change brought about by the enlightened elites who invented a new morality and sensibility for the rest of society? Was the

agent the modernizing State, which led the individual to internalize norms, refine manners and discover intimacy? Perhaps all three.

The last two explanations have the advantage of taking the entire period into account, of envisioning a long evolution instead of a linear one, and of adjusting to

André Burguière is directeur d'etudes *at the Ecole des Hautes Etudes en Sciences Sociales in Paris and co-director of the journal Annales. E. S. C. He has published* Bretons de Plozevet *[Paris, 1975],* Regards sur le France *[Paris, 1982], and is the co-author and editor of* Histoire de la famille.

fluctuation in demographic shifts as well as in the moral and religious atmosphere.

Characterized by demographic growth and a certain fluidity in social relations that allowed young people a fairly wide margin of freedom in their sexual lives and the choice of a mate, the rather exuberant sixteenth century was followed by a long, authoritarian and ascetic seventeenth century. The convergent efforts of Church and State imposed a uniformity upon behavior by using the family as a tool to impose morality on the social body. This morality favored the married couple and suppressed all extramarital sexual activity. The eighteenth century, however, experienced a loosening of religious control and the contagious effect of an ideology which, as an offspring of the *Lumières*, favored autonomy, the achievement of worldly happiness based on sentimental effusion, and pleasure. There was a rise of more permissive attitudes towards sexuality, and marriages of love were proposed as a social ideal. The rise in premarital conceptions and illegitimate births, which occurred during the first third of the century, followed the rhythm of economic growth and urbanization.

We can accept the idea of a permissive sixteenth century (that ended towards 1560), an austere seventeenth century, and a liberated eighteenth century (that drew to a close near 1740). This chronology approximates that of Europe as a whole. It is a nonlinear evolution composed of constraints and ruptures but it is not a simple oscillation between repression and loosening of control. It is during this long inculcation period of austere conjugal morality and surveillance of private life, that a barrier between a public and a private sphere became more apparent, forming a space within which the couple was no longer a simple unit of reproduction, but became a privileged focus of affection and solidarity. Paradoxically, it is also

due to the religious redefinition of the matrimonial union and the Church's efforts to restrict sexuality to a conjugal sphere, that the conditions for the emergence of marriages of love were created.

When we evoke marriages of love as a dominant matrimonial model, we confuse two distinct ideas which finally did fuse into one, but only after having evolved along different paths: (1) the idea that young people should be able to decide upon their marriages themselves; and (2) the idea that a love relation and a matrimonial relation are one and the same, that love is the best reason, if not the only reason, for marriage.

At the beginning of the sixteenth century, decision making in matrimonial matters became the object of contradictory pressures that reflected the chaotic vitality of the social fabric. Wedding negotiations continued to bring into play two family groups that needed to decide upon the transfer of a woman and eventually of goods. The *verba de futuro* constituted the heyday of marriage: a primarily civil ceremony during which the two negotiating families sealed their agreement (the marriage contract or "pact") in the presence of a notary, or when one was not available, in the presence of neighbors or close friends, to give their agreement a public nature.

The ecclesiastical authority had to be content with playing a complimentary role in the civil proceedings, respecting customary dispositions by blessing the couple (the *verba de presenti*) inside or in front of a church, in order to confirm the previously concluded agreement. Theological rituals and treatises like to remind us that marriage is the oldest of all sacraments, but it was a sacrament of only weak ecclesiastical tenor since it was "self-administered" by the husband and wife.

As long as the Church, by referring to Paulinian doctrine, continued to view marriage as a remedy for concupiscence and an institution desired by God to assure reproduction of the species, it had a tendency to combine the sacramental power held by husband and wife with the carnal union (*copula carnalis*). But with scholastic doctrine, the basis of the conjugal union passed progressively from a union of bodies to one of hearts, from copulation to mutual consent. Sacramental power tended to blend itself with the voluntary act of reciprocal pledges.

At the end of the Middle Ages, theologians began emphasizing the consensual nature of marriage, which led them to highlight the social dimension of the conjugal union, instead of its biological or prophylactic dimension. This is particularly evident in the debate concerning marriage between older people, which was defended, in a decidedly modern position, by Parisian theologians at the end of the fifteenth century. If procreation was the main goal of marriage, should the Church encourage or even authorize marriage between people who can no longer procreate? In the eyes of Martin le Maistre, such marriages were perfectly legitimate since they would allow husband and wife to assist one another in old age (Noonan, 1965).

During the same period, a similar line of argument led ecclesiastic authorities to encourage remarriages and to defend their legitimacy before reticent public opinion. This reticence, once shared by the Roman Catholic Church, was evident through charivaris—reprisal rituals and symbolic compensation that local society forced upon widows who remarried.

In synodic statutes of the fifteenth century, we find a large number of condemnations of charivari activity. Can this be attributed to a rise in popular resistance to remarriages, that let loose a veritable charivari epidemic? At least, it attests to the Church's insistence on favoring and accepting this type of marriage (Burguière, 1980).

Social conditions of the period—underpopulated cities, deserted villages, a general climate of insecurity—made solitude more improbable than ever, and greatly contributed to creating among critics the conviction that marriage was not a lesser evil, or a duty to the species, but rather a social necessity. The conjugal union could find its own justification by creating a relation of assistance and affection between two individuals. In the long run, this modification of ecclesiastical views laid the groundwork for the sacralization of marriage by Protestant doctrine. Lawrence Stone somewhat overestimates the innovations of Protestantism (particularly of English Protestantism) by attributing the precocious growth of a conjugal civilization in England mainly to the Puritan notion of "Holy Matrimony." Even if during the Council of Trent, when confronted by Protestant criticism, the Church reaffirmed its doctrine of marriage in its most traditional forms, its pastorals, dating from the end of the fifteenth century (a reading of ecclesiastical rituals will confirm this), nonetheless emphasized the reason for marriage as being "to form a society between two" ("se faire société l'un à l'autre")—a definition which had previously been ignored.

The Church could hardly emphasize the social value of the conjugal union without stressing the free consent and reciprocal vows between husband and wife. This would explain the extraordinary efflorescence of ecclesiastical marriage rituals at the end of the fifteenth century and its flourish of regional variants (Molin and Mutembe, 1974). Through gestures, exchanged symbolic objects and mutually spoken vows and commitments, husband and wife adopted an increasingly more active role, leaving priest and parents to merely witness and consent.

By emphasizing the role of husband and wife, ecclesiastic ritual showed itself to be more concerned with adapting to regional particularisms than to following fluctuations in theology. This intensive effort to modernize ritual at the end of the fifteenth and during the first third of the sixteenth century, preceded a systematic reduction of customs and their insertion into a register—"le grand coutumier." The strong wave of conjugality which ensued illustrates the success of the division of inheritance by "beds" in the case of remarriage according to Orleano-Parisian law, or of some kind of agreements such as the "sociètè d'acquets" or the brotherhood between spouses. Perhaps having originated in an urban environment, as shown in the case of Bordeaux (Lafon, 1972), but also favorably accepted by well-to-do peasants, these formulas accompanied economic and demographic recovery. In a society of high social mobility, they reflected the impact of "new men" with no familial past or lineal reflex. For these men, who were therefore free to choose, the conjugal union was precious both as an emotional refuge and as a unit of production at a time when salaries were high.

The *créantailles champenoises* (or *fiançailles*—engagements), in the case of clandestine marriages or engagement requests recorded by officials in Troye, give us a fairly good idea of the liberal climate which surrounded premarital relations and wedding engagements of the time.

We might doubt the sincerity of these depositions, but from one case to another, there is such similarity between the circumstances, the reported words, and the gestures, that we can consider them reliable testimony as to how a marriage was concluded among the popular classes in the sixteenth century. At that time, young people who wished to marry were allowed much autonomy in choosing. They did not decide alone, but the power to control marriages and to assure their validity was distributed among various agents who had neither the same system of values nor the same exigencies. Among the various sources of control were: the Church, the father or tutor, the network of relatives, friends and neighbors, the age group, the professional group, and so on. Amidst this variety of control factors, candidates for marriage could easily find a way to decide according to the dictates of their hearts.

These were competing authorities, but also tolerant ones. Marriage between young people was favored not only by a state of mind conducive to conjugality, or the voice of conscious choice (which is to say everything that encouraged individual determination), but also by a general climate of sexual permissiveness. This permissive attitude towards premarital sexual relations can be seen in the large number of clandestine or controversial engagements that accompanied *commerce charnel* ("carnal trade"). But also, with regard to extramarital relations, the phenomenon of illegitimate children (even if the paucity of serial sources does not allow us to measure its extent) was widespread and even admitted among both the aristocracy and the popular classes. Established prostitution was authorized and even regulated by urban authorities. Brothels and *étuves* ("bathhouses") were denounced by preachers but praised by poets, giving an air of venal gallantry to one of the privileged structures of masculine sociability.

This atmosphere was unlike what we would today refer to as sexual liberation. Its kindly disposition toward masculine instincts was accompanied by a reinforced sexual submission of women, who were exposed to prostitution and rape. Instances of rape and often of group rape were brought in great numbers before civil courts, but also before ecclesiastical ones, since the authors of these offenses were often young clerics, and the victims were known as *femmes de pretres* ("priests' women"). These crimes were punished with surprising leniency: mere fines were imposed and most often set according to the social status of the victim (Rossiaud, 1976).

Prostitution and rape were viewed by authorities as outlets for the sexuality and rebelliousness of young bachelors. Despite such institutions for young people as *abbayes de jeunesse* and *reinages*, bachelors were seen as unable to control their instincts and capable of attacking at any moment women, goods or the power of settled elders. Demographic growth, which made the pressure of upcoming generations more obvious, and urban growth, which drew an unstable mass of young bachelors to the city, added to this effect. Youth was regarded as a fearful menace.

The tolerance of authorities, therefore, did not originate in a liberal ethic, but rather in prudent resignation before a form of social turbulence impossible to control. To this can be added a naturalistic view of sexuality inherited from medieval Christianity. It is impossible not to be struck by the atmosphere of colorful and naive sensuality found in literary, iconographic and judicial sources concerned with the love lives of the famous or the humble. This atmosphere gradually died down and became less colorful during the last third of the century.

Sexual relations and love life were not confused with conjugality, however. The old Pauline conception of marriage as a remedy to concupiscence lived on, at least as an "accepted truth." The facts, and the permissive climate just described, show that the "carnal act" was left to err on the side of leisure beyond the matrimonial bed. But the conjugality promoted by the

Church and at certain levels of civil society, along with a growing tendency to allow young people to marry according to their hearts and to respect the couple's autonomy, took on a new meaning in the climate of tolerated sensuality and diffuse epicureanism. More precisely, these attitudes prepared the way for an inversion of the relationship between marriage and sexuality.

Marriage was not yet proposed as the goal of love, as was the case in what would later be called the model of romantic love. But already, marriage was no longer seen as an *end*, as a passage to a legal bond where the obligations of conjugal duty would extinguish the ardor of desire. Authorized by a low level of social control, by the ease with which they met one another, followed the call of nature and gave in to their desires, young people were also encouraged to make their own commitments. The temptation was great to confuse desire with choice, the immediate with the definitive. In the case of the *créantés champenois*, a simple object exchanged "in the name of marriage" was all that was needed to transform an innocent holiday flirt or roadside embrace into an indissoluble union. This rite regularized the engagement and invested the exchanged object with a magical force similar to an alchemic power, since it transformed an instant of emotional or physical fusion into an eternity of mutual obligations.

We cannot consider the extremely brief rituals involved in these clandestine or presumed engagements as being representative of normal practice, since it was precisely their insufficiency which made them the object of litigation. But the mere fact that debate concerning the validity of these pseudo-ceremonies was possible, shows that they were not too far removed from the norm. There was, however, an obviously disproportionate relationship between the insignificance of ritual and the judicial formalities to which the matrimonial engagement was subject, and the individuality of the bond between the husband and wife made during their engagement. The disequilibrium between the ease with which one could contract a bond of marriage and the irrevocability of the bond, appeared tolerable as long as the combined effects of low population growth and dynamic economic growth favored social mobility. The risk of a bad match was part of the flexibility of the social game that belonged to the atmosphere of the era. But as tensions reappeared, as class barriers were erected in a society that was becoming more rigid, this disequilibrium seemed more and more absurd and harder to bear. Its absurdity was denounced by humanists who considered the contradiction harmful to society. One criticism raised by Protestants when they rejected the sacramental dimension of marriage, was that it was a civil institution. It was holy not because of a sacredness administered by the priest, or even the husband and wife themselves, but because it was willed by God in the same way as other forms of organization in social life. It should therefore be considered as a revocable civil contract between two individuals and their families.

Challenged by the most innovative intellectual trends during the first half of the sixteenth century, the institution of marriage became an inexhaustible subject of discussion in the savy or jesting mode of the time (as can be seen in Panurge's discourses in Pantagruel). An institution such as marriage (and today we can speak of this from an excellent vantage point) can enter into a period of crisis in people's minds long before it disintegrates in practice.

It is possible, as is often claimed, that Henry II's edict of February, 1556, against clandestine marriages and the pressure

brought to bear upon the Council of Trent by the monarchy through French cardinals in order to obtain the nullification of all marriages contracted without parental consent, was directly caused by a matrimonial mishap at court. Henry II wanted to marry his illegitimate daughter Diane de France, age seven, to Francois de Montmorency, when he discovered that the young duke had secretly become engaged to one of the Queen's ladies-in-waiting (*fille d'honneur*). The lady-in-waiting was put in a convent and a nullification of the clandestine union was requested but Rome refused.

In reality the court's disarray joined a widespread panic in the upper classes and particularly in the nobility concerning the epidemic of clandestine marriages and the risks of bad matches that it entailed. Similar measures were taken in a large part of Protestant Europe. Between 1550 and 1592, the "Ehegericht" (the matrimonial affairs court) at Bâle, reformed by Zwingli, judged 167 cases of clandestine marriages and decided to annul 133 of them. We know that the Council of Trent remained faithful to the doctrine of consent and refused to follow the proposition of the French cardinals. The conflict between royal legislation and canon law was the main reason that France officially refused to "accept" the Council's decisions.

But we must not exaggerate the importance of this disagreement. Even if the "tridentine" Church refused to annul clandestine marriages, all the measures it took both during the Council and afterwards aimed at reinforcing the probability of marriage by subjecting them to stricter control by the priest and the head of the family. Changes in ritual and nuptial benedictions confirm this process. At the end of the seventeenth century, the Roman ritual of Paul the Fifth replaced local rituals which reflected the diversity of customs. The gestures and formulas of reciprocal gifts (*donation*) by which the couple affirmed the autonomy of their engagement, disappeared and was replaced by the "*ego conjugo vos*" of the officiant.

The struggle led by seventeenth-century bishops against noisy processions, charivari, "barrières," "dishonest" *chansons*, and other "indecent" manifestations of popular ritual that accompanied the religious ceremony, tended to impose a form of austere and internalized devotion. But this struggle was also aimed at destroying the power local forms of solidarity, village communities, age groups, etc., exercised over marriage alliances, especially since this power entered into competition with that of the Church, the State, and to a certain extent of families. The State, the natural enemy of local powers, could only congratulate itself that along with a rival authority, a situation of dispersion which had encouraged clandestine unions would also disappear.

Paradoxically, the weakening of control exercised by local society over engagements deprived young people who wanted to marry against their parent's will of a source of appeal, which thereby reinforced the autonomy of couples. By coming entirely under the authority of the family and a centralized apparatus, conjugal life turned its back on *voisinage* and took refuge behind the increasingly distinct boundaries surrounding private life. Couples internalized this transfer of authority and, through a reflex of introversion and privatization, became more and more hostile to interventions by the local community. From the end of the sixteenth century on, evidence of this growing hospitality can be found in the increasing numbers of charivaris that go awry and end up in court. Couples had once accepted these joking and cruel uproars as a rite that was both punitive and integrative. By breaking down the door or the roof of the newlywed's house, charivaris often symbolically affirmed the right to view the private lives of others. But during the end of the sixteenth century, couples began to refuse this local right, this "loi du milieu." The idea that neighbors could react noisily to the fact that a widow had remarried, that a woman had betrothed a younger or a poorer man, or that she chose a husband who was foreign to the community, grew to be regarded as an unbearable attack on the private lives of its victims.

In certain respects, the religious normalization that occurred in Catholic countries also aimed at limiting the decision-making power of families in marriage matters (an objective which might seem to go against those of the State). This, however, is how we must explain the disappearance of engagements (*fiançailles*), an old customary institution which often accompanied the signing of a marriage contract. To nonclerics, an engagement represented the legitimating sequence of the union since it sealed the agreement between the two families. In the hope of adapting religious ritual to civil practice, engagements became ever more elaborate, even to the point of becoming a ceremony almost as important as nuptual benediction. But engagements were reduced to a minor role by the Council of Trent, or were simply suppressed. In meridional France, families were less attached to engagements since they had long grown accustomed to making their arrangements coincide with the nuptual benediction. Bishops preferred to see them disappear. Engagements, however, were maintained in the north of France and even made obligatory where they didn't exist, but only as a simple session intended to verify the validity of the prospective marriage and to dispense moral pedagogy. In order to prevent fiancés from authorizing themselves to live together before marriage, priests were enjoined to celebrate the engagement only very shortly before the wedding (Pive-teau, 1957).

The main concern of the Roman Catholic Church, as well as of the Reformed Churches, was to render sexual life moral by confining it to the conjugal realm and imposing constraining norms upon it. This preoccupation, however, was not necessarily understood by the families involved, who were more concerned with controlling marital alliances than with regulating sexuality. Institutionalizing a certain amount of sexual permissiveness among young people was sometimes seen as the best way to maintain a hold over an age group that was unstable by nature, and to obtain their cooperation in familial strategies.

In certain regions, such as Corsica, premarital cohabitation was a direct result of the agreement reached between two families. The engagement contract, often concluded well before the "intended" reached the age of puberty and meant to conclude peace between two families who had been in vendetta, stipulated that the young girl was to be immediately transferred to the home of her future husband. Much to their horror, some priests of the Saint Vincent de Paul denomination discovered this practice when they were sent on a mission to the island in the late seventeenth century:

> There was yet a very disturbing custom amongst the inhabitants of the Isle concerning the sacrament of matrimony. When engaged or merely promised, the girl would lodge in the home of her future husband and they remained in this state of concubinage (illegitimacy) during two or three years, taking no pains to marry.

The price that Corsicans attached to their girls' virtue, and the cruelty with which they treated adulterous women, would seem to contradict the licentious impression that they gave the good priests from the continent. "Pawning" a young girl in order to guarantee the engagement corresponded to a very old custom in which the transfer of the woman constituted the essential part of the alliance.

Elsewhere, young people could visit one another and even live together while their families continued the negotiations. The girl was often pregnant at the time the agreement was reached and the wedding celebrated at the church. In this way, the husband and his parents had made the commitment having had assurance that the chosen girl could provide them with descendants. In 1567 during the Easter season, Richard Thomas, who was sowing wheat in the company of Maud Methewaye, one of his father's servants, declared to her that he "would like her to have a big stomach like that of Joan Asheman, a pregnant girl in the parish, and that if she carried a child of his, he would marry her" (cited in Houlbrooke, 1984). These probative premarital relations were frequent in England, and also in many parts of northern France and in the Aquitaine region. At the beginning of the sixteenth century, Pierre de Lancre, the demonologist from Bordeaux, denounced, among the Basques of the Labour region "the liberty with which they 'try out' their women a few years before marrying them, as if putting them to a trial test." According to him, this custom was not unrelated to the witchcraft practiced in the region. His colleague Jean d'Arrerac, who also noted this practice in the Labour region as well as in the *usances du pays de Sainctonge*, explained it primarily as a customary practice: "they marry their women for a trial period. They do not conclude their marriage contracts in writing and do not receive the nuptial benediction until after having lived with them for a long time, having closely observed their habits and verified their fertility" (cited in Flandrin, 1975).

There were *veillées paysannes* (peasant vigils) at which young girls would spin in the company of their mothers and boys would be let in to offer them words of gallantry. They were also *maraichinage vendéen*, when, according to an intricate code of flirtation, caresses could be exchanged in public but under the protection of the ritual umbrella. These vigils were surviving institutions of *ancien régime* beliefs, or, rather, resurgent features of the premarital freedom granted and controlled by local society. Trial marriage represented an extended form of these ancient customs.

The Church worked unceasingly for more than a century to suppress these practices but to no avail. Concerning the *veilleries* or *escreins*, the synodic statutes of the Diocese of Troyes in 1680 proclaimed: "Under threat of excommunication, we forbid all men and boys from mixing with women and girls in those places where they assemble at night to spin or work" (Statuts synodaux du diocese de Troyes, 1680). Six years later, a Bishop's mandate revoking the prohibition specified: "Let there be no future ambiguity as to what we mean by *veilleries ou escreins.* . . . We mean not only public places unattached to houses or dug into the ground where all sorts of people may enter indifferently, but also cellars, stables, bedrooms, or other domestic places where women and girls of several families gather together at night" (Mandement episcopal de l'êveque de Troyes, 1686). This condemnation was taken up again in 1744 by the Bishop of Boulogne against "those nocturnal groupings, commonly called *séries*, where women and girls gather ostensibly to work, but where men and boys are always let in and become a source of dissipation and disorder" (Statuts synodaux du diocese de Boulogne, 1744).

The "disorder" between boys and girls did not necessarily imply that flirtation always ended in *commerce charnel*, but it did raise the risk of conception out of wedlock. In those regions where this form of permissive premarital sociability was prominent, there was also a particularly high rate of illegitimate births and premarital conceptions. This was also true in those regions where girls of marriageable age were permitted to receive nocturnal visits from their suitors. These practices, known as *albergement* in Savoy, *Kiltgang* in Switzerland, *Fensterlin* in Austria and *Nachtfreien* in Bavaria, existed in a major portion of the "Alpine arc" and the Scandinavian countries. We know of these practices largely through descriptions left by nineteenth-century travelers or ethnographers. They are also confirmed by the very high rates of illegitimacy that we find during the same period. The maximum rate was reached by Carinthia, the veritable "Jamaica of Europe" (Mitterauer, 1983) where illegitimate births accounted for more than 80% of the total during the second half of the nineteenth century.

Illegitimacy was also aggravated in certain areas by legislation that practically forbade marriage among the poor. Although premarital permissiveness in England, the Vendée, and in the Basque region was a way of controlling relationships—from a distance and without force—in the hope of steering them towards a desired union, similar customs in the Alpine or Scandinavian countries were intended perhaps to provide young servants with a sexual substitute, as pointed out by a Frenchman traveling in Germany at the end of the sixteenth century, who noticed couples who spent the night together in this way. As the *maraichinage vendéen*, the *Kiltgang* combined intimacy with public viewing. *Maraichinage* meant several couples who mutually chaperoned each other; a girl's innocent flirt at a window; a more or less chaste night where young people slept together but without getting undressed, etc. It is not very probable that couples always contented themselves with this type of innocuous eroticism.

In 1603, the Bishop of Augsbourg denounced the *abus* of valets and servants who demanded that their contracts give them the right to go out at night to visit a person of the opposite sex or at least to be able to converse with them at the window. It appears that this was not merely a form of tolerance granted by a lax familial authority but rather a right claimed by an entire population of unmarried farm servants as one aspect of their living conditions. This custom was not related to any specific religious context since we find it in Catholic regions as well as in those secured by the Reformation. It does, however, seem closely tied to the existence of a pastoral economy employing a large indentured labor force of both sexes, who worked together in cow sheds or elevated pastures.

Campaigns on behalf of morals had to confront very strong resistance from a population that remained deeply attached to its vices, especially since they formed an integral part of their social system. These campaigns knew only provisional and mitigated success. The highest illegitimacy rates at the beginning of the nineteenth century are to be found in Bavaria and Austria, two Catholic countries where counter-reformation activity had been particularly intense (Mitterauer, 1983). On the other hand, the Church's efforts continually sought the State's approval and aid.

In France, in February, 1556, at the same time that he declared clandestine marriages nullified, King Henry II started a war against illegitimate births by an edict "contre les femmes qui cellent leur grossesse." Progressively, by royal or local initiatives, brothels, *étuves, maison de jeux*, and all other public areas that could

provide shelter for extramarital sexuality were ordered closed. In this effort Protestant states did not lag behind. During the second half of the sixteenth century, the marriage tribunal at Bâle ordered 133 illegitimate couples to separate for reasons of "fornication" (Safley, 1982). In England, at the beginning of the seventeenth century, courts began prosecuting those couples for premarital fornication who declared the birth of a child less than eight months after the marriage (Houlbrooke, 1984).

The imposition of these religious norms experienced unequal and provisional success. But it deeply transformed mentalities and behavior. In England, based on a sample of twelve parishes, we can see a noticeable drop in premarital conceptions: they represent 25.5% of all first births during the first half of the seventeenth century, but only 16.2% in the second half of the century (Houlbrooke, 1984). The drop in illegitimate births measured in a larger sample (98 parishes) is even more spectacular. The illegitimacy rate was 3.2% in the first decade of the 1600s, and only 1.7% in the 1640s at the beginning of the Revolution. It reached its lowest point of 0.94% during Cromwell's dictatorship and then rose progressively until the middle of the eighteenth century when it exceeded the level of a century and a half earlier (Laslett, 1977).

We do not have such early statistics for France. But the low level of illegitimate births and premarital conceptions that can be seen in the seventeenth century, and their fairly rapid rise from the middle of the eighteenth century on, seems to indicate that Catholic reform was able to discipline behavior and to impose a model of ascetic comportment for at least a century. The liberation of manners during the end of the *ancien régime* coincided with the decline in religious control.

It is also necessary to point out that the rise in illegitimacy is only really apparent in larger centers of rural industry such as Villedieu-les-Poeles (which had 0.1% rate of illegitimate births in the mid-eighteenth century and 4.1% between 1771 and 1790); in suburbs such as Ingouville of Le Havre (which had 3.5% illegitimacy from 1730 to 1773 and 5.7% at the end of the *ancien régime*); in the middle-sized cities such as Meulan (0.5% illegitimate births between 1670 and 1759; and 2.3% between 1760 and 1789) and St. Denis (8% on the eve of the Revolution); and metropolitan centers such as Lyon and Grenoble (10%) and Lille (12%) during the same period. In large cities, the rise in illegitimate births was a direct effect of urban growth and the unstable and badly integrated presence of a large immigrant population. This phenomenon was amplified by the migration of pregnant girls who chose the city to give birth discreetly or, if necessary, to abandon "le fruit du péché" ("the fruit of their sins") to institutions which existed for this purpose. The impact of illegitimacy in large cities, therefore, went beyond those illegitimate births that were declared. By adding abandoned children to the total, we reach perhaps a 25% illegitimacy rate in Toulouse and 30% in Paris on the eve of the Revolution.

Behavioral changes in the countryside during the eighteenth century are less noticeable. Sometimes illegitimacy rates there had the same pattern as urban centers: e.g., in Soudeiles in Quercy, where there was an illegitimate birth rate of 0.9% during the seventeenth century. The rate was 2.1% between 1700 and 1779, and more than 3% at the end of the *ancien régime*. But in most rural areas the rates remained stable. They stayed low in the Parisian basin (around 1%) and were even lower in West Brittany or Angevin. They were higher—and have continued to be— in Normandy: 3% in Troarn from 1658 to 1792; 2.6% at Tamerville from 1624 to 1740; 2.5% at Port-en-Bessin during the eighteenth century.

Structural disparities would seem to oppose northern, northwestern, and southwestern France, as being more indulgent towards illegitimacy; and western and Midi-Mediterranean France, as being more rigorous in this regard. Does this reflect traditional family differences towards premarital encounters between the young? At least it shows the unequal success of the attempts by seventeenth-century authorities to impose norms. In the countryside and in the upper classes success was limited and provisional. In the urban "middle classes" success was more durable, particularly where guilds existed and where the attempts to impose moral order revived traditions of conformity and the surveillance of the private lives of its members by the group.

This rigor was particularly striking in Germanic countries where it was aimed primarily against illegitimacy. In 1733, a tailor from Hildesheim was refused membership in a guild because he was an illegitimate child and was only later made legitimate by the marriage of his parents. Ten years later, the weaver's guild of Lünen forced one of its members to fire an apprentice for reasons of illegitimacy. Controls were no less strict in matters of premarital relations. In 1716, a master tailor from Kiel was expelled from his rightful professional community because his wife gave birth two months after their marriage. In 1726, a master shoemaker was threatened with the same sanctions because his wife gave birth five weeks too early (Möller, 1969).

The movement to impose norms was not equally extensive, efficient or durable in all social milieu or in all countries. For the moment, we should probably lay aside attempts to specify the impact of this phenomenon in statistical terms. But we cannot doubt the reality of this cultural mutation, which for over a century shrouded the emotional universe under a veil of suspicion. In retrospect, these changes can help us better understand the tearful and exaggerated sensibility which, during the second half of the eighteenth century, invaded painting and literature, as well as the most quotidian and unpolished forms of language such as epistolary exchanges, songs, and even the simple remarks (recorded in judicial sources) of those ignorant of written culture. Catholic propaganda, in its attempts at religious conversion especially in certain countries of Central and Mediterranean Europe, did not hesitate to appeal to the emotions to mobilize the masses. Certain people have viewed this inculcation strategy as the main resort of a Baroque aesthetic. But sensibility, manipulated and channeled in this way, was requisitioned for strictly mystic or devotional ends.

What appears to us today as insipid, obsolete, emphatic and perhaps insincere, was actually an affirmation of the will to trust one's own sensibility and to make relationships between individuals more transparent. This change occurred only after a long period of suppression which had made emotional life inadmissible.

In order to measure the change in sensibility during the eighteenth century, we would like to conclude by comparing this change with two indices of a serial nature: illegitimacy and premarital conceptions. The steep rise in "declarations of pregnancy" (a repressive measure aimed at girl-mothers and instituted by the monarchy as early as the sixteenth century), cannot totally be explained by reinforced police surveillance. The rise in illegitimate births in parish registers confirms the tendency. The circumstances of these unhappy love affairs, as recorded in the declarations, bear witness to a new state of mind. Sometimes they concerned female servants—young girls seduced by married

men or men of a social rank so far removed from their own that the relationship had no chance of leading to marriage. But most often, these seduced girls gave themselves to boys of their own age and background who promised marriage (Depauw, 1972). Previously, illegitimate births had been the fruit of amorous passions that were incompatible with conjugal life. From this point on, however, they revealed love stories that had involved a marriage project; in other words, they consisted of premarital relations that had gone awry.

As for premarital conceptions, they increasingly originated in illegitimate relations that went well. Within the global increase since the mid-eighteenth century, we can notice that the number of births occurring very shortly after marriage went up more quickly than those which occurred six and seven months later (Flandrin, 1975). In this latter case, we are dealing with couples who were going to marry, but for whom conjugal life had anticipated somewhat the nuptial benediction. The first case, however, might account for girls whose seductors agreed to marry them once they became pregnant.

In both of these cases, the love relationship preceded the marital one—which was, in theory, contrary to Church law. But it is significant that the illicit behavior which increased the most and which best illustrates the evolution of custom involved marriage as an almost accidental result of love.

The transformations affecting premarital life, both at the level of representation and of behavior, cannot easily be separated from those affecting marital life, most notably the appearance of birth control. Already noticed by such observers of eighteenth-century society as Moheau, who deplored "those fatal secrets [that] had even penetrated into the countryside," this innovation in the sexual life of couples (which France seems to have embraced much earlier than the rest of Europe), was first attributed to a loosening of traditional custom, as well as to dechristianization. The fact that the first statistical indices concerning the spread of birth control among the popular classes seem contemporary with the French Revolution gives credence to the dechristianization theory. The Church had always forbidden nonreproductive sexual relations and, in particular, the most widespread contraceptive practice of *coitus interruptus*, referred to by theologians as "Onan's sin." Some historians have therefore advanced the hypothesis that it was the internalization of this interdiction that made contraceptive techniques, as well as the mere idea of using them, "unthinkable." Once these techniques became shameful and clandestine, they continued to circulate only in the marginal world of prostitution (Ariès, 1960). Other recent studies show that birth control was widely used at the end of the seventeenth century in the upper classes, not only in France (among *ducs* and *pairs*), but also in the upper English nobility and in Geneva (in the patrician milieu). We could certainly explain this phenomenon by attributing it to a certain cultural advance among elites, but no longer by dechristianization.

A corpus of demographic research has led historians to place the introduction of Malthusianism among the masses of the population at a much earlier date. In Geneva and in the English countryside (Colyton), it appears as early as the second half of the seventeenth century, but only temporarily; by contrast, it appears in a durable way in Rouen during the last third of the century. In the mid-eighteenth century we observe it in several middle-sized cities of northern France such as Meulan or Châtillon-sur-Seine, and a bit later in the countryside of the Parisian basin.

Among the upper nobility, whose power was based on landed wealth, Malthusianism may have been brought on by a need to halt the division of patrimony at a time when a period of crisis had caused land revenues to drop. For the masses of the population, it may have been a way of reacting to the stresses of a crisis in high prices and high mortality, which Bardet considers to have been particularly serious in the case of Rouen following the crisis of 1694 (Bardet, 1983). The small French peasant who attempted to acquire micro-property during the unfavorable conjuncture of the second half of the eighteenth century indeed may have been concerned with savings and preserving his patrimony. Economic motivations for the rise of Malthusianism are not lacking. In Rouen, contraception seems to have been more precocious among immigrants than among the natives of the Normandy metropolis. It was widespread among notable and boutique owners as early as the beginning of the eighteenth century, but only reached artisan and working class groups towards mid-century. Nothing, however, in this regard, separates Protestants from Catholics. Should we attribute this change in people's attitudes toward life to the emergence of an entrepreneurial outlook? Should we refuse to consider religious attitudes as a possible explanation for the disappearance of something which was for so long a religious taboo?

Whether this was a radically new phenomenon in the seventeenth century, or whether it was simply a resurgence of an old practice, it is undeniable that the period of most active religious reform did coincide with the long respect for this interdiction. But the influence of reforms was unequal and ambiguous: post-Tridentine Catholicism, mainly through the influence of Casuist Jesuits, made an effort to provide the faithful with a detailed explanation of the Church's doctrine regarding conjugal sexuality and to demand respect for the "sanctity of the nuptual bed" by methods of inquisitional confession. Protestant authorities, on the other hand, displayed an attitude that was both rigorous and distant towards conjugal life. They tried to subject private life to morality by communicating to the individual a strict sense of fault and a deep awareness of his own responsibility, but they refused to see sexual life as the main and quasi-unique tendency of sin. They especially wanted to allow couples to freely assume responsibility for their daily lives: "You must know," declared *doyen* Bridel, "that we Protestant ministers will not allow ourselves to penetrate the mysteries of the conjugal sanctuary" (cited in Perrenoud, 1974).

In France, during the second half of the seventeenth century, rigorists of Jansenist Catholic clergy, who were very hostile to Casuist Jesuits, ended up adopting a similar attitude. Feeling no indulgence toward, but, instead, a sacred horror of everything that touched upon sexuality, this hyperpuritanistic clergy felt that the mere fact of speaking about it could be an invitation to sin. "It is necessary to interrogate them," wrote the curé Sauvegeon about his Solognot parishioners, "but it must be with a singular prudence for fear perhaps of teaching them of sins they have never committed nor even consequently had the thought of committing" (cited in Flandrin, 1970). The best solution was to cover conjugal life beneath a veil of silence.

In Jansenist regions, where the lower clergy maintained anti-sacramental tendencies among the faithful (particularly the refusal of confession), a chaste silence was progressively transformed during the eighteenth century into an indifference or at least a refusal to intervene in the intimate lives of couples. Starting from differ-

ent doctrinal positions, Protestantism and Jansenism led to the same results. By refusing to subject conjugal life to an exterior control, they created a sphere of intimacy in which husband and wife obtained the exclusive right to co-property. Conjugal sexuality, from here on, was placed on secular, morally neutral grounds. Since all risk of censure had been taken away, conjugal sexuality became the focal point of intimacy and the instrument of a more intense emotional relationship between husband and wife. There are good reasons to believe that certain Protestant groups (for example in Geneva) were among the first centers of western Europe's great conversion to Malthusianism.

It was not religious attitudes themselves, but their effects on couples and their intimacy which favored the appearance of contraception. This explanation joins the conclusions of several comparative studies on the introduction of birth control in different societies of the Third World. In Puerto Rico, a country of Catholic tradition, contraception diffused rapidly, whereas in India, the population remained largely hostile to birth control, even though its religious traditions did not forbid such practices. It is therefore not religious traditions, but the nature of relations within the couple, their degree of intimacy and equality, which could favor or hinder the transformation of sexual behavior.

In any case, we can say that in Europe, the invention of intimacy, the rise of "conjugal companionship," of a new model of relations within which couples were less distant if not more egalitarian, were the indirect results of new religious behavior.

REFERENCES

Ariès, P. 1960. "Interpretation pour une historie des mentalités." Pp. 311–327 in Hélène Bergues (ed.), *La prévention des naissances dans la famille*. Paris: Plon.

Bardet, J.P. 1983. *Rouen aux XVII et XVIII siècles*. Paris: S.E.D.E.S.

Burguière, A. 1978. "Le rituel de mariage en France: pratiques ecclesiastiques et pratiques populaires (XVI-XVIII siècles). *Annales E.S.C.* 33: 637–649.

—————. 1980. "The Charivari and Religious Repression in France during the Ancien Regime." Pp. 84–110 in R. Wheaton and T.K. Hareven (eds.), *Family and Sexuality in French History*. Philadelphia: University of Pennsylvania Press.

Casey, J. 1983. "Household Disputes and the Law in Early Modern Andalusia." Pp. 189–218 in J. Bossey (ed.), *Disputes and Settlements: Law and Human Relations in the West*. Cambridge: Cambridge University Press.

Depauw, J. 1972. "Amour illégitime et société à Nantes au XVIII siècle." *Annales E.S.C.* 27: 115–1182.

Elias, Norbert. 1978. *The Civilizing Process*. New York: Horizon Books.

Farge, A., ed. 1982. *Le miroir des femmes*. Bibliotheque bleue. Paris: Montalba.

Farge, A. and M. Foucault. 1982. *Le désordre des familles*. Paris: Archives-Gallimard.

Flandrin, J.L. 1975. *Les amours paysannes: amour et sexualité dans les campagnes de l'ancienne France, XVIe-XIXe siecle*. Paris: Archives-Gallimard.

Gillis, R. 1983. "Conjugal Settlements. Resort to Clandestine and Common Law Marriage in England and Wales (1650–1850)." Pp. 261–286 in J. Bossey (ed.), *Disputes and Settlements: Law and Human Relations in the West*. Cambridge: Cambridge University Press.

Houlbrooke, R.A. 1984. *The English Family 1450-1700*. London and New York: Longman.

Kaplow, J. 1972. *The Names of Kings: The Parisan Laboring Poor in the XVIIIth Century*. New York: Basic Books.

Lafon, J. 1972. *Les époux bordelais 1450-1850*. Paris: Mouton.

Laslett, P. 1977. "Long Term Trends in Bastardy in England." Pp. 102–159 in Peter Laslett, *Family Life and Illicit Love in Earlier Generations*. Cambridge: Cambridge University Press.

LeRoy, Ladurie, E. 1980. *L'argent, l'amour et la mort en pays d'oc*. Paris: Sevil.

Mitterauer, M. 1983. *Ledige Mutter. Zur Geschichte unehelicher Geburten in Europa*. München: C.M. Beck.

Molin, J.B. and P. Mutembe. 1974. *Le rituel de mariage en France du XII° au XVI° siècles*. Paris: Editious du cerf.

Möller, H. 1969. *Die Kleinbürgerliche Familie im XVIII*. Berlin: Walter de Gruyter.

Noonan, John T. 1965. *Contraception: A History of Its Treatment by the Catholic Theologians and Canonists*. Cambridge: Harvard University Press.

Perrenoud, A. 1974. "Malthusianisme et Protestantisme: un modeθle démographique wébérien." *Annales E.S.C.* 29: 975–988.

Piveteau, C. 1957. *La Pratique matrimoniale en France d'après les statuts synodaux*. Paris: Université de Paris.

Restif de la Bretonne, N. 1959. *Monsieur Nicolas*. Paris: J.J. Pauvert.

Rossiaud, J. 1976. "Prostitution jeunesse et societe dans villes du sud-est au XVe siècle." *Annales E.S.C.* 31: 289–325.

Safley, T.M. 1982. "To Preserve the Marital State. The Basler Ehegericht, 1550–1592." *Journal of Family History* 7: 162–179.

Shorter, E. 1975. *The Making of the Modern Family*. New York: Basic Books.

Stone, L. 1977. *The Family, Sex and Marriage in England 1500-1800*. London: Weidenfeld and Nicolson.

Demographic Patterns
and Family Organization

ANOTHER *FOSSA MAGNA:* PROPORTION MARRYING AND AGE AT MARRIAGE IN LATE NINETEENTH-CENTURY JAPAN

Akira Hayami

ABSTRACT: *Using several heretofore neglected but very significant sources of demographic information for late nineteenth-century Japan, the study investigates the statistics for proportions marrying and age at first marriage in all the Japanese prefectures. It establishes the existence of two patterns of marriage—one of early marriage in eastern Japan and one of late marriage in western Japan. Several explanations for this division are considered.*

INTRODUCTION

Japan has been regarded as a country consisting of a single race, single language and homogeneous culture. Compared with China, India or with the U.S. and the USSR, this may be true. In the premodern period, however, Japan exhibited many local differences in its social life. These local variations are particularly important for an understanding of Japan's history and modernization, and even contemporary Japan, since these local differences were utilized as a resource in the modernization of Japan. Economically, local differences resulted from local geographic conditions and they intensified local comparative advantages by maximizing local specialization in production. Culturally, during the Tokugawa period (1603–1868), when peace was maintained for more than two centuries nationwide, local differences stimulated people's curiosity, and many local gazetteers and studies were compiled. Travel became an industry.

Akira Hayami is Professor of Economics, Faculty of Economics, Keio University, 2-15-45 Mita, Minato-ku, Tokyo 108, Japan. His principal fields of research are comparative economic history and demography.

Among those regional variations, differences in social structure and in family life still remain unexplored. The present study investigates regional differences in age at marriage and proportions marrying, using the earliest national statistics available from the early Meiji period on.

AGE AT MARRIAGE

Age at marriage is an important variable in both historical demography and family sociology. Age at marriage, particularly age at first marriage for women, determines population size through the number of births. Of course, birth control can affect the relationship between age at first marriage and number of offspring, and, regardless of the presence or absence of birth control, late marriage will result in fewer births.

It is an important issue in social anthropology as well. Age at marriage interacts with issues of inheritance and family succession. Early marriage may speed up the family life cycle and increase the number of families consisting of three or more generations.

In the case of Japan, there have not been any noteworthy historical studies of age at marriage. As a result, the relationship between age at marriage and population change, inheritance and family succession, have yet to be analyzed. The reasons for this seem to be twofold. First, since birth control appears to have been rather commonly practiced, early marriage did not always result in an increase in population. Second, parents and children usually lived together until the middle of the twentieth century. This naturally provided for family succession without any particular need to consider age at marriage.

Before the first Japanese census of 1920, statistics on age at marriage were inadequate. This shortage in historical materials frustrated efforts to study the subject. Nevertheless, population records from the Tokugawa period can be used to study age at marriage and other demographic measures for small populations at the village and town level. The Tokugawa records are problematic in a number of ways: it is impossible to gather data on more than a few hundred individuals at a time, and it is difficult to estimate how representative the places studied were of the wider region or of Japan as a whole.

In the present study, the author will not use the aforementioned Tokugawa documents and will rely, instead, on records gathered by the Meiji government in the latter half of the nineteenth century. During the Meiji period (1868–1912) many of the social practices of the Tokugawa period were still present. We can, therefore, make inferences concerning the country as a whole in the Tokugawa period from Meiji-period documents. By using such documents, we can explore historical and spatial variation in age at marriage among many scattered communities and prepare more detailed local studies based on the registers of the Tokugawa period. We know that Tokugawa Japan was a society which had significant spatial and diachronic differences in age at marriage. By using Meiji-period documents, the author has been able to expand his investigation of several Tokugawa villages to a nationwide picture which may be multicolored.

The following three cases (two of them from the author's research) illustrate well these variations in the age at marriage. In Yokouchi village, Shinano Province, for example, the age at first marriage for females at the beginning of the eighteenth century was seventeen *sai*.[1] (Traditionally, age was counted in Japan in the following manner: one *sai* at birth and another *sai* each new calendar year. A person born in the last month of a year was considered two years old [*sai*] by the next month, i.e., the first month of the next year.)

In Yokouchi, age at first marriage for females gradually increased over time. By the middle of the nineteenth century, it had reached 22 *sai*. Until 1770, the population size of the village as a whole had been increasing, but it levelled off thereafter. It is clear that there was some relationship between age at marriage and population size in Yokouchi, even though it is not clear exactly what the nature of that relationship was. Comparing the number of births between wives in the two birth cohorts of 1651–1700 and 1801–1825, we find that number to be 6.4 and 3.8 respectively.[2]

In another case—Nishijo village in Mino Province—age at first marriage for the wives of the 1773–1835 cohort differed conspicuously according to landholding. In the upper class of peasants, age at first marriage was 21.5 *sai* while in the lower class of peasants, it was 24.5 *sai*. This age difference appears to come principally from the presence or absence of the experience of working away from the home (*dekasegi*). In the upper class, only 33 percent of female children who survived beyond eleven *sai* experienced *dekasegi*. In the lower class, 74 percent of the same group experienced *dekasegi*.[3]

Dekasegi usually began at age twelve or thirteen *sai* and continued for twelve to thirteen years in urban areas. Since women returned to their native village at age 24 or 25 *sai* for marriage, their age was naturally delayed relative to the age of those women who did not leave on *dekasegi*. The difference of three years in age at first marriage for upper- and lower-class peasant women was crucial. It is known through the historical demographic study of Nishijo that in order for the net reproduction rate (NRR) to exceed 1.0, women had to have more than 4.4 births per marriage. For this to happen, they almost had

to marry before age 24 *sai*. Thus, in those households where women married later than 24 *sai*, a successor could not be easily guaranteed.

Indeed, in Nishijo, there were no cases among the upper class of peasants where a successor could not be found during the period under study (1773–1869). But among lower-class peasants, when the head of the household died, a successor was not present 35 percent of the time and the family died out.[4]

In addition to such a demographic explanation, it should be pointed out that upper-class peasants had property and accordingly sought to find successors to the family estate. This resulted in the adoption of sons and daughters to be successors in the family. The difference of three years in the age at marriage was significant for another reason: women are most fertile between the ages of 21 and 25. Whether or not one marries during this period will have a major impact on the birth rate.

The third case comes from a village study using a very good series of registers in Tohoku.[5] The Tohoku district of northern Japan where this village is located experienced a sharp decline in population from the early eighteenth century on. Quite contrary to our expectations, however, the age at first marriage for females was surprisingly low. It was as low as 11.2 *sai* in the early eighteenth century. By the middle of the nineteenth century it had risen to 18.7 *sai*, still four years lower than in the other two cases from central Japan.

Age at marriage was thus significantly different depending upon the place and time of investigation. The lack of comprehensive data for the Tokugawa period makes it impossible to analyze the variation in age at marriage for the country as a whole. But the documents compiled by the Meiji government after its establishment in the last decades of the nineteenth century make it possible to study age at marriage systematically.

DATA AND ESTIMATES

Before analyzing them, it might be useful to make some observations about the nature of the data. The first census in Japan was compiled in 1920—a rather late date among the developed countries of the world. Because the quality of population data before the 1920 census was so poor, it has been said that demographers have generally ignored issues concerning the Japanese population before 1920. However, it is an exaggeration to think that population data from before 1920 is without any value whatever.

In 1872 the Meiji government initiated a household registration system which required that all inhabitants register their household circumstances at an appropriate level of local administration. Thereafter, for reasons of marriage or migration, the register was amended and the government was able to count the population on the basis of this "Registered Population" (honseki jinko).

The estimation problem in this "Registered Population" was created by that portion of the population which moved for a temporary period, the so-called kiryu jinko. According to the law, if persons moved for a period of longer than ninety days from their registered location, they were required to register as part of the kiryu population. This temporary migrated population was added to or subtracted from the registered population of each administrative unit, producing the genju jinko or residential population. However, many persons avoided the temporary registration requirement and, as a consequence, the figures for the residential population are not very reliable.

After 1890, when the urbanization and

industrialization of Japan began in earnest, the numbers of persons migrating locally in Japan increased dramatically and the reliability of the residential population figures slipped accordingly. Because of this, the government was unable to rely upon such demographic measures calculated at the local administration offices by the beginning of the twentieth century, and it used police population records created by the police independently to augment and revise the residential population figures, particularly in urban areas.[6]

Nevertheless, before 1890 or before Japan's industrialization and urbanization had become noteworthy, the kiryu jinko or temporarily displaced population was not so large, and the honseki jinko was rather close to the actually residential population. As a result, the reliability of the pre-1890 population data may be rather high.

Recently, bibliographic sources concerning the pre-1890 statistics have become more available, making it possible to cross-reference these materials with population records. This has generally increased the ease of use and reliability of such materials.[7]

The present study uses as its principal source the invaluable Table of Households and Population of Imperial Japan (Nihon Teikoku Minseki Kokohyo: hereafter NTMK), which was compiled first in 1886. It has been almost entirely overlooked as a source for the demographic study of Japan.[8] Among its many virtues, the NTMK lists the population at each age for each prefecture in Japan and how many of those persons at each age were marrying, using as the basis the honseki jinko. Thus, the December 31, 1886, compilation provides the first countrywide statistics about proportions marrying by age for the prefectures of Japan. Since 1920, the published census does not count the population at each age, but rather aggregates the data in five-year age groups. The value of the NTMK, which records each age if it was counted by traditional *sai*, is quite significant.

It is astonishing, therefore, that this valuable data source of *honseki jinko* (NTMK) has been entirely overlooked in demographic research so far. This may be a result of the absence of continuous uniform records from the termination of the *honseki jinko* register in 1897 and the commencement of the National Census in 1920. The intervening registers compiled every five years from 1898 to 1918, the Population Statistics of Imperial Japan (Nihon Teikoku Jinko Tokei: hereafter NTJT), contained different information from that in the NTMK.[9] It was almost impossible, therefore, to construct a systematic time series.

In addition to the NTMK, which forms the major data source for this study, the Table of Households and Population for Towns (Tofu Meiyu Kokohyo: hereafter TMK), will be used as well.[10] The TMK counted the urban population in 1884, and it is believed to provide highly reliable information. Finally, along with the NTJT of 1898, the 1899 Vital Population Statistics of Imperial Japan (Nihon Teikoku Jinko Dotai Tokei: hereafter NTJD), which connected age at marriage and proportion marrying, will also be used.[11]

PROPORTION MARRYING AND AGE AT MARRIAGE

Even if we do not have information on age at marriage, by using the method published by John Hajnal in 1953, it is possible to estimate the age at marriage from the proportion of persons marrying.[12] In his essay, Hajnal calculates the age at marriage from two different kinds of modern census data for the proportion of

unmarried persons. Because the census data was calculated in five-year age groups and because Hajnal wanted to estimate changing age at marriage over time, the calculations involved in his effort were no easy matter. Unfortunately, Hajnal's sophisticated technique is inappropriate for analyzing the single-year data from Meiji Japan.

In an earlier study on Japan the author used a simple estimate which calculates the age at marriage when the proportion marrying reaches 50 percent.[13] In this calculation I assumed that 100 percent of the population would marry, and that age at marriage was distributed evenly within a given five-year age group. But these assumptions are not always realistic. In Japan, although the proportion marrying was higher than in the West, it did not reach 100 percent at any age. Further, the age at marriage, particularly for women, was not distributed evenly within any five-year age group. An accurate distribution of ages at marriage for women would be skewed to the particular age with a long tail toward the right.

By contrast, in the present study I have used data which provide information on both age and proportion marrying in each age, and after calculating the relationship between these figures, I have applied the results to the NTMK. Unfortunately, there is no single source for obtaining these two figures of age at marriage and proportion marrying in one calculation. But by using the 1898 NTJT, one can get results for persons married and unmarried in 1898 and combine this information with the distribution of age at marriage obtained from the 1899 NTJD. Both these sources aggregate data for the country as a whole. Here, however, because I want to find the relation between proportion marrying and age at marriage as a whole, I will ignore the local differences that might exist (see Figure 1).

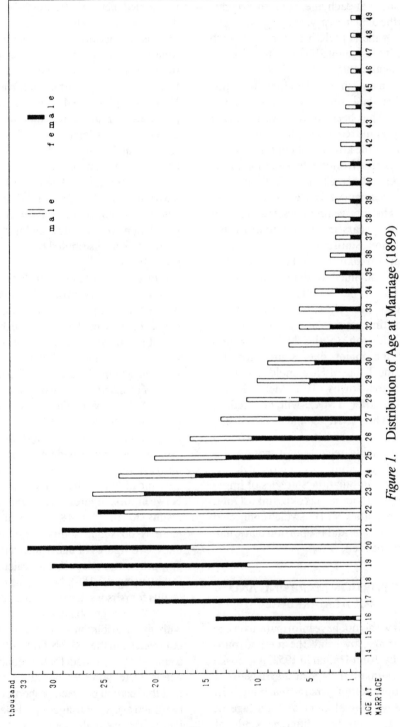

Figure 1. Distribution of Age at Marriage (1899)

By combining the data from these two records, we can reach the following conclusions. First, the proportion marrying did not reach eighty percent at the highest. For men, it reached 78.8 percent at age 44, and for women, it reached 79.4 percent at age 37. Second, the distribution of age at marriage reached its peak at age 23 for men and age twenty for women. Third, the shape of the distribution of age at marriage for women is more peaked and sharper than that for men. About 38 percent of men marry between the ages of 21 and 25. About 48 percent of women marry between 18 and 22. Because these ages at marriage include figures for remarriages, the distribution of ages at first marriage would be more concentrated in reality.

Of course, the average age at marriage will depend upon the length of time that one uses to calculate age at marriage. But we know from prior analyses of Tokugawa population records that almost all first marriages for both sexes occurred before age 35 *sai*.[14] By studying the NTJD and looking at persons who reach age 35, we calculate an average age at marriage for men of 25.7 and of 22.4 for women. Using the NTJT for obtaining figures for the proportion marrying at these ages, we find that 45 percent of men aged 26 were married, and 44 percent of women aged 22 are married. Although these figures are slightly higher than 40 percent, we can say that they resemble a half of the highest proportion marrying at any age for men and women.

According to the results above, even if the average age at marriage cannot be calculated directly from the data on hand, if the proportion marrying at various ages is known, the age that corresponds to half of the highest proportion marrying is approximately equal to the average age at marriage.

NTMK OBSERVATIONS

The NTMK records population data by prefecture for the number marrying and not marrying at each age on the basis of *honseki jinko*. First, the proportion marrying in each prefecture for men aged 28 *sai* and for women aged 23 *sai* was calculated and placed in Table 1. The results can be summarized as follows. For both sexes, there is more than a 30-point difference between the highest and lowest proportions. In particular, the difference for women is much greater than for men. The higher proportions can be found in the northern and eastern parts of Japan (except Tokyo and Kanagawa where urbanization was significant), and the regions east of and including Toyama, Nagano, and Shizuoka.[15] In these areas, except for Toyama for men and Yamanashi for women, the proportion of persons marrying was well over 55 percent. By comparison, to the west of these regions, except for a few prefectures where the proportions were slightly higher than the countrywide average, the proportion marrying was well under 55 percent.

The area with lower proportions marrying was, for both sexes, Kinki, where Osaka and Kyoto are located, and west Hokuriku and Chugoku Districts. Outside of that region, there are also Tokyo and Kanagawa, one of the most urbanized areas, and Hokkaido, which was growing rapidly in the late nineteenth century.

Thus the proportion marrying at certain ages has a pronounced regional bias. A similar sort of bias can be found displayed on Maps 1 and 2, which show age at marriage by prefecture, estimated from the proportion marrying of each age obtained in the above-mentioned way. The pattern of distribution of age at marriage corresponds closely to the pattern of distribution of proportion marrying shown

Table 1.
Proportion Marrying by Prefecture (1886)

DISTRICT Prefecture	MALE (age at 28 sai)			FEMALE (age at 23 sai)		
	population	marrying	proportion	population	marrying	proportion
HOKKAIDO	1604	715	44.6%	1932	856	44.3%
TOHOKU						
Aomori	4299	2985	69.4	4396	3217	73.2
Iwate	4763	3394	71.3	5159	3759	72.9
Miyagi	5533	3493	63.1	5820	3903	67.1
Akita	5889	3967	69.6	5886	4096	69.6
Yamagata	5333	3326	62.4	6130	3857	62.9
Fukushima	6191	4187	67.6	7664	5248	68.5
KANTO						
Ibaragi	7355	4566	62.1	8196	4781	58.3
Tochigi	4562	3018	66.2	5742	3349	58.3
Gunma	4413	3028	68.6	5544	3715	67.0
Saitama	7531	5137	68.2	9034	5317	58.9
Chiba	8550	5788	67.7	9367	6175	65.9
Tokyo	8624	3881	45.0	9882	4474	45.3
Kanagawa	5746	3197	55.6	7585	3700	48.8
HOKURIKU						
Niigata	11788	6826	57.9	12242	6935	56.6
Toyama	4520	2400	53.1	5953	3923	65.9
Ishikawa	5057	2260	44.7	6076	3204	52.7
Fukui	4093	1899	46.4	4882	2578	52.8
CHUBU						
Yamanashi	2993	1778	59.4	4044	2104	52.0
Nagano	7685	4656	60.6	9558	5816	60.8
Gifu	6552	2956	45.1	7215	3709	51.4
Shizuoka	7209	4600	63.8	8421	5531	65.7
Aichi	10294	5193	50.4	11117	6028	54.2
Mie	6493	3675	56.6	7507	3707	49.4
KINKI						
Shiga	4579	2130	46.5	5217	2262	43.4
Kyoto	6616	3046	46.1	6978	3316	47.5
Osaka	12220	5454	44.6	15376	5593	36.4
Hyogo	11807	5308	45.0	12375	5526	44.7
Wakayama	4897	1993	40.7	5415	1877	34.7
CHUGOKU						
Tottori	3190	1681	52.7	3152	1684	53.4
Shimane	5067	2410	47.6	5433	2818	51.9
Okayama	8564	4051	47.3	8654	4186	48.4
Hiroshima	10201	4958	48.6	10322	5027	48.7
Yamaguchi	6924	2964	42.8	8138	3749	46.1
SHIKOKU						
Tokushima	5530	2737	49.5	5660	2516	44.5
Ehime	12652	5777	45.7	13341	5925	44.4
Kochi	4508	2570	57.0	4573	3062	67.0
KYUSHU						
Fukuoka	8427	4042	48.0	11198	5127	45.8
Saga	4304	1842	42.8	4278	2001	46.8
Nagasaki	5328	2494	46.8	6617	2721	41.1
Kumamoto	7846	3973	50.6	9022	4169	46.2
Oita	5756	3110	54.0	6748	3605	53.4
Miyazaki	2737	1519	55.5	3592	1901	52.9
Kagoshima	6446	3088	47.9	8934	3563	39.9
Okinawa	3069	1798	58.6	3378	1488	44.0
TOTAL	287745	153870	53.5	327753	172096	52.5

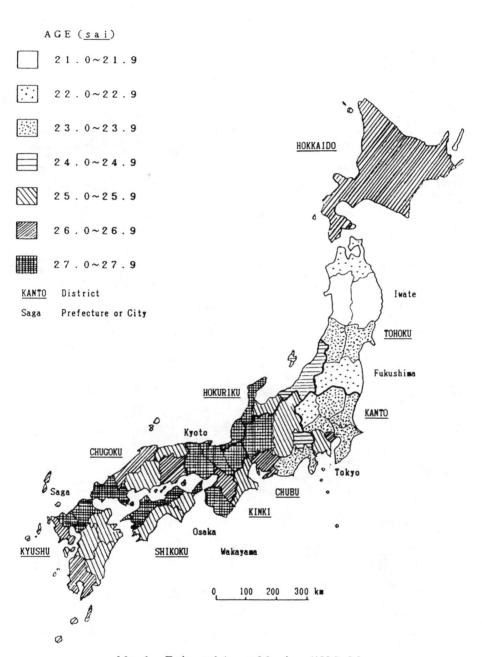

Map 1. Estimated Age at Marriage (1886): Men

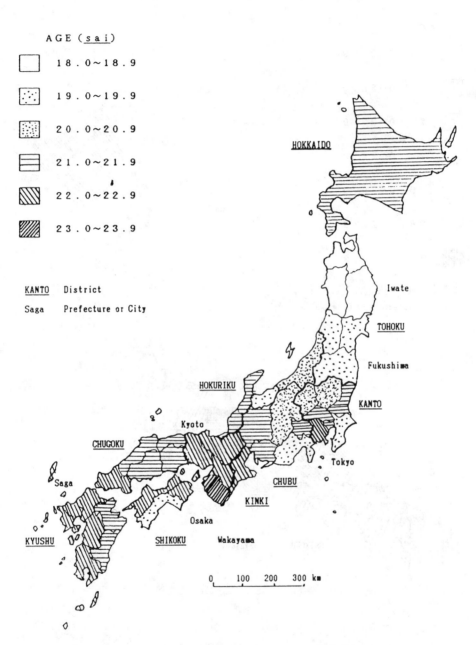

Map 2.   Estimated Age at Marriage (1886): Women

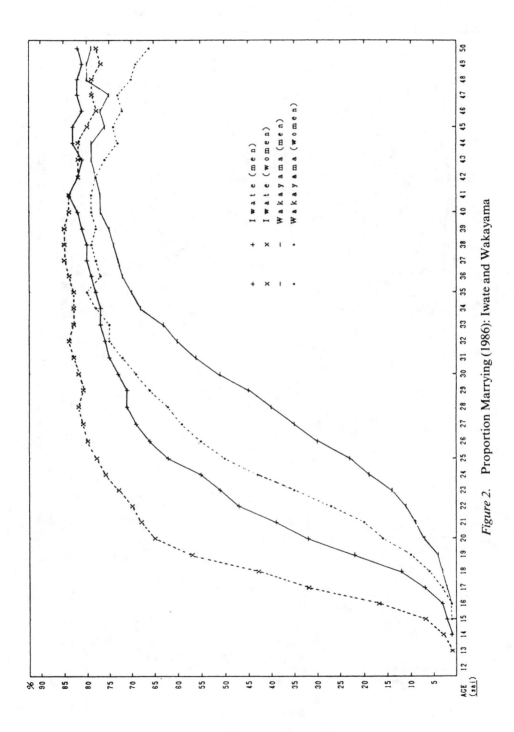

Figure 2. Proportion Marrying (1986): Iwate and Wakayama

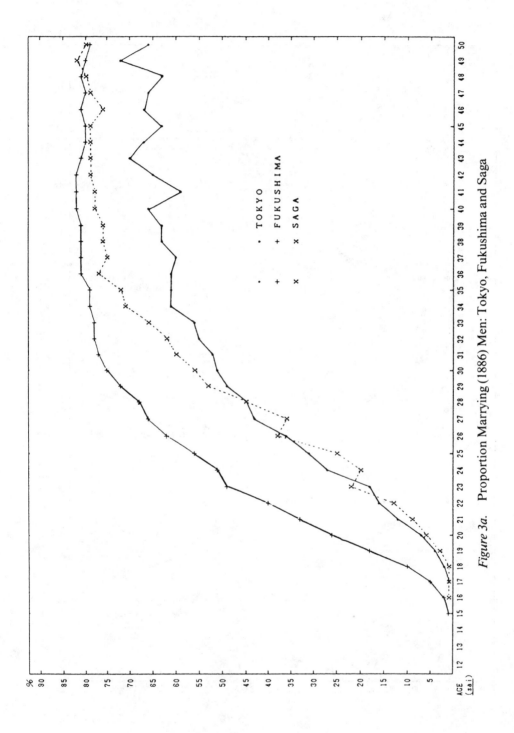

Figure 3a.   Proportion Marrying (1886) Men: Tokyo, Fukushima and Saga

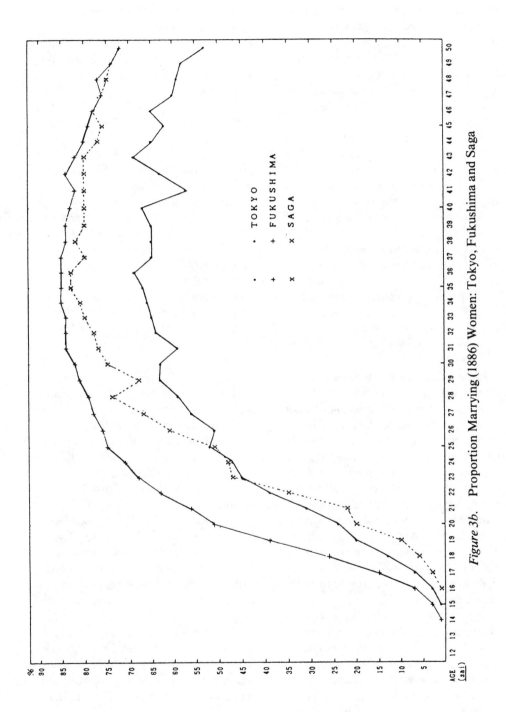

Figure 3b. Proportion Marrying (1886) Women: Tokyo, Fukushima and Saga

on Table 1. For men, the age at marriage was well over 25 *sai* in the areas to the west of Toyama, Nagano, and Shizuoka, except for Okinawa. East of this line, except for Tokyo, age at marriage was well under 25 *sai*.[16] For women, the age at marriage was well over 21 *sai*, except for Kochi, in the areas to the west of Toyama-Nagano-Shizuoka line. East of this line, except for Tokyo, the age at marriage for women was well under 21 *sai*.

For both sexes in Tohoku, age at marriage was significantly early. In the six prefectures that comprise this area, for males age at marriage was under 23 *sai* and for women under 19 *sai*. On the other hand, in the Kinki area and most of western Japan, late marriage was the rule. In the 21 prefectures making up this region, age at marriage for men was over 26 *sai* in thirteen prefectures, and age at marriage for women was over 22 *sai* in fourteen prefectures.

From these findings it is possible to suggest that there were two patterns of marriage in Japan in the late nineteenth century—a pattern of early marriage in eastern Japan and one of late marriage in the western Japan. By looking more closely at representative prefectures from each region—Iwate Prefecture in the east and Wakayama Prefecture in the west—it is possible to reach the following conclusions. As we can see from Figure 2, the pattern of early marriage in Iwate in the east and the pattern of late marriage in Wakayama in the west for both sexes holds true until age 40 *sai*.

In Iwate, for example, the proportion marrying for females age 20 *sai* was as high as 70 percent, but in Wakayama, it was a low 35 percent. The proportion of men marrying at age 25 *sai* was 50 percent in Iwate but 25 percent in Wakayama. Thus Iwate shows proportions marrying at the ages twice as high as Wakayama.

Another important consideration is the rural-urban comparison of the proportion marrying. We chose three prefectures: Tokyo, the most urbanized one where nearly three-quarters of the population were dwelling within the urban boundary; Fukushima, an eastern rural prefecture; and Saga, a western rural prefecture.

Figures 3a and 3b shows the proportion marrying from age 15 *sai* to 50 *sai* in these three prefectures. Tokyo was slightly higher than Saga in the younger age group, but after age 28 *sai* for men and age 25 *sai* for women, it became lower than that of Saga. This must be called an "urban type." By contrast, Fukushima started and reached the peak earlier than Saga, but the proportion was almost same as Saga, and much higher than that of Tokyo. This must be called a "rural type."

CONCLUSION

How can we explain these conspicuous regional differences in the proportion marrying and age at marriage? Geographical location—east or west—and degree of urbanization seem to be the decisive factors. The division line, incidentally, itself does fall on the Fossa Magna, a geological trough line which divides Japan into east and west. What we are interested in is the relationship between age at marriage and economic development. If age at marriage is dependent on economic circumstances, as is thought generally to be the case in the premodern world, such regional differences in the proportion marrying and age at marriage in Japan cannot be explained at all. This is because western Japan until the end of the nineteenth century was more prosperous and economically developed than eastern Japan.

Although detailed information on the input and output of each prefecture cannot be obtained for this period, the degree of urbanization and the proportion of urbanized population can be computed from the TMK of 1884. In Tokyo Prefecture where 73 percent of the population was urban, the proportion marrying was relatively low and age at marriage relatively high in the more urbanized areas. But, unexpectedly, the Tohoku region is found to have a higher proportion of urban population than the rest of Japan. Except for large urban concentrations like Tokyo, Osaka, and Kyoto, small and medium sized cities did not appear to have the expected attributes.[17]

The differential age at marriage and proportion marrying between eastern and western Japan may be partly affected by marriage customs. In the eastern part of Japan, primogeniture was more common. People married earlier and sons and their wives worked with their parents in the fields. Intensive labor in the relatively larger fields was needed especially in the shorter working season. A more compressed family cycle (earlier marriage and earlier child-bearing) was, therefore, more suitable.

By contrast, the western part of Japan contained a variety of inheritance customs, including ultimogeniture (inheritance by youngest son), and non-sex-selective inheritance. Consequently, people did not need to marry quickly. Heads of households wished to hold on their authority as long as possible, because their landholdings were more valuable than in the eastern part.

We suspect, therefore, that differences in age at marriage between eastern and western Japan and rural and urban areas were not strictly a result of geography and of degree of urbanization. Rather, they were related to differences in the family cycle and in inheritance customs as well as to differences in the type of agricultural production and size of farm. The exact nature of this relationship, especially where cause and effect are concerned, still requires systematic examinations. One is rather hard-pressed to find a consistent thread of explanation. In order to fully understand the context one should employ knowledge about agricultural technology as well as social-anthropological and cultural evidence for an explanation of these regional variations.

The relationship between age at marriage and economic circumstances was one of mutual interactions, rather than a one-way process. On the one hand, age at marriage was determined by demand for labor in family in the countryside; on the other hand, because of its regulatory power over population size, age at marriage also shaped economic conditions. My future research in this area will test this hypothesis.

ACKNOWLEDGMENTS

The author gratefully acknowledges the contributions made by Professor W. Mark Fruin, California State University, Hayward, and Professor Tamara K. Hareven, Clark University, to the translation and revision of this article. The latter also gave me many suggestions and comments. Without their patient assistance, this article would not have appeared. Of course, I am totally responsible for remaining mistakes.

NOTES

1. See Hayami, 1973a), Figure 11-2, p. 188.
2. Calculated from Hayami, 1973a), Table 12-16, p. 220.
3. See Hayami, 1973b, Table 1, p. 8.
4. See Hayami, 1983, Table 7, p. 27.
5. See Narimatsu, 1985, pp. 83–84.
6. For example, Nihon Teikoku Jinko Seitai Tokei (Population Statistics of Imperial Japan) of 1908, edited by Bureau of Statistics, Cabinet Office, inserted "residential population surveyed by police" as an appendix. In this survey, the population of

Tokyo Metropolitan Area was given as 2,328,791, but this was evidently an undercount because the survey of the Statistics Bureau estimated the population at 3,053,402, thirty percent higher than the police survey. The main reason for this gap appears to have been the double-counting of *kiryu jinko*, the population that had temporarily moved to Tokyo.

7. Hosoya, 1978, and Sorifu Tokeikyoku (Bureau of Statistics, Cabinet Office), 1976.

8. Naimusho (Ministry of Home Affairs), 1886.

9. Naikaku Tokeikyoku, 1898. Naikaku Tokeikyoku (Bureau of Statistics, Cabinet Office) compiled the statistics from 1898 for every five years until the year 1920 when the first census was carried out.

10. Naimusho (Ministry of Home Affairs), 1884.

11. Naikaku Tokeikyoku, 1899.

12. Hajnal, 1953.

13. Hayami, 1973a, pp. 123–127.

14. For Yokokuchi village, Shinano Province, see Hayami, 1973a, pp. 212–213.

15. The proportion marrying: for men age 26–30 *sai*, Tokyo 45.2, total 53.4; for women age 21–25 *sai*, Tokyo 33.9, total 50.5 percent.

16. The average age at marriage: for men, Tokyo age 26.0, total age 25.3; for women, Tokyo age 21.4, total age 21.3 *sai*.

17. For the variations of inheritance customs in Tokugawa Japan, see Homusho, 1877 and 1880.

REFERENCES

Hajnal, John. 1953. "Age at Marriage and Proportion Marrying." *Population Studies* 7(2): 111–136.

Hayami, Akira. 1973a. *Kinsei noson no rekishi jinkogakuteki kenkyu* (Historical Demography of a Rural Society in Tokugawa Japan). Tokyo: Toyokeizai Shinposha.

————. 1973b. "Labor Migration in a Pre-Industrial Society: A Study of Tracing the Life Histories of the Inhabitants of a Village." *Keio Economic Studies* 10: No. 2.

————. 1983. "The Myth of Primogeniture and Impartible Inheritance in Tokugawa Japan." *Journal of Family History* 8: 3–29.

Homusho (Ministry of Justice). 1877 (also 1880). *Zenkoku minji kanrei ruishu* (Surveys on the Customs of Civil Affairs) in Meiji bunka zenshu. (Collection of Meiji Civilization) Vol. 8: Law. Tokyo: Nihon Hyoronsha. (Reprinted in 1929.)

Hosoya, Shinji, ed. 1978. *Meiji zenki nihon keizaitokei kaidai shoshi: fukoku kyohei hen, jo-2* (Bibliography of Economic Statistics of Early Meiji Japan: Volume of Enrichment and Armament A-2). Tokyo: Institute of Economic Studies, Hitotsubashi University.

Naikaku Tokeikyoku (Bureau of Statistics, Cabinet Office), ed. 1898. *Nihon Teikoku Jinko Tokei* (Population Statistics of Imperial Japan), surveyed December 31, 1898. Tokyo: Naikaku Tokeikyoku.

————. 1899. *Nihon Teikoku Jinko Dotai Tokei* (Vital Statistics of Population of Imperial Japan), surveyed December 31, 1899. Tokyo: Naikaku Tokeikyoku.

Naimusho (Ministry of Home Affairs), ed. 1884. *Tofu Meiyu Kokohyo* (Table of the Population of Cities and Towns), Bureau of Geography, surveyed December 31, 1884. Tokyo: Naimusho.

————. 1886. *Nihon Teikoku Minseki Kokohyo* (Table of Civil Registration of Imperial Japan), Somukyoku Kosekika (Registration Section, Department of General Affairs), surveyed December 31, 1886. Tokyo: Naimusho.

Narimatsu, Saeko. 1985. *Kinsei tohoku noson no hitobito* (Peasants Life of a Village in the Northern Tokugawa Japan). Kyoto: Minerva shobo.

Sorifu Tokeikyoku (Bureau of Statistics, Cabinet Office), ed. 1976. *Sorifu tokeikyoku hayakunen shiryo shusei* (100 Years Collection of Documents of the Bureau of Statistics, Cabinet Office).

"EARLY" FERTILITY DECLINE IN AMERICA: A PROBLEM IN FAMILY HISTORY

Daniel Scott Smith

ABSTRACT: *A striking peculiarity of American demographic history is its comparatively early decline in fertility. Although some of the decrease before the Civil War may be attributed to later and less universal marriage, marital fertility also fell. Past scholarship on the subject has focused on alternative explanations and statistical approaches to cross-sectional variations in the child-woman ratio. After showing the inherent limitations of this approach, particularly at the level of states, this article draws on the findings of historians of political behavior and women's activities to suggest that the understanding of the early decline in marital fertility in the United States may be most profitably pursued through the study of the fertility behavior and values of the principal action-groups of antebellum America: religious, ethnic, and economic. Both the motivations for, and possibly the techniques of, family limitation were transmitted and sustained, this hypothesis contends, through membership and participation in these groups.*

From a comparative perspective, the early decline in fertility is a central problem in American demographic and family history. Starting with the highest rates of childbearing ever estimated for a large population—a crude birth rate well over 50 per 1,000 in 1800 or a total fertility rate above seven children per woman—the United States, along with France, led the western world in the secular decline in fertility. By the eve of the Civil War in 1860, the total fertility rate had dropped to 5.2 and by 1900 reached 3.6 a fifty-percent decrease over the course of the nineteenth century (Coale and Zelnik, 1963). By contrast, fertility decline in Europe outside of France did not begin until the 1870s. Not only was the decline in American fertility early by comparative

Daniel Scott Smith is a member of the History Department of the University of Illinois at Chicago and is editor of the journal Historical Methods. *His research deals with the demographic, family, and social history of America from the seventeenth century to the present.*

standards, but it also apparently preceded the secular fall in mortality by some eight decades (Haines, 1979). The timing of the reduction in these two components of natural population increase in the American case reverses the sequence depicted by the theory of demographic transition. Finally, explanations of the early fall in American fertility have focused on marital fertility rather than on other demographic variables; the transition in marital fertility is, of course, of central concern for population policy, since it is the key to the reduction of rapid rates of population growth (Knodel and van de Walle, 1979).

Given these manifest peculiarities of the American case, the consensus on the early decline in fertility among historical demographers and family historians is surprising, particularly since the evidentiary bases are problematic and the estimates derived are indirect. Further, the major explanatory efforts have utilized data and methods that are tangential to the theoretical understanding of the reasons for the decline of marital fertility in the United States in the antebellum period.

Anomalous cases are of particular interest in social science for they may provide important clues to crucial factors in causation; deviations from general patterns are also, or so most historical demographers assume, inherently suspect and thus deserving of critical reexamination. E.A. Wrigley (1985), for example, recently subjected the early French decline to such scrutiny, noting both the remarkably constant rate of population increase both nationally and regionally, and the ski-jump trajectory of the decline of marital fertility in many departments, first observed by van de Walle (1974), in which fertility remained level for several decades after a period of decline. Both results differ from the usual patterns of post-1870 population change and fertility transition, leading Wrigley to argue that the French

case before 1870 should be included in the old demographic regime of homeostatic balance, even though it exhibited patterns of marital fertility that are usually interpreted to mean the use by couples of conscious birth limitation. The early fertility decline in France remains peculiar, but its peculiarities differ from those of classic declines in marital fertility experienced elsewhere in Europe and the rest of the world.

This article will, first, examine skeptically the evidence for an early, pre-1860 decline in marital fertility in the United States; despite obvious uncertainties in the data and their interpretation, it will not entirely reject the notion that there remains a real problem to be solved, at least for a large group within the American white population. Second, it will review the literature on the correlates of fertility in this period; most of these studies compare ecological units at one point in time. Although both economic and cultural variables have been shown to have statistical importance, this section concludes that the data and methodology used in these studies limit their explanatory potential. Drawing on a suggestive result of one of the few analyses of fertility change, the final section will outline a new interpretive approach to American fertility decline. Arguing that fertility behavior is a collective or group phenomena, it attempts to sketch, using findings from political and women's history, the possible definitions of the core action-groups that composed American society during the antebellum period and the relevance of these groups to the phenomenon of early fertility decline in the United States.

VARIATION IN THE CHILD-WOMAN RATIO

Most of what is known about American fertility change in the nineteenth century rests on a single source: the age structure reported in the decennial United States census, with a decrease in fertility inferred from the declining ratio of children to women. Although various series have been calculated (Thompson and Whelpton, 1933; Yasuba, 1962; Coale and Zelnik, 1963), all depend on the child-woman ratio. Most of interpretive literature on fertility change explicitly or implicitly focuses on childbearing within marriage, but data on levels and trends in nuptiality are scattered in coverage and uneven in quality. Further, there is no viable way of ascertaining the relative under-enumeration of children and women of childbearing age in each census. The pattern of change in the ratio, among whites, of children under ten to women aged 16–44 between 1800 and 1860 shows two decades of relatively rapid decline, the 1820s and 1840s (Table 1). Perhaps by coincidence the 1830 and 1850 censuses were the only two that changed the method of recording of children. In 1830, enumerators recorded the numbers of children under age five, and the number from age five and under ten; previously they had counted the number of children under age ten for each household. In 1850 for the first time, enumerators recorded the name and identifying information of each free person in the population, not just those who headed households. From these manuscript schedules, clerks then tallied the numbers in each age group. It is not obvious, of course, why the recording procedures employed in 1830 and 1850 should have increased the undercount of children; a reduced undercount would seem to have been just as likely. However, the calculation by McClelland and Zeckhauser (1982: 68–71, 144–155) of a radically lower death rate during the 1850s of those aged 10–19 in 1860, compared to previous decades, suggests that the 1850 census undercounted children more than other censuses of the period.

The uneven decennial rate of decline in the child-woman ratio between 1800 and 1860 could, of course, be genuine. Decades of relatively more rapid westward movement in the north and relatively lesser increases in urbanization in the northeast (the 1830s and 1850s) experienced lesser rates of decline in the child-woman ratio than decades (the 1820s and 1840s) of more rapid northeastern urbanization and relatively slower movements to the west within the northern section of the United States (Fishlow, 1965). This temporal relationship is consistent with two of the major emphases—urbanization and declining land availability—in the explanation of cross-sectional variations in fertility in the antebellum era.

A real decrease in the child-woman ratio does not necessarily mean, however, that fertility within marriage actually declined. At least some of the decrease is doubtless due to an increasing fraction of the female population who never married and a rising age of first marriage. Additionally, increases in mortality rates, if

Table 1.
Children Under Age 10 per 1,000 White Women Aged 16–44, United States, United States, 1800 to 1860.

Year	1800	1810	1820	1830	1840	1850	1860
Child-Woman Ratio	1844	1824	1735	1556	1514	1335	1308
Percent Change		−1.1	−4.8	−8.6	−4.5	−7.8	−2.0

Source: Yasuba, 1962: 62.

they occurred in the first half of the nineteenth century, will appear as reductions in fertility as measured by the child-woman ratio; a higher mortality level means that relatively more children than adults die, the average age of the population increases, and the child-woman ratio declines (Coale, 1964).

The absence of data on marital status and the consequent neglect of the effect of changing nuptiality on overall fertility are major flaws in the literature depicting an early decline in American fertility. What most impressed contemporary observers of pre-nineteenth century American demography, such as Benjamin Franklin and T.R. Malthus, was a very high fertility that resulted from early and near universal marriage for women. The early age of entry into marriage derived from the frontier conditions of the American economy and society. Both in Western Europe and America, marriage required the establishment of new households, and access to an independent means of livelihood was needed to form a household. Cheap land, therefore, meant a low cost of household formation and early marriage for both men and women. As the population of the United States rapidly increased, density and land prices also increased; inevitably, the ratio of persons living in settled areas to those living in frontier areas also grew. Declining fertility as a consequence of later and less universal marriage requires no special theory of the uniqueness of the American experience; America was simply becoming Europeanized in its fundamental economic environment.

Unfortunately there are no adequate national data on nuptiality until the 1890 census. Quite clearly, nuptiality has an important influence on the overall level of fertility. One index of the proportion, by state, of adult females married in 1890 accounts for 77 percent of the variance in the child-woman ratio among the 32 states that existed in 1860 (also see Guest, 1981). This correlation overstates the magnitude of the influence of nuptiality on overall fertility, since later marriage ages and lower marital fertility were spatially associated in the United States (Guest, 1981). While there are local data on female marriage age for the late eighteenth century, showing averages just above 20 for southern and middle states and closer to 22 or 23 for New England, no sample of marriage ages exists that would represent the United States as a whole. Genealogical and especially family reconstitution-based studies cover long-settled areas, those in which marriage ages were higher than in places that were settled more recently.

Similarly, the direction and magnitude of mortality change between 1800 and 1860 remains largely a mystery. Increase, decrease, or fluctuations without a trend are all possibilities. However, to make relatively extreme assumptions about the magnitude of the rise in the proportion of persons who never married and of the increase in mortality requires an increase of unlikely magnitude in female age at first marriage to account for all of the decline of the child-woman ratio. Specifically, the calculation first postulates that life expectancy at birth decreased from fifty years to forty years at birth for females between 1800 and 1860. In the Coale and Demeny (1966) model life tables, this change corresponds to a shift from Level 13 to Level 9 in the NORTH variant. Fogel (1986) argues for such a major increase in mortality during the first half of the nineteenth century. In addition, the proportion never-marrying among females was assumed to have doubled between 1800 and 1860, from 3.65 to 7.3 percent, the latter being the 1890 figure. Assuming, finally, that married women bore children at a rate of 0.4

children per year, then age at first marriage would have to increase from 19.2 years in 1800 to 21.9 years (the singulate age in 1890) by 1860; a national average of female first marriage of 19.2 years in 1800 seems implausibly low. Although this calculation employed simplifying assumptions and approximations, this result very likely overstates the importance of the impact of decreases in nuptiality and increases in mortality on the child-woman ratio. Although a significant portion of the 26 percent decline in the total fertility rate from 7.0 to 5.2 between 1800 and 1860 may be attributed to factors other than the decline in marital fertility, the entirety of the decline cannot be. Also, using an indirect calculation, Sanderson (1979) concludes that marital fertility must have declined during the nineteenth century. Indeed, this indirect conclusion is supported by a direct estimate of a 16.7 percent decrease in the number of births per 1,000 married women aged 16-44 as tabulated by the 1825 and 1845 New York state censuses (Yasuba, 1962: 188–189).

CORRELATES OF FERTILITY IN ANTEBELLUM AMERICA

Yasuba initiated the systematic inquiry into American fertility variations, and his assessment of the main patterns still stands. He argued that the best predictor of cross-sectional differences was an index of land availability, a factor which differentiates the long-settled eastern states from the frontier western states and which most plausibly operates through its effect on the age and incidence of marriage. On the other hand, as Yasuba showed, land availability was not the entire story, especially in the decades closer to the Civil War, and measures of economic and cultural development are also associated with lower fertility, as others (Forster and Tucker, 1972; Vinovskis, 1976a; Sund-

strom and David, 1985; Garey, 1985) have shown.

Data on interstate differences in fertility and other variables obviously have quite limited potential for assessing competing interpretations. There were only thirty-two states in 1860, and many of the independent variables are substantially intercorrelated. In addition, the results are sensitive to the formulations used to tap the alleged causal mechanisms. For example, using the price of an average farm to measure land availability (Vinovskis, 1976a) greatly reduces the apparent influence of this factor relative to an index of the degree of settlement (the ratio of currently improved acres or number of farms to the maximum number of acres ever-improved or the maximum number of farms ever operated in a state [Schapiro, 1982]). The latter indices are consistent with an understanding of the evolution of an area from frontier to fully-settled, while the former conforms to a more abstract economic conception of the cost of becoming a farm owner. The three states of northern New England, for example, had relatively low land prices but a very high fraction of farm acres ever-improved in 1860; they also had low levels of fertility. Thus it was relatively easy to become a farmer in northern New England at the end of the antebellum period, but Yankee farmers and their children voted with their feet to indicate that they preferred the possibilities of making a better living to a meager way of life (Barron, 1984).

Factor analyses performed on different combinations of the usual set of variables used in these interstate analyses underscore the limited analytical possibilities in these data (see Table 2). Two factors, which typically accounted for about 80 percent of the variance, emerged. One of these captures the gap in fertility between eastern and western states, the other a dimension that distinguished lower

Table 2.
Factor Analysis of Variables Used in Study of Interstate Variations
in the Child-Woman Ratio.

	Rotated Factor Matrix	
	Factor 1 *East-*	*Factor 2* *North-*
Variable	*West*	*South*
(1) White sex ratio, aged 15–49 in 1860	−.933	−.041
(2) White female illiteracy, aged 20+ in 1860	−.051	−.857
(3) Percent foreign-born in 1860	−.183	.912
(4) Percent in places over 2,500 in population in 1860	.546	.662
(5) Percent white females aged 20–29 who were single in 1890	.645	.722
(6) Singulate mean age at first marriage of white females in 1890	−.101	.938
(7) Farm value in 1860	.454	.019
(8) Acres in farms in 1860/maximum of acres ever in farms before 1910	.971	.065
(9) Number of farms in 1860/maximum number of farms at any date before 1910	.949	−.175
Percent of variance explained	45.9%	33.3%

Region	*Mean Factor Scores*	
(1) New England	0.925	0.753
(2) Middle Atlantic	0.782	0.805
(3) Old South	0.518	−1.353
(4) New South	−0.726	−0.835
(5) Old Northwest	−0.412	0.451
(6) West North Central	−1.498	0.816
(7) Border	0.585	−0.177

Notes: States in Regions: (1) Maine, Vermont, New Hampshire, Massachusetts, Connecticut, Rhode Island.
          (2) New York, New Jersey, Pennsylvania.
          (3) Virginia, North Carolina, South Carolina, Georgia, Alabama, Tennessee.
          (4) Florida, Mississippi, Louisiana, Arkansas, Texas.
          (5) Ohio, Indiana, Michigan, Illinois;
          (6) Wisconsin, Minnesota, Iowa, Kansas, Missouri.
          (7) Delaware, Maryland, Kentucky.
Sources: (1) U.S. Secretary of the Interior, Population of the United States in 1860 (Washington, 1864): pp. 592–93.
        (2,3) U.S., Secretary of the Interior, Superintendent of the Census, Ninth Census: The Statistics of the Population of the
        United States (Washington, 1872): (2) vol. I, Table IX, pp. 396–397; (3) vol. I, Table IV, p. 299.
        (4) U.S., Bureau of the Census. U.S. Census of Population: 1950. (Washington, 1952): Table 15, vol. I, Section 1, pp.
        17–23.
        (5,6) U.S., Department of the Interior, Census Office, Compendium of the 11th Census: 1890 (Washington, 1897):
        Part III, Table 20, pp. 130–178.
        (7,8,9) U.S., Bureau of the Census. Thirteenth Census of the United States taken in the Year 1910. (Washington,
        1914): (7) V, Table 32, pp. 84–89; (8,9) V, Table 24, pp. 68–72.

northern from higher southern fertility. The East-West factor includes the sex tio, the ratio of farms in 1860 to the maximum number and, to a lesser degree, average farm value. Illiteracy, percentage foreign-born, and the mean marriage age in 1890 load on the North-South dimension. Perhaps the most interesting finding is that urbanization is not captured by either factor. Inasmuch as both East-West and North-South dimensions of American fertility variation rest on differences in marriage patterns, urbanization might be an indicator that distinctly taps variations in marital fertility in contrast to nuptiality. However, the proportion of women aged 20-29 who were single in 1890 also loads on neither of the first two factors.

All of the indicators that tap nuptiality may also incorporate variations arising from differences in marital fertility.

Factor analysis is an appropriate statistical technique when one does not wish to pretend that the indicators have obvious substantive meaning or when the proxies represent different levels of phenomena and thus are not comparable (Kim and Mueller, 1978). And the variables used in the analysis reported in Table 2 are a hodgepodge. The sex ratio in 1860 and the nuptiality index in 1890 measure the fraction of the female population most at risk to have children. These compositional variables are thrown in with those, such as urbanization or illiteracy, about which a more complex story must be told. Higher levels of literacy or education probably do not reduce fertility because couples spend their evenings reading rather than having sexual intercourse. Scholars can tell stories about how education lowers fertility based on plot outlines supplied by the disciplines of economics or sociology, but these theoretical plots can be no more than illustrated by the statistical analysis of empirical data. Utilizing apples and oranges, so to speak, factor analysis is a conservative way of examining the fruit salad of empirical indices for ecological units such as states.

Factor analysis thus is an appropriate technique for dealing with an eclectic melange of indicators, and to discuss each indicator separately, as is often done in multiple regression analyses, represents an over-interpretation of the information in the analysis. All of the indicators exhibit strong regional patterning, a fact obscured by the absence of the mapping of variables or residuals or a listing of the variables by state; in these studies history is divorced from geography. Most historians of the antebellum United States will not be surprised by the conclusion that the country differentiated on both an East-West and a North-South dimension. The evidence is consistent with both this regional interpretation and the perspectives, based on multiple regression analyses, that purport to sort out the influence of different factors.

One may prefer an interpretation cast in terms of a theoretically preferred variable or list of variables, but the merits of such interpretations do not rest unambiguously on the data being analyzed. The strongest statistical relationship between the child-woman ratio and a single theoretically-grounded independent variable was reported by Leasure (1982) who used change in the child-woman ratio between 1800/1810 and 1860 as the dependent variable (a welcome innovation in approach); and, as the independent variable, a modernizing religious culture defined as the fraction of church seats held by five Protestant denominations—Congregational, Presbyterian, Quaker, Unitarian, and Universalist—that allegedly favored religious and personal autonomy, education, and a more active role for women.

The strength of this variable derives from its unique ability to tap both the North-South and East-West regional dimensions. In the North, these denominations were particularly strong in New England, the region of lowest fertility, and adherents were much more numerous in the North than in the South. Leasure's emphasis on culture, like that of other scholars who stress different indicators, may or may not be correct. The regional differentials in the child-woman ratio can be related to any and all of the historical elements that make regions distinctive entities, or units that reflect the sharing by a population of an environment over time.

While ecological analyses of counties within states (Leet, 1976, 1977; Vinovskis, 1976b; Laidig et al., 1981) are less susceptible to the criticism that they merely capture the factors that differentiated the United States regionally, smaller units are more influenced by migration and thus differentials in fertility are more likely to be influenced by variations in nuptiality. While the New York data allow children per married woman to be the dependent variable, Vinovskis used the proportion married as an independent variable rather than the number of married women as the denominator of the dependent variable. And none of these works can isolate variations in marital fertility from those in the overall child-woman ratio.

One major study, however, does use individual-level data to show that personal characteristics do not account for the ecological relationship between the fertility of farmers' wives and the stage of settlement. Working with a sample of farm households from 102 northern counties in 1860, Richard Easterlin (1976) and his associates (Easterlin et al., 1978) have shown that not only were wives younger in more newly settled areas, but that women in their thirties were more likely to have children under age five in their households than farm women in counties in which more of the available farm land had been improved. This is the only study indicating that the fertility difference between the East and West in the antebellum United States involved differences in marital fertility as well as in patterns of nuptiality.

Despite beginning with data on wives in individual households, Easterlin actually analyzes five aggregations grouped on the basis of the index of future land availability. This procedure necessarily captures whatever the unmeasured individual differences are that covary with the settlement indicator. Further, the ecological index of land availability logically could be a proxy for another factor at that level, e.g. distance to a significant urban center. Contextual variables often show statisti-

cally powerful effects, but their interpretation is difficult (Hauser, 1974; Lieberson, 1985).

Easterlin does not argue that land availability has a straightforward influence on nuptiality or fertility at the individual level. According to his hypothesis, parents attempt to provide children with a start in adult life equivalent to that they themselves enjoyed. Thus poor farm couples who began their marriages in meager material circumstances will have the same number of children on average as wealthy farmers who were affluent at the inception of their adult lives. An individual-level test would involve, for example, the comparison of the fertility of wives in their thirties in whose families wealth had increased, decreased, or remained the same relative to the standing they inherited from their parents at the start of their marriages; no such test has been performed to date.

ACTION-GROUPS AND EARLY FERTILITY DECLINE

One major peculiarity of the literature on the early decline of American fertility is that the theoretical explanations have been cast at the level of the individual household or couple, but the readily available data exist at a high level of aggregation. While there are a few individual-level studies (Osterud and Fulton, 1976; Temkin-Greener and Swedlund, 1978; Byers, 1982; Logue, 1983), these necessarily are based on groups or localities that are relatively homogeneous in cultural terms. The second oddity of the literature is its strong internal orientation; much effort has gone into modifying Yasuba's indicators for the cross-sectional analysis of interstate variations. Neither the results of scholars studying the European fertility decline nor the interpretations of historians studying other aspects of the history of the antebellum United States has had influence. The distinction between the effects of nuptiality and of marital fertility, so central to the Princeton project on the decline of fertility in Europe (Coale and Watkins, 1986) has been virtually ignored. And the important arguments and findings in political, intellectual, and women's history have not been considered as relevant to the study of American demographic history.

Despite the growth of individualism, the basis of antebellum society was not the individual but the group, defined by the sharing of ethnic origins, denominational affiliation, and perhaps socioeconomic status. Adherence to political party, for example, was voluntary, but partisan regularity was prized and defectors scorned. Indeed, aspirations for modernity were as much a characteristic of groups as of individuals within the white American population. Biologically, of course, women do bear children, and conjugal family units, husbands and wives, are also actors. However, as Ryder (1980) argued, these units are not the only answers to the question, "Where do babies come from?" Central to persistent variations in fertility and inclination to initiate family limitation are social identifications, often based on ascription, that locate people into groups. If we direct our attention away from the narrow literature of American demographic and family history to other areas of experience in the nineteenth century, the case for a focus on the action-groups becomes compelling.

The concept of action-groups has several interpretative implications beyond its emphasis on the collective character of behavior. First, it transcends the usual historiographical distinction between ethnocultural and class interpretations of nineteenth-century phenomena. Second, it directs attention both to the membership in groups and the differences in behavior among people in different groups, and to the motivations or values of individuals in these groups. This perspective avoids the circular reasoning that allows, for example, Yankees to have low fertility because they are "modern" and for their modernity to be illustrated by their practice of family limitation; both group and action are operative aspects of the notion of action-groups. Finally, the focus on action demands an analysis of the reasons for action. Scholars must consider both the methods of family limitation and their rationale to understand the decline of marital fertility; the latter includes such matters as the definition of women's roles and the value placed on children by the various action-groups. Historians who have analyzed the non-demographic behavior of nineteenth-century Americans provide implicit support for pursuing this social-psychological approach.

In politics, religious and ethnocultural groups supplied the core for political parties. Reform-minded, pietistic-religious and ethnic groups tended to be Whigs and later Republicans, while more conservative, liturgical groups favored the Democratic Party. Regionally, these differences ultimately polarized aggressive Yankee and defensive white Southern political cultures (Kelley, 1979). And there is little doubt that Protestants in New England had the lowest fertility of any large group in the American population in 1860. Indeed native-born Massachusetts females born around 1830 did not come close to replacing their numbers; their replacement rate was only 0.78 (Uhlenberg, 1969). The marital fertility of white Southerners, on the other hand, very likely did not begin to decline before the Civil War (Steckel, 1985). Further, it is unlikely that Irish- and German-born Catholics, both strongly Democratic in politics, initiated fertility control within marriage before 1860.

This rough fit between the ethnocultural interpretation of American political division and the plausible patterning of early control of marital fertility raises as many questions as it answers. At a superficial level, fertility control within marriage is a reform analogous to temperance, abolitionism, and the extension of public schooling. All of these reforms and the Whig-Republican strain in American politics can be mapped into an interpretation of a modern world view (Foner, 1970; Jensen, 1978; Kleppner et al., 1981) that struggled against traditional habits and beliefs.

Observing an ecological relationship between fertility and the geographic location of these religious and ethnic groups provides only a promising lead; Leasure's demonstration that the indicator of modern denominations was a powerful predictor of interstate fertility variation is, as argued above, only one of several empirically plausible delineations of the North-South and East-West regional patterning of American fertility and other phenomena. To advance and refine this interpretation, demographic historians will require both behavioral data on fertility and attitudinal data relevant to fertility of these groups. For this project, the most interesting groups are the different denominations of Northern native-born Protestants, since no shift toward lower marital fertility is to be expected among other groups in the population.

A major advantage of this focus is that the interpretation of the divisions among Northern Protestant groups needs refinement and revision. Among the possible sources of modern tendencies, including family limitation within marriage, are evangelical religion and liberal, individualistic ideas deriving from the Enlightenment. Recent historians of women's activity and politics have stressed the dynamic role of evangelical religion as the matrix of reform. Evangelical revivals, it is claimed, activated men and women to social action and to reorganize their personal lives on a more disciplined and rational basis. The terms "evangelicalism" and "pietism" however, are used very loosely, even incorporating such liberal religious groups as Unitarians. Further, southern Baptists and Methodists were evangelical but not oriented toward reform or family limitation. Historians of women have also noted that many antebellum feminists who developed the most advanced positions concerning women's rights rejected or modified considerably their youthful religious orientations (Hersh, 1978; Hewitt, 1984). Within the Republican Party, there was a distinctly liberal, secular element that was more interested in economic development and other such programs than in temperance or moral reform.

If evangelical denominations are the central concern of the religious interpretation, the emerging American middle class is the focus of the individualistic emphasis. "Middle-class," however, is a category used as loosely as "evangelical," and both are intertwined with the Yankee culture of New England and natives of that region living elsewhere in the United States.

Future research ideally will examine the marital fertility of persons in different religious and occupational groups, although information on the former is difficult to obtain (see, however, Juster, 1985). Since family limitation is the focus, samples can be limited to women over age thirty. Some analytical leverage may be gained through the analysis of county-level variations in child-woman ratios, with cultural and religious indicators being employed in conjunction with the land availability indicators.

Just as important is the exploration of attitudes about women's roles, children, and family life in different denominational and occupational groups. It is not clear that the sources can be read closely enough to detect the differences that are probably quite subtle; the usual tools of intellectual and cultural history are too crude for such a study (Smith, 1985). Isolating the attitudes that supported the precocious modernity of American fertility behavior has interest not just for the study of that demographic subject but for the more general cultural and social history of antebellum America.

REFERENCES

Barron, Hal S. 1984. *Those Who Stayed Behind: Rural Society in Nineteenth-Century New England*. Cambridge: Cambridge University Press.

Byers, Edward. 1982. "Fertility Transition in a New England Commercial Center: Nantucket, Massachusetts." *Journal of Interdisciplinary History* 13: 17–40.

Coale, Ansley J. 1964. "How a Population Ages or Grows Younger." Pp. 47–58 in R. Freedman (ed.), *Population: The Vital Revolution*. New York: Anchor Books.

Coale, Ansley J. and Paul Demeny. 1966. *Regional Model Life Tables and Stable Populations*. Princeton: Princeton University Press.

Coale, Ansley J. and Susan Cotts Watkins, eds. 1986. *The Decline of Fertility in Europe*. Princeton: Princeton University Press.

Coale, Ansley J. and Melvin Zelnik. 1963. *New Estimates of Fertility and Population in the United States*. Princeton: Princeton University Press.

Easterlin, Richard A. 1976. "Population Change and Farm Settlement in the Northern United States." *Journal of Economic History* 36: 45–75.

Easterlin, Richard A., George Alter, and Gretchen Condran. 1978. "Farms and Farm Families in Old and New Areas: The Northern States in 1860." Pp. 22–84 in T.K. Hareven and M.A. Vinovskis (eds.), *Family and Population in Nineteenth-Century America*. Princeton: Princeton University Press.

Fishlow, Albert. 1965. *American Railroads and the Transformation of the Ante-Bellum Economy*. Cambridge: Harvard University Press.

Fogel, Robert W. 1986. "Nutrition and the Decline in Mortality Since 1700: Some Additional Preliminary Findings." Working Paper No. 1802, National Bureau of Economic Research.

Foner, Eric. 1970. *Free Soil, Free Labor, Free Men: The Ideology of the Republican Party Before the Civil War*. New York: Oxford University Press.

Forster, Colin and G.S.L. Tucker. 1972. *Economic Opportunity and White American Fertility Ratios, 1800-1860*. New Haven: Yale University Press.

Garey, Anita Ilta. 1985. "An Examination of Explanations for Fertility Decline and Differentials on the United States Frontier, 1800–1860." Program in Population Research Working Paper No. 16, University of California, Berkeley.

Guest, Avery M. 1981. "Social Structure and U.S. Inter-State Fertility Differentials in 1900." *Demography* 18: 465–486.

Haines, Michael R. 1979. "The Use of Model Life Tables to Estimate Mortality for the United States in the Late Nineteenth Century." *Demography* 16: 289–312.

Hauser, Robert M. 1974. "Contextual Analysis Revisited." *Sociological Methods and Research* 2: 365–375.

Hersh, Blanche Glassman. 1978. *The Slavery of Sex: Feminist-Abolitionism in America*. Urbana: University of Illinois Press.

Hewitt, Nancy A. 1984. *Women's Activism and Social Change: Rochester, New York, 1822-1872*. Ithaca, NY: Cornell University Press.

Jensen, Richard J. 1978. *Illinois: A History*. New York: W. W. Norton.

Juster, Susan. 1985. "Religion and Fertility in the Nineteenth Century: A Woman's Sphere." Unpublished conference paper, University of Michigan.

Kelley, Robert. 1979. *The Cultural Pattern in American Politics: The First Century*. New York: Alfred A. Knopf.

Kim, Jae-On and Charles W. Mueller. 1978. *Introduction to Factor Analysis: What It Is and How To Do It*. Beverly Hills: Sage Publications.

Kleppner, Paul et al. 1981. *The Evolution of American Electoral Systems*. Westport, CT: Greenwood Press.

Knodel, John and Etienne van de Walle. 1979. "Lessons from the Past: Policy Implications of Historical Fertility Studies." *Population and Development Review* 5: 217–245.

Laidig, G.L., W.A. Schutjer, and C.S. Stokes. 1981. "Agricultural Variation and Human Fertility." *Journal of Family History* 6: 195–205.

Leasure, J. William. 1982. "La baisse de la fécondité aux Etats-Unis de 1800 a 1860." *Population* 37: 607–622.

Leet, Don R. 1976. "The Determinants of the Fertility Transition in Antebellum Ohio." *Journal of Economic History* 36: 359–378.

————. 1977. "Interrelations of Population Density, Urbanization, Literacy, and Fertility." *Explorations in Economic History* 14: 388–401.

Lieberson, Stanley. 1985. *Making It Count: The Improvement of Social Research and Theory*. Berkeley and Los Angeles: University of California Press.

Logue, Barbara J. 1983. "The Whaling Industry and Fertility Decline: Nantucket, Massachusetts, 1660–1850." *Social Science History* 7: 427–456.

McClelland, Peter D. and Richard J. Zeckhauser. 1982. *Demographic Dimensions of the New Republic: American Interregional Migration, Vital Statistics, and Manumissions, 1800-1860*. Cambridge: Cambridge University Press.

Osterud, Nancy and John Fulton. 1976. "Family Limitation and Age at Marriage: Fertility Decline in Sturbridge, Massachusetts 1730-1850." *Population Studies* 30: 481–494.

Ryder, Norman B. 1980. "Where Do Babies Come From?" Pp. 189–202 in Hubert M. Blalock, Jr. (ed.), *Sociological Theory and Research: A Critical Appraisal*. New York: Free Press.

Sanderson, Warren C. 1979. "Quantitative Aspects of Marriage, Fertility and Family Limitation in Nineteenth-Century America: Another Application of the Coale Specifications." *Demography* 16: 339–358.

Schapiro, Morton O. 1982. "Land Availability and Fertility in the United States, 1760–1870." *Journal of Economic History* 42: 577–600.

Smith, Daniel Scott. 1985. "Notes on the Measurement of Values." *Journal of Economic History* 45: 213–218.

Steckel, Richard H. 1985. *The Economics of U.S.*

Slave and Southern White Fertility. New York and London: Garland Publishing.

Sundstrom, William A. and Paul David. 1985. "Old-Age Security Motives, Labor Markets, and Farm Family Fertility in Antebellum America." Working Paper No. 17, Stanford Project on the History of Fertility Control.

Temkin-Greener, H. and A.C. Swedlund. 1978. "Fertility Transition in the Connecticut Valley, 1740–1850." *Population Studies* 32: 27–41.

Thompson, Warren S. and P.K. Whelpton. 1933. *Population Trends in the United States*. New York: McGraw-Hill.

Uhlenberg, Peter R. 1969. "A Study of Cohort Life Cycles: Cohorts of Native Born Massachusetts Women, 1830–1920." *Population Studies* 23: 407–420.

van de Walle, Etienne. 1974. *The Female Population of France in the Nineteenth Century: A Reconstruction of 82 Departments*. Princeton: Princeton University Press.

Vinovskis, Maris A. 1976a. "Socioeconomic Determinants of Interstate Fertility Differentials in the United States in 1850 and 1860." *Journal of Interdisciplinary History* 6: 375–396.

————. 1976b. *Demographic History and the World Population Crisis*. Worcester: Clark University Press.

Wrigley, E.A. 1985. "The Fall of Marital Fertility in Nineteenth-Century France: Exemplar or Exception?" *European Journal of Population* 1: 31–60, 141–177.

Yasuba, Yasukichi. 1962. *Birth Rates of the White Population in the United States, 1800-1860: An Economic Study*. Baltimore: Johns Hopkins University Press.

The Cross-Cultural
Perspective

ADVANCES IN ITALIAN AND IBERIAN FAMILY HISTORY

David I. Kertzer
Caroline Brettell

ABSTRACT: *In the past decade a tremendous increase in family history research in Italy, Spain and Portugal provides new insight into family processes and has many implications for generalizations regarding the course of European family history. In this article many of these new findings are detailed and their historical and theoretical implications assessed. Previous generalizations regarding Mediterranean family history are examined in light of this new evidence. Among the topics discussed are the sources and methods employed in recent research, the household formation systems operating in Italy and Iberia, the role played by inheritance norms and by dowry, changing childrearing practices—especially as regards child abandonment, marriage patterns, the family lives of the elderly, and the impact of migration on family life. The benefits of considering certain cultural topics in understanding the course of southern European family history are also considered.*

Recent historical family research in southern Europe has undermined a number of generalizations, popular not long ago, regarding the course of western European family life. While this fact has not yet been recognized by all scholars, there have been a number of recent attempts to

David I. Kertzer is Professor of Anthropology at Bowdoin College (Brunswick, Maine 04111). His most recent book is Family Life in Central Italy,

1880-1910 *(Rutgers, 1984) and he is currently continuing his research on the social and demographic transformation of nineteenth-century Bologna.*

Caroline Brettell, a social anthropologist, is project director at the Family and Community History Center, Newberry Library (60 W. Walton St., Chicago, Illinois 60610). Her most recent book is Men Who Migrate, Women Who Wait: Population and History in a Portuguese Parish *(Princeton, 1986) and she is currently conducting a study of several French Canadian immigrant communities in central Illinois.*

discern a pattern of family life distinctive from that found further north in western Europe. In these pages we take stock of just what has been learned in recent years regarding family history in Italy, Portugal and Spain, and we assess the validity of recent generalizations about the area. We also draw conclusions regarding the most productive theoretical approaches to historical family study, and we suggest fruitful directions for future research. Our focus is on the eighteenth and nineteenth centuries, although we make note of relevant work dealing with earlier centuries, as well as selected studies of the twentieth century. A complete overview of southern European family history would have to include discussion of work done in Yugoslavia, Greece, and Mediterranean France. However, given space limitations, we must leave to others a review of recent work in those other areas.

OVERCOMING THE PERILS OF GENERALIZATION

Although generalizations regarding *the* western European marriage pattern or *the* western European family system may still be readily found in the current sociological and historical literature, some of those who bear responsibility for formulating the generalizations have since disclaimed them. For example, while Wrigley (1982) has recently predicted a continued interest in Hajnal's (1965) "western European marriage pattern," Hajnal himself now recognizes that a single east-west boundary is inadequate to describe the complexities of marriage and family life in Europe. Accordingly, Wrigley, as well as Hajnal (1983) and Laslett (1983), now recognize a "Mediterranean" pattern of marriage and household formation. This is said to characterize much of southern Europe, including Spain, parts of Portugal, most of Italy, and portions of the Balkans. How-

ever, while Wrigley argues that the "Mediterranean pattern persisted until a very late date," Hajnal suggests that the distinctiveness of southern Europe was eroded by the nineteenth century. This issue of whether Mediterranean Europe's distinctive characteristics represented a survival of a more ancient European pattern, which merely was extinguished later in southern Europe than in the north, has been raised by Smith (1981). Smith asks whether the classic case provided by fifteenth-century Tuscany (Herlihy and Klapisch-Zuber, 1985) demonstrates a distinctive Mediterranean family system, or simply a medieval family system.

These recent attempts at generalization have been valuable in highlighting the fact that the southern European family experience is often quite unlike that documented for northwestern Europe. However, with the benefit of the proliferation of recent historical family research in southern Europe, we are now in a position to examine in greater detail just how distinctive this area is and what generalizations are tenable. In doing this, we argue that no family system can be understood apart from the political economic context in which it is found. As a corollary, where within a region we find political economic differentiation, we would expect to find differences in family life. Nor should it be assumed that such economic differentiation is a product of differential timing of the advent of industrialization, for there was no single pre-capitalist form of political economy or family economy in southern Europe. Hence, differences in family forms found there were not simply a product of the degree of capitalist penetration.

We begin our review by discussing the sources and methods recently employed in family historical studies in Italy and Iberia. We then turn to the household formation systems found there, and we inquire into the role played by inheritance norms and by the practice of dowry. Looking at the history of the family in a life-course context, we briefly discuss the changing practices of childrearing, especially child abandonment; the age at marriage and the practice of permanent celibacy; the choice of a spouse and of postmarital residence; and the questions of widowhood, remarriage, and the situation of the elderly. We then turn to the issue of the impact of migration on family life in this area, as well as the family determinants of migration patterns. Some benefits of considering certain cultural issues in southern European family history are also discussed. Finally, we try to summarize what recent research in this area contributes to our larger knowledge of family history in Europe and beyond.

SOURCES

Although to date the bulk of work in family history has been done in northern Europe—and especially in Britain and France—it could be argued that more possibilities for family history research exist in southern Europe because of the wealth of sources available covering a long period (Aymard and Delille, 1977). In this section, we attempt merely to give some idea of the range of these sources.

The nature of research sources, and their richness, is of course related to the historical period in question. Records for the medieval period are occasional and of variable quality and utility. Some of these consist of census-like documents which often pertain to a limited segment of the population (e.g., Ortalli, 1981; Herlihy, 1985), while others consist of individual genealogies or family chronicles (de la Roncière, 1981). Dillard (1984) draws upon a series of settlement charters and codes of customary law normally used by legal and economic historians to study the lives of women in medieval Castile, and

in the process provides a rich understanding of family life in central Spain between 1100 and 1300. Finally, there are more traditional literary and historiographic sources (Belmartino, 1968). Certainly, the most important late medieval source to be used for family history is the Florentine *catasto* of 1427, subject of the exhaustive and ambitious study of Herlihy and Klapisch-Zuber (1985). This document enumerates 260,000 individuals, their household situations, and provides considerable economic information, much of which has been put into machine-readable form.

With the end of the medieval period, a variety of other sources, found more widely and more regularly, have increasingly been employed by family historians. As elsewhere in Europe, notarial records—beginning especially in the 1500s—provide valuable information on family processes, especially the transmission of property. This has permitted insight into marriage strategies, dowry, and inheritance (Levi, 1976, 1985; Merzario, 1981). Worthy of special note in this regard is the unusual archive of the Florentine dowry fund of 1425-1545 (Kirshner and Molho, 1978). Although such sources exist for Spain and Portugal, with three exceptions which only skim the surface (Brandão and Rowland, 1980; Brandão, 1983; Brettell, 1986) they have yet to be explored to the same extent as in Italy. Beginning in this period, too, it was not uncommon for large landowners to keep account books which provide information on families living on their land, and allow insight into the family dynamics of the peasantry (Balugani and Fronzoni, 1979; Caiati, 1984).

A variety of church records also have proved useful, especially in the period beginning in the mid-sixteenth century when the Council of Trent mandated a system of statistical record-keeping by parish priests. This involved not only the keeping of ledgers of births, deaths and marriages, but also, in many areas, of annual parish censuses enumerating the entire population by household (Doveri, 1983; Felix, 1958; Kertzer, 1984). The quality and format of such records improves by the seventeenth century, particularly by the mid- to late-eighteenth century when, at least in the Iberian Peninsula, the names and places of origin of all grandparents and the deaths of all individuals (not just those over seven years) are included (Brettell, 1986; Reher and Robinson, 1979).

The Church kept other records which have proven useful to family historians. Noteworthy in this regard are the records of requests for dispensation from the church prohibition on marriage between kin. Merzario (1981), in a recent study of endogamy and marriage strategies in a northern Italian community in the 1500s and 1600s, makes good use of this source. In addition, the Church kept annual lists of communicants fulfilling their Easter duty. In Madrid these were recorded street by street, house by house, and floor by floor. Although Larquie's (1974) interest in these lists is as a source for a study of urban density, clearly they could be used by family historians interested in household structure, and recently have been employed in four studies in Portugal (Amorim, 1983; Brettell, 1986; Nunes, 1985; O'Neill, 1984).

Indeed, with the onset of the nineteenth century, the number of sources available for historical studies of the family in southern Europe begins to mushroom. The Napoleonic invasions at the beginning of the century increased the attention paid to keeping population records, and the new sense of state (as opposed to church) responsibility has left a rich archival legacy. This may be illustrated with the case of Florence. Gozzini (1984) has drawn upon the rich marriage records (1808–1812) compiled by the city officials

of the Napoleonic era to study not only age at marriage, but also occupational endogamy and transmission of occupation. Not only were the occupations of both husband and wife recorded in these documents, but also those of the fathers of bride and groom. Both Ciacci (1980) and Woolf (1984) have made use of another Florentine document from the Napoleonic period to study family life. This is the list of requests for poverty assistance compiled between 1808 and 1814. Both economic information and information on household composition for the poor of the city are included.

Even before modern decennial censuses were conducted, civil authorities occasionally undertook an enumeration of the population, as they had in Tuscany in 1427, often for purposes of taxation. To date, these have been used primarily by strictly demographic historians (Vilar, 1965a, 1965b) and by economic historians (Bennassar, 1968; Castillo, 1965; Ringrose, 1970); although, as in the case of the *Catastro* of the Marques de la Ensenada (1749–1752), they frequently contain valuable data on the family. Civil enumerations became increasingly numerous in the nineteenth century. A number of these have been examined by family historians with a primary emphasis on questions of household composition (Angeli and Bellettini, 1979; Jiménez-Chacón, 1983; Reher, 1984; Torti, 1981; Tittarelli, 1980). Rowland (1981) drew upon a military list of 1827 to study, in addition to household composition, age at marriage and population mobility.

The studies of LePlay and the group of scholars associated with him resulted in a large quantity of household budgets, compiled from the mid-nineteenth century on in various parts of southern Europe. Much of this information is now readily available to family historians, though to date the source has not been used much (Somogyi, 1945). In Portugal, the LePlay tradition continued into the twentieth century, and two books in particular provide detailed, though primarily qualitative, data on family structure (Teles, 1903; Descamps, 1935).

With the dawning of the modern statistical era during the second half of the nineteenth century, the sources available for family history in southern Europe become even more abundant. Not only is there a more systematic keeping of vital statistics, and the introduction of regular censuses, but a variety of other records were maintained which have only recently been explored by family historians. Especially notable in the Italian case in this regard is the population register (*anagrafe*). Although experimented with in some parts of the peninsula earlier in the century, it became mandated for all communes of the new nation in the 1860s. The population register of each commune records the entrance of each individual, the sequence of demographic events and changes of household situation that occur during residence in the commune, and the date and place of emigration and with whom emigration occurred. Kertzer and Hogan (1985; see also Hogan and Kertzer, 1985a, 1985b; Kertzer, 1985) have used the population registers of Casalecchio, near Bologna, for the period 1865 to 1921 to follow family and other changes through people's life course. As yet, few other scholars have explored this source, but it promises to yield insights into family processes which cannot be as directly obtained through the more common cross-sectional sources, or through vital statistics data alone.

For the twentieth century, in addition to the sources already described, some scholars have made use of oral historical materials (Barbagli, 1984; Brettell, 1986; Schneider and Schneider, 1984). Given the rapidity of changes in family life in many areas of southern Europe, such an approach is particularly helpful, for among the elderly are those who can recall childhoods and young adulthoods lived in social, economic, and political conditions radically different from those of today. Blending oral historical sources with various kinds of archival sources offers an especially promising route for the family history of the first half of the twentieth century.

METHODS

The methods employed by southern European family historians over the past decade have been profoundly affected by methodological developments elsewhere in Europe. In particular, the family reconstitution approach pioneered in France and the household typological approach promulgated by the Cambridge Group in England have had major impacts.

Merzario (1981), for example, has been able to use parish birth, death, and marriage records to reconstruct the history of 585 marriages celebrated in a northern Italian community for the period 1597 to 1810. Similarly, Anelli et al. (1979) have followed the Fleury/Henry reconstitution method in reconstructing families in forty parishes of the Parma valley beginning in 1750. In Spain and Portugal where, until recently, parish records were used solely to document broad demographic trends (e.g., Gonzalez Muñoz, 1974; Nadal, 1966), family reconstitution has been used by Amorim (1973, 1984), Vaquer Benassar (1984), and Brettell (1986). In an interesting and productive variation of this approach, Schneider and Schneider (1984) combined family reconstitution methods with a variety of other archival and oral historical data to examine the history of fertility reduction in rural Sicily.

Even more dramatic, though, has been the impact of the typological approach pioneered by Laslett and his associates. In Italy alone, there have been literally scores of studies in the past decade which have utilized census-type data and the Laslett typology to shed light on household composition in the past (e.g., Angeli and Bellettini, 1979; Doveri, 1983; Ciacci, 1980; Rowland, 1981). As a result, we now know much more about coresidential arrangements in the past, especially the distribution and prevalence of complex family households in southern Europe. However, as elsewhere in Europe, some southern European family historians have begun to express doubts about the future of such studies (Ferrante, 1984:623). We may be reaching the limit of potential benefit from such cross-sectional investigations. New methods of analysis are necessary to capture the dynamic relations between family life, economic, demographic, social and cultural changes over time, as well as to address more fully kinship relations that extend beyond household boundaries (Kertzer, 1985).

HOUSEHOLD COMPOSITION

In recent years perhaps the most striking finding to come from southern European family history has been the high incidence of complex family households found there. Yet, before any broad generalization of Mediterranean Europe as a region characterized by complex family households takes hold, the important variability found in the area must be plotted. While southern European family historians are called upon to explain the high incidence of complex family households, their distribution, and their historical evolution, part of their task is to explain why some portions of the population did not share in the complex family household system.

In Italy, which has provided the best known examples of complex family household organization, this system has a long

history. Ring (1979:17), for example, found that in ninth-century central Italy the joint family household system was the ideal and was followed whenever possible. Herlihy and Klapisch have similarly demonstrated a high frequency of complex family households in the rural areas of fifteenth-century Tuscany. However, Barbagli (1984) has recently demonstrated that while complex family household organization had long been widespread in the countryside in central and northern Italy, it reached its high point during the nineteenth century, and was linked to a progressive transformation of the peasantry from nucleated settlements to dispersed sharecropping households on the land. Poni (1978:226) points out that the lowering of mortality rates in the nineteenth century resulted in larger families with more opportunities for extension. In earlier centuries, periodic plagues and epidemics led to considerable changes in the proportion of households that were complex in composition (e.g., Merzario, 1981:137–138).

What is perhaps most instructive theoretically about household composition in southern Europe are the differences found within the region. There are not only differences among different areas, but also differences among different social or occupational groups within any single area. While this complexity makes simple generalization of a single Mediterranean family pattern unwise, it gets to the heart of the issue of what factors lead to complex family household organization.

Anthropologists in Iberia and Italy have divided the area roughly into a northern northern and a southern zone, with complex family households common in the north and nuclear family households predominant in the south. Thus, for example, Lison-Tolosana (1977) described a patrilocal stem family as prevailing in much of northern Portugal, in the northwestern provinces of Galicia and Asturias, in the Basque country of northeastern Spain, and in Aragon and Catalonia. He contrasted this with the rest of the peninsula, typified by nuclear family arrangements. Rowland (1983, n.d.) seems to concur. Interestingly enough, a similar pattern has been noted for Italy, where complex family households were especially characteristic of the sharecropping sector in central Italy but extended well beyond it in the center and north, while the southern Italian household was thought to be atomistic and typified by nuclear family organization (Silverman, 1968).

As for the differences in household composition found within local areas, the fifteenth-century Tuscan data provide us with perhaps our earliest evidence. Herlihy and Klapisch-Zuber (1985:298) found that 31 percent of the sharecropper households consisted of two or more kin-related nuclear family components, accounting for the majority of people living in sharecropper households. In contrast, nineteen percent of the households of rural artisans and shopkeepers had two or more nuclear family components. Four centuries later in Tuscany, Torti (1981: 190) found 76 percent of the component nuclear family units in sharecropping households living in multiple family households, with 28 percent of these nuclear family components living in households having three or more such units. In contrast, in households headed by day laborers, only thirty percent of the nuclear family units were in multiple family households, and only four percent lived in households having three or more such units.

In terms of local-level differentiation in household composition, the case of the sharecroppers and agricultural wage laborers of central Italy is especially instructive. Here we have two segments of the same population participating in the same economic system, sharing in the same culture, and having various social ties with each other. Yet, the evidence overwhelmingly indicates that sharecropper households were predominantly complex and patrilocally extended, while the households of agricultural wage laborers were typically nuclear. For example, Angeli (1983:731), in a study of thousands of individuals living in the Bologna plains in 1847, found that three-quarters of those living in sharecropper households lived in multiple family households, while just one-sixth of the agricultural wage laborer-headed households were multiple family units. The same pattern is documented for the Pisan area in the eighteenth century (Doveri, 1982), and many other areas of central Italy (e.g., Della Pina, 1983). One striking feature of the sharecropping households, from a comparative point of view, is the large number of *frérèches*, or households composed of two or more married brothers and their wives and children. Indeed, in some areas of the nineteenth-century Bologna plains, fifteen percent of sharecropper households were of this type (Angeli, 1983:732).

At the root of the complex family organization of the sharecroppers was an economic system in which the household was the unit of production and where there was strong pressure to maximize the number of adults working the farm. This pressure, in fact, grew during the late eighteenth and nineteenth centuries as population growth and the spread of capitalism led to increased competition for sharecropped farms. With landowners interested in maximizing their half of the produce, and hence eager to have large numbers of adults on each farm, nuclear family units were at a great disadvantage in getting or retaining the annually renewable sharecropping contracts (Kertzer, 1984). On the other hand, for the agricultural wage laborers, the household was not the unit of production, nor were they (for the most part) provided with houses by their employers. Hence, there was much less reason to come together in large, complex residential units.

But it is not sharecropping alone that explains the high proportions of complex family households in southern Europe. Not only is the proportion of complex day laborer households—though much lower than the sharecroppers—considerably higher than that found in northwestern Europe, but a variety of other family economies support multiple family households. For example, in the Biella zone of the Italian north, many families survived by combining farming small plots of their own land with doing piece work at home for the wool industry in the nineteenth century. Ramella (1977, 1983) found a large proportion of these households to be complex in composition, with the predominant pattern being a single son bringing his wife into the parental household. The explanation given by Ramella for this pattern is that it permitted the families to divide the risks of both the protoindustrial and the small farming sectors, allowing a more predictable livelihood. In still another area of the Italian north, in Veneto, Mabilia (1980:587) found in a community having a high proportion of ambulatory livestock traders, almost two-thirds of the households were multiple family units as recently as 1931, and just a quarter of the households were nuclear. As elsewhere in Italy, these were extended patrilocally. Mabilia explains this organization as an adaptation to an economy in which men were often away from home doing their business, while the women were left to tend the homes and the small pieces of farmland. Finally, in a study of a mountain village in northwestern Portugal where the majority of the population combined farming their own small plots of land with the farming of rented plots,

Feijó (1983) found that, in 1830, 30 percent of the households were multiple and 11.6 percent were extended. He demonstrates a positive correlation between wealth and household complexity.

While most of the work on complex family household organization in southern Europe has focused on economic determinants—especially labor demands and inheritance patterns—some recent work has suggested that other factors may be relevant to an explanation of complex family patterns in portions of the area. In the northwestern Portuguese parish of Lanheses, for example, neolocal residence was the stated cultural norm. Yet, in 1850, fourteen percent of the households contained two or more conjugal units, with another twelve percent of the households having kinsmen beyond the nuclear family present. Almost eighty years later, the proportion of multiple family households had fallen to five percent, but the proportion of extended family households had risen to eighteen percent. At both ends of the period, about 54 percent of the households were of the simple family type, and hence conformed to the cultural norm.[1] Households made up of solitaries were seven percent of the total in 1850 and ten percent in 1927, reflecting in part the high rates of permanent celibacy—especially for women—in the region.

Brettell (1986) explains this pattern through a combination of economic, cultural, and housing factors. She shows that a high proportion of couples lived in multiple family households at some point in their lives,[2] and argues that, in this region, residence patterns have less to do with land tenure arrangements and more to do with the availability of housing, the economic possibility of setting up a separate household, migration patterns, and culturally-specific attitudes about the appropriateness of women living alone.

To date, fewer studies of household

composition—at least outside of the elite—have focused on the urban areas of southern Europe. However, Barbagli (1984) has recently contrasted the high proportion of complex family households in much of rural central and northern Italy with a low proportion of such households in the cities in the eighteenth and nineteenth centuries. While he adduces considerable data in support of this generalization (Barbagli, 1984:172), some reservations are in order. Tittarelli (1980), for example, found that 42 percent of the households in the most urban part of the city of Perugia in 1782 were complex in composition, presumably containing a majority of the population in that area. However, clearly the cities in general had a much higher proportion of nuclear family households than did the countryside.[3] In Italy, the great majority of historical household studies have focused on the center and the north. Despite previous generalizations that in the south the nuclear family household predominated and complex family units were rare, recent evidence indicates a more complicated situation. Most notable in this regard is Douglass's (1980) study of the town of Agnone, in the Molise area. While he found the settlement pattern (nucleated) and the organization of agriculture (fragmented small landownership) in accordance with historical generalizations of southern Italian society, he found a high "incidence of joint family domestic groups and an attendant extended family ethos" (1980:345). Indeed, in 1753 a majority of all conjugal units were living in complex family households. He explains this pattern in terms of family economy—especially the advantages accruing to peasants and artisans for whom the household was a unit of production.

Much work remains to be done in southern Italy before we can accurately characterize the family history of the region. In many areas, cultural norms related to the family contrasted sharply with those found further north. For example, in large parts of the south, it was not considered proper for women (and especially married women) to work outside the house (Calise, 1979). The contrast with northern regions of the peninsula, where women were a crucial part of the agricultural labor force, could not be more acute. A similar statement could be made for the north of Portugal.

INHERITANCE AND POSTMARITAL RESIDENCE

In attempting to explain the principles which have influenced the structure and dynamics of the family within different regions of southern Europe, numerous scholars have taken their lead from Goody et al. (1976) and directed their attention to strategies of heirship. In Iberia, most of the considerable body of this research concentrates on the nineteenth and twentieth centuries, largely because the work has been done by anthropologists. Yet, even the questions posed by those anthropologists who focus primarily on present-day community relations can provide a context within which to frame appropriate historical questions. In Italy, thus far, there has been less attention paid to these questions, though the historical studies that do exist cover a longer period of time. While we can by no means survey all of this work, we look here at selected cases in order to demonstrate the variation within the region as a whole and the way in which these variations are linked to different family forms.

Strategies of heirship involve a number of basic decisions, many of which are defined by law or custom. Among these are: the sex of the heir, the time at which the legacy is given (e.g., at marriage or at death) or at which a favored heir is actually specified, the rights retained by the parent or parents making the legacy, the degree to which heirship is partible or impartible, and precisely *what* is divided or kept intact—essentially what happens to the farmland. Differences in family and household structure, in kinship relations, and in other demographic phenomena are related to the way in which property is transferred according to some or all of these choices. We will use these choices to frame the following discussion, beginning with Iberia and then turning to the Italian peninsula.

Iberia

The most basic decision is whether property is to be divided equally among all legal heirs or whether it is to be passed on intact to a single heir. Throughout much of southern Europe there is a tendency to partibility, but with significant variations and conditions. In Portugal, for example, the portion of property which can be freely disposed of has been regulated by law and, at least since the nineteenth century, varies between a third and two-thirds. The remaining portion (the *legitima*) has been divided equally among all descendents. How strictly these laws were observed is, of course, open to question and depended on the importance given by the parents to keeping their property intact. Often this depended on the emphasis placed on the family patrimony as opposed to individual family members. In many situations, what looks like partibility is in fact a disguised impartibility.[4]

O'Neill (1983, 1984, 1985) provides one of the most interesting discussions to date of the delicate balance between partibility and impartibility in his study of inheritance in a parish in the mountainous northeastern Portuguese district of Trás-os-montes. Given the bleak economic conditions of the region, strict adherence to the legal prescription of equal division of property among all heirs would, in O'Neill's words, "result in a collective economic suicide." Although not entirely deterministic, since there are exceptions to the rule, the limited productivity of the land may help explain why the tendency to impartibility and to the complex households associated with it are frequently found in mountain communities throughout southern Europe.

The goal of maintaining an economically viable piece of property intact, and the fact that transmission occurs at death rather than at marriage, are associated with a number of demographic and family features which have been noted for other regions of both southern and northern Europe: late marriage, celibacy, large domestic groups, and high ratios of illegitimacy—all of which operate to limit the number of offspring in future generations with legal claims to the family patrimony. The basic system of inheritance described by O'Neill is "primonuptiality" —the patrimony goes to the child who marries first. It can be an eldest, middle, or youngest sibling of either sex who, upon marriage, comes to live in the natal household.[5] Yet, only at the parent's death does he or she gain title to the patrimony and in return for the expectation of title, he or she is obligated to care for the aged parents. By the time that death occurs, other heirs, who legally have a right to two-thirds of the patrimony, may have emigrated or established themselves elsewhere. Thus, their interest (attitudinal, not legal) in the patrimony is reduced.

The preference for impartibility in some form is equally prevalent in northwestern Spain, particularly in the province of Galicia. Here, Lison-Tolosana (1976) has described several different ecological zones, each with its own characteristic patterns of land tenure and domestic group structure. In the mountainous zones, the general rule is for the eldest son, or at least one of the sons, to bring his bride home. A daughter brings her husband into her home only when there are no sons. This gives the heir a right to two-thirds of the total estate of the parents and an equal share of the remaining third which is divided equally among all offspring. This is a pre-mortem transfer in the sense that the heir becomes the legal owner. His parents, however, retain usufruct rights until their death and the heir has specific obligations to them and to any unmarried siblings. This pattern of heirship is associated with a stem family structure wherein the son and heir is neither independent nor the major decision maker. In short, succession is not accompanied by a real transmission of either property or authority. This is an extremely important distinction to make because it influences the nature of family relationships within the household. The contrast with Ireland (Arensberg and Kimball, 1940), where the parental generation retires to the "west room" when the son and heir marries, is quite apparent. A similar contrast can be made with Austria (Berkner, 1976).

Bauer's (1981, 1983) research on "preferential partibility" in the mountainous Sierra Caurel in eastern Galicia, where the practice of differentiating among offspring dates back to the sixteenth century, demonstrates a particularly illuminating difference in this regard. Between 1800 and 1879, the mean age at marriage for eldest sons was 27.0, compared with 30.2 for second sons and 29.9 for third sons and those higher in the birth order. If full authority were passed on from father to son at the time of marriage, would the age at marriage of eldest sons have been higher?

In the coastal areas of Galicia another pattern predominates. A daughter, and not necessarily the eldest daughter, is the heir. Normally she is bequeathed the house and a field as well as an equal share in the remainder of the property. She lives with her husband and children in her parents' home and has the same rights and obligations as male heirs. In this area residence is uxorilocal, the transmission of rights is matrilineal, and authority belongs to the wife. Lison describes a form of extreme subordination of sons-in-law. This uxorilocal stem family is closely associated with a maritime economy.[6]

In the parish of Lanheses in the northwestern Portuguese province of Minho studied by Brettell (1986), women are also frequently favored heirs of the third share (*terço*) although this is primarily an agricultural village, fourteen kilometers from the coast. However, it is equally a parish which has been affected by sex-biased (primarily male) seasonal or temporary migration for several centuries. Thus, as in the fishing communities, it is the women who are left to tend the fields and to take care of parents. Brettell believes that the granting of the *terço* in this northwestern Portuguese parish is used primarily as a form of old age insurance, and not as a mechanism for maintaining a family patrimony intact through a matrilineal or patrilineal line. This is evident in the fact that not infrequently spinster daughters are favored recipients of the *terço* and that in this region it was not uncommon to buy and sell land. Indeed, the nature of the land market has not been fully explored with respect to its impact on family forms. Clearly it almost precludes the kind of corporate ownership prevalent in parts of northeastern Spain where stem-family households are also associated with some form of impartibility or preferential partibility. Based on research in two villages further to the southwest in the province of Minho, Pina-Cabral (1984) offers a slightly different perspective. There, too, daughters, and often youngest daughters, are favored heirs, but a distinction is made between property near the household (to be kept intact) and that in more outlying regions (subject to division).

One of the best documented examples of heirship in northeastern Spain is the Basque region (Douglass, 1971, 1974, 1984) where farm owners are free to select a single heir to the patrimony from among their offspring. They may provide non-heirs with dowries, but not necessarily, and the amount is entirely at the owners' discretion. The heir or heiress and spouse hold joint ownership in the patrimony, but the legal owner of the farm (*baserria*) is merely the usufructuary of the patrimony. Actual ownership is vested in a particular line of descendants. However, Douglass identifies a fundamental difference by drawing our attention to the importance of the time in the domestic cycle at which the major heir is designated, apart from the time at which property is in fact bequeathed. If this decision is made at birth—usually clear male primogeniture—it has a completely different impact on residence and migration patterns than does a decision made later in the domestic cycle and totally at the parents' discretion.

A similar emphasis on the corporate household, on preferential male primogeniture, and on a major heir who marries and remains at home is described by Iszaevich (1975, 1981a, 1981b) and Hansen (1977) for rural Catalonia, and by Fine-Souriac (1977) and Poumarède (1979) for the Spanish Pyrenees. Among all social strata, the main concern of this corporate *casa* had been to improve or at least to maintain social standing by appropriate marriages. The cultural ideal is a marriage between two main heirs with similar land holdings (Iszaevich, 1981b:154). Succession does not imply marriage; nor does marriage and the taking up of residence with the parental generation imply full

rights to the patrimony. These are gained only at the death of the grantors. The curious practice in Catalonia, at least curious in comparison with other regions of Iberia where major heirs are chosen, is the use of birth control to avoid more than one heir. Catalonia, according to Iszaevich, has followed the French demographic pattern.

Indeed, Iszaevich (1981a:286) takes issue with the emphasis on descent in discussions of the stem family. Instead, he argues, the emphasis should be on continuity over time.

> The contrast between the family of (rural Catalonia) and that of southern Spain, for example, is not based on a dichotomy of extended or nuclear, or upon its dimensions, but rather on a contrast between the corporate character of one and the temporal character of the other. While the latter disappears with the death of the founder, the former endures through time. While the nuclear family has temporal limits, the corporate household remains for generations.

It is the structure of authority and the relationships within the household, not overall household form or residence patterns per se which are primary. The important question, it appears, is why a sense of corporateness emerges in some regions and not in others. Does it have to do with the proportion of the population who are landed, or with the average size of farms they work? The direct correlation between the size of farms and the size of households is not new. Yet, any categorical statements about the relationship between inheritance, marriage patterns, and family structure should take the amount of land actually owned by a peasant family and the social group to which they belong into account. Some families may simply not have had enough land to matter and thus, property ownership would have little to do with decisions about the timing of marriage or residence after marriage.

Italy

Outside of the elite, partible male inheritance upon the testator's death, supplemented by a system of dowry, has long been the rule in Italy.[7] Ring's (1979) study of ninth-century central Italy attributes the already existing system of partible male inheritance to the Lombard legal tradition. Herlihy and Klapisch-Zuber (1985:282) similarly found a system of male partible inheritance and dowering of the daughters to prevail at the end of the Middle Ages. With the expansion of sharecropping from the end of the Middle Ages through the nineteenth century in central Italy, this system continued to influence family relations, the attainment of wealth, and household composition. Since sharecropping required a certain amount of equipment and supplies, the partible inheritance system and dowering of daughters encouraged all sons to remain in the parental home, with daughters expelled on marriage to the parental household of their new husbands. It also made it more difficult for any one son to accumulate enough wealth to rise from sharecropper status to become a landowner (Poni, 1978).

Where peasants owned their own land, however, there were forces acting against partible inheritance, namely, the obvious ruin which came with extreme land fragmentation. In some cases, it seems, partible inheritance led to just such extreme fragmentation and poverty, often, but not always associated with nuclear family household organization as well. In the southern Italian case discussed by Douglass (1980:144), fragmentation due to partible inheritance among sons was compounded by the practice of sometimes including land in the dowries of

daughters. However, in some northern regions, where peasant landownership was common, partible inheritance had the effect—like impartible inheritance elsewhere—of slowing or preventing the marriages of all but a single son. This is perhaps best described for the Biella area in the north where the practice was for land to be inherited jointly (not fragmented) by all sons. Not only did this have the effect of keeping sons living together in the parental home, it also discouraged more than one son from marrying, for the land could only support a limited number of family members. In many cases, as in Iberia, nonmarrying sons emigrated either for a limited period of time, or for good (Ramella, 1977, 1983).

One of the few descriptions of a system in Italy where both men and women acquired land from their parents is provided by Davis (1973) for the southern town of Pisticci, although much of his description relates to the twentieth century after laws requiring inheritance of daughters as well as sons had gone into effect. Davis describes a system of pre-mortem succession (with daughters provided with land as part of their marriage contract) which, along with partibility, he claims, leads to almost universal marriage and a proliferation of nuclear families. Because both men and women inherit, and because land is transferred at marriage, division of land is counteracted by a tendency to seek out spouses with rights to property near one's own. This had a number of ramifications, including a propensity for consanguineous marriages. Land rights are shared by intermarrying kin and affines.

Although women throughout most of Italy were historically excluded from inheritance, the practice of dowry was widespread and, as elsewhere in Europe, was seen in part as a way to compensate daughters for the fact that they would not inherit the family patrimony. If we look again at the case of sharecropping central Italy, the legal status of women is reflected in the 1577 statute of the city of Bologna which stated that wives were excluded from the family's obligations to repay all debts to the landowner. In this area, the dowry consisted of bedroom furniture, linens, a few pieces of jewelry, and a sum of money, which, for wealthier share-croppers, could be greater than the annual wages of an agricultural day laborer. While the trousseau and the furniture were considered the wife's property, money became household property, under the household head's control (Poni, 1978: 221–222).

The content and, hence, significance of the dowry did vary throughout the peninsula. In the Piedmontese (northern) area studied by Levi (1976), in the seventeenth and eighteenth centuries, a major portion of the dowry consisted of ploughing equipment. The cost of the dowry to the family was such that families with more than one daughter were constrained to allow considerable spacing between their marriages. In the nearby agricultural and protoindustrial area of Biella in the nineteenth century, families also had to make sacrifices to provide a dowry for their daughters, with the dowry including a bed with linens and, for the more well-to-do, a wardrobe (Ramella, 1977, 1983).

In many of these areas, the size of the dowry was proportionate to the wealth of the peasant family, and the dowry became the currency which measured the appropriateness of marriage between children of two families. The higher the dowry, the greater the status of the daughter's family, and the higher the status of the family from which the husband would come. Merzario (1981), along these lines, documents the interesting situation of the Como (northern) area in the seventeenth century where, lacking a dowry considered fitting of the family's status, the

family might contract with kinsmen for a marriage for their daughter to ensure a status-homogamous marriage. The implication is that in marriages between kin the size of the dowry was considered less important.

In contrast to this relatively historically uniform system of inheritance and dowry among the Italian masses, clear historical changes have now been documented for the inheritance system among the elite. Barbagli (1984) provides us with an excellent overview of these changes, focusing on the aristocracy and bourgeoisie of urban central Italy, and links them as well to historical changes in the household composition of the Italian elite.

Until the mid-sixteenth century, partible male inheritance was practiced, leading to multiple family households. Indeed, even after the father's death, married sons from the time of the Middle Ages continued to live together in order not to divide the patrimony. Daughters were provided with dowries which, in the case of noble families with modest incomes, could greatly exceed their annual family income. The burden of these sizable dowries led fathers with many daughters to send some of their daughters to convents and keep others at home as spinsters.

Around the middle of the sixteenth century, the prevailing inheritance system shifted to impartibility. Just one son was to be given the inheritance, generally the eldest, and he was pledged to keep it intact, passing it on intact to one of his own heirs at his death. While this system began among the aristocracy, it diffused among other wealthy urban classes as well. Its major impact on household composition was the disappearance of the *frérèche*. The inheriting son brought his bride into his parental home, and he became household head on his father's death. His brothers could not bring their wives into the household, and many of them remained unmarried, living in their brother's household.

But this system proved unstable, both because it created considerable tensions within families (between the inheriting son and his siblings and between the non-inheriting siblings and their father) and because it led to the extinction of many lines of noble families, for each generation was putting all its eggs in a single basket. The push toward partibility was aided at the beginning of the nineteenth century by the Napoleonic occupation of Italy and the spread of the Napoleonic code, which specified bilateral, partible inheritance. Although this was legally nullified in the Restoration period which followed, and although the equal rights of inheritance of daughters were never fully established, the system of impartibility was severely undermined.

FAMILY RELATIONS AND THE LIFE COURSE

While much of the southern European family history literature of the past decade has focused on questions of household composition, many other issues are now being examined in addition to the issues of inheritance and dowry discussed in our previous section. In this section, we employ a life-course framework in our attempt to address some of these newer issues—first, as an organizing aid in discussing the various strands of historical family work; and second, as an approach which promises to bring new insight into historical family study in southern Europe. An emphasis on the life course not only serves to identify important and little-studied issues in this field, but also can help scholars move beyond the static framework so many have lamented yet relatively few have overcome.

Although the history of birth and infancy has attracted considerable attention in other parts of Europe (and elsewhere in the world), rather little historical attention has thus far been paid to these topics in southern Europe. While many studies of breastfeeding, for example, have now been conducted in France and Germany, such studies are rare in southern Europe. The one important exception to this lacuna is the topic of foundlings, an extremely important social phenomenon in both Italy and Iberia, especially in the eighteenth and nineteenth centuries. Until a decade ago, this topic was little explored, but thanks to the work of Corsini (1976), Hunecke (1978), Della Peruta (1979), Tonizzi (1983), and others this is perhaps the most exciting current research topic in family history in Italy.

The proportion of infants who were left at the Church-run foundling homes (*ospizi*) in Italy was low but rising from the middle of the sixteenth to the middle of the eighteenth centuries, and then began a dramatic increase which peaked in the middle of the nineteenth century. For example, in the city of Florence, 43 percent of the children born in the 1830s were abandoned. Nor was this phenomenon limited to the north; in the city of Cosenza (Calabria) in the 1820s, 39 percent of all newborns were abandoned (Da Molin, 1983:104).[8] Increasingly, too, these consisted of legitimate births, the children of working class families which found they could not support all their offspring. Although many of these families made efforts to reclaim their children later, in most cases this proved futile since the infant mortality rate was so high. However, it is notable that by 1841 in Florence, 24 percent of the foundlings were later reclaimed by parents (Corsini, 1977:9).

Although systematic studies of this topic in Spain and Portugal have yet to be published, similar evidence suggests that many children abandoned at the foundling wheel (*roda*) were the offspring of parents who could not support them or mothers who claimed their breastmilk had run dry. They were often left with items of clothing and notes attached indicating that they would be reclaimed. In Portugal, the extensiveness of the problem of foundings (*expostos*) led, during the 1860s, to a general outcry against the foundling homes which were thought to encourage the practice of abandonment. As sharper restrictions were placed on these institutions throughout southern Europe, after 1870 abandonment on this massive scale abated.[9] Despite the upsurge in interest in this topic, much remains to be done. Fortunately, foundling institutions in Spain, Italy and Portugal kept records detailing the lives of their charges, and these promise to allow research not only into the circumstances in which babies were abandoned, but also the implications for a person's life of being abandoned at birth.

Aside from the massive number of children who left their parents at birth, a tremendous number left at a tender age in order to enter some form of service. While there is as yet no work comparable to that done further north in Europe on this topic (e.g. Kussmaul, 1981), we now know that in many parts of southern Europe it was common for boys and girls to leave their parental home around age twelve to work in service for a wealthier (or less poor) family. This was apparently more common in northern and central Italy than in the south; in the large area devoted to sharecropping, servants were taken in to make up for life-cycle downward fluctuations in the family labor force (Poni, 1978:217). In one Portuguese village in the nineteenth century, twenty percent of households were found to have servants and 55 percent of these were women (Nunes, 1985). Yet, although service (especially in the agricultural sector) affected a large proportion of all people in certain areas, we as yet know very little about how children were placed in homes as servants, or what impact this phase had on the rest of their lives. For example, how extensive were the formal contractual arrangements between employer and servant described by Jiménez-Chacón (1983) in his study of Murcia and Orihuela in southeastern Spain?

One of the indicators commonly used in differentiating among historical family systems is age at marriage. Indeed, Laslett (1983:526) has recently distinguished Mediterranean Europe from the rest of western Europe by the low female age at marriage. This is a questionable generalization, however, because it lumps together both different historical periods and different subareas and subgroups within southern Europe. The major source for Laslett's characterization is apparently the fifteenth-century work of Herlihy and Klapisch-Zuber, who refer to the pattern found in Tuscany as follows: "a young age at first marriage for women, with almost no permanent spinsters in the community outside the convents; an advanced age at first marriage for men, with a significant number of permanent bachelors; and, as a consequence of all this, a very extended age difference between husband and wife" (Herlihy and Klapisch-Zuber, 1985:215). But, a close reading of their data shows the slippery nature of any broad generalizations. For example, Klapisch (1981:183) presents detailed data for the Prato area showing the mean age at marriage for 1427 (the year of the *Catasto*) and 1470. While the mean age of women at marriage in the earlier year was 17.6, less than a half-century later it was 21.1.

By the eighteenth century, female age at marriage in central and northern Italy was over 21 in most areas, and in the nineteenth century it was close to 25 in many areas. In the south, the pattern is less well known. Yet the claim that female age at marriage in the south was low is an oversimplification. It is true that Delille (1977: 44) found 44 percent of all marriages in Capitanata in 1865 involved females under twenty, but in nearby Principato Citra this proportion was just 23 percent. In his more recent study, Delille (1984) plots a range of female age at first marriage from 15.2 to 26.4 in various southern communes in the sixteenth and seventeenth centuries and 16.6 to 25.7 in the eighteenth. Douglass (1980:350), in his study of Agnone in the Molise, also found a mean female age at first marriage of 24.5 in the 1850s. As these authors note, these marital age differences are due to differences in economic arrangements.

Similarly, while some areas of the Iberian peninsula tend to conform to the 'Mediterranean pattern' in the sixteenth and seventeenth centuries, with women marrying under age 21 (Amorim, 1973; Bennassar, 1967; Casey, 1979; Vaquer Benassar, 1984), there are other areas that demonstrate a marriage pattern closer to the 'western' pattern for *both* men and women by the eighteenth century (Amorim, 1973, 1980; Brettell, 1984), and certainly by the nineteenth century (Bauer, 1983, G. Collier, 1983; Livi Bacci, 1971). Indeed, studies of age at marriage in various regions of Iberia preclude any attempt at facile categorization (Livi Bacci, 1968; Valero Lobo, 1984; Poza Martin, 1985; Rowland, n.d.). Clearly there is much research that needs to be done to link age at marriage to family economy, demographic variables, and cultural norms throughout southern Europe.

Laslett (1983) has also distinguished Mediterranean Europe from the rest of western Europe by the higher proportions of people who ever married in the former area. This, too, is suspect, at least if it is taken to mean that in southern Europe high proportions married in all social groups and in all geographical areas. In Italy, for example, high rates of permanent celibacy characterized the elite from at least the seventeenth century. Indeed, in those years in Milan, about half the men and three-quarters of the women over age fifty from patrician families had never married (Barbagli, 1984:198).

In Portugal, high rates of permanent female celibacy have been documented by Brettell (1984). By the latter part of the nineteenth century, 27 percent of all women over fifty died as spinsters. During the first half of the twentieth century, this proportion rose to 32 percent. In the Sierra Caurel, Bauer (1981) found nearly one-third of all men over age fifty and more than one-third of all women over fifty in the permanently celebate category by the end of the nineteenth century. Studies by O'Neill (1981, 1984), Iturra (1980), and Iszaevich (1975) substantiate the conclusion that the never-married population on the Iberian peninsula was by no means insignificant.

While some of this permanent celibacy can be linked to patterns of inheritance and migration, Brettell (1986) suggests that family historians must also be attentive to the cultural norms and attitudes surrounding the status of permanent spinster or bachelor. The anthropologist Brandes (1976), in an article on spinsterhood in Spain, has some valuable insights to offer in this regard; and another anthropologist, Jane Collier (1983), discusses the important role of spinster aunts in raising orphaned children in a village in southern Spain. Both these studies represent attempts to raise the question of permanent celibacy from an entirely different perspective and they open up numerous avenues for research. Not only do we need to collect more data on the extent of the unmarried adult population in southern Europe, but also on their living arrangements, their economic and social roles, and their rights to property.

Choice of spouse is a crucial area for historical family research, and this too has begun to attract increasing attention in southern Europe. In the more isolated and mountainous areas, marriage between kinsmen has been the topic of some recent research. Since such marriages required formal church dispensation, they left behind records which not only tell who married kin and what the kinship relation was, but also what reason was given for the need to break the Church prohibition on kin marriages. Merzario (1981), in a study of a mountain community in northern Italy in the sixteenth and seventeenth centuries, refers to the phenomenon of the *paese stretto*, the long inbred isolated communities where a goodly proportion of the people are kin-related, and where exclusion of kinsmen from the marriage pool would prevent many people from marrying at all. A good example of this is provided by the Aeolian Islands off southern Italy, where by 1900, thirty percent of all marriages were consanguineous within the fourth degree (Delille, 1984).

Nor is this phenomenon limited to earlier centuries or isolated areas. In a study of the northern Italian area of Biella, Ramella (1983:102) has found that thirty percent of all marriages in the 1850s required dispensation of consanguinity, and this was an area where protoindustrial labor was important. Similarly, Brettell (1984) has found that thirteen percent of marriages contracted between 1700 and 1799 in a northwestern Portuguese parish had dispensations of consanguinity within the fourth degree. During the first half of the nineteenth century this proportion rose to twenty percent, and between 1850 and 1899 it was seventeen percent. She suggests a relationship with progressive land fragmentation during the nine-

teenth century. In fact, marriages within closer consanguineal relationships (second and third degree) were most common among the more prosperous peasant landowners.[10]

Along with the phenomenon of the complex family household discussed in a previous section, one of the major life-course events connected with marriage was the movement of the bride to the home of the groom's family. Scholars are making considerable progress toward sketching out the geographic and social-economic contours of this patrilocal pattern, which was much more developed in some areas than in others. That this is an ancient pattern, though, should now be clear. In his study of a ninth-century Italian community, for example, Ring (1979: 19) found that in "most households where the eldest son married he and his wife lived in his paternal household...." Wherever complex family households were found in Italy—and this involved a good deal of the peninsula—patrilocality was the norm. This contrasts somewhat with Iberia.

Lison-Tolosana (1976), Brettell (1986), and Feijó (1983) have described a practice of the groom moving in with the bride's family in northwestern Spain and northwestern Portugal, and O'Neill (1984) discusses a rather unusual pattern of natalocal residence—that is, of married siblings continuing to live in their own natal households and to work for and eat with their own parents. In such domestic arrangements, the husbands of the younger generation are merely 'night visitors' in the homes of their brides, where their children also live. It is not clear whether this form of natalocality is a recent pattern, but it is nevertheless provocative in the southern European context.

While much research on the older end of the life course has been done for the northern parts of Europe by family historians, relatively little has been done in southern Europe. This may be due in part to the fact that in northern Europe peasant landownership has led to research on the transmission of the family farm and the problem of retirement (e.g., Gaunt, 1983), while many of the most intensively studied areas in southern Europe have lacked significant peasant landownership and formal retirement. Furthermore, the emphasis on post-mortem transfer throughout much of the region obviates the issue of retirement, although it does not mean that there is no period of old-age dependency. As was made clear in the previous section, when peasants did own land, they used their right to bequeath that land as a form of old-age insurance.

The phenomenon of widowhood in particular is of great historical importance, yet not well-studied to date. In many areas, a woman, upon widowhood, took up residence (if not already coresiding) with a married child (Klapisch, 1981:179; Nunes, 1985). Presumably, widowhood had a very different impact on an individual who was living in a complex family household from one who was left alone or with his or her young children. With the kind of continuous household material available in some regions of southern Europe (population registers, Easter duty lists), it is sometimes possible to document the movement of the 'senior generation' from household to household and thereby arrive at some understanding of the responsibilities of different offspring towards their parents or widowed parent. They may not, necessarily, have resided continuously with one child in their later years.

The difficulty a man without a wife faced is evident in the speed with which he remarried in some areas. For example, in southern Italy in the nineteenth century, a quarter of all remarriages of widowers involved weddings celebrated within six months of the previous wife's death while another fifth took place within the next six months (Livi Bacci, 1981:353). Livi Bacci found that in Italy in this period 43 percent of widowers and twenty percent of widows remarried, and that women widowed after age forty rarely remarried. Corsini (1980:173) found a similar situation in his study of Tuscany in the eighteenth and nineteenth centuries, where eighty percent of the men and 42 percent of the women widowed before their thirtieth birthday remarried, while, for example, 39 percent of men and just two percent of women widowed in their forties remarried. Brettell (1986) notes the impact that these varying rates of remarriage by sex can have on both age at marriage and the extent of marriage. For example, had it not been common for men widowed in their thirties, forties, and sometimes even fifties and sixties to remarry, the proportion of spinsters in the population would have been higher.

In general, there is some evidence that rates of remarriage declined over time (Bellettini, 1981). As for the link between remarriage and the family economy, Livi Bacci's (1981:357–359) speculations are instructive. He tentatively links the substantial Italian regional variations in remarriage rates in the nineteenth century to the distribution of the sharecropping economy. In the sharecropping areas, remarriage rates were lower because widowed individuals often found themselves in the supportive environment of large complex family households.

MIGRATION AND FAMILY LIFE IN SOUTHERN EUROPE

New research throughout Europe reveals that migration has long been a fundamental part of the people's experience no matter what the prevailing system of inheritance or the prevailing form of economic organization. However, exploration of this issue is at an early stage and the methodological problems—especially the challenge of documentation and measurement—are enormous. Furthermore, we are not interested simply in describing migration patterns, but also in determining the relationship between migration and marriage, fertility, and household structure.

Within southern Europe both internal and international migration have long been fundamental aspects of family life. And yet, only recently have studies of the historical impact of migration on the family been undertaken. For example, the association between rural-urban migration and household residence has been addressed by Kertzer (1984) in a study of internal migration in central Italy. Nineteenth-century Bertalia, a primarily agricultural parish situated just beyond the walls of Bologna, experienced significant population growth during the late nineteenth and early twentieth centuries due to short-distance migration.

Kertzer is interested in exploring the hypothesis of whether industrialization, urbanization, and migration cause the nuclearization of households. He demonstrates that the extended or multiple family households may, in fact, have facilitated rather than impeded migration and that in 1910 immigrants were more likely to be living in complex households than persisters (non-immigrants). To some extent the complex coresidential patterns of immigrants were more characteristic of young adults and the elderly, the latter a direct result of a life-course process wherein the elderly move in with children once their working lives are over. In general, however, just as sociologists and anthropologists demonstrate for present-day migration, kinship links were fundamental to the migration process in central Italy during the nineteenth century.

Few studies demonstrate, as Kertzer and Hogan (1985; Hogan and Kertzer, 1985a) have, the extensiveness of internal spatial mobility in southern Europe.[11] Rather, it is longer-distance international movement which has received more attention, although the impact of emigration on household and family structure has been addressed with much less rigor than the obverse. The growth of international emigration within southern Europe during the nineteenth century is frequently explained by the increasing penetration of the countryside by capitalism and by the significant population pressures during the nineteenth century. However, the relationship between economic organization, household organization, family structure, and emigration patterns is not clearcut. Gabaccia (1984), for example, found greater emigration from the *latifondo* areas of southern Italy than from those areas characterized by smaller and more diverse peasant and sharecropping household economies. She used this to argue against the necessary association between familism, low levels of agrarian organization and militance, and migration. Quite different emigration patterns characterize Portugal's history. There, the greatest population mobility is to be found in the areas where small-scale peasant agriculture has predominated for centuries and only in recent times, particularly with the industrialization of the Lisbon region, have agricultural laborers from the southern *latifundias* become involved in rural outmigration on a significant scale.

In northwestern Portugal men emigrate both before and after marriage, a pattern which influences not only ages at marriage and the extent of female spinsterhood, but also marital fertility levels. In this region, it has long been customary for married women to dress themselves in black when their husbands departed and, as "widows of the living" (*viuvas dos vivos*), to wait for years for the safe return of migrant spouses.

One impact of male migration has been a tendency toward uxorilocality, with married women taking up residence in their parents' homes. This is a feature of northwestern Portuguese society that also relates to the fact that women do much of the agricultural work. When husbands migrate, young wives who may have been living neolocally often move back with their parents. Yet, here too, diversity is evident. Merzario (1981:135) found, in the northern Italian commune of Peglio around 1600, that when men migrated, leaving wives and children behind, the patrilocal pattern was kept intact, and the remaining family lived with the absent husband's parental family. The relationship of male migration to patterns of postmarital residence and household composition obviously depends heavily on the timing of the male migration. Douglass (1980:353), for example, links the pattern of migration in Agnone (southern Italy) to a declining frequency of complex family households. In Agnone, most migrants were single males under the age of marriage. Even if they ultimately returned, the lag in time meant it was less likely that the parental generation was still alive, and, hence, made complex family coresidence less common.

Although Douglass does not suggest the matricentrality of Agnonese society to the extent that it is suggested by Brettell for northwestern Portugal, the relationship between a history of male migration and matricentric characteristics is one worth exploring further in the southern European context. Indeed, it is a hypothesis proposed several years ago by Boissevain (1979:92) which has not received much attention. Based on his study of Malta, Boissevain has argued that where attachment to landed property for economic purposes is minimal and where

there is a strong village-outward economic orientation, the ties between mothers and daughters are given freer rein and matrifocal-uxorilocal patterns tend to emerge.[12]

More studies of marital migration patterns are also necessary. Establishing regional variations in virilocal or uxorilocal (husband's village or wife's village) preferences may provide a clue to domestic relationships, division of labor, and the character and strength of kinship networks beyond the conjugal unit. Furthermore, changes in overall patterns of village exogamy and endogamy may be an indication of the changing composition of rural communities vis-à-vis the world outside the community. Goldey (1981), for example, describes an increasing pattern of village endogamy in a northern Portuguese parish from the late nineteenth into the twentieth century as emigration replaced the regional cattle trade as the primary source of cash, and as pastoralism and the population of day laborers declined. Emigrants, men without land, became attractive marriage prospects. Similarly, while only one percent of the baptismal godparents between 1941 and 1968 were from another parish, between 1850 and 1877 the proportion was 17.5 percent.

The differences between pre- and postmarital migration, and between a move at the time of marriage and a move made to find new employment underscore the importance of the life-course model. For example, if a woman is left with very young children when her husband goes abroad, she may be more likely to move back in with her parents than if she has older children, particularly older male children. Douglass (1984) notes the tendency among Italians at the turn of the century to undergo a stage migration process of family members. Older children often joined fathers abroad before mothers and younger children emigrated or before the father returned to Italy. Similarly, some children were sent back for schooling, a practice not uncommon today among southern European immigrants in northern Europe. The essential point is that, at different stages of the domestic cycle, varying kinship ties may be activated to support the migration process both in the sending community and in the receiving community.

CULTURAL CONCEPTS

Five years ago, in a rather playful analysis of 'anthropologyland' and 'historyland,' Cohn (1980:220) concluded that "the units of study in anthropological history should be cultural and culturally derived: honor, power, authority, exchange, reciprocity, codes of conduct, systems of social classification, the construction of time and space, rituals." "One studies these," he continued, "in a particular place and over time, but the study is about the construction of cultural categories, and the process of that construction, not about place and time." Although we do not believe that anthropological or historical study should be limited to these cultural categories, we do think the history of southern European family life could be advanced through a more systematic study of them. In anthropology, much recent soul-searching about just what, if anything, defines the Mediterranean as a unit for study, has involved discussion of just such cultural concepts (Boissevain, 1979; Davis, 1977; Gilmore, 1982). It is worth considering how some of these concepts have come into southern European family history, and where future research in this area might profitably be directed.

In his study of demographic patterns in four Italian towns, three in the south and one in the north-central region of Emilia-Romagna, Bell (1979) explored the relationship between powerful elements of the Italian peasant's world view—fate, honor, familism, and parochialism (*campanilismo*)—and demographic behavior. While Bell's approach is novel in its attempt to use culture to explain specific demographic trends, it is at times confusing, and the socioeconomic differences among his four towns which clearly contribute to an explanation of variations in population patterns are frequently submerged if not entirely lost. Yet, he places the emphasis where it has rarely been placed and in the process raises a number of new questions for the family historian.

Bell is interested in the way in which fate, honor, familism, and *campanilismo* have influenced the timing of demographic events. For example, the seasonality of marriages is explained not only by the practicalities of the annual economic cycle, but also by fate, as it is manifested in specific beliefs about fortunate and unfortunate months for taking nuptial vows. The fatalistic view of cyclical time is also apparent in the recycling of Christian names (see also Mabilia, 1980). The importance of *la famiglia* is equally embodied in the recycling of names, and, in addition, serves as a strategy for maximizing resources, as a source of labor, as a vehicle to accumulate wealth, get a job, migrate, form a group at social occasions, and as an arena for conflict. Male honor and male dominance of the family are the basis for significant proportions of marriages where the groom is appreciably older than the bride, and *campanilismo* is reflected in extraordinarily high rates of marital endogamy across all age groups (see also, in this regard, Destro, 1984). A number of changes in these demographic patterns between 1800 and the mid-twentieth century can be documented, and Bell links these changes to subtle shifts in some of the cultural concepts which make up the world view of the Italian peasantry.

Religious sponsorship, or godparent-hood, is a subject that has interested anthropologists at least since the time Mintz and Wolf (1950), Foster (1953), and Pitt-Rivers (1954) first described its importance in the Latin American and southern Spanish context. Indeed, godparenthood is often referred to in the anthropological literature with a Spanish word—*compadrazgo*. *Compadrazgo* forms the basis for a series of extra-kinship social links and, in much of the literature, it is the special relationship of 'ritual' or 'fictive' kinship established between the parents of a child and the baptismal godparents that is emphasized. Because the lateral connection at the level of the parental generation is so important, godparents are frequently chosen from among people of higher status— thus setting up an important patron-client relationship as the basis for the extension of both political and economic favors and services. Godparenthood can be the foundation for the formation of important alliances.

In the early days of family history, there was some interest in looking at the godparents of baptisms or marriages. However, perhaps because the cultural emphasis on godparenthood in the Catholic areas of northwestern Europe is not as great as it is in the Mediterranean region, interest soon waned. It is within the southern region that further research on this important form of extra-domestic, if not extra-kinship, association can be more fully explored. Such research should begin by addressing the most fundamental question: Who served as godparents? Were they kinsmen or non-kin, and if the former how close were the genealogical relationships? If the latter, were godparents chosen from among status equals or status unequals? Once these questions have been answered, a range of additional questions can be raised, questions which

we will illustrate by looking for a moment at the particular case of Portugal.

In the north of Portugal, unlike Latin America or parts of southern Spain, the link at the level of the parental generation between *compadres* is not as important as that between the godparent and the godchild. Historical data drawn from baptismal records indicate that from at least the mid-eighteenth century godchildren were frequently named after the godparent of the appropriate sex. Furthermore, although systematic quantitative data are lacking, it appears that godparents were and continue to be chosen most often from among fairly close kinsmen, an aunt or uncle, sometimes an older brother or sister. Anthropological data indicate that once this close kinsman has been chosen, he or she is generally addressed by the godchild with the godparental term. Thus, a mother's sister who genealogically is an aunt (*tia*) is addressed as *madrinha* (god-mother). A special relationship is embodied in this shift of terminology—the child is more than one of many nieces or nephews; he or she is a godchild. Embedded in this layering of a consanguineal relationship with a ritual relationships is an expectation of special regard which is two-directional. For example, evidence drawn from nineteenth century household lists indicates that, as today, some godchildren went to live with spinster aunts who were their godmothers. Presumably, they helped with household chores, and took care of the godmother as she aged. In return, as may be seen in wills from the eighteenth and nineteenth centuries, the spinster aunt—godmother often favored this godchild over other potential heirs in the property bequests made at her death. In a society where permanent spinsterhood is common and where women have rights to property which are equal to those of men, the choice of a spinster aunt as godmother to a child is not an unwise strategy, particularly for a couple with a number of children to provide for.

Although a preference for kinsmen as godparents in the south of Portugal is clearly expressed (Cutileiro, 1971), anthropological data demonstrate that it is not uncommon in this region for parents to look beyond the kinship network in their search for appropriate godparents. In this search, parents often choose someone of more importance and wealth. As in Latin America, this forms the basis for a patron-client relationship between *compadres*. Indeed, while the term *compadre* to signify a relationship between parents and godparents is rarely used in the north, it is much more current in the south. Although differences of wealth exist in the north of Portugal, they are not as extreme as they are in the south and the patronage which landless laborers, sharecroppers, and small landowners can receive from those higher in the social scale is sometimes crucial to their survival—often more crucial than what they can expect or get from kinsmen who are as poor as they are. The social distance between those richer and those poorer is bridged through ritual kinship. Regional variations similar to those described for Portugal have been described in Spain by Pitt-Rivers (1976). He expressly notes that in Andalusia, where classes are sharply divided, *compadrazgo* "provides the possibility of intimacy and trust between persons whose difference of class would otherwise make this difficult" (1976:324). In contrast, the dyadic relationships of godparenthood established in the western Mediterranean area differ dramatically from the corporate group/ritual kinship relationships embodied in *kumstvo* which have been described by Hammel (1968) for the Balkans. *Kumstvo* is an inherited right which binds different households (*zadrugas*) to one another in long-term relationships. Its

very existence underscores the importance and centrality of the agnatic joint household and its duration over time.

Godparenthood as a mechanism of social linkage may provide a different angle from which to examine the dynamics of heirship and therefore of family structure within the southern European region. The potential questions are many. In regions where stem families predominate, for example, do grandparents serve as godparents, and if so, is this a way to reinforce a designation of heirship? Is there any variation between a husband's side of the family and his wife's, and if so, what does this tell us about the importance of gender differentiation and its possible ramifications in other realms of family relationships and household structure? In those regions of the western Mediterranean where joint households are found, is ritual kinship similar to that found in the Balkans? Or are godparents chosen from among members of the domestic group in order to assuage potential tensions inherent in this form of household? At the very least, a study of godparenthood will help us to get at the importance of kinship relations beyond the domestic household group.

Honor and shame have been described as central values underlying Mediterranean culture (Peristiany, 1965). In Schneider's (1969) view, honor is an ideology held by property-holding groups which struggle to define, enlarge, and protect their patrimonies. Although manifested differently in different regions of the Mediterranean area, Schneider (1971) argues that honor and shame are mechanisms of social control which have most often emerged in the absence of full-fledged state control. In some contexts, the major focus is upon honor as an attribute of wealth; in others, honor is a measure of prestige and social status without economic overtones; and in still others, honor is primarily associated with masculinity and with the protection of women. Indeed, linked to the concepts of honor and shame are distinctions between the public domain of men (the community) and the private domain of women (the family, the household), and sharp gender differentiation in status and roles. In some situations, a man's honor has to do with his ability to keep his women at home. Thus, if women work, if honor does not depend on a man's ability to support his wife in the fullest sense of the word, a different household structure and a different set of family dynamics will emerge than in a situation where male honor is primarily linked to the behavior of women. The acceptability of female labor outside the home, as it is embedded in an ideology of male honor, may contribute to an explanation, for example, of varying distributions of nuclear as opposed to joint family households. It may also help to explain the timing of marriage. Yet, in the Sicilian case at least, the symbolic expression of family honor through female domestic toil on the embroidered textiles of the dowry itself has an economic component. According to Schneider (1980), such labor results in marketable wealth which serves as a safety reserve against the possibility of hard times.

Where male honor is weak as an attribute of wealth, prestige, and masculinity, or as an aspect of intergroup/interfamilial relations, the emphasis on female virginity may also assume less importance. Clearly, this will have an effect on the extensiveness of extramarital sex in the form of premarital pregnancy, illegitimacy, and adultery. For example, the concept of male honor is weak in the northern Portuguese context. While virginity is an expressed ideal, it does not assume the ideological proportions that it has in the eastern Mediterranean where an emphasis on lineage

and property is greater. Rates of illegitimacy in Portugal are high, especially in comparison with other regions of the Mediterranean area, including Spain and Italy. While the absence of a strong emphasis on male honor defined through the behavior of women, or as a measure of social prestige, does not offer a total explanation for these varying rates of illegitimacy, it certainly cannot be ignored. There is probably a connection between the flexibility of heirship, the possibility of matrilocal/uxorilocal (as opposed to patrilocal/virilocal) households, and the relative importance of female virginity as a cultural value. In addition, the degree to which shame is an effective mechanism of social control may influence the extent to which conceptions out of wedlock result in legal births, and therefore the demographic ratios of pre-marital pregnancies to illegitimate births.

The hierarchical and dichotomous models of sex roles within southern Europe have other applications to the understanding of family dynamics in history. Again, a determination of the extent to which private and public domains are culturally distinct will help us to differentiate between kinship relations within the household and those without it—a differentiation, we might add, which is particularly important in the "outdoor cultures" of the Mediterranean world. What are the differences in the connections which a man has with his kinsmen, and a woman has with hers? The opposition between men and women is a fundamental aspect of southern European anthropology (Saunders, 1981), and should therefore become integral to the analysis of family history in the region as well. To what extent, for example, is the strong mother-son bond in Italian culture—indeed, the entire concept of "La Mamma" (Giovannini, 1981)—borne out in the historical past? Where this particular symbolic vector of the Italian woman is strong (in Sicily, for example), does it help to explain the existence of nuclear family households because it underscores a relationship of extreme tension between mothers-in-law and daughters-in-law?

As Giovannini (1981) notes, woman as mother and madonna are only two aspects of a complex symbolic configuration of the female sex. Woman, from the southern European male's perspective, also connotes a whore, a highly sensual being who must be controlled. This particular perception of the female sex carries over into other heavily culture-laden concepts which may affect aspects of family dynamics in the historical past as in the present. One such concept is the evil eye which embodies all kinds of deep-rooted fears about the indominable women in an ideally male-dominated society. The degree to which there is a culturally expressed interest in the evil eye and 'woman-as-sorceress' may contribute to an explanation of attitudes towards widowhood and remarriage, and may in turn influence the cultural acceptability of women living alone (see Press, 1979). There appears to be, for example, a strong geographical correlation between female seclusion and the strength of the evil eye belief (Maloney, 1976).

Our discussion here of culturally constructed categories and family history has touched briefly on only a few of the many potential areas for historical research. We have omitted, for example, any discussion of the nature of Catholicism in southern Europe and its relationship to family norms. It is hoped that, along with the further development of more behavioral and demographic studies of southern European family history, progress can be made in plotting the distribution of family-related cultural conceptions in all their variety, and determining the nature of the links between these cultural ideas and historically changing family behavior patterns.

CONCLUSIONS

There has been a healthy upsurge in family history research in Italy and Iberia over the past several years, attributable in part to the impetus given by studies done elsewhere in Europe. Perhaps inevitably, many of the methods and conceptual frameworks guiding these southern European studies were borrowed from this earlier family history tradition. Having surveyed some of the major observations to result from these recent southern European studies, we would like here to take stock briefly of where we are and in what directions we might profitably move.

As mentioned earlier, there has been a welcome movement over the past decade away from lumping southern Europe with northwestern Europe in revisionist pronouncements of the 'myth' of the complex family household. With the recognition that southern Europe may show a different historical pattern, however, there has been a tendency to construct an alternative model of family organization to characterize southern Europe, one which contrasts with the model constructed for the northwest. Although this has served the useful purpose of highlighting possible areas of difference in Europe, and has pointed to important regional distributions of various family characteristics, it is now clear that many of the generalizations encompassed in such a model are not supported by the historical evidence.

More important, though, we must now raise the question of whether a trait list approach (what in anthropology earlier in this century was identified with the "cultural area" approach linked to a diffusionist perspective) is the most productive theoretical direction in which to go.[13] The diversity of family forms and family-related processes in Italy and Iberia that we have demonstrated should alert us to the dangers of generalizing about regions such as southern or Mediterranean Europe. On a more theoretical level, if one accepts the proposition that family processes are intimately linked to political economic arrangements, as we have argued, the uniformities to be sought are not regional at all, but uniformities linking certain political economic forms to certain family organizational patterns.

Yet family historians can still ask, as anthropologists have done before them, whether there are not some characteristic features of family life in southern Europe. We have raised this question in addressing cultural codes in Italy and Iberia, for while we view cultural forms as being strongly influenced by political, economic, and historical forces, we also see cultural conceptions exerting an influence over people's family lives. Moreover, we can look to ecological similarities in Mediterranean Europe and inquire into the extent to which these similarities are linked to similarities in family life. Of course, similar ecological situations are often associated with similarities in economic arrangements, and much work remains to be done in this regard. For example, mountainous areas of Greece and Italy long hosted pastoralist peoples (Campbell, 1964), yet to date little historical attention has been paid to these peoples or to the similarities among them across Mediterranean Europe. While some work has been done on fishing communities in southern Europe, the nature of family patterns in these communities remains similarly obscure.

The issue of ecological similarities in southern Europe also recalls the matter of settlement pattern and its effects on family organization. Douglass offers a hint of the importance of settlement patterns in arguing that peoples living in nucleated communities could support a system of partible inheritance (as they did in many parts of southern Italy) more easily than peoples living on the land they farmed. If it can be argued that the settlement pattern is determined by various political (security), economic (land ownership) and health (e.g., malaria) factors, we might argue that inheritance patterns are determined by these various factors as mediated in part by settlement. More specifically, for example, we note that both southern Italy and southern Portugal were characterized by agrotowns, and these are the areas where large, complex family households were, in general, least frequent. As for similarities in family life in the cities of southern Europe, we must await the publication of work in Iberia for, while a fair amount of work has now been done in urban family history in Italy, with a few exceptions (Reher, 1984, 1986; Napal, 1985), very little has yet been undertaken in Spain or Portugal.

We also see promise in the increased use of a life-course approach to address many issues in southern European family history. This comes not only from a desire to interpret the processes that lead to certain family patterns, but also from a desire to relate generalizations of social organization to the actual experience of individuals in the past. Take, for example, the question of childhood in the past. We would like to know not only what proportion of children were abandoned, but what became of the ones who were? It happens that many of the foundling institutions kept records following their charges through a goodly portion of their lives. What kind of handicap was it for an individual to be a foundling in terms of later family life, including marriage? Similarly, it is not enough to know what proportion of youths entered service. We would also like to know how they came to be servants, how long they remained servants, and what impact this service stage of their lives had on their subsequent marriage.

A life-course perspective would also be valuable in pursuing an issue which has thus far received too little attention in southern European historical family studies, namely, changes in the status and roles of women in the family context. Barbagli (1984), for example, argues that central Italy was long a highly patriarchal society, while Brettell, in her work in northwestern Portugal, shows a society where women enjoyed considerable autonomy, status and power. Such differences, insofar as they exist (we have our doubts regarding Barbagli's generalization), may be linked to differences in women's property rights. But these property rights themselves are linked to life-course factors insofar as the individual is concerned. For example, although designating sons as heirs may be the official norm, wives may in effect inherit from deceased husbands. Whether they inherit, and how much influence this has over their lives, is linked to the point in their lives when they become widowed. This, itself, is linked to differences in age at marriage between husband and wife and the norms regarding remarriage. Research linking political economic, life-course and cultural factors can take us far in gaining a richer understanding of family life in the past.

In short, family history research in Italy and Iberia has mushroomed over the past decade, involving a mix of historians, anthropologists and sociologists. The diversity that has been documented thus far argues for the potential theoretical interest of southern European family historical study at the same time as it provides us with a caution against premature generalization.

ACKNOWLEDGMENTS

David Kertzer's contribution to this essay is based, in part, on work supported by NICHD grant No. 1R01 HD18976. The authors would like to thank William Douglass for allowing them to read his unpublished paper on the stem family household in northern Iberia.

NOTES

1. In nearby parishes, Rowland (1981) has found 88 percent of the households with only one or two generations and the remaining twelve percent with three or four in 1827. However, the source used by Rowland (a listing for military purposes) excludes almost all single women. In the mountainous parish of Montaria, complex families were sixteen percent of the total; in the coastal parish of Ancora, they were 20 percent.

2. Reher (1984), in his study of the Spanish town of Cuenca in the nineteenth century, has also found that following people through different points of their lives reveals a much higher proportion who lived at some point in complex family households than is indicated by looking at single-year proportions of simple and complex family arrangements.

3. On the nuclear family household organization of the poor of Florence in the early nineteenth century, see Woolf (1984). For urban-rural comparisons in Spain see Jiménez-Chacón (1983).

4. This is a point which has, of course, been noted in studies of heirship in western Europe. See, for example, Cole and Wolf (1974) and Berkner and Mendels (1978).

5. Although O'Neill implies that the stem-family arrangement has been the pattern most characteristic of this region, in 1977 only five of fifty-seven households were multiple, and three of these involved cases of illegitimacy. Beyond the household lists (*Rois dos Confessados*) kept by the parish priest between 1870 and 1909, no systematic quantitative data on household structure for the latter nineteenth century is given.

6. The southern province of Orense is unique in Galicia in its emphasis on strict partibility. The rights and duties toward parents are shared equally. Newlyweds can live where they choose and it is not particularly important who remains in the family house.

7. On the development of dowry in Mediterranean Europe, see Hughes (1978).

8. These figures can be misleading, since many women from the surrounding rural areas came into the city to give birth when they planned to abandon their newborns.

9. In Italy, for example, the *ruota*, or wheel which allowed infants to be deposited anonymously at the *ospizi*, was banned in this period.

10. For some historical insights into consanguineous marriages in Spain, see Abelson (1979, 1980), Calderon (1983) and Pinto-Cisternas et al. (1979).

11. Although covering but a brief time span (1843–1847), Reher's (1986) work in Spain leads him to similar conclusions.

12. A different link of migration to family patterns has recently been described by Viazzo (1984) in his study of a German-speaking community in the Piedmontese Alps. There a large jump in illegitimacy in the latter half of the nineteenth century is directly tied to the families of the immigrants who found jobs in the local mining industry.

13. Such a diffusionist model may also be seen to underlie the Princeton European Fertility study, with its identification of cultural variables with "linguistic frontiers."

REFERENCES

Abelson, Andrew. 1979. "Population Structure in the Western Pyrenées: I. Population Density, Social Class Composition and Migration." *Journal of Biosocial Science* 11:353.

_____. 1980. "Population Structure in the Western Pyreneés: II. Migration, the Frequency of Consanguineous Marriage and Inbreeding, 1877 to 1915." *Journal of Biosocial Science* 12: 93–101.

Amorim, Maria Norberta. 1973. *Rebordãos e a Sua População Nos Séculos XVIII.* Lisbon: Imprensa Nacional.

_____. 1980. *Métoob de exploráçao dos livros de registos paroquiais: e Cardanha e a sua populaçāo de 1573 a 1800.* Lisbon.

_____. 1983. *Exploração de Rois de Confessados duma Paróquia de Guimarães (1734-1760).* Guimarães.

_____. 1984. "Comportamentos demograficos do norte de Portugal durante o antigo regime." *Boletin de la Asociación de Demografia Histórica* 2: 20–30.

Anelli, Aldo, Enzo Siri and Lamberto Soliani. 1979. "Analisi della fecondità per strutture familiari." *Genus* 35: 173–187.

Angeli, Aurora. 1983. "Strutture familiari nella Pianura e nella Montagna Bolognese a metà del XIX Secolo. Confronti territoriali." *Statistica* 43: 727–740.

Angeli, Aurora and Athos Bellettini. 1979. "Strutture familiari nella campagna Bolognese a metà dell'Ottocento." *Genus* 35: 155–172.

Arensberg, Conrad and Solon Kimball. 1940. *Family and Community in Ireland.* Cambridge: Harvard University Press.

Aymard, Maurice and Gerard Delille. 1977. "La Démographie historique en Italie: une discipline en mutation." *Annales de Démographie Historique* 1977: 447–461.

Balugani, Angela and Silvio Fronzoni. 1979. "Poderi e Mezzadri di una 'Impresa' Bolognese, 1720–1770." *Quaderni Storici* No. 40: 105–129.

Barbagli, Marzio. 1984. *Sotto lo Stesso Tetto: Mutamenti della Famiglia in Italia dal xv al xx Secolo.* Bologna: Il Mulino.

Bauer, Rainer. 1981. "Property, Marriage, and Population Change in the Sierra Caurel during the 19th Century." Paper presented to the Society for Spanish and Portuguese Historical Studies, Toronto, April.

_____. 1983. *Family and Property in a Spanish Galician Community.* Unpublished Dissertation, Anthropology, Stanford University.

Bell, Rudolph. 1979. *Fate and Honor, Family and Village: Demographic and Cultural Change in Rural Italy Since 1900.* Chicago: University of Chicago Press.

Bellettini, Athos. 1981. "Les remariages dans la ville et dans la campagne de Bologne au dix-neuvieme siecle." Pp. 259–272 in Jacques Dupaquier et al., eds., *Marriage and Remarriage in Populations of the Past.* New York: Academic Press.

Belmartino, S. 1968. "Estructura de la familia y edades sociales en la aristocracia de Leon y Castilla según las fuentes literarias e historiograficas (siglos X-XIII)." *Cuadernos de Historia de España* 47–48: 256–328.

Bennassar, Bartolome. 1967. *Valladolid au Siècle d'Or. Une Ville de Castille et sa Campagne au XVIe siecle.* Paris.

_____. "Economie et société à Segovie au milieu du XVI siecle." *Anuario de Historia Social y Economica* 1: 185–205.

Berkner, Lutz K. 1976. "Inheritance, Land Tenure and Peasant Family Structure: A German Regional Comparison." In Jack Goody, Joan Thirsk and E.P. Thompson, eds., *Family and Inheritance.* Cambridge: Cambridge University Press.

Berkner, Lutz K. and Franklin F. Mendels. 1978. "Inheritance Systems, Family Structure, and

Demographic Patterns in Western Europe (1700–1900)." In Charles Tilly, ed., *Historical Studies of Changing Fertility*. Princeton: Princeton University Press.

Boissevain, Jeremy et al. 1979. "Towards a Social Anthropology of the Mediterranean." *Current Anthropology* 20:81–93.

Brandão, Fatima. 1983. "Death and the Survival of the Rural Household in a Northwestern Municipality." Pp. 147–162 in Rui Feijó et al., eds., *Death in Portugal: Studies in Portuguese Anthropology and Modern History*. Oxford: Oxford University Press.

Brandão, Fatima and Robert Rowland. 1980. "História da propriedade e comunidade rural: questões de método." *Análise Social* 16: 173–207.

Brandes, Stanley. 1976. "La Solteria, or Why People Remain Single in Rural Spain." *Journal of Anthropological Research* 32: 205–233.

Brettell, Caroline B. 1984. "Nupcialidad en un Pueblo de la Provincia del Miño, 1700–1970." *Boletin de la Asociacio¹n de Demografia Histórica* 2: 2–19.

———. 1986. *Men Who Migrate, Women Who Wait: Population and History in a Portuguese Parish*. Princeton: Princeton University Press.

Caiati, Vito. 1984. "The Peasant Household under Tuscan Mezzadria: A Socioeconomic Analysis of Some Sienese Mezzadri Households, 1591–1640." *Journal of Family History* 9: 111–126.

Calderon, R. 1983. "Inbreeding, Migration and Age at Marriage in Rural Toldeo, Spain." *Journal of Biosocial Science* 15: 47–57.

Calise, Mauro. 1979. "Strutture familiari e mobilitaθ del Lavoro: alle origini della industrializzazione in Italia." *Rassegna Italiana di Sociologia* 19(3): 439–460.

Campbell, John. 1964. *Honour, Family and Patronage*. Oxford: Oxford University Press.

Casey, J. 1979. *The Kingdom of Valencia in the Seventeenth Century*. Cambridge: Cambridge University Press.

Castillo, Alvaro. 1965. "Population et richesse en Castille durant la seconde moitié du XVIe siècle." *Annales, E.S.C.* 20: 719–733.

Ciacci, Margherita. 1980. "Precarietà economica e strutture familiari nella Firenze del Primo '800." *Storia Urbana* 13: 55–75.

Cohn, Bernard. 1980. "History and Anthropology: The State of Play." *Comparative Studies in Society and History* 22: 198–221.

Cole, John W. and Eric R. Wolf. 1974. *The Hidden Frontier: Ecology and Ethnicity in an Alpine Village*. New York: Academic Press.

Collier, George. 1983. "Late Marriage and the Uncontested Reign of Property." Paper presented to the American Anthropological Association, Chicago.

Collier, Jane. 1983. "Children and Property in an Andalusian Village." Paper presented to the annual meetings of the American Anthropological Association, Chicago.

Corsini, Carlo A. 1976. "Materiali per lo studio della famiglia in Toscana nei secoli XVII–XIX: gli esposti." *Quaderni Storici* 33: 998–1052.

———. 1977. "Self-regulating Mechanisms of Traditional Populations before the Demographic Revolution: European Civilizations." Pp. 5–23 in *International Population Conference*, Volume 3. Liège: International Union for the Scientific Study of Population.

———. "La mobilità della popolazione nel settecento: fonti, metodi e problemi." Pp. 401–433 in Athos Bellettini, ed., *La Popolazione Italiana nel Settecento*. Bologna: CLUEB.

Da Molin, Giovanna. 1980. "Mobilità dei contadini Pugliesi tra fine '600 e Primo '800." Pp. 435–475 in Athos Bellettini, ed., *La Popolazione Italiana nel Settecento*. Bologna: CLUEB.

———. 1983. "Les enfants abandonne¹s dans les villes italiennes aux XVIIIᵉ et XIX ᵉ siècles." *Annales de Démographie Historique* 1983: 103–124.

Davis, John. 1973. *Land and Family in Pisticci*. London: London School of Economics Monographs on Social Anthropology, No. 48.

———. 1977. *The People of the Mediterranean: An Essay in Comparative Social Anthropology*. London: Routledge and Kegan Paul.

de la Roncière, Charles M. 1981. "Una famiglia Fiorentina nel XIV secolo: I Velluti." In Georges Duby and Jacques Le Goff, eds., *Famiglia e Parentela nell'Italia Medievale*. Bologna: Il Mulino.

Delille, Gérard. 1977. *Agricoltura e Demografia nel Regno di Napoli nei Secoli XVIII e XIX*. Napoli: Guida.

———. *Famille et Propriété dans le Royaume de Naples (XVe-XIXe Siècles)*. Rome: École Française de Rome.

Della Peruta, Franco. 1979. "Infanzia e famiglia nella prima metà del ottocento." *Studi Storici* 20(3): 473–491.

Della Pina, Marco. 1983. "Famiglie di lavoratori e famiglie di pigionali nel contado Pratese all fine del sec. XVIII." Paper presented to the Conference on Family Structures and Relations in Modern Times, Trieste, September 5–7.

Descamps, Paul. 1935. *Portugal: La Vie Sociale Actuelle*. Paris: Firmin-Didot.

Destro, Adriana. 1984. *L'Ultima Generazione: Confini Materiali e Simbolici di una Comunità delle Alpi Marittime*. Milan: Angeli.

Dillard, Heath. 1984. *Daughters of the Reconquest: Women in Castilian Town Society, 1100-1300.* London: Cambridge University Press.

Douglass, William A. 1971. "Rural Exodus in Two Spanish Basque Villages: A Cultural Explanation." *American Anthropologist* 79: 1100–1114.

_____. 1974. *Echalar and Murelaga: Opportunity and Rural Exodus in Two Spanish Basque Villages.* New York: St. Martin's Press.

_____. 1980. "The South Italian Family: A Critique." *Journal of Family History* 5: 338–359.

_____. *Emigration in a South Italian Town: An Anthropological History.* New Brunswick, N.J.: Rutgers University Press.

Doveri, Andrea. 1982. "Famiglia Coniugale e Famiglia Multinucleare: Le Basi dell' Esperienza Domestica in Due Parrocchie delle Colline Lungo il Secolo XVIII." *Genus* 38(1)59–96.

_____. 1983. "Famiglie di contadini e famiglie di pigionali del contado Pisano nel secolo XVIII. Struttura ed evoluzione." Paper presented to The Conference on Family Structures and Relations in Modern Times, Trieste, Italy, September 5–7.

Feijò, Rui. 1983. "Household Structure and Labor Organization in Carreço (NW Portugal) c. 1830." Paper presented to the Social Science History Association, Washington D.C.

Felix, M. 1958. "Les registres paroissiaux et l'état civil au Portugal." *Archivum* 8:89–94.

Ferrante, Lucia. 1984. "Strutture o strategie? Discussione sulla storia della famiglia." *Quaderni Storici* 56:613–626.

Fine-Souriac, A. 1977. "La Famille souche Pyrenéene au XIX siècle: quelques reflexions de méthode." *Annales E.S.C.* 32:478–487.

Foster, George. 1953. "Confradia and Compadrazgo in Spain and Latin America." *Southwestern Journal of Anthropology* 9: 1–28.

Gabaccia, Donna R. 1984. "Migration and Peasant Militance: Western Sicily 1880–1910." *Social Science History* 8: 67–80.

Gaunt, David. 1983. "The Property and Kin Relationships of Retired Farmers in Northern and Central Europe." In Richard Wall, Jean Robin and Peter Laslett, eds., *Family Forms in Historic Europe.* Cambridge: Cambridge University Press.

Gilmore, David. 1982. "Anthropology of the Mediterranean Area." *Annual Review of Anthropology* 11: 175–205.

Giovannini, M.J. 1981. "Women: A Dominant Symbol within the Cultural System of a Sicilian Town." *Man* 16: 408–426.

Goldey, Patricia. 1981. "Emigração e estrutura familiar—estudo de un caso no minho." *Estudos Contemporâneos* 2–3: 118–128.

Gonzalez Muñoz, Maria del Carmen. 1974. *La Población de Talavera de la Reina (xvi-xx): Estudio Socio-Demográfico.* Toledo: Publicaciones del Instituto Provincial de Investigaciones y Estudios Toledanos.

Goody, Jack, Joan Thirsk and E.P. Thompson, eds. 1976. *Family and Inheritance: Rural Society in Western Europe.* Cambridge: Cambridge University Press.

Gozzini, Giovanni. 1984. "Matrimonio e Mobilità Sociale nella Firenze di Primo Ottocento." *Quaderni Storici* 57: 907–939.

Hajnal, J. 1965. "European Marriage Patterns in Perspective." In D.V. Glass and D.E.C. Eversley, eds., *Population in History.* London: Edward Arnold.

_____. "Two Kinds of Pre-Industrial Household Formation System." In Richard Wall, Jean Robin and Peter Laslett eds., *Family Forms in Historic Europe.* Cambridge: Cambridge University Press.

Hammel, Eugene. 1968. *Alternative Social Structures and Ritual Relations in the Balkans.* Englewood Cliffs: Prentice-Hall.

Hansen, E.C. 1977. *Rural Catalonia under the Franco Regime: The Fate of Regional Culture Since the Spanish Civil War.* Cambridge: Cambridge University Press.

Herlihy, David. 1985. *Medieval Households.* Cambridge: Harvard University Press.

Herlihy, David and C. Klapisch-Zuber. 1985. *Tuscans and Their Families.* New Haven: Yale University Press.

Hogan, Dennis P. and David I. Kertzer. 1985a. "Migration Patterns during Italian Urbanization." *Demography* 22: 309–325.

_____. 1985b. "Longitudinal Approaches to Migration in Social History." *Historical Methods* 18: 20–30.

Hughes, Diane Owen. 1978. "From Brideprice to Dowry." *Journal of Family History* 3: 262–296.

Hunecke, Volker. 1978. "Problemi della demografia Milanese dopo l'unità: la chiusura della ruota ed 'Crollo' della nascite." *Storia Urbana* 5: 81–90.

Iszaevich, Abraham. 1975. "Emigrants, Spinsters and Priests: The Dynamics of Demography in Spanish Peasant Societies." *The Journal of Peasant Studies* 2: 292–312.

_____. 1981a. "Corporate Household and Ecocentric Kinship Group in Catalonia." *Ethnology* 20: 277–290.

_____. The Perils of Prosperity: Affluence and Demographic Depletion in Catalonia." Pp. 150–159 in Richard Salisbury and Elizabeth Tooker, eds., *Affluence and Cultural Survival.*

Proceedings of the American Ethnological Society.

Iturra, Raul. 1980. "Strategies in the Domestic Organization of Production in Rural Galicia." *Cambridge Anthropology* 6: 88–128.

Jiménez-Chacón, Francisco. 1983. "Introducción a la historia de la familia Española: el ejemplo de murcia y orihuela (Siglos XVII–XIX)." *Cuadernos de Historia* 10: 235–266.

Kertzer, David I. 1984. *Family Life in Central Italy, 1880-1910*. New Brunswick, N.J.: Rutgers University Press.

_____. 1985. "Future Directions in Historical Household Studies." *Journal of Family History* 10: 98–107.

Kertzer, David I. and Dennis P. Hogan. 1985. "On the Move: Migration in an Italian Community, 1865–1921." *Social Science History* 9(1): 1–24.

Kirshner, Julius and Anthony Molho. 1978. "The Dowry Fund and the Marriage Market in Early *Quattrocento* Florence." *Journal of Modern History* 50: 403–438.

Klapisch, Christiane. 1981. "Declino demografico e struttura della famiglia: L'Esempio di Prato (fine XIV sec.-fine XV sec.)." In Georges Duby and Jacques Le Goff, eds., *Famiglia e Parentela nell'Italia Medievale*. Bologna: Il Mulino.

Kussmaul, Ann. 1981. *Servants in Husbandry in Early Modern England*. Cambridge: Cambridge University Press.

Larquie, C. 1974. "Quartiers et paroisses urbaines: l'exemple de Madrid au XVIIe siècle." *Annales de Démographie Historique*, 165–195.

Laslett, Peter. 1983. "Family and Household as Work Group and Kin Group: Areas of Traditional Europe Compared," In Richard Wall, Jean Robin, and Peter Laslett, eds., *Family Forms in Historic Europe*. Cambridge: Cambridge University Press.

Levi, Giovanni. 1976. "Terra e strutture familiari in una comunità Piemontese nel '700." *Quaderni Storici* 33: 1095–1121.

_____. 1985. *L'Eredità Immateriale. Carriera di un Esorcista nel Piemonte del Seicento*. Torino: Einaudi.

Lison-Tolosana, Carmelo. 1976. "The Ethics of Inheritance," In J.G. Peristiany, ed., *Mediterranean Family Structure*. Cambridge: Cambridge University Press.

_____. 1977. *Invitacio¹n a la Anthropologia Cultural de España*. La Coruña: Editorial Adara.

Livi Bacci, Massimo. 1968. "Fertility and Nuptiality Changes in Spain from the Late 18th to the Early 20th Century." *Population Studies* 22: 211–237.

_____. 1971. *A Century of Portuguese Fertility*. Princeton: Princeton University Press.

_____. 1981. "On the Frequency of Remarriage in Nineteenth Century Italy: Methods and Results." Pp. 347–361 in Jacques Dupaquier et al., eds., *Marriage and Remarriage in Populations of the Past*. New York: Academic Press.

Mabilia, Mara. 1980. "Struttura familiare e uso del soprannome in une communità dell'alto Padovano." *Rassegna Italiana di Sociologia* 21: 585–605.

Maloney, C., ed. 1976. *The Evil Eye*. New York: Columbia University Press.

Merzario, Raul. 1981. *Il Paese Stretto: Strategie Matrimoniali nella Diocesi di Como, Secoli XVI-XVIII*. Torino: Einaudi.

Mintz, Sidney and Eric Wolf. 1950. "An Analysis of Ritual Godparenthood (compadrazgo)." *Southwestern Journal of Anthropology* 6: 341–368.

Nadal, Jordi. 1966. *Historia de la Población Española*. Madrid.

Napal, Pedro Luis Iriso. 1985. "Estrutura económica, desarrollo urbano y comporta-mientos demográficos en el siglo xix, Requena 1787-1910." *Boletin de la Asociación de Demografia Histórica* 3(3): 21–61.

Nunes, João Arriscado. 1985. "Is there *one* household formation system in northwestern Portugal?" Paper presented to the workshop on Family Forms and Demographic Patterns in the Western Mediterranean," Oeiras, April.

O'Neill, Brian. 1981. "Proprietários, jornaleiros, et criados numa Aldeia Transmontana desde 1886." *Estudos Contemporâneos* 2/3: 31–74.

_____ "Dying and Inheriting in Rural Trás-Os-Montes." *Journal of the Anthropological Society of Oxford* 14: 44–74.

_____. 1984. *Proprietários, Lavradores e Jornaleiros: Desiqualidade Social numa Aldeia Transmontana, 1870-1978*. Lisbon: Publicações Dom Quixote.

_____. "Family Cycles and Inheritance in Rural Portugal." *Peasant Studies* 12 (3): 199–213.

Ortalli, Gherardo. 1981. "La Famiglia tra la realtà dei gruppi inferiori e la mentalità dei gruppi dominanti a Bologna nel XIII secolo." In Georges Duby and Jacques Le Goff, eds., *Famiglia e Parentela nell'Italia Medievale*. Bologna: Il Mulino.

Peristiany, John G., ed. 1965. *Honor and Shame: The Values of Mediterranean Society*. London: Weidenfeld and Nicolson.

Pina-Cabral, João de. 1984. "Comentários criticos sobre a case e a familia no alto minho rural." *Análise Social* 20: 263–284.

Pinto-Cisternas, J., G. Zei, and A. Moroni. 1979. "Consanguinity in Spain, 1911-1943: General Methodology, Behavior of Demographic Variables, and Regional Differences." *Social Biology* 26: 55–71.

Pitt-Rivers, Julian. 1954. *The People of the Sierra*. London: Weidenfeld and Nicolson.

————. 1976. "Ritual Kinship in the Mediterranean: Spain and the Balkans." In J.G. Peristiany, ed., *Mediterranean Family Structures*. Cambridge: Cambridge University Press.

Poni, Carlo. 1978. "Family and *podre* in Emilia Romagna." *Journal of Italian History* 1: 201–234.

Poumarède, J. 1979. "Famille et tenure dans les Pyrenées du moyen age au XIX siècle." *Annales de Démographie Historique*, 347–360.

Poza Martin, Maria del Carmen. 1985. "Nupcialidad y fecundidad en valle de Tabladillo entre 1787 y 1860. Una nota de investigación." *Boletin de la Asociación de Demografia Histórica* 3 (3): 32–50.

Press, Irwin. 1979. *The City as Context: Urbanism and Behavioral Constraints in Seville*. Urbana: University of Illinois Press.

Ramella, Franco. 1977. "Famiglia, terra e salario in una comunità tessile dell'ottocento." *Movimento Operaio e Socialista* 23: 7–44.

————. 1983. *Terra e Telai: Sistem di Parentela e Manifattura nel Biellese dell'Ottocento*. 2nd ed. Torino: Einaudi.

Reher, David Sven. 1984. "La Importancia del analisis dinámico ante el analisis estático del hogar y la familia: algunos ejemplos da la ciudad de Cuenca en el siglo XIX." *Revista Española de Investigaciones Sociológicas* 27: 107–135.

————. 1986. "Mobility and Migration in Pre-Industrial Urban Areas: The Case of 18th Century Cuenca." Paper given at the IUSSP Seminar on Urbanization and Population Dynamics in History, Tokyo.

Reher, David Sven and David J. Robinson. 1979. "The Population of Early Modern Spain: A Review of Sources and Research Questions," Discussion Papers, Syracuse University Department of Geography 59: 1–27.

Ring, Richard R. 1979. "Early Medieval Peasant Households in Central Italy." *Journal of Family History* 4: 2–25.

Rowland, Robert. 1981. "Ancora e Montaría, 1827: duas frequesias do noroeste segundo os livros de registro das companhias de ordenação." *Estudos Contemporaneos* 2/3: 199–242.

————. "Family and Marriage in Portugal (16th–20th Centuries): A Comparative Sketch." Paper presented to the Social Science History Association.

————. n.d. "Sistemas matrimoniales en la peninsula Ibérica: una perspectiva regional. In V. Perez Moreda y David S. Reher, eds. *La Demografia Histórica de la Peninsula Ibérica, Siglos XVI-XX*. Madrid: Editorial Tecnos (forthcoming).

Saunders, George R. 1981. "Men and Women in Southern Europe: A Review of Some Aspects of Cultural Complexity." *Journal of Psychoanalytic Anthropology* 4 (4): 435–466.

Schneider, Jane. 1971. "Of Vigilance of Virgins: Honor, Shame, and Access to Resources in Mediterranean Societies." *Ethnology* 10: 1–24.

————. 1980. "Trousseau as Treasure: Some Contradictions of Late Nineteenth-Century Change in Sicily." Pp. 323–356 in Eric B. Ross, Ed. *Beyond the Myths of Culture*. New York: Academic Press.

Schneider, Jane and Peter S. Schneider. 1984. "Demographic Transition in a Sicilian Rural Town." *Journal of Family History* 9: 245–272.

Schneider, Peter. 1969. "Honor and Conflict in a Sicilian Town." *Anthropological Quarterly* 42: 130–155.

Silverman, Sydel. 1968. "Agricultural Organization, Social Structure, and Values in Italy: Amoral Familism." *American Anthropologist* 70: 1–20.

Smith, Richard M. 1981. "The People of Tuscany and Their Families in the Fifteenth Century: Medieval or Mediterranean?" *Journal of Family History* 6: 107–128.

Somogyi, Stefano. 1959. "Cento anni de bilanci familiari in Italia (1857-1956)." *Annali Istituto Giangiacomo Feltrinelli* 2: 121–263.

Teles, Basilio. 1903. *A Carestia da Vida nos Campos*. Porto: Livraria Chardron.

Tittarelli, Luigi. 1980. "La mobilità territoriale della popolazione di una parrocchia ternana nel XVIII secolo: uno studio basato sugli stati d'anime nominative." Pp. 477-500 in Athos Bellettini, ed. *La Popolazione Italiana nel Settecento*. Bologna: CLUEB.

Tonizzi, M. Elisabetta Bianchi. 1984. "Esposti e balie in Liguria tra otto e novecento: Il caso di chiavari." *Movimento Operaio Socialista* 6(1):7–31.

Torti, Cristiana. 1981. "Struttura e caratteri della famiglia contadina: Cascina 1841." In Giovanni Cherubini et al., ed., *Contadini e Proprietari nella Toscana Moderna, Età Contemporanea*. Firenze: Olschki Editore.

Valero Lobo, Angeles. 1984. "Edad media de acceso al matrimonio en España, siglos XVI-XIX." *Boletin de la Associación de Demografia Histórica* 2 (2): 39–48.

Vaquer Benassar, Onofre. 1984. "La Nupcialidad en Felanita (Mallorca) en los siglos XVI y XVII." *Boletin de la Asociación de Demografia Histórica* 2 (2): 31–38.

Viazzo, Pier Paolo. 1984. "Tra antropologia e demografia storica: illegitimità, struttura sociale e mutamento etnico in un villaggio delle Alpi Italiane." *L'Uomo* 8: 163–196.

Vilar, Pierre. 1965a. "Quelques problèmes de démo-

graphie historique en Catalogne et en Espagne."
Annales de Démographie Historique, 11–30.
————— 1965b. "Essai d'un bilan démographique
de la periode 1787-1814," *Annales de Démographie Historique*, 53–65.

Woolf, Stuart J. 1984. "Charité, pauvrété et structure des ménages a Florence au debut du XIXe
siècle." *Annales, E.S.C.* 39: 355–382.
Wrigley, E. Anthony. 1982. "The Prospects for
Population History." In Theodore K. Rabb and
Robert I. Rotberg, eds., *The New History: The
1980s and Beyond*. Princeton: Princeton University Press.

RURAL HOUSEHOLD ORGANIZATION AND INHERITANCE IN NORTHERN EUROPE

David Gaunt

ABSTRACT: *By focusing on morphological continuity, family historians may be neglecting long-term changes within the family that are documented in non-numerical sources. Evidence from Finland suggests that researchers need to reexamine the history of the* suurperhe *("large family"). Similarly, evidence from the Scandinavian peninsula suggests that the early modern centuries witnessed the growth of privacy in generational relations, the emergence of the father-son dyad as the preferred method of land transfer, the separation of landownership from household authority, and the use of the courts to solve family problems. Thus there may have been transformations in family life in the long term that unchanging measures of mean size do not capture.*

The following survey of writings on rural family relationships and inheritance in the Nordic past may seem a bit odd. It concentrates on admittedly curious cultural phenomena such as multi-family households in eastern Finland, generational conflicts in stem families and various tricks used to avoid official inheritance laws. I have made such a peculiar choice in order to discuss sources and human problems not ordinarily treated in the common garden-variety history of the European family. In addition, I shall take up the difficult question of the periodization of varying family forms.

These choices of subject matter and perspective take us away from the mainstream of modern family history to pick up threads of thought from more than twenty years ago. In some ways the historical sociology of the family during the last two decades has made an exaggeratedly radical break with past knowledge and reduced the latter too quickly to the realm of myth. This may have been justified

David Gaunt is Lecturer in history at the University of Umeå and a research director at the Secretariat for Future Studies in Stockholm, Sweden.

when family history was fighting for recognition and needed to present itself as a major breakthrough in the study of social development. But now that family history is properly established, there is good reason to return to some of the neglected issues which troubled our predecessors.

Writing and research on the family and household in the Nordic countries started in the late nineteenth century. International interest in the subject came mostly from Germany. This meant that the scientifically precise Le Play was ignored while misty romantics, such as Wilhelm Heinrich Riehl, whose work on the family was translated into Swedish (Riehl, 1856), Ernst Grosse, author of *Die Formen der Familie* (Grosse, 1896), and the Grimm brothers were known and admired. Then, also, the German legal historians had an interest in what they called *die Sippe*, a clan-like kinship structure they believed to have been the original organization of the Teutonic tribes. They submerged themselves in the vast corpus of medieval Nordic law codes in order to uncover fragments of this cultural ruin. Works such as Karl von Amira's *Nordgermanisches Obligationenrecht* (von Amira, 1882, 1895) and Konrad von Maurer's *Die Berechnung der Verwantschaft nach altnorwegischen Rechte* (von Maurer, 1877) were widely read, and the authors became celebrated corresponding members of several Nordic scientific academies. A similar influence from France was exerted by Ludovic Beauchet and his *De propriété familiale dans l'ancien droit suédois* (Beauchet, 1900-1901).

Other influences worth mentioning came from Fustel de Coulanges, H.S. Maine, J.F. McLennan and L.H. Morgan who were searching for a common Indo-European primary group connected with agrarian communal living. This line of reasoning was attractive in Scandinavia because most scholars assumed that primi-

tive forms had survived here well into historical times. It led to studies of the laws and customs of the "primitive" and "classic" cultures in the hope of finding a general evolutionary pattern and stages parallel to medieval Nordic phenomena. Here we can name the Danish Carl Nicolai Starcke's *Die primitive Familie in ihrer Entstehung und Entwicklung* (Starcke, 1888), the Finnish sociologist-anthropologist's Edvard Westermarck's *History of Human Marriage* (Westermarck, 1891) and his colleague's Gunnar Landtman's *Kulturens ursprungsformer* (Landtman, 1918).

The role of Maxime Kovalevsky should be mentioned also. His 1887 lectures in Stockholm were published as *Tableau des origines et de l'evolution de la famille et de la propriété* by a Swedish foundation (Kovalevsky, 1890). Kovalevsky was a well-known Russian professor, a reform politician and the brother-in-law of a leading Swedish cultural figure. His book is actually very informative about households in the Caucasus mountains.

With the exception of Westermarck, these writers seldom ventured into recent historical times. Others, such as the Dane Vilhelm Grønbech in *Vor Folkeaet i Oldtiden* (Grønbech, 1909-12) and the Norwegian Emil Birkeli in *Fedrekult, fra norsk folkeliv i hedensk og kristen tid* (Birkeli, 1943), attempted to graft ancient Nordic archaeological and mythological evidence onto a general evolutionary tree-trunk through comparisons between the Nordic area and other cultures.

The dominance of this type of scholarship created an atmosphere in which it was accepted that human family forms passed through successive stages of development. This was the "state of the art" at the turn of the nineteenth century in ethnology, religious and legal history and the tiny embryonic social history.

This great interest in mythical clan society, either among ancient Teutonic tribes or in contemporary isolated mountain villages, makes these older works tedious and unconvincing. The period preceeding the Second World War left no runestones unturned, no saga unread, no legal code unthumbed, no royal decree undeciphered—all with the goal of piling up, at best, circumstantial evidence on clan-like structures. Very little attention was paid to source criticism even though the documents discussed were often highly ambiguous: Bertha Phillpotts' useful antidote, *Kindred and Clan in the Middle Ages and After: A Study in the Sociology of the Teutonic Races* (Phillpotts, 1913), appears to have had no impact.

The arrival of the new discipline of sociology allowed scholars of the family to leap easily from the middle ages to modern urban settings. Evolution could be preserved in the form of "before-after." The American sociologist William I. Thomas and his wife Dorothy had good contact with the Swedish parliamentary commissions of the 1930s establishing the ground rules for building up the welfare state. In the wake of this reception the works of W.I. Thomas and Florian Znaniecki, Robert and Helen Lynd, William F. Obgurn, Margaret Mead and others became touchstones for judging the development of the family.

However, very few dark academic clouds lack a silver lining. Sometimes even the legal-romantic-evolutionary scholars stumbled across the real thing. One well-known case is that of the Balkan *zadruga*. Similar to the *zadruga* is the much less famous *suurperhe* (a neologism coined from the Finnish words for "large" and "family") system in Carelia in the eastern parts of what is now Finland and the northwestern parts of what is now the Soviet Union.

The first to study the Finnish extended family was Väinö Voionmaa who published *Suomen karjalaisen heimon historia* in 1915. The title of the book is typical for its time and translates as "The History of the Carelian Tribe in Finland." The Carelians, like many other small peoples, were dispersed throughout several countries, and they considered themselves to be separate from but related to the Finns. Older encyclopedias will inform the reader that Carelians are "lively and happy, love pleasure, singing and telling tales, are easily influenced and less inclined to hard work than the Finns." In short, in the older literature they were described in the stereotypical manner of nineteenth-century evolutionary thought.

Voionmaa used Grosse's typology of family forms. In particular, he adopted the diffuse concept of *Grossfamilie*, which meant any household with more than two generations or with more than two married couples within the same generation. Sometimes these principles were ignored and the large family for Voionmaa was any household with more than eleven members, even though it was unclear how many married couples were living together. Voionmaa split the large family into several different household types according to kinship constellations: a father and his married sons (which could be either a stem type, or a multiple type if several married sons lived together); brother-families (which combined two or more married siblings or a stem family composed of married uncles and married nephews); and, finally, the "living team" (from the contemporary documentary term *bolag*, which today is only used to denote a business enterprise), which was a group of several married non-relatives sharing a dwelling. He was thus mixing a whole series of structures which modern family historians try to keep separate in categories such as stem, extended, and multiple family households and that strange unit, the houseful.

Voionmaa's study is important because he actually did some quantitative analysis of tax records based on hearths and farmsteads, which in some localities went back to the early sixteenth century. While complicated family household forms could be found scattered throughout all of Finland, Voionmaa came up with dramatic figures for some eastern and northern districts. For instance, he said that in 1500, in the county of Käkisalmi, 32 percent of all households were extended in one way or another; in Lappee farther west 31 percent were extended in 1558; and in the county of Häme in 1634 nearly 22 percent were extended. In the following year 37 percent of the households were extended in Jääski parish on the Isthmus of Carelia. In 1680, over a large part of southern Ostrobothnia, 22 percent of the households were extended. Since most of these regions had sizeable Carelian settlements, Voionmaa concluded that this people had a family structure that differed from the more nuclear form of the Finns proper who lived in the south-west.

A modern historian would probably play down the cultural tradition explanation and point to the differences in agricultural technology in the different areas. The predominant Carelian form of cultivation was swidden or slash-burn in sparsely populated forests. But in the densely settled southwest, agriculture was based in permanent fields. In the west, land was a limited and highly valued resource, whereas in the east land was so plentiful it had minimal value.

Swidden farming in Finland was done in several different ways. In its most basic form, it involved slashing or cutting down virgin forest, allowing it to dry, burning the wood and then sowing rye in the ashes. This procedure gave astonishing yields: about five times as much per acre compared with permanent field cultivation. A heavy plow was

not needed. But after only two or three seasons the soil became thoroughly depleted and was therefore abandoned. Swidden fields were shifted to new parts of the forest. As time went on and settlement grew denser it became common to repeat burning at shorter intervals before trees had grown fully. Eventually this led to some permanent fields near the farm house and these had the classic problem of needing continual fertilization, fallowing, and plows capable to turning the soil. The Finnish literature on swidden is vast (cf. Suomen, 1980: 202–218 and Åström, 1978).

The swidden method of land cultivation is therefore very expansive, forcing workers away from the home in search of suitable patches of forest, sometimes for great distances. A large number of people in the household enable better exploration of the forest, quicker felling of trees and better control of fires. Especially during a period of transition when some fields were being rendered permanent, it was good to have several outdoor teams: one doing plowing another doing swidden. Traditionally land was not considered property. A farm was simply a dwelling for those who lived there. No one thought of farms as something to be claimed permanently. Women usually left their household of origin at marriage, and the males remained. Daughters took a small symbolic dowry of clothing, beds and cows, but had no other claim on rights to their parents' farm. This was well-known regional practice and even the high courts of appeal recognized the custom despite the fact that it was in conflict with Swedish law which already in the medieval period had granted females inheritance rights (Hemmer, 1953).

Voionmaa's figures have not gone unchallenged. Several historians have objected to the vagueness of the category "large family" and have tried to separate

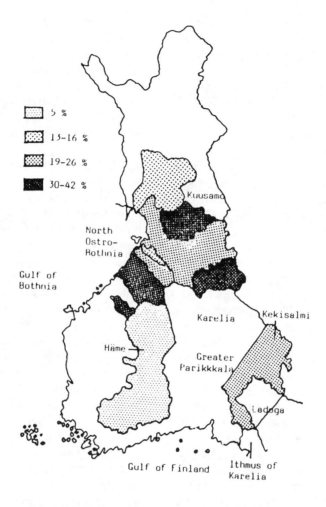

Figure 1.   Areas With Complex Households in Finland, 16th-17th Centuries.

Note: Percentages represent proportion of complex households of all households.
Source: Adapted from Tornberg (1972:10).

stem families from the extended and multiple. Pentti Virrankoski reduced the percentage for Käkisalmi in 1500 to 23 percent and Eino Jutikkala put the 1634 figure for Häme at five percent—the remainder being stem families (Virrankoski, 1973; Jutikkala, 1957). Virrankoski insisted that Voionmaa's "large family" was too inclusive and that it should be reserved for households in which "more married couples than the farm owners

and their married son or daughter live."

Despite these reductions and distinctions, places where 23 percent of all households are multiple and a further nine percent are stem family are still rather unusual in historic Europe. Additional investigations have been made and some of the results for the sixteenth and seventeenth centuries are shown on the map in Figure 1 (adapted from Tornberg, 1972:10).

The nineteenth-century situation in the large parish of Parikkala on the present Soviet border has been investigated, and since Parikkala is close to Käkisalmi it can illustrate the continuity of large household complexes over three centuries. During the 1820s there were in this parish households consisting of more than fifty persons and more than ten married couples. Of all households, those with more than 21 members made up twelve percent, although this percentage declined rapidly in following decades. After 1830 there were no households consisting of more than five married couples.

Elli Jantunen has calculated that the proportion of greatly extended households in Parikkala was 34 percent in 1820, fifteen percent in 1830, seventeen percent in 1840 and 21 percent in 1850. These figures exclude stem families. By far the most common form of extended household was that of several married brothers. During the mentioned years between 73 and 92 percent of the extended households contained married siblings. In the 1820s 23 percent of the complex households involved the coresidence of two or more non-related couples. The largest household, containing only two generations, had 47 members belonging to nine married coresident brothers (Jantunen, 1955). Virrankoski has found similar results for some parishes in Ostrobothnia in the eighteenth century. Little wonder that the first major Finnish novel, Aleksis Kivi's *Seven Brothers* (1870), deals with how seven brothers cooperated throughout their lives.

But even in Finland the Carelian extended *suurperhe* household was an extreme. If one is interested only in mean household size over large areas such as the central province of Savolax, then the sizes drop to between 4.0 and 4.6 individuals. Households with more than fifteen members account for less than four per-

cent of all. But there are things to be learned from these exotic settings about how domestic units could have been organized had western Europeans chosen other alternative ways of dwelling. Analysis of the material background of the *suurperhe* households provides perspective for the connection between the west European family pattern and specific agricultural regime.

Thirty years ago the ethnologist Gabriel Nikander described the residence problems of some very complex households in the province of Savolax. His basic sources were reports from local parish constables proposing the awarding of medals to successful agrarian improvers. This was part of a general official campaign to reward agriculture. The constables would write to the provincial governors and describe in detail the farm, the fields and buildings and equipment; calculate how great recent improvements had been; and often characterize the main families of the household. Sometimes the award proposals were accompanied by maps and drawings of the farms and dwellings. Many of the proposals described farms with large and complex households. The complex households are probably overrepresented in the reports since the large number of workers gave them an advantage in labor-intensive improvements such as draining and clearing new fields, and little wealth was removed through inheritance.

Figure 2 is a drawing from 1820 of Kotila farm in Rautasalmi parish and Figure 3 is a crude sketch of the kin relationships of the inhabitants. In the sketch in Figure 3 circles indicate males, and triangles females. Circles with a cross inside mark family members who have already inherited but who have chosen not to separate their inheritance from the communal wealth. In 1824 this household contained 42 persons (Nikander, 1953).

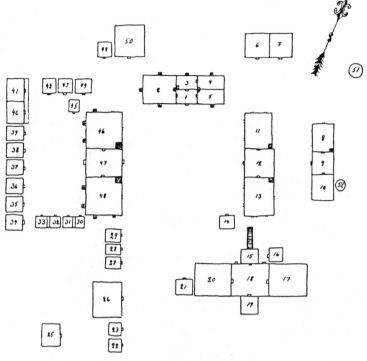

Figure 2.   Kotila Farm in Rautasalmi Parish, 1820.

Key

1-5	guest house built 1803	21	fodder store
6	larder	22	storage
7	grain store	23	storage
8	sauna	25	kiln
9	hall	26	stall
10	kitchen	27-29	sleeping sheds
11	living room	30-33	sleeping sheds
12	hall	34-40	sleeping sheds
13	living room	41	grain shed
14	kitchen for barn	42-44	sleeping sheds
15	pig-stye	45	shed
16	stall	46	living room
17	barn	47	hall
18	wagon-room	48	living room
19	pig-stye	49	bait-house
20	barn	50	kiln
		51-52	wells

Source: Nikander (1953:62).

The constable described the difficulty of managing such a household. The household, however, over the past twenty years had doubled its number of cattle and had experienced a five-fold increase in grain and hay production. The elected leader was Lars Staffansson and he had responsibility for economic decisions. But he was also aided by his uncle, Lars and his cousin's son Lars Fredrik in keeping track of money. Uncle Lars supervised the potato, hemp and flax fields; Lars Fredrik watched over the other outdoor work and fishing. Leadership of the women's work

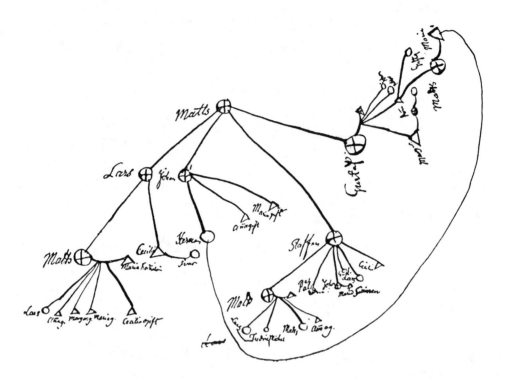

Figure 3:   The Kinship Relationships of Household Members On Kotila Farm in 1820.

Circles indicate men, and triangles women. A circle with a cross inside demarcates an heir. This sketch was drawn by the local constable and was sent with a letter to the provincial governor. Source: Nikander, 1953:64.

rotated, but the prestigious and important job of tending cows was always supervised by Maria, the widow of Lars Staffansson's brother. The constable made a special point of mentioning Maria, since she was childless and thus had no material interest in the farm to pass on to a direct heir. Ordinarily, such childless widows would return to their household of origin as elderly aunts. But Maria worked "only for the common good of the household. For which she is respected by all for her calm manners—which has made all her family so well known that they never have any unmarried daughters."

A look at the buildings in Figure 2 indicates that all 42 persons probably did not live under the same roof or behind the same lock, at least not all year long. The small sleeping sheds (numbered in the sketch from 27 to 40 and from 42 to 44) were only in use during the warmer months: they could not be heated. The only stoves or fireplaces were in the larger buildings containing rooms one through five, eleven through thirteen and 46 through 48. Perhaps the building with rooms numbered one through five was not in use since it is labeled "guest house." Probably, in the winter, this kin group of 42 persons lived in only four heated rooms. There may not have been much privacy, and the room was probably smelly and filled with smoke, but it was warm. This enforced togetherness would probably explain the eagerness to move out to the sleeping sheds in the spring. Teenagers would have sheds all for themselves. Beyond the "guest house", only the room numbered ten is called a kitchen, though presumably cooking would be done over the fireplaces in the other rooms.

All of these people living close together a large part of the year, working effectively with a strict division of labor and not claiming individual inheritance clearly deserved a medal. Such complex households were hardly the way of the future, however, but some of them could still be found in eastern and northern Finland on the eve of the Second World War. Matleena Tornberg describes one such family in an oral history she recorded (Tornberg, 1971). This household, near Kuusamo, began as a nuclear family and then gradually added a son-in-law and other extensions as the sons married but declined to start their own households. At its largest, the household contained twenty persons grouped around three married siblings and their spouses. As in the other cases mentioned above, property was held in common, and the only personal possessions were clothing and the cows a wife had brought in as dowry.

More working hands in the large households meant both higher neighborhood status and greater collective wealth. But size was also a solution to practical problems since farming was difficult and natural resources were scattered over the landscape. Bogs had to be drained for plow-land, pastures were far away in the forest, meadows were spread here and there in small patches along lakes and streams. By-employments were essential as a source of cash and even these took household members far away from the hearth. There was carting of goods across the border to Russia, the floating of timber down to the coastal sawmills, and the cutting of trees for a daily wage. The number of nights all twenty slept at home must have been very few.

The head of the household was always the oldest brother and this forced him to remain close to the homestead at all times. He did status chores such as sowing seed and guarding the money-box. Housekeeping and cooking were led by the wife who had lived the longest time in the family even if she was not married to the man who was the head. The great number of laborers allowed work to proceed quickly and enabled some persons to specialize in tasks like tar burning, fishing and logging. As was usual in this sort of arrangement, there were several buildings—one dwelling for the winter, one for the summer. During the warmer months children slept alone in the sheds.

Most of the scholarship discussed above was conceived and carried out before the start of the great international expansion in family history in the late 1960s. This expansion has had two facets. On the one hand, family dynamics have become central to social history and the analysis of societal change, but, on the other, the orientation of pure research has shifted into a narrow stream. As in so many areas of the arts and sciences, the last fifteen years have experienced a drift away from content and toward morphology. We now have a whole series of studies on the form of the domestic group, but considerably fewer than one would like that deal with the facts of life.

This trend fits into a larger pattern of international comparison, with statistics used for broad description combined with eclectic or negligent interest in theory. A few "vulgar" superficial arguments have made an almost universal impact: for example, that extended family households are a myth, that there is a definite European family pattern to be used as a touchstone for comparison, that average household size has been unchanging as far back as can be measured.

In Scandinavia, family historians made

a strategic retreat into church records to obtain quantitative description. Problems of measurement (combined with the problems of record-linkage by computer) came into the front line: how many, how big, how old and so on. A new rivalry in family history grew up: instead of trying to find the largest possible households in order to show the extremes of change over time, historians competed to find the smallest households in order to reveal the continuity of and absence of change within our basic domestic unit. Since small neo-local rural households were seen as a precondition for the rise of industry, finding small households became a way of measuring the degree to which a country participated in general European economic progress.

In Finland, this has meant a shift from the Carelian area to the westernmost islands of Åland and other areas on the Baltic coast. Often these were places with Swedish-speaking populations, living from fishing and permanent field agriculture. They were drawn early into the sphere of urban markets because of their central position on various well-established trading routes.

In contrast with the Carelian complex households, the islander families appeared to fit into a general European pattern. Here one could find masses of servants—up to seventy percent of households had them, whereas in Carelia there were none. Households had, on average in the seventeenth century, six or seven persons (excluding children under five). But still, there were complications which did not fit in: only a minority of households were simple nuclear families plus servants. Many were extended with close kin present; in some places a majority had two married couples (Moring, 1984).

Local officials supported the formation of double-family households. A court case from the first half of the seventeenth century involved two married brothers living together. They were in conflict and wished to split the homestead "because of the disagreement between them, since they are both together in one house with their wives and children." But the court commanded them to remain together until the youngest children were old enough to be sent away as servants. In the eyes of the court a partition would cause economic ruin (cited in Winberg, 1985:225).

This pattern of slightly extended households persisted into the eighteenth century (Nerdrum, 1978). However the tendency was for extension to become less frequent. In Finström parish there were in the 1760s almost seventy percent multiple and extended family households; by 1840 this proportion had declined to 35 percent. This fall had been connected with the founding of landless cottages, which had been prohibited before the middle of the eighteenth century but became very common thereafter. As yet we know very little about the background to the multiple family households of these islanders. Two lines can be investigated: either they were caused by an unwillingness of the tax officials to partition (but then why did the other brother not move?); or there was a cultural pattern in the twilight zone between nuclear family households and the massively complex households.

Looking from Finland west toward Sweden or southwest toward Denmark researchers have discovered households which are progressively less complex and increasingly smaller. In the final analysis the only variations worth noting have to do with the degree to which some households had servants and with the pressure on some families to push their children into service. There are many monographs which treat household structure as a part of a local study. But the main aims of these efforts have not been the analysis of the household, but rather to see if there was any special arrangements for subgroups within the population. Hans Christian Johansen has collected extensive data from two Danish censuses in 1787 and 1801 (Johansen, 1975). Mean household size in his nationally representative sample is 5.2 in 1787 and 5.0 in 1801. The figure varies depending on the wealth of the household: farm owners had as many as 6.6 persons in the household, day-laborers as few as 3.6. A few older kin, mostly infirm fathers or mothers, gave a small number of families an upward extension. Several studies of manorial organization touch upon the households of the married servants (Eriksson and Rogers, 1978) or variations between holders of different types of tenure (Winberg, 1975; Jonsson, 1980). However, the overall interest is in describing the dynamics of population increase and this aim has not been conducive to probing deeper into relationships within the households.

Studies of variations within the same general family form do not need to confront the problem of transition from one form to another. Differences in size and composition can be quickly connected with variations in wealth or temporary changes in economic organization. They fit well within the idea that there was one universal and normal family melody. But the history of the disappearing *suurperhe* suggests that there are types of family change which can be ascertained morphologically. Size does change over time and so do, obviously, the value systems that underlies such change. Is it possible that these changes also affected what we call the classic west European family but that these changes are hidden and cannot be seen because of the relatively stable household structures?

The most ambitious modern Scandinavian attempt to describe a stage-like development is Börje Hanssen's painstaking research on parishes in southern Sweden (Hanssen, 1952, 1976). He worked out his ideas and methods during the 1940s independently of any established scientific tradition. He followed a region in detail from the 1600s to modern times and termed his dissertation a "social anthropology."

Hanssen's approach was to uncover continuous series of historical documents on the household and follow them over three centuries by making detailed cross-tabulations at certain intervals. His ability to combine parish records, tax registers, market prices, auction sales, land transfers, probate records, insurance applications, and so on, make his studies similar to the most advanced local demographic history monographs of today. His thoughts on household transformation were presented in an article written in 1976.

Hanssen identified three separate stages in household development since 1500. The first, lasting until about 1750, he called "feudal". During this stage, he argued, family and kin relations were unimportant in organizing everyday household life. Domestic units were complex and many totally unrelated married couples dwelt on the same farm and pooled their economic resources. These combinations were in Sweden and Denmark not as complex as in Carelia—but were similar in type to Voionmaa's "living team" built around two unrelated nuclear families. In Hanssen's area the families did not live in the same room but had separate compartments within a connected building. Barns and stables were used in common, and the families shared the kitchen and the bread oven. In 1694, in the large villages of Hagestad and Löderup, 24 of 54 and 22 of 33 farm households, respectively, had two married couples. One reason was practical: the adults cooperated in work and in paying the taxes which were heavier on real estate than on individuals. Often it was impossible for one family to have enough draught animals to pull the heavy plows. Even so, the size of the households was small, ranging from 7.8 in the two-family households down to 3.3 in the single family households. Behind this lay a high mortality regime, punctuated by famine and wars throughout the century. This meant that very few elderly relatives and children survived, and adults were sometimes forced to move away from their place of birth.

Turnover of farmers because of illness or death was great. Between 1694 and 1702 half the farms changed hands. Widows and widowers were encouraged, at times obliged, to remarry. Remarriage seems to have been almost mandatory for tenants who leased their land (Hallan, 1961; Gaunt and Löfgren, 1981). Children left home between eight and ten years of age. Neighbors rather than kin were the most important source of help and a considerable amount of work was exchanged between households. The rapid changes in farm possession indicated that there was little feeling of personal or familial attachment to the soil or indeed even of ownership of landed property. In addition, there was no strict class differentiation into landed and landless. Just about anyone at some point in his or her life-cycle had possession of land. Owners of large estates were hard pressed to find peasants willing to take over a farm (Christiansen, 1978).

There was no reason to limit the number of births. Non-sterile wives averaged 10.2 children—but the ranks of children were reduced by disease, famine and negligence. Some infants died in strange circumstances, smothered in the parents' bed. In some places it was not normal to breastfeed and infant mortality was especially high (Guttormsson, 1983).

The "feudal" stage was followed by a period Hanssen termed "mastery" to denote a paternalistic large farming household basic form whose was similar to what we would now call a stem family.

The active farmer exercised a dominance over his own children, his wife, and his elderly parents living as inmates or separately maintained from the farm produce, plus a growing group of servants. This stage lasted from about 1750 to about 1870 and thus covered the era of agrarian revolution when grain and dairy farming became very profitable. Farm owners and large tenants became increasingly important in national, political, and business affairs. These were important changes in the peasant economy involving the growth of urban markets, increased efficiency and the subsequent increases in the value of land. By the nineteenth century a lively rural land market had evolved. This was the first time land had a market value for the farming population—could be bought and sold freely—and therefore became an attractive possession. The peasants began to think in terms of property rights and succession and the benefits of improvements within a limited kin group. The latter involved singling out a line of relatives to be given priority of access to the land. Some children, either the youngest-born males (on the island of Bornholm) or the oldest-born males were considered presumptive heirs and given privileged treatment. In Norway property transfers went from father to son in 51.7 percent of cases before 1700, but after 1800 the proportion was 74.9 percent (Helland-Hansen, 1964:193). A major consequence of this lineage reorientation was that remarriage of widows and widowers was discouraged. If the son took over remarriage was unnecessary and, in any case, remarriage in a bilateral kinship system made for messy heirship strategies.

The number of servants increased and supply often exceeded demand. Functionally, servants were household members with no claim of inheritance. There could have been affectionate feelings between the owners and the servants—little was done to separate them by eating or sleeping arrangements—but they were effectively excluded from property. Class differences sprang up between those who possessed land and those who probably never would get access to it. Often several younger children were given only a symbolic inheritance and were forced into the ranks of day laborers. This downward mobility of farmers' children has been well studied in the early nineteenth century (Martinius, 1977; Winberg, 1981). Even if the younger siblings did inherit a little land they often sold it quickly and thus had no attachments to keep them from drifting into the proletariat. Considerable conflict developed between privileged and non-privileged siblings. Even youth peer groups split into those who were certain to inherit and those who might not (Gaunt, 1983b:29).

The size of households in Hanssen's district increased to between 7.7 and 8.4 persons, even though the number of two-family households declined rapidly. Behind this development lie the facts that children stayed longer in the household and that the many non-kin inmates and older people living on the farms were replaced by the parents of the possessor. It became very common to have parents or in-laws within large farm households. Labor became gradually divided among the active adults. The farmers' wives did only light indoor work while maids and daughters did rough work in the barns and fields. By the second half of the nineteenth century visible distinctions appeared here and there between "family" and servants. Separate sleeping quarters for servants were built, at times even a separate dinner table with different food. The family might even have their own "privy" while the servants were obliged to use the traditional manure pile. A farmer might begin to call himself "patron" and do very little manual labor.

Neigborliness decreased as social life became a matter of taking Sunday rides to visit kin in nearby parishes or of trips into villages to participate in voluntary organizations. This kind of family life can be well studied in peasant diaries of the time. One such diary is that of a young farmer's daughter—Helene Dideriksen—from the Danish island Møn. It reveals a progressive narrowing of friendliness even within the kin group as class barriers became increasingly obvious. The kin of the father who were rather poor had frequent contact with Helene's household, but not the relatives of the mother who were large farm owners. Helene, a young girl of fifteen, was perhaps more sensitive to these slights than the adults. She wrote, after having witnessed the confirmation of two of her cousins:

> The two girls Kirstine Pedersen and Eline Marie Olsen are both my cousins. The one is poor or almost that and a daughter to a craftsman. The other a proud, haughty and rich farmer's daughter. Her father is not as rich as mine, but she does not think much of me. She was dressed in an expensive, but actually not pretty, gray-brown dress fringed with a fashionable brocade collar and with a broad green silk apron fastened with a gold broach. Her clothes were very costly, but not at all pretty. Kirstine looked much more pretty and elegant in her simple black dress with a pale red silk ribbon on its white collar. (Dideriksen, 1984, entry for 1875; Balle-Petersen, 1980:114).

Hanssen's stage of "mastery" thus treats both the initial building-up of family ties and then the steady erosion of ties with non-kin and groups of relatives. This is a process which fits well into a vision of the emancipation of the individual or the privatization of the family in the late nineteenth century. "Mastery" was followed by the rural nuclear household prevalent today, which began to appear at the end of the previous century. Rapidly, servants began to disappear from the household;

first the men, then the women. Many farms started to specialize either in dairy, grain or meat production and acquired the machines or equipment necessary to run the enterprise with just the family's labor force alone.

Higher wages and better work conditions in industry meant that landless men had an alternative to remaining in the rural areas. The farmer, despite integration into the national cash economy, had no chance of matching industrial or commercial wages. In the end this was not possible even for females. Pooling neighborhood resources was difficult since no one had the time to spare and most machines had to be in use simultaneously. The impossibility of borrowing and cooperating of course increased barriers between neighbors. The household became smaller. Systematic contraception kept the number of heirs low. Old farmers sold their property and created a pension fund out of the purchase price. Often they moved into nearby railway centers where they had better, although more expensive, service.

Hanssen's developmental thesis is stimulating since it gives an approximate chronology to the various forms of the household found in Scandinavian environments. At first, demography, especially the high mortality rates, was the crucial factor. In the next stages the commercialization and then industrialization of agriculture were the major formative influences. It is relatively easy to fit the findings of other researchers into Hanssen's scheme, especially if one takes his dates as proximate. Quite possibly 1750 is a trifle too late as the start of the "mastery" stage. And it may also be true that we are dealing not with well-defined stages but with a slow drift which appear as "stages" only if one does cross-sectional analysis of the continuous flow of data.

Most ethnographic and historical re-

search has dealt with the period of "mastery" and the modern period. Very little household analysis has been done on the period before 1750. Therefore Hanssen's surmise that before 1750 property succession and kinship inheritance was unimportant remains to be fully tested. This will certainly prove to be a tricky matter as it involves an *argumentum ex silencio*. Certainly his statements must be qualified since court records are filled with quarrels over property.

One can complement Hanssen's findings by studying other districts to see how varying forms of household economy influenced the structure of inheritance and household formation (Gaunt, 1977a). Parishes in central Sweden often had totally different economies even though they were quite near to each other, had close contact, and belonged to the same larger administrative unit. I have studied one parish where farmers also owned shares in nearby iron mines and operated small-scale smelting works producing pig iron. Not far away was a parish where farmers had the off-season by-employment of carting the pig iron from the north to the ports in the south and bringing back additional grain for the miners. Along the coast were small manor-dominated parishes where tenants produced a surplus of grain to be sent northwards.

People in this area can be followed throughout their lives between the years 1580 and 1700 in unusual church records (burial books) which contain short biographies. Household structures in this period varied locally depending on the volume of work to be done in each primary unit and according to how agrarian by-employments coincided with the growing season. The largest households—which were not very large—were those of the miner-farmers, having a mean household size of over seven. The households of farmers who combined transport with grain-growing had on average between five and six persons. Both of these groups had great need of labor throughout the year. Mining, charcoal burning and smelting took place in the winter and spring. Transport on sleds was done while the earth and lakes were frozen, making hauling easier. But households which depended on grain production only—as was the case for manorial tenants—had very small size, averaging fewer than five persons. In these there was very little to do during the off-seasons and estate owners discouraged by-employments.

One can find stem families throughout the whole area. But the greatest concentration was in the places where by-employments were essential and where the farmers owned their land. Of all people dying over the age of sixty about 75 percent lived with either married or unmarried children at the moment of death. In manorial parishes this figure was much lower, varying between a third and forty percent. Behind this lower proportion lies the fact that even here manorial peasants seemed to have few ties to the soil. Usually over a fifth were born in places more than fifty kilometers away, and in one parish nearly half had moved that distance. Only a tiny minority farmed the same land on which they had been born. By contrast, very few people had moved into or out of parishes where by-employments flourished and where farmers owned their land.

Most likely we must include a discussion of ownership in any chronology of family dynamics. The high mobility of manorial tenants fits well into Hanssen's picture of the "feudal" stage. But tenants did not form double family households of non-kin as in other parts of Scandinavia. On the other hand, there were many solitaries and inmates among the tenants, as well as elderly couples living by themselves. Perhaps it is too soon to draw the conclusion that inheritance did not matter before the commercialization of agriculture.

Inheritance did play a role, but the whole concept in reference to the period before the eighteenth century needs clarification. What we mean by "inheritance" today is a particular type of wealth transfer between generations. The assumption is that each transfer is a one-time unrevocable transaction. Grandfather gives to father; father gives to son. In order for this to be socially acceptable all concerned must recognize that first the grandfather, and then the father are the sole and individual owners of what is being transferred. Before the seventeenth century, however, the ideology of landownership gave the descendents of previous possessors a claim—a so-called birth-right—on the disposal of land. Sometimes they could revoke sales and even dictate the inheritance settlements of families who had taken over the property later. Possession was therefore insecure and the current possessors had little defense against such claims even when they had bought the land (Winberg, 1985).

Most Nordic governments in the past preferred dividing inheritance equally among males. Women were not excluded but received a share half the size of their brothers'. At times women were not permitted to receive landed property. At any rate, the administration of the woman's share was turned over to her husband. Governments liked partitioning since it was believed that the siblings would all improve their shares and create in due course a larger base of wealth to tax. At the same time, governments discouraged turning over the main part of the farm to one kinsman while setting up smaller cottages and landless houses for other descendants. This was thought to decrease the tax base. At times laws were passed which prohibited farmers from keeping all their adult children at home. This meant that the siblings had to receive a proportion of the inheritance early in life and move on. Since such portions were difficult to calculate equitably, most received only a token payment such as a cow, a promise of help at marriage, or some cash. All of this was further confused by uncertainty about the actual value of the farmland.

Transfer of wealth within families became a problem by the latter half of the eighteenth century. As long as high mortality kept the number of heirs low, there was hardly a land market. Access to property was not a real problem. The stem family of a modified sort, with elderly parents being close by but in a separate lodgings, solved some problems. The stem family was at its height from 1700 to 1850. But then population increased and good land grew increasingly scarce, yet equality remained the official inheritance principle. In the nineteenth century this principle was strengthened when the sexes were set on par with each other. If one saw the farm as an economic entity—and this was the way farmers saw it—one needed to find a way of avoiding division of the collective wealth. In some areas, such as Gotland contraception was already used in this period (Gaunt, 1973). Other areas opted for complete division but forced most of the heirs to leave all land in the care of one of them. And still others found a way to get around the law by turning over the farm to an heir within the lifetime of the owner or tenant. Inheritance in a legal sense was avoided.

Although the authorities were well aware of these arrangements among the peasants, they never sought to regulate them. I have elsewhere described the custom by which a farmer either through an outright gift or through a fictive sale transferred his farm to one designated heir (Gaunt, 1983a). The heir then assumed control of the farm and bound himself to deliver to the father annually a specified quantity of food, clothing, firewood, alcohol, and money. The elderly might remain in their childrens' households but ordinarily they lived in a separate specially prepared cabin on the farm. The generations might eat together, but it was more common for them to eat separately.

The confusion about property possession marking the period before 1700 gradually disappeared. And transfers of wealth between generations became clearcut negotiations between sovereign individuals. All other familial or collective claims were disregarded. When ownership was simplified so was property disposal. But clarity on this level brought the psychological stress in generational conflicts out into the open. The parent-child dyad became a cauldron of social conflict. Two examples can illustrate its extent.

Recently there was published a manuscript autobiography of a Danish peasant born in 1776 (Schousboe, 1983). Søren Pedersen describes in detail the transfer of his parents' leasehold in Zealand in 1811. The parents had both become elderly and infirm. The farm was declining rapidly. Søren was in the army when his parents, in 1808, first mentioned their intention to retire and let him take over. He was 32 and unmarried. The parents had previously resisted his arguments and had also refused an offer from the estate owner to convert their lifetime lease, for a fee, into heritable tenancy.

Once the parents were convinced, Søren had to persuade the army—he was otherwise bound to military service until the age of 45. He needed to negotiate with the estate for the terms of his lease and entrance fee. The army proved to be the easiest. But the estate insisted that the tenancy was not heritable and that Søren must pay a high entrance fee. The estate manager hinted that the farm could possibly be made heritable, but not until after two or three years of Søren's management, and maybe not even then.

At the same time, Søren wrote up a contract guaranteeing his parents two barrels of rye, two barrels of barley, one barrel of malt, the upkeep of a cow, two sheep, a goose plus meat, flax, free lodging and fuel. He promised his brother 100 dalers in cash, a cow, and bed-clothing. All of these land transfers and contracts involved registration and legal fees. The estate increased pressure by increasing the amount of the yearly lease by 100 dalers over what the parents had paid and by repossessing some important farm equipment. The assumption of the tenancy thus involved considerable economic burden as well as the additional psychic disturbance of an agreement among so many parties. Further, there was only one real solution to Søren's economic problems and it involved even more stress. According to family and friends, the only way for Søren to get out of his difficulties was to find a rich girl with a sizeable dowry and marry her.

It might be imagined that transfer for farmers who owned their own land was less complicated than for manorial tenants. But the pressure appears to have been just as great. In 1871 an American tourist, Paul Du Chaillu, was passing through the way-station of Husum in central Norway. He participated in the wake and burial of the old farmer Halvor's wife. On one of the following days he observed the subsequent mealtime ceremony.

> All the family came in and sat down. The father as usual at the head of the table. I knew that people are usually silent during meals, but I sensed the serious faces of all those present. Suddenly Roar who had not taken his place stepped up to his father and said, 'Father, you are old. Let me take your place.' 'No, my son', answered the farmer, 'I am not too old to work, it is not yet time. Have patience.' Roar insisted, 'Father it hurts me and all your other children to see how tired you are when the day's work is done. Responsibility for the farm is too much for you. It is time to rest and do nothing. Allow yourself a little peace in your old age. Let me take your place at the head of the table.' Now everyone was completely serious. There were tears in many eyes. 'Not yet, my son.' 'Yes, father.' Then the whole family said, 'Now is the time—let your rest begin.' The proud old farmer who had led the household so long, felt it hard to comply. But he rose and Roar took his place and assumed leadership. His father had thus stepped down and no longer needed to work. He would live in a comfortable cabin and yearly received a determined amount of grain or flour plus potatoes, cheese, milk, butter and meat. (cited in Gaunt, 1983b:144)

This is one of the very few observations we have of Nordic peasants relinquishing the authority of the household. Probably the visitor did not disturb the process, since the farm was a way-station and used to the constant presence of strangers.

It is possible to imagine what lay behind this scene. This ritual was only the last phase of a long and drawn out process of authority transfer. Roar had married eleven years before. At that time Halvor, the father, had given him half the farm, promising the rest later if he behaved well. But Halvor was then only 42 and had no intent of retiring. Six years later, in 1866, Halvor transferred the title of the whole farm to Roar and registered a written contract concerning his and his wife's maintenance. But this contract did not go into effect because Halvor remained the head of the family. Legally , of course, Roar was the owner. But he only got authority when his mother died and a new mistress of the household was needed.

Obviously, within the family legal formalities had little to do with the everyday running of the household. Transfer of ownership without ensuing transfer of authority was a tradition on this and other Norwegian farms. In 1808 Halvor's father and grandfather had concluded a written agreement to turn over the ownership to the younger man. But an important clause read: "Nevertheless, this farm shall not be delivered to my son until I myself find it suitable to let him have it." And the son bound himself not to put pressure on the father (Helland-Hansen, 1964:185–187).

These two stories are extreme examples of how many generational transfers took place, and they supply the complicated background to straightforward official documents. Hans Christian Johansen has attempted to compare the number of extended family households enumerated in the oldest Danish censuses with a demographic calculation of how many such households could have been formed. He found that extended households were far from the rule. "Only about half of the people who were sixty years or more and who had married children lived in the same household as the children" (Johansen, 1978:129). He points out the social norm that required old people to set up their own household—geriatric neolocality—once children had taken over.

The period when pensioners' households became privatized appears to have been the end of the seventeenth century. During the middle ages Norwegian documents hardly ever speak of a separate room or cabin. Instead there are phrases such as "getting care," "taking in," "care," "going the rounds," "food and clothing." These expressions are supplemented in the fifteenth and sixteenth centuries by "going in others' bread," "giving oneself in," "becoming among." One of the most common terms was *framføsel*, a word which today means only the foddering of cattle through the winter. The phrases indicate that the initiative lay with the elderly and that they remained in or entered into an existing social network. Separation is not emphasized.

But by the seventeenth century a new set of terms came into use, stressing separateness: "give up," "give over," "life price," "renounce," "take up," "set up," "life bread." There is a slight shift in meaning from "going in my son's bread" and "getting my life-bread" or "getting set up." The latter things one had earned individually during the active period of one's life (Helland-Hansen, 1958:173–177).

Detailed written contracts became common in the late seventeenth and early eighteenth centuries. Before that time documents contained imprecise statements of the intention to turn over property and the promise to care for the elderly. Simultaneously, there was a shift from the earlier period's transfers evenly distributed between close kin, distant kin and strangers, to a concentration on the parent-child connection in the seventeenth and eighteenth centuries. In the period before 1600 only 33.7 percent of the transfers with retirement documents involved parents and children, but in the 1700s, 66.1 percent involved them (Helland-Hansen, 1964:192).

In fifty manors in Denmark during the eighteenth century 63 percent of the voluntary transfers of land occurred between parents and children. About a third of all transfers of leases involved retirement contracts. But these figures were true of only a certain type of tenant. If tenants were poor and infirm and the holding probably run down, transfers to children occured only 25 percent of the time. Also, if the holding was very wealthy the transfer tended to be made to strangers (Skrubbeltrang, 1961: 242–45). Not all contracts were registered with the estate because they were private agreements among tenants. The estate did not consider retirement payments when setting leases. Probably the majority of agreements were oral (Pedersen, 1984:51, 54).

During the nineteenth century payments delivered to elderly retired farmers tended to increase in size (Kiviahlo, 1927; Koskikallio, 1927; Högnäs, 1938). Receiving a farm thus became a real economic burden as the number of mouths to feed grew in time. There were the elderly with their clearly stated demands. The family had its own small children, which could mean that the wife could not work at farming all the time. This situation could only be ameliorated when the children were old enough to support themselves or if the retirement maintenance was reduced. And this happened only when the elderly parents died.

One unfortunate side to retirement was that the care of the old parents when they were ill was also the responsibility of the young farmer and his wife. Yet they had an interest in having the old people live a short life. Care may or may not have been good. But there was always a suspicion that it was not. Rural court records are full of complaints about deliverance of bad food, wet firewood and constant quarreling. Some cases of outright violence had been recorded (Gaunt, 1977b). A folklore revolving around the alleged cruelty to elderly parents grew up either in the form of rough jokes about arsenic being "retirement-medicine" or symbolic tales of "family-mallets" used by relatives to kill the elderly with ceremony (Gaunt, 1983a).

This literature survey serves several purposes beyond presenting some curious ethnography of Nordic family life in the past. It points to aspects of family life in the seventeenth and eighteenth century which suggest significant changes. Such changes might have taken place as well in other parts of Europe but they would be hidden behind statistics showing morphological continuity. Especially worth exploring is the growth of privacy in generational relations, partiularly in lodging and eating ; the emergence of the father-son

dyad as the prefered method of land transfer; the separation of landownership from household authority; and the use of the courts to solve family problems. It may be that these early modern centuries witnessed changes in family life that were connected with the better-known transformations of world-views of the period. The changes in family life may have been as dramatic as those that took place during industrialization some hundred years later.

REFERENCES

von Amira, Karl. 1882. *Nordgermanisches Obligationsrecht. 1. Altschwedisches Obligationsrecht.* Leipzig: Veit

————. *Nordgermanisches Obligationsrecht. 2. Westnordisches Obligationsrecht.* Leipzig: Veit.

Åström, Sven-Erik. 1978. *Natur och byte. Ekologiska synpunkter på Finlands ekonomiska historia.* Ekenäs: Söderström.

Balle-Petersen, Poul. 1980. "Gården, slaegten og naboerne: sociale relationer i et lokalsamfund i Danmark o. 1880." *Folk og Kultur.* Pp. 106–150.

Beauchet, Ludovic. 1900-1902. "De propriété familiale dans l'ancien droit suédois." *Nouvelle revue historique de droit francais et étranger* Dec. 1900-Jan. 1901.

Birkeli, Emil. 1943. *Fedrekult, fra norsk folkeliv i hedensk og kristen tid.* Oslo: Dreyer.

Christiansen, Palle Ove. 1978. "The Household in the Local Setting." Pp. 50-60 in Sune Åkerman et al. (eds.), *Chance and Change.* Odense: Odense University Press.

Dideriksen, Helene. 1984. *Dagbog og breve 1875-1891.* Edited by Bodil K. Hansen. Odense: Landbohistorisk Selskab.

Eriksson, Ingrid and John Rogers. 1978. *Rural Labor and Population Change. Social and Demographic Developments in East-central Sweden during the Nineteenth Century.* Uppsala: Almqvist and Wiksell.

Gaunt, David. 1973. "Family Planning and the Pre-industrial Society: Some Swedish Evidence." Pp. 28-59 in Kurt Ågren, et al. (eds.), *Aristocrats, Farmers, Proletarians: Essays in Swedish Demographic History.* Uppsala: Almqvist and Wiksell.

————. 1977a. "Pre-industrial Economy and

Population Structure." *Journal of Scandina-vian History* 23: 183–210.

————. 1977b. "I slottets skugga. Om frälse-bönders sociala problem i Borgeby och Löddek-oppinge under 1700-talet." *Ale.* Pp. 15–30.

————. 1983a. "The Property and Kin Relations of Retired Farmers." Pp. 249–280 in Richard Wall et al. (eds.), *Family Forms in Historic Europe.* Cambridge: Cambridge University Press.

————. 1983b. *Familjeliv i Norden.* Stockholm: Gidlund.

Gaunt, David and Orvar Löfgren. 1981. "Remarriage in the Nordic Countries: The Cultural and Economic Background." Pp. 49–59 in Jacques Dupaquier et al. (eds.), *Marriage and Remarriage in Populations of the Past.* London: Edward Arnold.

Grønbech, Vilhelm. 1909-12. *Vor Folkeaet i Old-tiden.* 4 volumes. Copenhagen: Pio.

Grosse, Ernst. 1896. *Die Formen der Familie und die Formen der Wirtschaft.* Freiburg: J.C.B. Mohr.

Guttormsson, Loftur. 1983. *Bernska, ungdómµr og uppeldi á einveldisöld.* Reykjavik: Sagnfraedis-tofnun Háskóla Islands.

Hallan, Nils. 1961. "Ordet sytning." *Heimen* 12:111–122.

Hanssen, Börje. 1952. *Österlen. En studie över social-antropologiska sammanhang under 1600-och 1700-talen i sydöstra Skåne.* New edition 1977. Stockholm: Gidlund.

————. 1976. "Hushållens sammansåttning i österlenska byar under 300 år." *Rig* 59:33–60.

Helland-Hansen, Kjeld. 1958. "Follog, føderåd, kår." *Heimen* 11:173–177.

————. 1964. "Kårskipnaden." *Heimen* 13: 182–195.

Hemmer, Ragnar. 1953. "Kungl.Maj:ts brev till Åbo hovrätt den 6 mars 1690 angående de finska allmogedöttrarnas arsvraått." *Juridisk förening för Finlands tidskrift* 96:69–74.

Högnäs, Hugo. 1938. *Sytning och arvslösen i den folkliga sedvänjan uti pedersöre- och nykarleby-bygden 1810-1914.* N.p, Åbo.

Jantunen, Elli. 1955. *Parikkalan suurperhelaitos vv 1820-1850.* Unpublished thesis. Helsinki University.

Johansen, Hans Christian. 1975. *Befolkningsudvikling og familiestruktur i det 18. århundrede.* Odense: Odense University Press.

————. 1978. "The Position of the Old in the Rural Household in a Traditional Society." Pp. 122–130 in Sune Åkerman et al. (eds.), *Chance and Change* Odense: Odense University Press.

Jonsson, Ulf. 1980. *Jordmagnater, landbönder och torpare i sydöstra Södermanland 1800-1880.* Stockholm: Almqvist and Wiksell.

Jutikkala, Eino. 1957. *Väestö ja yhteiskunta.* Hämeen historia 2:1. Hämeenlinna.

Kiviahlo, K. 1927. *Maatalouskiinteistöjen omistajan-vaihdokset ja hinnanmudostus Halikon tuomio-kunnassa 1851-1910.* Taloustieteellisiä tut-kimuksia 35. Helsinki.

Koskikallio, Onni. 1927. *Maatalouskiinteistöjen eläkerasituksesta Pirkkalan ja Rouveden tumio-kunnissa vuosina 1800-1913.* Helsinki: Yliopisto väitoskirja.

Kovalevsky, Maxime. 1890. *Tableau des origines et de l'evolution de la famille et de la propriété. Skrifter utgivna av Lorénska stiftelsen 2.* Stockholm: Samson and Wallin.

Landtman, Gunnar. 1918. *Kulturens ursprungs-former.* Helsingfors: Helsingiin uusi kirjapaino.

Martinius, Sture. 1977. *Peasant Destinies. The History of 552 Swedes Born 1810-12.* Stockholm: Almqvist and Wiksell.

von Maurer, Konrad. 1877. *Die Berechntung der Verwantschaft nach altnorwegischen Rechte.* München: Sitzungsberichte der könig. bayer. Akademie der Wissenschaften. Philosophie-Philologie.c.1.

Moring, Beatrice. 1984. "Hushåll i periferin - ett bidrag till diskussionen om den europeiska fa-miljen." *Historisk tidskrift för Finland* 69:1–12.

Nerdrum, Monica. 1978. "Household Structure in Finström Parish, βland 1760-62 and 1840-42." Pp. 136–142 in Sune Åkerman et al. (eds.), *Chance and Change.* Odense:Odense University Press.

Nikander, Gabriel. 1953. "Bebyggelsetyper och storfamiljsgårdar i Savolax." *Finsk museum* 60: 41–69.

Pedersen, Karl Peder. 1984. *Vestfynske faeste-bønder.* Odense: Landbohistorisk Selskab.

Phillpotts, Bertha. 1913. *Kindred and Clan in the Middle Ages and After: A Study in the Sociology of the Teutonic Races.* Cambridge: Cambridge University Press.

Riehl, Wilhelm Heinrich. 1856. *Familjen.* Lund: Berlingska.

Schousboe, Karin ed. 1983. *En faestebondes liv. Erindringer og optegnelser af gårdfaester og sognefoged Søren Pedersen, Havrebjerg (1776-1839).* Odense: Landbohistorisk Selskab.

Skrubbeltrang, Fridlev. 1961. "Faestegården som forsørger: aftaegt og anden forsorg i det 18. århundrede." *Jyske samlinger.* New series. 5: 237–274.

Starcke, Carl Nicolai. 1888. *Die primitive Familie in ihrer Enstehung und Entwicklung.* Leipzig: Brockhaus.

Suomen. 1980. *Suomen taloushistoria 1: Agraa-rinen Suomi.* Edited by Eino Jutikkala et al. Helsinki: Tammi.

Tornberg, Matleena. 1971. *Kuusamolainen suur-perhe työ- ja elinyhteisönä.* Turku: Scripta etnologica.

————. 1972. "Storfamiljinstitutionen i Finland." *Nord-nytt.* Pp. 4–17.

Virrankoski, Pentti. 1973. *Pohjois-Pohjanmaan ja Lapin: 1600-luvulla, 3.* N.p., Oulu.

Voionmaa, Väinö. 1915. *Suomen karjalaisen heimon historia.* Helsinki: Kansanvalistuseura.

Westermarck, Edvard. 1981. *History of Human*

Marriage. London: Macmillan.

Winberg, Christer. 1975. *Folkökning och proletarisering. Kring den sociala strukturomvandlingen på Sveriges landsbygd under den agrara revolutionen.* Göteborg: Historiska Institutionen.

————. 1981. "Famili och jord i tre västgötska socknar." *Historisk tidskrift.* pp. 278–309.

————. 985. *Grenverket. Studier rörande jord, släktskapssystem och ståndsprivilegier.* Stockholm: Rättshistoriska Instituatet.

HAJNAL AND THE HOUSEHOLD IN ASIA: A COMPARATIVIST HISTORY OF THE FAMILY IN PREINDUSTRIAL JAPAN, 1600–1870

L.L. Cornell

ABSTRACT: *When Hajnal (1982) argued that different types of household formation rules determine whether fertility is adjusted to economic conditions in traditional
peasant societies, he deliberately ignored societies with stem family formation rules.
This study examines the relationship between household formation, fertility, and
family relations in such a society—eighteenth- and nineteenth-century Japan. It sum-
marizes previous work on the history of the family in Japan and discusses the role
life-cycle service played in adjusting fertility to economic conditions.*

The history of the family in Japan can be
divided into four great periods marked by
the dates 1600, 1870, and 1945. The practitioners of Japanese family history can be
similarly subdivided into four large
groups: the legal theorists who wrote the
first Civil Code; the early Japanese sociologists and ethnographers; the American anthropologists who succeeded them
after World War II; and the amorphous
group of historians, demographers and
anthropologists who are now writing the
new family history of Japan. My intent in
this article is to concentrate on the family

in traditional Japan and on what we have
learned about it in the last ten to fifteen
years. My argument will be structured
around an article by John Hajnal (1982)
in *Population and Development Review*
entitled "Two Kinds of Preindustrial
Household Formation System." This article is important because it links three
areas crucial to the study of family history: household structure, marriage, and

*L.L. Cornell, Assistant Professor of Sociology,
Cornell University, Ithaca, NY 14853, USA, is a
social anthropologist who works on demography
and family relations primarily in early modern
Japan.*

fertility. Its use enables me both to set the traditional Japanese family in a theoretical and comparative context and to suggest fruitful avenues for future research.

SOURCES OF FAMILY HISTORY IN JAPAN

The three dates which I have chosen to mark the eras of Japanese family history mark, respectively, the initiation of peace after centuries of civil war, the opening of Japan to foreign influence after two centuries of seclusion, and Japan's defeat in World War II and subsequent resurrection.

Our knowledge of the family in Japan prior to 1600 is limited by a paucity of source materials. Those which remain are primarily either literary or legal documents pertaining to the elite classes. Cornell (1980) outlined that literature up to 1976. The work of Farris (1985), which discusses population patterns from the eighth to the tenth centuries, and that of Mass (1983) on inheritance in the eleventh and twelfth centuries are both valuable additions to the literature. Murakami, Kumon, and Sato's recent book *Ie Society as a Pattern of Civilization*[1] also provides a general theory of the Japanese family which deals with this early period.

The coming of peace and the unification of Japan after 1600 meant a transformation in agricultural technology which also transformed the family system. More efficient seeds and tools meant the rise of a household economy governed by a single couple, and the decline of the large, cooperative household which was necessary to farm efficiently the local ecological niches (T.C. Smith, 1959). This ushered in an era first of rapid population growth, and then of stagnation, as more couples became able to marry and then, apparently, began deliberately limiting the size of their families.

The 1870s mark the intrusion of Western industrial technology into a burgeoning commercial economy, and the subsequent effort to catch up with the West, culturally as well as economically. One aspect of this modernization was the construction of a unified national legal system on the Napoleonic model, the most contentious part of which was the codification of family law. The system promulgated in the 1899 Civil Code imposed a family model derived from elite feudal traditions on a society which was undergoing rapid industrialization.

Japan's devastating defeat in 1945 and the efforts of its occupiers to turn it into a democratic nation forced a new constitution and civil code on the country, one which reflected contemporary American values. This date is the watershed which marks the beginning of "modern" Japan.

This study will ignore the Japanese family before 1600 and after 1870, except as later research illuminates aspects of the earlier period. I will concentrate on that Japan which was rural, had a young age structure, relatively high levels of fertility and mortality compared with today, and where the household was the locus of most economic activity. This preindustrial Japan is the kind of society from which Hajnal's conclusions are drawn and it yields the best comparisons with Europe and its environs in the seventeenth, eighteenth, and nineteenth centuries. In addition, it is the traditional Japan of myth and legend, the "golden age" against which the decadence of contemporary society is measured.

In the modern period four sets of scholars have written about the character of the Japanese family.[2] The first were those statesmen and legal scholars entrusted with the drafting of the 1899 Civil Code. Some parts of the legal system, such as the criminal and commercial codes, could be borrowed wholesale from foreign countries, but the proposed importation of European family norms caused an uproar. Revisions delayed promulgation of the Civil Code for a number of years, and its provisions remained controversial until the onset of militarization in the 1930s. From the original controversy we have the results of a nationwide field survey of family relations (Wigmore, 1969), annotations on the code itself (Gubbins, 1899), and a general treatise on the family system (Hozumi, 1940), but systematic analysis of how the Civil Code crystallized family relations is yet to come.[3]

Japan's early sociologists, ethnographers, and folklorists were the next body of scholars to discuss families. Ariga, Oikawa, and Kitano, among others, produced a large body of literature which examined the structure of *ie* (household) and *dōzoku* ("lineage") institutions in traditional village society. They engendered thereby a research tradition which continues to flourish. Yanagita Kunio, the preeminent Japanese folklorist, likewise began a research tradition in Japan which emphasizes the collecting and contrasting particulars of local custom (see Nakane, 1967:176–197 for discussion and references).

The end of World War II brought American anthropologists to Japan to apply structuralist-functionalist methods to the analysis of local rural communities. Their works, especially those which are restudies (R.J. Smith, 1978a; Dore, 1978; Beardsley et al., 1959, is the classic study in this tradition) contain excellent information about how traditional families have fared in post-traditional society.

Finally, Japanese sociologists, borrowing the conventions of American family sociology, have produced a large number of works contrasting the modern nuclear family with the traditional household. The titles of such works frequently use the contrast between *ie* (traditional family)

and *kazoku* (modern family): a single term fails to express the whole of family history. Long (1982) provides a fine review of this literature and a recent issue of the *Journal of Comparative Family Studies* (Vol. 12, No. 3, 1981) includes representative articles.

A more recent interest in demographic and family history draws on all these traditions but grows out of a separate one, namely, the work of a series of economic historians located at Keio University in Tokyo. These scholars have used the village-level religious investigation registers of the Tokugawa period to study a variety of topics, most of them demographic, but some pertaining more directly to family relations. Unfortunately, the first substantial work in this line of inquiry by the progenitor of this school Akira Hayami—*Historical-Demographic Analysis of Villages in Early Modern Japan* (1973a)—is available only in Japanese, though much of his later work is in English. Hanley and Yamamura (1977), *Economic and Demographic Change in Preindustrial Japan: 1600-1868*; T.C. Smith (1977), *Nakahara: Family Farming and Population in a Japanese Village, 1717-1830*; and Hanley and Wolf (1985) *Family and Population in East Asian History* are the major English-language works in this field (see Cornell and Hayami [1986] for a more detailed review of the literature and discussion of sources). The dramatic change in perception which these works represent can be best captured by comparing their optimistic view of eighteenth- and nineteenth-century Japan with Taeuber's (1958) pessimistic one.

In summary, the history of the family in Japan can draw on a large body of research from a variety of fields. Yet so far no one has produced a synthesis, controversial or not, on the order of Stone, (1977) *The Family, Sex, and Marriage in*

England 1500-1800, Shorter, (1975) *The Rise of the Egalitarian Family* or even Laslett (1965), *The World We Have Lost*. One reason is that scholarship, especially about the traditional period, is still in its infancy, and the scholarly literature still tends to be more demographic than anthropological. Another is that specialists on Japan have yet to make a convincing argument of why Japan's family history should be of interest to those examining the entirely different and separate history of the family in Western civilization.

HAJNAL IN ASIA: THE STEM HOUSEHOLD FORMATION SYSTEM

How can information that is both historically specific and comparative be integrated into a history of the family in Japan? My response is to turn to John Hajnal's (1982) article "Two Kinds of Preindustrial Household Formation System." In this article he explicitly links two of the major concerns of family history: household structure and demographic levels. He argues that the rules for creating households determine the rapidity with which marriages are contracted; and age at marriage is, of course, one of the principal determinants of levels of fertility in the traditional societies with which he is concerned (Bongaarts and Potter, 1983).

Hajnal postulates two fundamental sets of rules for forming households. In the one system, upon marriage the new couple joins an existing household, commonly the household in which the husband has resided since childhood. This system permits early marriage and higher fertility, since the couple sustains itself by using preexisting resources. It also inhibits adolescent economic activity. In the other system a couple establish an independent household upon marriage. This requires a conjugal fund. Amassing one

takes time, which both delays marriage and fosters adolescent labor force participation. In addition, under this system population growth is regulated by economic conditions. When times are bad couples delay marrying and reproducing; when times are good they marry earlier and thus bear children more quickly. This regulating mechanism is entirely absent in the other type of system. The former system Hajnal terms the joint household formation system and identifies it in India and China; the latter, the simple household formation system, said to be characteristic of northwestern Europe in the seventeenth and eighteenth centuries.

Hajnal substantiates his argument by showing that while households can be the same size under both systems, their composition is quite different. Joint households contain relatives, many of them married; simple households contain few relatives but many servants, mostly unmarried. In addition, Hajnal uses age at becoming household head to demonstrate that in the joint system new households are created by fission, when a man is older; in the simple system, by marriage when he is younger. The differences between these two systems have a number of implications, in addition to the link between household formation and levels of fertility. These are that adolescent employment may foster the independence of women; a marriage made by mature adults is likely to have a different character than one made by the young; and the poor and indigent can be subsumed in existing households under the one system, but may need to be provided for by public welfare under the other.

Hajnal explicitly excludes the stem family household from his discussion. How then is his work useful for understanding Japan, where the stem household system prevails?

First, Hajnal provides a general model

for household structure that escapes the limitations of Peter Laslett's conceptualization of the problem (see Netting et al., 1984, for specific criticisms). "Formation" is the crucial word here: Hajnal invites us to examine the constraints on behavior and kind of choices individuals can make. Luckily, the Japanese household has largely escaped scrutiny by means of the Laslett method. The initial forays reported in *Household and Family in Past Time* (Hayami and Uchida, 1972; Nakane, 1972; R.J. Smith, 1972) have not been followed up, though R.J. Smith (1978b) made an abortive attempt to classify the developmental cycle. Hajnal's concern with process matches the concerns of recent anthropologists, who argue, for example, that inheritance in traditional Japan is governed not by a strict rule, such as male primogeniture, but by a series of strategies such that if all could be followed choice of the eldest son would result (Kitaoji, 1971; Bachnik, 1983).

A second contribution is Hajnal's specification of household *formation* as a significant social activity. This makes it possible to elevate the concept of household formation systems to the status of a principle of social organization akin to that of lineage systems. Doing so points out that the household may be a significant analytic unit in some societies and not in others. This is a great improvement on Laslett whose classification scheme assumes that households are important everywhere. It leads us to ask "Is the household a significant unit in the domestic, politico-jural, economic, and ritual domains?" and "What are its boundaries?" It also suggests that there are societies in which the household is not a significant unit of social organization and where use of household concepts is not fruitful. West African societies (see Arnould, 1984) are an example.

This isolation of "household formation system" as a type of social organization also resolves a problem in Japanese ethnography: how is the Japanese family system to be conceptualized? The early American anthropologists and some of their Japanese counterparts identified Japan as a society characterized by a lineage system, of which a group of economically and ritually cooperating households, termed the *dōzoku*, was the prime example. For example, Matsumoto writes:

> Traditionally, the Japanese family was based on patrilineal descent, patriarchal authority, and patrilocal residence. Great emphasis was placed on the ideal of the biological perpetuation of the patrilineal lineage in order to maintain the unity and continuity of the family (1962:55).

Nagai, analyzing Ariga's work, says: "the regulation of inheritance is served by the patrilineal descent system . . . " (1953:10); and Embree states that "the family system is patrilineal in pattern but, through the customs of adoption, often matrilineal in practice" (1939:85). Finally Befu observes that "patrilineal descent in Japan is a means of continuing the corporate group called 'family' " (1962:39).

However, in explaining the evidence, this approach encountered insuperable difficulties. Befu (1962), for example, argued that Japan had a patrilineal primogenitural rule of descent but that various demographic and economic exigencies, such as lack of sons or the need for a competent successor to a family business necessitated deviation from this rule. He concluded that the needs of the household corporation took primacy over the perpetuation of the geneological relationship. He argued further that by distinguishing between social structure, which is a model, and social organization, which is actual behavior, the contradictions between the Japanese system would resolve themselves.

Brown (1966) resorted to a similar distinction in his analysis of a rural hamlet in northeastern Japan. After analyzing the constituent units of the *dōzoku* and the requirements for membership in it, he concluded that there was a difference between the phenomenal order, which is the statistical pattern of activity, and the ideational order, that is, the norms and values. He concluded that *dōzoku* were cognatic descent groups although succession within them was patrilineal. Fukutake (1967: 170), reacting to the observation that the so-called lineages were far less prevalent in some parts of the country than in others, went so far as to postulate the existence of a northeast-southwest dichotomy.

The organization of villages in the former area centered on *dōzoku* groups, while villages in the latter were characterized by neighborhood associations in which equal relationships between households obtained.

Thus the evidence argued against a lineage model of Japanese society. Nakane gave this paradigm the final blow when she pointed out, through a diagram which contrasted a *dōzoku* with a patrilineal descent group (Figure 1), that the principles of membership in each were quite different. For example, only the children of the second son were members of his patrilineal descent group, but his wife and his children's spouses all belonged to the

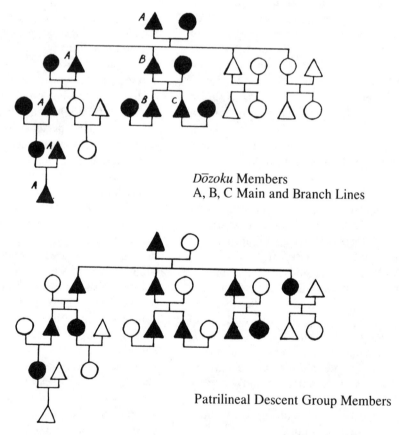

Dōzoku Members
A, B, C Main and Branch Lines

Patrilineal Descent Group Members

Figure 1.   Membership in Patrilineal Descent Groups and *Dōzoku*.

dōzoku. The structure of Japanese kinship terminology also argues against a lineal model (R.J. Smith 1962a, 1962b).

The observation that *dōzoku* were made up of households points to the household as a fundamental unit of social organization. Indeed, its boundaries are quite clear in all the domains of social organization: domestic, economic, politico-jural and ritual. The polysemic character of the concept of household (*ie*) is indicated by the definition given in the standard dictionary of current Japanese, the *Kojien* (2nd. rev. ed, author's translation, examples omitted):

ie
1. A building used for residence. A house.
   i. (Usually for a single family) A structure in which people reside.
   ii. Especially, one's own house. One's home.
2. An aggregate of people like those who live in the same house.
   i. A domestic group. . . .
   ii. A group made up of the whole family. Especially in Meiji civil law, the polity composed of the household head and family members who fall under the household head's jurisdiction.
   iii. (Implying "the mistress of the house") wife. Housewife . . .
3. The house passed down from generation to generation, also, an object which can be likened to it.
   i. A kinship group descended from the ancestors.
   ii. A family or professional name passed down from the ancestors. Good reputation, family occupation, or a school of art, martial arts, etc. . . .
4. The household's state of affairs.
   i. family property . . .
   ii. a distinguished family. Pedigree . . .
   iii. the main line of a family.
5. (In contrast to a priest) a layman. The worldly life . . .
6. A case for storing various small objects. In tea ceremony, a container for tea-serving equipment such as the tea canister, etc.

The household is an architectural unit with certain distinctive features. It is the dwelling place of a family: the word itself derives from that for "hearth" (Nakane, 1967:2). The building itself may also have a name attached to it, and its residents may be referred to by that name.

In the Tokugawa period the peasant household was an economic entity, the unit of the production and consumption. It owned or had usufruct rights to paddy field, dry land, and forest, and these rights were attached to the household as a whole rather than to any individual member. The household provided the labor force for cultivating these properties, and members jointly consumed their products.

In the politico-jural domain, a person has no legal or social status except as a member of a household (Embree, 1939: 79; Beardsley et al., 1959:216–217). One can be a member of only one household at a time (Brown, 1966: 1140). The household was also the smallest unit in the political system, any member of it being qualified to represent its interests in village affairs. The sizes of villages were often stated in terms of the number of households, rather than the number of persons they contained.

The *ie* is also a unit of reproduction, both physical and social. A person obtains civil status at birth only by being registered as a member of a household. Marriage is a transaction between households, rather than between individuals.

Finally, the household is the preeminent unit in the ritual domain. At death an individual is memorialized by a tablet at the household altar, and he or she is eventually subsumed to the ancestors of the household as a whole. However, one worships not all of one's genealogically related predecessors, but (1) only those who were resident in one's household at death and (2) all those who were permanent household members, whether biologically related or not (R.J. Smith, 1974). Hence, the boundaries of the economic unit, the politico-jural unit, the domestic group, and the ritual unit are all coextensive with the boundaries of the household.

The identification of the household as a fundamental unit returns it to the preeminence it was accorded by the Meiji legal scholars and is the conceptual path followed by recent ethnographers (Bachnik, 1983; Kitaoji, 1971). It follows that the entity that the population registers recorded was a real entity with important social meanings, and not a construct of the compiler's imagination. Thus the record of an anomalous household, such as one consisting of only a two-year-old boy, may not be a slip of the brush at all, but the record of an entity which had politico-jural viability in the form of a "vote" in the village polity, if not economic viability as well. Identifying the household as a significant unit of social organization thus aids in the interpretation of the population registers.

But this still leaves the problem of linking the structure of Japanese society with societies elsewhere. Nakane abjured this problem, arguing that Japan was unique and its social structure incongruent with that of societies elsewhere (1967:176ff.). Japanese analysts have frequently adopted this approach. However, when one identifies the household as the fundamental unit of social organization and postulates a class of societies where households, rather than lineages, form the skeleton of social relationships, Japan looks much like a number of other societies. Principal among them are the Iban of Borneo (Freeman, 1970), and especially the stem family household systems of continental Western Europe, of which Douglass's work on the Spanish Basques provides the best contemporary example (1971, 1975). Concentrating on the household in traditional Japan both resolves a number of

ethnographic anomalies and makes Japan's principles of social organization comparable to those of societies elsewhere.

Yet Hajnal explicitly rejects examining the stem family class of household formation principles (1982:486, n. 8). How is the stem household to be conceptualized? What are its consequences? Let me begin by reviewing the principles of the simple and joint household formation systems.

Household Formation Rules in Simple and Joint Household Societies

The fundamental rule for household systems is captured by the question "How many couples in how many generations are allowed to comprise a household?" The rule for simple household formation systems is that a household contains only one married couple; under a joint household formation system a household may contain more than one married couple. This element of structure implies rules for obtaining household members and for getting rid of them. These rules apply, in the first instance, to the children produced by a married couple. Under the simple system the rule is "all children leave"; under the joint one "all children stay." The latter rule is modified when brothers and sisters are prohibited from marrying each other. Then the rule becomes "all siblings of one sex remain; all of the others leave to become spouses in other households "; most commonly it is the brothers who remain while the sisters go as wives to other households. The households of preindustrial England provide a good example of the former system; the *zadruga* of traditional Yugoslavia of the latter.

What differences would we expect to find if these two systems operated perfectly in reality? We can predict a number of them. First, we would expect differences in an individual's life course, especially in the "convoy" (Plath, 1980) of persons who share household membership with him or her throughout the course. In the joint system a child would share the household with cousins, aunts and uncles; in adulthood with brothers, sisters, nephews and nieces; and in old age with members of younger generations. In a simple household system one has only parents, servants, or children. Social psychologists have not yet documented the individual and social consequence of sharing a household with many, rather than few, but such intimacy has long been the aim of utopian thought in the Western intellectual tradition.

The relative position of men and women is likely to differ under the two systems. Where members of one sex stay permanently in the household while members of the other move at marriage as in the joint system, the former, usually males, will have considerable advantages over the latter. The male will have a long-standing relationship with the other members of the household and the local community, and will be familiar with its political workings and financial resources. The female will enter a household as an outsider and an unknown, who must prove herself in order to gain access to resources. It is not surprising that in such societies women are often considerably disadvantaged. In simple-household societies the partners at least enter marriage with a similar lack of experience.

Conflict is also likely to occur in different junctures and to be perceived differently in the two types of societies. Societies based on the joint household formation system are often buttressed by an ideology that holds that brothers live together harmoniously throughout their lives. Once a man has his own family, however, its interests are likely to conflict with those of his brothers' families. The household is likely to break apart, particularly after the death of their father, the kingpin who held the group together. This kind of fission is always unexpected, and frequently leads to conflict, often bitter and intractable. The sisters-in-law are often identified as the source of trouble. In the simple household formation system, by contrast, departures are regular events as children attain adulthood. Hence they are not a major source of conflict: it is the husband and wife who are more likely to have incompatible interests.

Adulthood and old age also differ in the two systems. In the joint system a person does not become master or mistress of a household until the older generation has died and fission has occurred, an event which may not happen until he or she is well into middle age. This subservience of adults to their elders gives the system a strong patriarchal flavor. This contrasts with the simple system where individuals gain control of a household—their own newly established household—when they marry. Independence comes early. On the other hand, the master or mistress of a household under a joint household formation system remains in that powerful position until death, and extracts support from the junior members of the household. In a simple system, one's children are born, grow up, and depart, leaving one in old age dependent on the resources amassed throughout one's lifetime. This accounts for the early development of welfare schemes to protect the indigent elderly in simple system societies, and their absence elsewhere. Widows and orphans received similar support in early modern England; in other societies they were expected to be embedded in households. Those who by virtue of their junior position had not yet created strong bonds, such as young widows in China, suffered abandonment.

Where one expects to receive old age support from one's children, it makes sense to have as many children as possible.

The prolific man is revered, the barren wife scorned. In the opposite case no children are, in theory, necessary. Prolificacy goes unrewarded; women need not marry, and some may never do so, finding other sources of support instead.

One further aspect of these theoretical systems is discussed by Hajnal: the relationships between age at marriage, household formation, and economic conditions. In the Asian societies characterized by joint household systems he describes— India and China—marriage means the transfer of young adults between existing households. Provision of a conjugal fund sufficient to support an independent household is unnecessary, and the newly married couple depends on the resources of the household in which it resides. Since accumulating a fund is unnecessary, marriage can occur early, and few remain unmarried. Marriage also tends to be under the control of older members of the household, who work to minimize the difficulties of incorporating an unfamiliar person into an already functioning enterprise.

In northwestern Europe, characterized by the simple household formation system, marriage means creating a new household. This requires a fund, much of which the couple amasses independently, often by working as agricultural servants in adolescence. Because such efforts take time, marriage is delayed; with the gradual attrition of the marriage market, and the experience of self-support, some persons never marry. The new couple is alone in a new household; parents play a role in the marriage only in proportion to the share of the conjugal fund they have provided.

In the latter kind of society, fertility is directly linked to economic conditions. When times are good, more people marry, and marry earlier, thus producing more children; when times are bad, a larger proportion never marry at all, and fewer children are born. In the former kind of society, fertility is only tenuously connected to economic conditions. The economic rationality inherent in the simple household formation system clearly has broad consequences for the desire to adopt methods of family limitation, and for other aspects of what is called modernization or development. Indeed, some would argue that modern economic theory seems to be based almost entirely on the behavior patterns arising in societies whose basis is the simple household.

Household Formation Rules in Stem Household Societies

How are households created under the stem family rule? The rule of household formation under this system is that a household can contain any number of married couples, but it can have only one in each generation. Among siblings, the rule of affiliation is more complicated than either "all stay" or "all leave." It is that one stays and brings his or her spouse into the household, and all the others leave for other households elsewhere. One must consider both sides of this latter rule. Analysis which asks only "Who stays?" is flawed because it ignores the range of choices which the system presents.

What are the consequences of this system? Following the outline above, we would expect to find that one's "convoy" in the life course is wider than that in the nuclear system, but narrower than what is found under the joint principle. As a child, one may grow up with grandparents as well as with parents and siblings; adulthood finds one with spouse, perhaps parents, and own children, and old age with two generations of descendants. The crucial transition point occurs at marriage, when one either bids goodbye to one's siblings or leaves for a different household oneself.

The power of men and women within the household is also affected by this system. We expect to find that it is the spouse remaining in his or her household of birth who has greater access to resources, and the in-marrying one who is disadvantaged. It is not necessarily either the female or the male who suffers. This is because parents recruit the child who stays from their existing children. When they have only daughters it will be a husband who enters the household to marry a daughter, rather than vice versa. Hence women are severely disadvantaged only when a local rule strictly mandates that it is a son who must remain.

Conflict is also handled in a different way. As in the simple household formation system, fission is a regularly expected event. When the child who is to remain is designated, conflicts over access to household resources are muted. Those whose interests are most likely to conflict are the in-marrying members of different generations, namely, the mother-in-law and the daughter-in-law.

In the joint formation system, when one becomes household head, one remains head until death to keep the household from dissolving. In the nuclear system one remains a head because there is no one else. The stem household formation system falls between these. When an heir is designated, the head of household may turn over his responsibilities and retire, but this event can take place at any time between the marriage of the heir and the death of his predecessor. Where timing is strictly mandated, conflict will be minimal; when timing is left to individual proclivities, conflict may be severe. Retirement also means that elderly persons are relieved of domestic responsibilities and may be free to follow their own pursuits. Rebel (1978) gives an excellent example of this freedom in his discussion of the preindustrial Austrian stem family system.

An elderly person in a stem system does garner support from children. However, this does not put a premium on high fertility, for if one can bear a child, raise it to adulthood, and persuade it to stay, only one child is necessary. Other children are only burdens who cannot remain in the household, who must be established elsewhere, and who are unlikely, as adults, to serve as sources of support. However, the corollary to the necessity of having at least one child is that there should be numerous strategies for assuring that that child is recruited to stay, if this does not come naturally.

Finally, what about the relationship between age at marriage, household formation, and economic conditions? Hajnal posits a direct relation and considerable economic rationality in nuclear systems, and none at all in joint ones. Simple systems throw all children out into the world to make their own way; joint ones establish them carefully under the control of their elders. The stem system does both. Consider a couple with three children. One of them, let us say a son, remains in the household, and brings a wife in from elsewhere. The second, a daughter, leaves her household of birth, but marries into an existing household, substituting for the woman who left and became her brother's wife. It is the third child, the excess one, who is problematic. He or she cannot stay in the natal household, for all positions within it are filled. He or she cannot move to another existing household either, for their sister has already filled the one available married couple position in the appropriate generation there. Hence it is these excess persons on whom the relationship between marriage and economic conditions hinges. If land is available or jobs are plentiful they may be able to amass capital, establish a new household, and marry; if not, they can become lifelong servants in the village, or depart for the cities where adult mortality is high. Hence a pattern of departure from home in adolescence, life-cycle service, and an age at marriage as that in preindustrial northwestern Europe will exist, but among a much smaller proportion of the population. The population of those who marry includes both those who stay and are likely to marry earlier, and those who leave and marry later. Consequently, the mean age at marriage is likely to fall between the ages posited for the other two systems, and to have a large variance.

THE STEM HOUSEHOLD AND LIFE CYCLE SERVICE IN PREINDUSTRIAL JAPAN

Does the Japanese system accord with this model? I have described earlier how the household in Japan was a salient social unit with well-defined boundaries. In addition, the Japanese system has long been described as one in which stem households were formed. The Meiji Civil Code clearly described a system where one child remained and others left. This scattering of siblings to the households in which they will spend their adult lives is suggested in the proverb "the sibling is the beginning of the stranger" (Nakane, 1967). It also accounts for the confusion over the obligations owed to and expected from the grandchild (*mago*): one has close contact with those who are resident in one's own household, but little to do with the grandchildren who are progeny of those children who left for other households (R.J. Smith and John M. Roberts: personal communication, 1982). Kinship terminology also differentiates strongly between lineal kin and others, and, within the same generation, by seniority (R.J. Smith, 1962a, 1962b).

Laslett's (1972) investigation of the Japanese town of Nishinomiya demonstrates that the stem household was a reality as well as an ideology. Mean household size was only 4.95 (1972:76), but complex households were common (1972:85); the reason for that complexity was primarily the coresidence of the mother and the grandchildren of the head of household, rather than the coresidence of married brothers and sisters, as in a joint household population like Belgrade (1972:81). Indeed, Laslett concludes that the Japanese are the only population among those reviewed which successfully maintained a statistical predominance of complex households (1972:68–70).

Other features of a stem household formation system can also be found in the evidence. There is a regular method of dealing with non-inheriting children who remain in the locality. They are established in what are known as "branch households" (*bunke*) (Nakane, 1967; Brown and Suenari, 1966). A husband enters an inheriting daughter's household, and suffers the opprobrium that such a reversal of roles entails, except in the service where management of the household enterprise is properly entrusted to the daughter who has grown up knowing its secrets (Befu, 1962). And the practice of adrogation, in which an adult is incorporated into a childless household as an heir, is also well-developed (Cornell, 1982). The experiences of old age in this system are not as well known. Elsewhere I have argued that household heads usually relinquish the headship to their heirs at a set time (though not before the heirs are married), and without conflict (Cornell, 1983). The ex-heads' roles afterwards are unclear, though they seem to retire from domestic duties and pursue ritual and political ones (Ishihara, 1967). Hence, the Japanese family seems to follow the outlines of the stem household formation system rather closely.

But what about life cycle service, the lynchpin of Hajnal's argument linking household structure with fertility and economic growth? I have argued earlier that it ought to have played a similar, though less significant, role in stem household formation systems. What about traditional Japan?

Casual perusal of the existing literature is not favorable to this hypothesis. Life cycle service itself has not been identified as a topic of inquiry. However, I believe that further analysis will reveal that it does exist. I will concentrate on women, because it is principally they whose marriages must be delayed in order to reduce fertility.

Let us remind ourselves of the characteristics of life cycle service in England. First, it did not entail domestic service, but agricultural labor. Second, it was a regular part of adolescent life. Most young men and young women experienced it, whatever their origins: it was not a lower-class phenomenon. Third, it lasted for a short time; and, fourth, it happened before marriage (Hajnal, 1982:473; Kussmaul, 1981).

The present pattern of labor force participation of women in Japan gives us a clue to the existence of life cycle service in the Tokugawa period. Basically, women pursue full-time employment in the interval between education and marriage; they leave with marriage or childbearing; and employers treat them as temporary workers (Cook and Hayashi, 1980). This pattern is echoed in World War II mobilization of women for factory labor: Edicts identified only unmarried women as appropriate, and one could avoid being mobilized by becoming married (Havens, 1975). Kidd (1978) gives similar evidence for workers in Japan's cotton mills around the turn of the century: they were primarily young, unmarried women from rural areas who were employed on short-term contracts. All of these activities can be broadly classed as life cycle service.

Documenting this pattern as early as 1800 suggests that it might have existed earlier as well.

But before we examine the earlier period we must remember the character of Tokugawa economic development. As outlined above, the period from 1600 to 1870 witnessed the decline of large cooperative farming, the emergence of single family farms, the growth of commerce and a national market, and the development of by-employments which enhanced a peasant household's income (T.C. Smith, 1959, 1969). Servants certainly did exist in agricultural households at the beginning of the Tokugawa period. But these were hereditary servants or persons indentured for life who were called *genin*, *nago*, or *fudai*. They disappeared by the middle of the Tokugawa period. The village of Yokouchi, for example, had thirteen such persons in 1672 (seven percent of its population), but none after 1729 (Hayami, 1973a:147–148). However, temporary labor migration (*dekasegi*) increased enormously, and its direction was increasingly toward large distant cities rather than nearby villages. In Yokouchi in 1840 some thirty percent of the male population aged 15–59 were absent (Hayami, 1973a:167). Hence the nature of the service we are discussing may involve not only agricultural employment but also work in rural and urban handicraft industries. In addition, there is a gradient running from northeast to southwest Japan and from the central mountains to the coastal valleys in the extent of economic development and market penetration, such that in the same years different localities exhibited quite different characteristics. In the central hinterlands, for example, large cooperative farming seems to have survived into the twentieth century (Befu, 1968a, 1968b). Hence one must be careful to specify the location of change.

The evidence for life cycle service by women in traditional Japan is sparse but suggestive. Laslett's figures for Nishino-miya show that servants appear in only about ten percent of the households, far below the English standard of one-third. Males outnumber females four to one—a contrast with England where the sex ratio is more nearly equal. However, both men and women are concentrated in the appropriate age groups, ten to nineteen and 20-29, rather than being dispersed over the entire range of ages as the Serbian servants are (1972:82).

Hayami's discussion of labor migration in Nishijo from 1772 to 1869 (1973b) is very significant. Hayami does not discuss life cycle service explicitly, but he gives us statistics that enable us to discern it. First, he shows that many people experienced migration: 48 percent of the men, 62 percent of the women (1973b:9). Men left home at ages thirteen to sixteen, women at thirteen or fourteen, returning about ten to fifteen years later. They moved around from place to place on one-year contracts. In the later years of the period, 1851–1868, it appears that women went mostly to towns five to seven miles east, where there was a nascent textile industry. All this points to a pattern quite similar to the northwestern European one. However, the most persuasive evidence is to be found in Hayami's table on "Reasons for Terminating *Dekasegi*." He had not discussed the marital status of these migrants, but when we see that 55 percent of the women ended their service because of marriage it is clear that migration is primarily an adolescent phenomenon. Its demographic consequences are spectacular. Women with labor migration experience marry at an age of 26.3; women without it at age 20.7, thus averting two births.

But is this correlated with economic development? Examination of mean age

at marriage for women suggests that it is. The basic argument is that as employment opportunities for adolescent women increase, their value to their natal households will rise, and marriage will be delayed. This assumes that the primary value of women to their households of origin and of marriage in preindustrial societies is as producers of children, and that their secondary value is as laborers. When we examine the distribution of mean age at first marriage for women in preindustrial Japan, we find that it is low in the underdeveloped northeast (T.C. Smith: personal communication, 1976) and high in the commercially developed southwest (Hanley and Yamamura, 1977). More conclusive is the striking rise in marriage age in Yokouchi in the period from 1671 to 1871: mean age at first marriage for women jumped from 18.8 to 21.7 years over the period. This parallels an increase in by-employment, especially in sericulture, traditionally a woman's task. This transformation should also mean a decrease in female-specific infanticide and the disappearance of differential female mortality in childhood. T.C. Smith substantiates this by observing that

> ... there was a significant nationwide fall in the sex ratio during the eighteenth century that can be most convincingly accounted for as a shift in the sex incidence of infanticide, reflecting the increased economic value of women as a result of the growth of secondary and tertiary employment (T.C. Smith, 1977:148).

Additional evidence for this change can be obtained by examining two of Hajnal's indicators: household composition and age at attaining headship. As mentioned above, servants appeared in the earlier years of Yokouchi's population register, but not in the later ones. Household structure also changed from more to less complex, as Table 1 shows. Households

Table 1.
Household Structure in Yokouchi, 1720 and 1828

Year	Single	Married Couple	Nuclear	Stem	Joint	Other	Total Percent	Number of Households
				Type				
1720	—	2.0	32.0	30.0	26.0	10.0	100.0	50
1818	3.0	6.1	29.3	37.4	13.1	11.1	100.0	99

consisting of married siblings made up a quarter of all households in 1720, but only slightly over a tenth a century later. In the earlier period, when land was abundant, there were many examples of the delayed fission Hajnal's model of the joint household formation system predicts (see example in appendix of present article). With the constriction of opportunities for establishing new agricultural enterprises, the pattern disappears. Not as many children are produced, and sons leave much earlier, many for employment in the cities. (The ratio of daughters to sons surviving to age ten also improves [Cornell, 1981].) This accounts for the decline in the mean age of household heads, the decrease in elderly heads, and the increase in the younger heads that Hayami's figures revealed (1973a:176–177). In the earlier period a man became the head of household long after marriage, at fission. In the later period many left and it is only those who remained in the village to assume leadership of a household who remained in the statistics. Hence, it seems quite likely that life cycle service not only existed in Tokugawa Japan but played an important role in linking household formation to economic conditions.

CONCLUSION

This article has had three objectives: to discuss the sources for family history in Japan; to expand Hajnal's concept of household formation system to include the stem household; and to outline how household structure and fertility were linked in preindustrial Japan. The argument is intended to inspire research in Japan to go beyond the demographic foundations already established, and to make clear why Japan should be of interest to researchers on other societies.

With respect to research, my call is for less statistical investigation of household structure and more discussion of what might be termed "family relations." As the discussion of Hajnal in Japan indicates, we know very little about topics central to his inquiry: the determinants of age at marriage, the prevalence of servanthood, the household position of the elderly and indigent, and so on. Hajnal's argument suggests that it was not only the capital-maintaining properties of the stem household system which was crucial to Japan's industrialization, but also the rapid flow of young unattached workers to commerce and industry.

The other part of my argument was to show how knowledge of family structure can inform our interpretation of economic and demographic events. This reinterpretation of Hajnal is only preliminary and requires much modification. However, Hajnal's work points to the crucial questions of social analysis. What kinds of constraints are set by cultural conditions? How do people make choices within these constraints? This approach also implies a theory of change, for as individual choices fall more and more at the boundaries of possibilities, they push the constraints into a new alignment. Japan, in fact, may be one of the best places for examining Hajnal's propositions, for there, unlike in northwestern Europe, it may be possible to observe the origin of life cycle service as well as its decline.

Using his notion of constraints and choices we may also be able to develop a more coherent theory to explain how parents come to lose control over resources significant to their children, and how the old rules for household formation became impossible to enforce. Understanding this will not only serve our intellectual curiosity about the family in the past, but will also provide direction for policy governing our own contemporary families.

NOTES

1. See Murakami (1984) for an English summary. See also Hayami (1981).
2. The Neo-Confucianists and the popular writers of the Tokugawa period who produced an abundance of agricultural manuals, diaries and moralistic treatises undoubtedly discussed appropriate and inappropriate family relations. Except in Kojima (1985), this topic has not received much scholarly attention.
3. The same is true of the transformations of family relations wrought by the 1945 Civil Code; Steiner (1950) is one of the few sources. Havens (1975) gives excellent examples of how neotraditional notions of appropriate family relations served to limit women's wartime mobilization. Japanese legal scholars have continued to be a rich source of commentary on the family: see the bibliography in Nakane (1967) and Coleman and Haley (1975) for references.

APPENDIX
Serial Fission in Japanese Households

In the earliest period of Yokouchi's population registers there is a regular pattern of a brother marrying, becoming household head, and leaving to establish his own household when a younger brother marries. Figure 2 shows this process occurring in a single household. Following Laslett (1972:41), we consider each group of persons enclosed by a squared boundary a household unit listed in the registers. Persons missing in subsequent years marry or die in the interim.

Kanbei, the eldest son of Shōhei, becomes head of household when his father dies in 1693, and remains in this position through 1701. He and his wife and children establish their own branch household in 1702, and his younger brother Sōemon becomes household head. He heads the main household until 1706, when his youngest brother marries and Sōemon's family becomes independent. The third brother, Shōhei, is now head of the main household, which includes his widowed mother and his married younger brother, Kihei. Shōhei and his family establish a third branch in 1733. Since Kihei has dropped out of the records, Kihei II, his son, becomes head of the household run by his grandfather Shōhei until 1694. The same process also occurs in Kanbei's household.

This pattern looks strange to persons who expect the eldest son to inherit the household. However, this example is not a mistake or an aberration. It accurately depicts household fissions as recorded in the population registers. One reason that older sons, rather than younger sons, leave is that last son succession is the rule in this area.

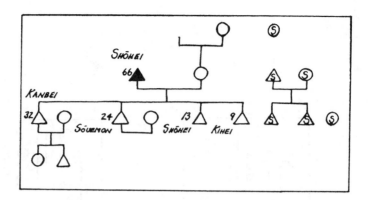

1693

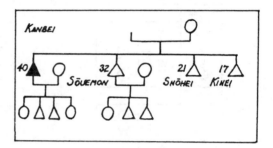

1701

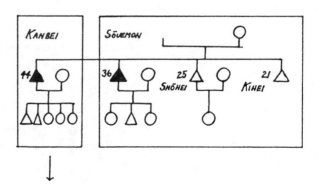

1705

Figure 2. Serial Fission of Brother's Households.

Source: Cornell (1981: 70).

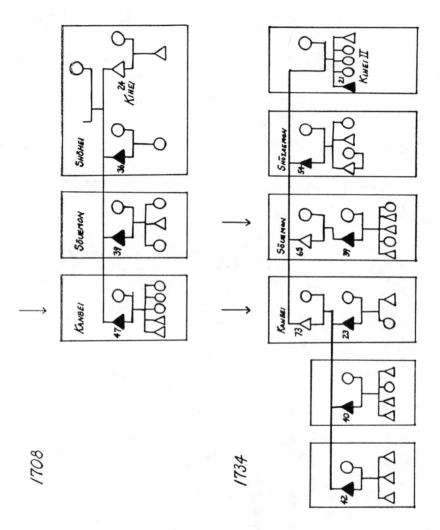

Figure 2 (continued).

REFERENCES

Arnould, Eric J. 1984. "Marketing and Social Reproduction in Zinder, Niger Republic." Pp. 130–162 in *Households: Comparative and Historical studies of the Domestic Group*, edited by Robert McC. Netting, Richard R. Wilk, and Eric J. Arnould. Berkeley: University of California Press.

Bachnik, Jane M. 1983. "Recruitment Strategies for Household Succession: Rethinking Japanese Household Organization." *Man* 18:160–182.

Beardsley, Richard K., John W. Hall, and Robert E. Ward. 1959. *Village Japan*. Chicago: University of Chicago Press.

Befu, Harumi. 1962. "Corporate Emphasis and Patterns of Descent in the Japanese Family." Pp. 34–41 in *Japanese Culture: Its Development and Characteristics*, edited by R.J. Smith and R.K. Beardsley. Chicago: Aldine.

————. 1968a. "Ecology, Residence and Authority: The Corporate Household in Central Japan." *Ethnology* 7:25–42.

————. 1968b. "Origin of Large Households and Duolocal Residence in Central Japan." *American Anthorpologist* 70:309–319.

Bongaarts, John, and Robert G. Potter. 1983. *Fertility, Biology, and Behavior: An Analysis of the Proximate Determinants*. New York: Academic Press.

Brown, L. Keith. 1966. "*Dōzoku* and the Ideology of Descent in Rural Japan." *American Anthropologist* 68:1129–1151.

Brown, Keith, and Michio Suenari. 1966. "Bunke no bunshutsu ni tsuite." (The Establishment of Branch Households.) *Minzokugaku Kenkyū* 31:38–48.

Coleman, Rex, and John Owen Haley (compilers). 1975. "An Index to Japanese Law." *Law in Japan, Special Issue* 1975:1–167.

Cook, Alice H., and Hiroko Hayashi. 1980. "Working Women in Japan: Discrimination, Resistance, and Reform." Cornell International Industrial and Labor Relations Report No. 10. Ithaca, NY: New York State School of Industrial and Labor Relations, Cornell University.

Cornell, L.L. 1980. "Japan." Pp. 265–271 in *History of the Family and Kinship: A Select International Bibliography*, edited by Gerald L. Soliday. Millwood, NY: Krause International Publications.

————. 1981. "Peasant Family and Inheritance in a Japanese Community, 1671 to 1980." Ph.D. dissertation, Johns Hopkins University.

————. 1982. "Getting and Begetting Children: Adoption, Childlessness and Risk in Preindustrial Japan." Paper presented at the Seventh Annual Meeting of the Social Science History Association, Bloomington, Indiana, November 4-7, 1982.

————. 1983. "Retirement, Inheritance and Intergenerational Conflict in Preindustrial Japan." *Journal of Family History* 8:55–69.

Cornell, L.L., and Akira Hayami. 1986. "The *Shūmon Aratame Chō*: Japan's Population Registers." *Journal of Family History* 11:311–328.

Dore, Ronald P. 1978. *Shinohata: A Portrait of a Japanese Village*. New York: Pantheon Books.

Douglass, William A. 1971. "Rural Exodus in Two Spanish Basque Villages: A Cultural Explanation." *American Anthropologist* 73:1100–1114.

————. 1975. *Echalar and Murelaga*. London: C. Hurst & Company.

Embree, John F. 1939. *Suye Mura*. Chicago: University of Chicago Press.

Farris, William Wayne. 1985. *Population, Disease, and Land in Early Japan, 645-900*. Cambridge: Harvard University Press.

Freeman, J.D. 1970. *Report on the Iban*. London School of Economics Monographs on Social Anthropology No. 41. London: Athlone Press.

Fukutake, Tadashi. 1967. *Asian Rural Society*. Seattle: University of Washington Press.

Gubbins, John Harrington (translator). 1899. *The Civil Code of Japan*. Tokyo: Maruya and Company.

Hajnal, John. 1982. "Two Forms of Preindustrial Household Formation System." *Population and Development Review* 8:449–494.

Hanley, Susan B., and Arthur P. Wolf (eds.). 1985. *Family and Population in East Asian History*. Stanford: Stanford University Press.

Hanley, Susan B., and Kozo Yamamura. 1977. *Economic and Demographic Change in Preindustrial Japan, 1600-1868*. Princeton: Princeton University Press.

Havens, Thomas R.H. 1975. "Women and War in Japan, 1937–1945." *American Historical Review* 80:913–934.

Hayami, Akira. 1973a. "Kinsei nōson no rekishijinkōgakuteki Kenkyū" (Historical Demographic Analysis of Villages in Early Modern Japan). Tokyo: Tōyō Keizai Shinpōsha.

————. 1973b. "Labor Migration in a Preindustrial Society: A Study Tracing the Life Histories of the Inhabitants of a Village." *Keio Economic Studies* 10:1–17.

————. 1981. "Review of *Ie Society as a Pattern of Civilization*." *Journal of Japanese Studies* 7:415–420.

Hayami, Akira, and Nobuko Uchida. 1972. "Size of Household in a Japanese County Throughout the Tokugawa Era." Pp. 473–515 in *Household and Family in Past Time*, edited by Peter Laslett and Richard Wall. Cambridge: Cambridge University Press.

Hozumi, Nobushige. 1940. *Ancestor Worship and Japanese Law*. 6th ed. Tokyo: Hokuseido Press.

Ishihara, Kunio. 1967. "Nōson chokkei kazoku no sedai kotai ni okeru shotainushi kengen no ikō." ("Status Transfer of the Head of the Stem Family System.") *Shakaigaku Hyōron* 67:2–16.

Kidd, Yasue Aoki. 1978. "Women Workers in the Japanese Cotton Mills: 1880-1920." East Asia Papers No. 20. Ithaca, NY: Cornell University.

Kitaoji, Hironobu. 1971. "The Structure of the Japanese Family." *American Anthropologist* 73:1036–1057.

Kojima, Hideo. 1985. "Japanese Concepts of Child Development from the Mid-17th to Mid-19th Centuries." Paper presented at the Biennial Meeting of the Society for Research in Child Development, Toronto, Canada, April.

Kussmaul, Ann. 1981. *Servants in Husbandry in Early Modern England*. Cambridge: Cambridge University Press.

Laslett, Peter. 1965. *The World We Have Lost*. New York: Charles Scribner's Sons.

————. 1972. "Introduction: The History of the Family." Pp. 1–89 in *Household and Family in Past Time*, edited by Peter Laslett and Richard Wall. Cambridge: Cambridge University Press.

Long, Susan Orpett. 1982. *Family Change and the Life Course in Japan: A Review of Japanese Historical and Sociological Studies*. New York: Social Science Research Council. Manuscript.

Mass, Jeffrey P. 1983. "Patterns of Provincial Inheritance in Late Heian Japan." *Journal of Japanese Studies* 9: 67–95.

Matsumoto, Y. Scott. 1962. "Notes on Primogeniture in Postwar Japan." Pp. 55–69 in *Japanese Culture: Its Development and Characteristics*, edited by R.J. Smith and R.K. Beardsley. Chicago: Aldine.

Murakami, Yasusuke. 1984. "Ie Society as a Pattern of Civilization." *Journal of Japanese Studies* 10:279–363.

Nagai, Michio. 1953. "*Dōzoku*: A Preliminary Study of the Japanese 'Extended Family' Group and Its Social and Economic Functions." Interim Technical Report No. 7. Columbus: Ohio State University Research Foundation.

Nakane, Chie. 1962. "Nihon Dōzoku Kōzō no Bunseki." ("Analysis of Japanese *Dozoku* Structure.") *Tōyōbunka Kenkyūjo Kiyō* 28:133–167.

————. 1967. "Kinship and Economic Organization in Rural Japan." London School of Economics Monographs on Social Anthropology No. 32. London: Athlone Press.

————. 1972. "In Interpretation of the Size and Structure of the Household in Japan Over

Three Centuries." Pp. 517–543 in *Household and Family in Past Time*, edited by Peter Laslett. London: Cambridge University Press.

Netting, Robert McC., Richard R. Wilk, and Eric J. Arnould (eds.). 1984. *Households: Comparative and Historical Studies of the Domestic Group*. Berkeley: University of California Press.

Plath, David W. 1980. *Long Engagements: Maturity in Modern Japan*. Stanford: Stanford University Press.

Rebel, Hermann. 1978. "Peasant Stem Families in Early Modern Austria: Life Plans, Status Tactics, and the Grid of Inheritance." *Social Science History* 2: 255–291.

Shorter, Edward. 1975. *The Making of the Modern Family*. New York: Basic Books, Inc.

Smith, Robert J. 1962a. "Japanese Kinship Terminology." *Ethnology* 1:349–359.

————. 1962b. "Stability in Japanese Kinship Terminology." Pp. 25–33 in *Japanese Culture: Its Development and Characteristics*, edited by R.J. Smith and R.K. Beardsley. Chicago: Aldine.

————. 1972. "Small Families, Small Households and Residential Instability: Town and City in 'Pre-modern' Japan." Pp. 429–471 in *Household and Family in Past Time*, edited by Peter Laslett and Richard Wall. Cambridge: Cambridge University Press.

————. 1974. *Ancestor Worship in Contemporary Japan*. Stanford: Stanford University Press.

————. 1978a. *Kurusu: The Price of Progress in a Japanese Village, 1951-1975*. Stanford: Stanford University Press.

————. 1978b. "The Domestic Cycle in Selected Commoner Families in Urban Japan: 1757–1858." *Journal of Family History* 3:219–235.

Smith, Thomas C. 1959. *The Agrarian Origins of Modern Japan*. Stanford: Stanford University Press.

————. 1969. "Farm Family By-Employments in Preindustrial Japan." *Journal of Economic History* 29:687–715.

————. 1977. *Nakahara: Family Farming and Population in a Japanese Village, 1717-1830*. Stanford: Stanford University Press.

Steiner, Kurt. 1950. "The Revision of the Civil Code in Japan: Provisions Affecting the Family." *Far Eastern Quarterly* 9:169–184.

Stone, Lawrence. 1977. *The Family, Sex, and Marriage in England, 1500-1800*. New York: Harper and Row.

Taeuber, Irene B. 1958. *The Population of Japan*. Princeton: Princeton University Press.

Wigmore, John Henry. 1969. *Law and Justice in Tokugawa Japan*. Tokyo: University of Tokyo Press.

INTERACTION BETWEEN THE HOUSEHOLD AND THE KIN GROUP IN THE EASTERN EUROPEAN PAST: POSING THE PROBLEM

Andrejs Plakans

ABSTRACT: *The households of traditional eastern Europe were frequently complex, containing a variety of kin beyond the members of the head's conjugal family unit. In these households, the domain of family roles was fused with the domain of kin roles. The interaction between the household and the kin group therefore means, in these coresidential units, the interaction of different role domains, and to understand this interaction we have to know more about the nature of each domain and more about how roles were enacted. This appears to be the next step in micro-level structural research for Eastern Europe.*

Few areas of the European continent have remained untouched by historical-microstructural inquiry of the sort launched by family historians in the mid-1960s. The most heartening consequence, from the vantage point of eastern European history, has been the emergence of a corpus of research in which an unapologetic empiricism combines with an agnosticism about outcomes. This research, surveyed in this article, cannot rival its western European counterpart in geographical coverage, application of now-standard techniques of analysis, or the variety of used archival materials. Still, information that was scarce a few decades ago is now, if not plentiful, then certainly sufficient enough to have encouraged the creation of typologies of regional patterns (Laslett, 1983). In the comparisons, historical eastern Europe has emerged as a

Andrejs Plakans is Professor of History at Iowa State University, Ames, Iowa 50011, and Associate Editor of the Journal of Family History. *His research concerns the social structures of Eastern European peasant societies in the eighteenth and nineteenth centuries.*

region in the study of which researchers should not be surprised to find family forms and familial behavior differing considerably from those of western Europe:

> In contrast to the western European family type, an eastern European type can be posited. It should include a large proportion of multiple-family households, with a significant number consisting of three or more generations; the units should be relatively large, with mean household size significantly greater than 5.0, and contain an average 2.0 conjugal family units. Near-universal early marriage and childbearing would be additional features of the eastern European family type (Czap, 1983:145).

These observations, based on close studies of serf estates in the very center of the Russian Empire are meant, of course, to be a starting point. From them, research can continue in several directions, only one of which will be pursued here. If we can indeed think of historical eastern European populations as frequently living in complex coresidential groupings, and if, as can be expected, a "resident kin" analysis of such communities would yield high proportions, then a series of questions about the interaction of the household and the kin group moves into view. Certainly the first is whether the general characterization of the eastern European domestic group as large, complex, and multi-generational is valid throughout the region. Second, we would want to know about which of the various kinds of kinship analysis is appropriate to the commonly available eastern European historical sources. Third, we need to ask about the concept of "interaction," and whether the sources explored to date have yielded reliable interactional evidence. Finally, we must assess, in a general way, what the larger contexts are in which the interaction problem needs to be studied. A breakdown of the central theme into these components should yield a useful

survey of the eastern European research accomplished to date and of the types of inquiry that have to be carried out in the future.

THE EASTERN EUROPEAN HOUSEHOLD

The study of eastern Europe has always involved the problem of boundaries, not only for researchers viewing the region from an external vantage point but also for those working within the various past and present indigenous scholarly traditions (Halpern and Kideckel, 1983). In micro-studies of historical populations the problem is especially acute because findings, being local, do not answer the question of whether generalization based on them can be made to apply to the region (which may not include the entire ethnic group [Smith, 1981]), the ethnic group (which may be, in the local study, only a fragment defined by a political boundary), or the state unit (which, certainly in the eighteenth and nineteenth centuries, was likely to be experiencing constant boundary changes). So complicated is this problem that in many cases it is sidestepped, which is a precedent we will follow here. Fortunately, most of the useful recent studies are based on materials from localities which unquestionably are in "eastern Europe," however the external boundaries of the region as a whole, or of the subunits within it, are defined.

All boundary problems cannot be sidestepped, however, because they recur in a different sense, at the micro-analytical level, in the application of the Hammel-Laslett household classification scheme to eastern European materials (Laslett and Wall, 1971:1–89; Hammel and Laslett, 1974). Undoubtedly the utility of the scheme has been amply demonstrated and, indeed, it can be viewed as the catalyst for the last decade-and-a-half of eastern European micro-level research. With household listings from the Russian interior the use of the scheme has been unproblematic (Czap, 1978, 1982, 1983), while in similar listings from the western borderlands of the Empire, interpretations of the basic (household/houseful) unit have had to differ (Plakans, 1975; Palli, 1983). Still elsewhere, as in the Balkan peninsula, researchers have often used schemes of their own devising (Halpern and Wagner, 1980). It is possible to raise the question of whether a standard definition of the household can be evenly applied across data which include places that have a high degree of coresidential choice and others that have physically fixed premises among which a population is forced to circulate, e.g., the Balkan peninsula and the Baltic littoral, respectively. Nonetheless, when the entirety of the research using the Hammel-Lasslet classification scheme is surveyed, a broadbrush comparison does become possible and Peter Czap's characterization of the "eastern European family household" is largely sustained.

In view of the many comparative tables now available in the literature a recital of statistics would be redundant. Suffice it to say that a high enough proportion of multiple family households (upwards of 20 percent) reappears over the eastern European places studied for this feature to be regarded as a regional characteristic. If the proportion of extended family households is added to the proportion of multiple, and both together considered as the proportion of "complex" households, the level of complexity is throughout extremely high (upwards of 40 percent). It is now well known, of course, that areas outside eastern Europe—southern France, for example, and regions of the Italian peninsula—also achieved high levels of household complexity in the past. Complexity therefore is not uniquely eastern European, but eastern European households historically have tended toward complex forms of internal organization. Using the "resident kin of head" analysis, and excluding from the counted 'kin' members of the head's family of marriage, we repeatedly obtain proportions of resident kin ranging from 25-20 percent in the western areas of eastern Europe to an extreme of 66.6 percent in Mishino estate in central Russia (Czap, 1982:20). These are the proportions of the population *in households* that for one reason or another have failed to disperse (if we hold them up to western European standards) or have been retained or recruited by the head (if we work with an eastern European model).

Stated more precisely, these findings mean that in those scattered moments of past time at which analyzable sources were created, the phases of the developmental cycle of the family household visible in the source aggregatively suggest a pattern of repetitious complexity. That complexity was a constant condition throughout all phases of the developmental cycle has been demonstrated convincingly in the Russian case (leading Czap to speak of the 'perennial multiple family household' there [Czap, 1982]) and to a less convincing extent in Serbian materials (Halpern and Halpern, 1972). Elsewhere, for example in the Russian Baltic provinces (Plakans, 1983) and Hungary (Andorka and Balazs-Kovács, 1986) (though cyclical analyses in these areas are too sporadic for solid generalizations), it was not at all uncommon for family households to experience phases of nuclearity, and 'perennial complexity' was seldom the experience of all the people all of the time. In the Russian Baltic provinces, the experience of familial complexity appears to have been for many people a vicarious one: only those peasant families which headed farmsteads had complex phases of the cycle, while the landless farmhands' families remained nuclear regardless of the age of the husband. The unevenness of information at this time, however, does not permit the phenomenon of complexity to be described unambiguously as class-specific, because we are not yet certain of how upward and downward social mobility worked out.

Similar restraints at this time must be recognized for general statements about long-term trends in complexity in eastern European household-level data. The work of Hammel on medieval Balkan listings (Hammel, 1972, 1980) has established a longer time frame for that area than exists for any other in eastern Europe and has convincingly demonstrated the recurrence of similar patterns of complexity at scattered points within it. Hammel's current analysis of the censuses of the Croatian Military Border, covering the period from about 1820 to 1860, is not expected to alter the existing picture (Hammel, 1984). At a different level of analysis, the work of Joel and Barbara Halpern on the Serbian village of Orašac, using data files covering the period from about 1800 to the present, has permitted them to show how complexity changed its character from lateral to lineal (Halpern and Halpern, 1972; Halpern and Anderson, 1970). Peter Czap's soul-revision sources, supplemented by aggregated data, cover a bit more than a century (1780's to 1880's) and detail the situation in a handful of serf estates. The recently reported work of Hoch (1986) and Bohac (1985) uses the same sources as Czap and hence covers the same period of time, but the Russian historian Daniel Kaiser has recently begun to explore Russian sources from the fifteenth to the seventeenth centuries. The research of the Estonian historical demographers includes, at the provincial level, sources that span the period from the mid-seventeenth to the mid-nineteenth centuries (Palli, 1980). Comparative statements

about long-term trends in complexity are therefore forced to rely on information from very different levels of analysis, from widely scattered sites, and from widely dispersed points in past time. The expectation that the same locality will supply data for more than a few generations has been frustrated, except in a few instances. Even so, the studies that have been carried out have reinforced the overall picture for eastern Europe. The likelihood that randomly surfacing eastern sources will continue to demonstrate a high degree of complexity remains at this time as great as initially postulated in continent-wide comparisons (Laslett and Wall, 1972:xi).

To state the matter in terms of probable outcomes is to recognize the possibility of local, provincial, and regional variations in levels of complexity. Research on variation in eastern Europe, however, has not yet moved much beyond the recognition that it exists and that it needs to be accounted for. The challenge is analogous to that faced by the east-west marriage-age age contrast posited by Hajnal's pioneering essay (Hajnal, 1965), which has led subsequent researchers to point to differing levels of early marriage ages in eastern Europe, ranging from the late teenage years in Russia proper (Czap, 1978) to the early and mid-twenties in the Russian Baltic provinces (Plakans, 1984a) and in other areas of eastern Europe (Sklar, 1976). The explanation of different levels of "early" marriage and of different proportions of never-married in the population still needs to be discovered; as do the relatively high household complexity levels. The Baltic provincial data have shown that in the same province, in the same year (1797), in a collection of forty different communities of serfs, levels of household complexity can range overall from zero to 95 percent, if outliers are included, and from 6 to 65 percent when outliers are not considered (Plakans, 1983:180). Similarly, seven Hungarian villages from the period 1747 to 1816 show complexity levels ranging from eleven to 54 percent (Andorka and Farago, 1983:293). What local- or provincial-level characteristics such differences are associated with is at this time far from clear, nor has it been shown convincingly whether variations of this range are persisting features of a given site or a temporary response to short-run conditions. Explanations of variation in levels of relatively high complexity, however, still leave the discussion within the overall phenomenon of the complex household, or, as was said earlier, within the problem area of retained or recruited kin. Because the objective of this article is to explore the interaction of the household and the kin group, we must now assay the discussed findings from a different direction and consider the extent to which they can be seen as evidence about interactive processes.

HOUSEHOLD ROLES AND KINSHIP ROLES

To understand dynamics of social interaction requires that we first specify exactly what is being brought together within the analytical framework. In the case of the eastern European household, the framework has normally been set by the empirical data: that is, by a cluster of names which is believed to be a coresidential group because the relational terminology in the source suggests as much. In the analyses of such evidence (presented in the form of tables of various kinds), distinction is drawn, though not always systematically, between relational terms deriving their meaning from the household as such and those whose meaning comes from other domains of social experience, such as affinity and descent. The activity of sorting relational terms in various ways therefore has always been part of the ana-

lytical methodology, with the result that the same set of persons is described from different vantage points. One table analyzes structure, which is determined by looking at the connection between the head and other residents; another counts the number of conjugal family units, a procedure that explicitly ignores, among other things, the tie to the head. Implicit in all of these evaluations, and sometimes buried very deeply in the description of the mechanics of classification and reclassification, is the concept of social roles.

Thinking in terms of social roles is inescapable with nominal level historical sources, even if the researcher, for a variety of reasons, does not reflect on it. It is impossible, operationally, to convert a cluster of names into a "household" and to attribute a "structure" to that new entity without thinking of role relationships. One can, of course, consider these matters to be preliminary, and put them aside for the main task at hand; or one can stop at them and ask if new understanding might be obtained if the sorting process were done with more careful attention to the meaning of dyadic links and the configuration emerging from the linking of many dyads. Approached in this manner, a cluster of names (a coresidential group) poses the question of whether all links stated or implied in the relational terminology derive their social meaning from the same domain of social experience, and the corollary of whether analytical precision is not gained by specifying what the different domains might be.

It is at this point that we first glimpse what direction to take in dealing with the problem of "household-kin group interaction." Generally, in household listings from eastern Europe (in contrast to many western European sources) relational terms are plentiful, sometimes describing the same person simultaneously as a "farmhand," a "husband," a "father," a "brother," a "brother-in-law," a "brother of the head," and so forth. Such descriptions of individuals are a legion in the regimes of high-level household complexity we are dealing with. The labels are role labels, but their relative importance for determining a person's structural position is seldom clear. The meaning of the different labels, and sets of labels, is being supplied by analytically separable domains of the local social world, including that which Meyer Fortes has called the "kinship domain" (Fortes, 1969). Recognizing this is to mark a step forward in understanding the "household-kin group interaction" problem. In these sources the evidence on its face reveals that the domain of household authority which supplies meaning to such dyads as head-farmhand is not the only supplier of meaning; there is also the kinship domain which gives meaning to brother-brother dyad, the domain of the conjugal family unit which supplies meaning to the husband-wife dyad, and so on. The meanings of these different role dyads cannot be deduced from each other, nor is it productive to assume, at the beginning, that any particular dyad is more or less important than any other.

In these sources, in other words, we have a tangible expression in the historical record of what Fortes, who has used the concept of "structural domain" extensively, means by "fused domains":

> In my formulation structural domains, even when they are recognizably distinct by the criteria of norms and customs, tend to be fused together in simple societies, whereas in complex societies they tend to be numerous and structurally differentiated (Fortes, 1969:99).

Whether the eastern European evidence comes from societies that are "simple" in terms that anthropologists would accept,

and whether Fortes' contrast between "simple" and "complex" societies can be substantiated are questions we shall put aside at this time. The idea of "fused structural domains" however is a useful one, and it will guide the line of thought being developed. In eastern Europe, we would not expect, in describing household-kin group interaction, to find all members of the household necessarily residentially separated from all members of the "kin group." Because of this, it is useful to view the household records of eastern Europe as supplying evidence about more than a single domain. In them, the households domain and the kinship domain are seen to have interpenetrated each other, generating the dense role descriptions referred to earlier.

What is also very clear in the case of these records is that they do not provide direct evidence about "interaction." To do so, they would have to state how embeddedness by an individual in one role system (defined by kinship ties) make a difference for that individual's embeddedness in another (defined by household membership). The sources position an individual in various role systems, sometimes with great precision, but they require the behavioral meaning of these simultaneous involvements to be inferred. We can demonstrate from the records, at least in principle, that a particular household is but a fragment of a larger genealogically connected subpopulation living in many different households, but "interaction" in the dynamic behavioral sense would still remain undescribed even at this point (Plakans, 1984b). One is not being unnecessarily harsh in observing that the study of the "household-kin group interaction" problem, taking eastern Europe as a whole, has arrived at this juncture but has not pushed very far beyond it. We have a much better understanding of the extent to which role systems interpenetrate in the eastern European coresidential group, but we have not yet begun to explore what social significance this fact had.

When the domestic group is conceived of in this manner—as a unique domain with rules of its own, yet also one whose inhabitants enact kin roles—the question immediately arises as to what other information we need to understand the roles which do not derive their meaning from household membership. Or, put another way, are the kin roles we identify by use of a normal household listing (household kinship) all that is necessary to talk about kinship? Given the ubiquity of coresident kin in many eastern European areas, one might conclude that the identification of kin ties across household boundaries is not worth the effort if the labor involved results in understanding only a few additional kin roles, enacted by household members toward non-coresidents. A close examination of the Russian and Balkan listings could easily lead to the conclusion that for any given individual all or nearly all of the most significant kin were already in the same coresidential group as that individual; and, since these lists seldom employ non-kinship relational terminology, we could easily surmise that the coresident group *was* the kin group (Baric, 1967:1). The head of the coresident group, in this line of reasoning, occupied that position by virtue of his position in the kin group; his authority as household head derived from his authority as kin group head. The interpenetration of these two role domains in such cases would be total: the structure of the coresident group would be identical with the structure of the kin group. The precise placement of any individual in a grid of kinship ties could be accomplished by looking solely at the coresidential position.

The extent of the interpenetration of these two role domains in all eastern Eu-

ropean areas has to be researched much more before we are enabled to study interaction in the dynamic sense. There is at least one area—the Baltic provinces of the Russian Empire—where the members of a coresident unit (a farmstead) were not all linked by kin ties either to the head or to each other, and where a substantial proportion of presumably important kin roles were being enacted toward persons in other coresidential groups (Plakans, 1982). Remembering that all that is of interest at this juncture is the most precise positioning of persons in role-yielding systems of social relationships, we can note that in the examined Baltic serf estates enumerators systematically employed several different types of relational terminology to describe ties among domestic group members. Some terms such as *Wirth* (farmstead head), *Knecht* (married male farmhand), and *Magd* (unmarried female farmhand) derived their meaning from the 'constitution,' as it were, of the farmstead, which, in turn depended upon the farmstead's position in the estate economy. Other terms were of the kinship type—*Bruder* (brother), *Schwiegersohn* (son-in-law), etc.—and these were frequently attached to the same set of persons as the other terminology. The description of *"Bruder als Knecht"* and *"Schwesterstochter als Magd"* occurs very frequently in these documents. But, just as frequently, farmhands were described as having kin in other domestic groups, and perhaps none at all in their own places of residence. In these serf estates, then, the extent of interpenetration of the two role domains *in the domestic group* was far lesser than in Russian estates examined by Czap and in the Balkan materials. The focal point (two oldest males, let us say) of a reconstructed Baltic kin group could be in one farmstead while many of its "members" could reside in other farmsteads. In the Baltic estates very clearly we cannot know all we would wish to know about the kinship domain if all we looked at were coresident kin. Here we might very well have to oppose "household" to "kin group" in order to study interaction.

As I have observed elsewhere (Plakans, 1984b: Ch. 9), the study of the kinship domain in European sources has to involve reconstructions of genealogical relationships, which, in and of themselves, are only grids or maps with no prima facie social meaning. They are essential for positioning people in potentially role-yielding systems of relationships, but, when this line of investigation is concluded, the reconstructions themselves may have to be discarded. The reasoning we are following at this point certainly indicates the need for such reconstruction if the problem of "household-kin group interaction" is to be resolved.

INTERACTION OF ROLE DOMAINS

"Household-kin group interaction" means, in the final analysis, how the people comprising these groupings deal with each other. If the members of both groups are the same people, or if the membership overlaps considerably (as is frequently the case in eastern European data), then by "interaction" we must mean the ways in which the implicated persons coordinated the enactment of different roles, deriving meaning from different domains of their social world. If the household head, acting in that capacity, sought to improve the household as a work group, but, at the same time, understood his coresident brother to be an indifferent worker, he would have needed to coordinate these different demands. This example is of role conflict, but coordination did not necessarily have to involve the resolution of conflict. It could have involved as well the processes of adjustment, voluntary sub-

ordination or superordination of roles to each other, resigned toleration of conflictful roles, or others. The point is that in describing interaction we must have evidence about how such situations were handled among people long since deceased, and it must be evidence that, in a given community, is coextensive with the already mentioned, and far more easily obtained, evidence about positions.

This is a very heavy burden to place on the historical data at hand, and in that connection two questions arise. Might it not be possible to assume that the two domains had no connection, that is, did not interact to the extent that it would be incumbent upon the researcher to analyze the connection? Peter Laslett, for example, has agreed with the anthropologist Michael Verdon that residence "is a distinct and autonomous social phenomenon" and not "as is often claimed, simply an epiphenomenon of marriage, kinship, or economics (Verdon, 1979, cited in Laslett 1983:515). In eastern European sources, the fact of residence is very frequently "distinct" because the sources organize their information on the basis of residence. Whether residence is "autonomous" and what its relation is to other aspects of social life must be viewed as empirical questions, given the information in the sources as we have described it. The data are too full of relational terms pertaining to familial and kinship connections (or, only kinship connections, if familial ties are considered a subset of kin ties) for the researcher to regard coresidence as autonomous at the outset (it may be regarded as autonomous for analytical purposes, of course, as a temporary expedient). The assumption of full autonomy would require the further assumption that the multitude of easily documented kin connections did not insinuate themselves in the working of the coresidential group: in other words, that the two domains were mutually exclusive in spite of the fact that the same set of persons were enacting roles in both simultaneously. Whether to make the two domains coequal, or to see the one as an epiphenomenon of the other, therefore, has to be an empirical question.

Second, is it necessary to deal with interaction as a dynamic of role relations at all, when, as can be easily shown from the literature, descriptions of interaction can be kept at the unit level? We can speak, in other words, of the household as having recruited or retained kin, and of the kin group as having extruded some of its members or as having served as a kind of recruitment pool. In this approach, acknowledging the difficulties role analysis entails, the researcher attributes volition to the groups, making them the actors, thus avoiding the thorny evidentiary problems about how such allegedly collective decisions come into being. Alternately, interaction can be presented as a *fait accompli*, and the results discussed as attributes or tendencies, as Laslett has done in his survey of "tendencies in domestic group organization in traditional Europe" (Laslett, 1983:526–527). In this strategy one of the groups—in this case the household—is recognized as a supplier of personnel but is not characterized in any particular way. We learn from such a listing that the eastern European household can be compared to households elsewhere by looking at female age at marriage (low in eastern Europe), proportion of multiple family households (high), mean number of adults per household (maximal), addition to household of kin as workers (universal), formation of household by fission or fusion of existent household(s) (always), proportion of resident kin (high), and so on. Many of these attributes imply that some kind of interaction, in the sense understood above, has taken place. A household could not be de-

scribed as having a high proportion of kin as workers without the implication that in the process of producing such a result the head had to enact his (her) role as head and as kinsman (kinswoman). The result implies choices having been made and it is the process of choosing that we would like to know more about.

The answers to these two questions have to await future research. Whether analysis of interaction can succeed by way of role analysis requires that much more work be done along this line than has been accomplished. When we turn to the micro-level work about eastern Europe produced during the past twenty years, and ask about social roles, we find that at this level research on western European historical communities has far outdistanced what is available for eastern Europe. The descriptive precision one looks for is the sort found in such studies as Macfarlane's close analysis of Ralph Josselin's diary (Macfarlane, 1970), Linda Pollock's discussion of parent-child relationships (Pollock, 1983), and Martine Segalen's interpretation of husband-wife relations (Segalen, 1983). The counterparts for eastern European of historical studies of this kind are to be found in the work of those few anthropologists (or ethnographers, in eastern Europe) who have deliberately used and interpreted archival sources (e.g., Halpern and Halpern, 1972; Fél and Hofer, 1969) and who are in any case trained to view dyadic relations as an important area of analytical concern. These works, however, are very few in number and with few exceptions deal with the recent rather than the distant past. The wish to avoid anachronistic interpretation of role relations in eastern Europe cannot at this time be realized very well.

The possibilities, however, are more promising than the existing eastern European studies would suggest, because of the demonstrable availability of certain inter-action sources that have been used profit-ably elsewhere. The voluminous folklore collections have not been systematically exploited as yet, nor has there been any-thing like full usage of available notarial sources (such as wills), ecclesiastical vis-itation reports, the records of manorial courts, and the memoir literature of the new nineteenth-century eastern European intelligentsia. In underlining the utility of these materials, however, one needs to make clear that the information they con-tain must be used in conjunction with the evidence from household lists and ecclesi-astical registers; otherwise there is a risk of repeating the mistakes of earlier users of such sources in areas outside eastern Eu-rope. The analyzed role relationships must not be dealt with as part of some disembodied realm of "culture," in the hope that they "must have had" meaning somewhere on the ground in the past. For maximum advantage, they must be used as part of the analysis of concrete household-kinship relations, which pro-vide control over the incidence of particu-lar relationships and structural informa-tion about their multiplexity.

In the absence of immediately accessi-ble interactional evidence, we are obliged at this time, and probably for some time to come, to draw inferences from the posi-tional data we have. In this, there are three major problems to overcome. The first concerns the meaning to be assigned to the fact that both sets of relational terms needed to study household-kin group in-teraction are not always present in the sources for all eastern European areas. More frequently than not, kin terminol-ogy is present, but the terms designating household roles are lacking. This situa-tion obtains throughout the period of available sources in some cases; in others, earlier sources use both sets while later ones use only kin terms. Whether this

characteristic of the evidence is purely ac-cidental or has some deeper meaning for the changing relationship between house-hold and kinship remains to be seen. But one consequence of its presence is that household roles are frequently entirely hidden from view. Since households func-tioned as labor groups and divided the required labor in various ways among their members, this problem is a very se-rious one.

The second problem concerns the diffi-culties inherent in evidence about role changes at the individual level. The very concept of interaction implies passage of time during which people lost and gained both household and kinship roles. The best serial listings for any eastern Euro-pean locality to date are the Russian soul revisions, in which usable enumerations were made at roughly fifteen-year inter-vals over a period of about eighty years. The prospect of detecting and describing role changes any individuals experienced in these data, therefore, are better than in other areas. That role changes took place is patently clear, not only logically but also empirically, as experimental thrusts in this direction have shown. But reliable generalizations would require more, and the necessary evidence is lacking at present.

The third problem for interaction stud-ies concerns population at risk at the mo-ments when interaction is said to have taken place. If the proportions of resident kin is in the range of thirty to sixty percent we know that there is considerable inter-penetration of role domains, but we do not understand clearly enough whether the non-kin are present because the kin pool has been exhausted or because choi-ces have been made between kin and non-kin in favor of the latter. To detect what choices have been made we have to be able to reconstruct genealogical configur-ations that include related people residing not only in the household but in all households, and this task is virtually impossible unless listing sources provide the key for links across household boundaries or if several data sources can be linked. In both cases, accomplished research has been only partially successful and the results clearly provisional.

THE LONG-TERM IN EASTERN EUROPE

The overarching question of all eastern European micro-level research concerns the long-term duration of patterns that emerge in short-run data collections. Our covering theoretical concept of 'fused domains,' when inserted in the differing histories of eastern European peoples raises the problem quite naturally. We surmise that historical processes were at work that brought such fusion into being (unless it was there from time immemorial), managed to keep it the 'normal' state of affairs for a long period (including the short time periods when we see it in the sources), and then, perhaps brought about a separation of the household and kinship domains. Whatever the actual interaction process—still to be described—we must at this point note that explaining interaction historically will be no easy matter.

The problem of the long duration of patterns has already been broached in the research literature on eastern Europe from at least two different vantage points: the demographic and the socioeconomic. E.A. Hammel, in his magisterial essay on "the zadruga as process" argued that this complex institution was best understood when

historical changes in household organization in the Balkans are attributed largely to alteration in demographic rates and external constraints, rather than to changes in underlying principles of organization which have

remained remarkably constant (Hammel, 1972: 337).

Hammel's observation covers a period of time of about five hundred years, from the fifteenth century to the present. A somewhat reduced time frame—about one hundred years, roughly from the mid-eighteenth to the mid-nineteenth centuries—has been used by researchers concerned with the link between micro-structures and "the end of the old order in rural Europe" (Blum, 1978), specifically the ending of formal serfdom, or, in Marxist–Leninist formulation, the "transition from feudalism to capitalism" (Kahk, 1982). In all these works the elements of the long-term story are all noted as being important, though they are differently assembled in each. Most, save the expected ones, have kept open the question of which element has primacy—which is the phenomenon and which the epiphenomena—but all of them present historical change as a complex, placing microstructures in the demographic, socioeconomic, and cultural contexts that made up the totality of the past.

The factors mentioned by Hammel—demographic rates, external constraints, underlying principles of organization—mark the directions which research on household-kin group interactions must take. In due course we are bound to have demographic histories of those eastern European areas which, excepting Russia (Coale, Anderson, and Härm, 1979), are not represented in the published reports of the Princeton Fertility Project. We are also bound to gain a much better understanding of what Hammel calls "external constraints": the policies, institutions, laws, and economic arrangements in eastern Europe that resulted in low marriage ages, high marriage rates, low rates of local population turnover, and the remarkably high mean of coresidential group sizes that have been found with great regularity. As work proceeds we are also likely to have more on-the-ground descriptions of kinship organization in eastern Europe, particularly of the differing combinations of kinship principles from region to region. (In the Russian Baltic provinces, in the same community, household complexity could be produced by lineal relatedness of married coresident couples in some households, and affinal relatedness in others; such a mixture of principles evidently never occurred in the Balkans.) By themselves these findings will not however answer the questions of household-kin group interaction, because they concern the movement of carriers of roles, the fusion and separation of role domains, and the meanings with which various roles were invested. Findings about interaction will have to demonstrate that the simultaneous possession of roles in both the household and kinship domains made a difference in the way that these roles were enacted in both. At this juncture, twenty years after the start of the effort, there is little reason to be pessimistic.

REFERENCES

Andorka, Rudolf, and Tamas Faragó. 1983. "Preindustrial Household Structure in Hungary." Pp. 281–308 in Richard Wall, Jean Robin, and Peter Laslett (eds.), *Family Forms In Historic Europe.* Cambridge: Cambridge University Press.

Andorka, Rudolf, and Sandor Balazs-Kovács. 1986. "The Social Demography of Hungarian Villages in the Eighteenth and Nineteenth Centuries (With Special Attention to Saπrpilis, 1792-1804." *Journal of Family History* 11:169–192.

Baric, Lorraine. 1967. "Levels of Change in Yugoslav Kinship." Pp. 1–24 in Maurice Freedman (ed.), *Social Organization: Essays Presented to Raymond Firth.* London: Frank Cass.

Blum, Jerome. 1978. *The End of the Old Order in Rural Europe.* Princeton, NJ: Princeton University Press.

Bohac, Rodney. 1985. "Peasant Inheritance Strategies in Russia." *Journal of Interdisciplinary History* 16:23–41.

Coale, Ansley, Barbara Anderson, and Erna Härm. 1979. *Human Fertility in Russia in the Nineteenth Century.* Princeton, NJ: Princeton University Press.

Czap, Peter, Jr. 1978. "Marriage and the Peasant Joint Family in Russia." Pp. 103–123 in David Ransel (ed.), *The Family in Imperial Russia.* Urbana: University of Illinois Press.

——— 1982. "The Perennial Multiple Family Household, Mishino, Russia, 1782-1858." *Journal of Family History* 7:5–26.

——— 1983. "'A Large Family: The Peasant's Greatest Wealth': Serf Households in Mishino, Russia, 1814-1858." Pp. 105–151 in Richard Wall, Jean Robin, and Peter Laslett (eds.), *Family Forms In Historic Europe.* Cambridge: Cambridge University Press.

Fél, Edit, and Tamas Hofer. 1969. *Proper Peasants.* Chicago: Aldine.

Fortes, Mayer. 1969. *Kinship and the Social Order.* London: Routledge.

Hajnal, John. 1965. "European Marriage Patterns in Perspective." Pp. 101–143 in D.V. Glass and D.E.C. Eversley (eds.), *Population in History.* London: Edward Arnold.

Halpern, J.M. , and David Anderson. 1970. "The Zadruga: A Century of Change." *Anthropologica* 12:83–97.

Halpern, J.M., and B.K. Halpern. 1972. *A Serbian Village in Historical Perspective.* New York: Holt Rinehart.

Halpern, J.M., and David Kideckel. 1983. "Anthropology of Eastern Europe." *Annual Review of Anthropology* 12:377–402.

Halpern, J.M., and Richard A. Wagner. 1980. "Anthropological and Sociological Research on the Balkans During the Past Decade." *Balkanistics* 4:13–62.

Hammel, E.A. 1972. "The Zadruga as Process." Pp. 355–373 in Peter Laslett and Richard Wall (eds.), *Household and Family In Past Time.* Cambridge: Cambridge University Press.

——— 1980. "Household Structure in Fourteenth-Century Macedonia." *Journal of Family History* 5:242–273.

——— 1984. "Fertility Patterns in the Croatian Military Border in the Nineteenth Century." Working paper of the Program in Population Research, University of California, Berkeley.

Hammel, E.A. and Peter Laslett. 1974. "Comparing Household Structure Over Time and Between Cultures." *Comparative Studies in Society and History* 16:73–108.

Hoch, Steven. 1986. *Serfdom and Social Control In Russia.* Chicago: University of Chicago Press.

Kuhk, Juhan. 1982. *Peasant and Lord in the Process*

of Transition from Feudalism to Capitalism in the Baltics. Tallinn: Eesti Raamat.

Laslett, Peter. 1983. "Family and Household as Work Group and Kin Group: Areas of Traditional Europe Compared." Pp. 513–563 in Richard Wall, Jean Robin, and Peter Laslett (eds.), *Family Forms in Historic Europe*. Cambridge: Cambridge University Press.

Macfarlane, Alan. 1970. *The Family Life of Ralph Josselin*. Cambridge: Cambridge University Press.

Palli, Heldur. 1980. *Estesvennoe dvizhenie selskogo naseleniia estonii 1650-1799*. Tallinn: Eesti Raamat.

_____. 1983. "Estonian Households in the Seventeenth and Eighteenth Centuries." Pp. 107–216 in *Name of Publication?* edited by Wall, Robin, and Laslett. City: Publisher?

Plakans, Andrejs. 1975. "Peasant Farmsteads and Household in the Baltic Littoral, 1979." *Comparative Studies in Society and History* 17:2–35.

_____. 1982. "Ties of Kinship and Kinship Roles in an Historical Eastern European Peasant Community: A Synchronic Analysis." *Journal of Family History* 7:52–72.

_____. 1983. "The Familial Context of Early Childhood in Baltic Serf Society." Pp. 167–206 in Richard Wall, Jean Robin, and Peter Laslett

(eds.), *Family Forms In Historic Europe*. Cambridge: Cambridge University Press.

_____. 1984a. "The Demographic Transition in the Russian Baltic Provinces and Finland: Prospects for a Comparative Study." *Journal of Baltic Studies* 15:171–184.

_____. 1984b. *Kinship in the Past: An Anthropology of European Family Life 1500-1900*. Oxford: Basil Blackwell.

Pollock, Linda. 1983. *Forgotten Children: Parent-Child Relations from 1500 to 1900*. Cambridge: Cambridge University Press.

Segalen, Martine. 1983. *Love and Power in the Peasant Family*. Chicago: University of Chicago Press.

Sklar, June. 1976. "The Role of Marriage Behavior in the Demographic Transition: The Case of Eastern Europe Around 1900." *Population Studies* 18:231–247.

Smith, Anthony. 1981. *The Ethnic Revival*. Cambridge: Cambridge University Press.

Verdon, Michael. 1979. "Sleeping Together: The Dynamics of Residence among the Abutia Ewe." *Journal of Anthropological Research* 35:401–425.

Wall, Richard, Jean Robin, and Peter Laslett, (eds.), 1983. *Family Forms in Historic Europe*. Cambridge: Cambridge University Press.

The Life Course
and Family Patterns

FAMILIES AND LIVES: SOME DEVELOPMENTS IN LIFE-COURSE STUDIES

Glen H. Elder, Jr.

ABSTRACT: *As a theoretical orientation, the life course brings a contextual, dynamic, and temporal perspective to studies of families and lives in the past and present. Building upon literature reviews in the mid-1970s, this essay examines some elementary distinctions of life-course analysis, including the links between age, temporality and the life course; the dynamics of interdependent lives; and the unit of analysis problem. Emerging conceptual and research approaches to the household exemplify these distinctions. The relation between social change and the life course remains one of the more central and challenging areas of life-course study.*

Over the past two decades, theoretical developments in family studies have drawn attention to the contextual variation of family life, to family dynamics over time, and to the family as an actor that makes choices in constrained situations. The life-course perspective exemplifies this movement by highlighting the interlocking nature of individual trajectories within the family, the formation and dissolution of family patterns over time, and the relation between family and social change.

The life course has become a prominent framework for demographic analysis, especially in relation to family transitions generally and the adult transition in particular (Hogan, 1981; Hernandez, 1986; Hogan and Astone, 1986; Rindfuss, Morgan, and Swicegood, 1987). By compari-

Glen H. Elder, Jr. is Howard W. Odum Professor of Sociology at the University of North Carolina, Chapel Hill, N.C. and is also currently a NIMH Research Scientist Fellow. He is engaged in long-term studies on the effects of the Great Depression and World War II on family and life patterns.

son, cultural influences on the life course remain noteworthy for their acknowledged importance *and* lack of development. We still lack research on the normative patterning of the life course. Since the 1960s, life-course studies of the family have benefited from the rapidly expanding number of longitudinal data archives and from the innovative application of statistical models to the dynamics of life-course patterns (Featherman, 1986) such as multivariate life-table techniques.

In 1977 the *Journal of Family History* published an essay which outlined some basic features of life-course study as applied to the family and family history (Elder, 1977). These features view the life course as interlocking trajectories, indicate differences between the family cycle and life course, and propose ways of thinking about linkages between the family and social change. Originally this essay came to life in a multidisciplinary project that joined a common framework on the life course to the diverse analysis of archival data on late-nineteenth-century Essex County, Massachusetts (Hareven, 1978). For purposes of the study, the life course (Elder, 1978:21) refers to "pathways through the age differentiated life span, to social patterns in the timing, duration, spacing, and order of events; the timing of an event may be as consequential for life experience as whether the event occurs and the degree or type of change."

Before the Essex County project in the 1970s, research on age and the life course consisted of a small, fragmented literature of relevant studies (Riley, Johnson, and Foner, 1972; Elder, 1975). The field has expanded greatly since then. This essay explores some aspects of this growth, including greater awareness of important analytic issues. I begin with some perspectives and elementary distinctions in life-course study, as it has emerged over the past decade or so (Elder, 1985; Riley,

Foner, and Waring, 1987). These distinctions include historical eras of life-course study; the link between age, temporality, and the life course; the usefulness of both age and kinship perspectives on the life course; and the concept of interdependent lives in family dynamics. The second part of the essay shows how concerns over family process and temporality have been expressed in views of the domestic household, once the most static and acontextual territory in family history. In conclusion, we come to a topic that had much to do with the rise of life-course thinking in the 1960s, namely, the realization that individual change is linked to social change. This connection has been studied intensively, but it remains a puzzle on the agenda of future research.

PERSPECTIVES AND ELEMENTARY DISTINCTIONS

Periods of rapid change and dislocation tend to orient the study of families and lives to distinctions that are fundamental in life-course analysis—elements of time, process, and context. By disrupting routine, events mark transitions from one state to another and heighten awareness of the passage of time. Families acquire a distinct past, defined as "before the change or event"; and also a distinct "future" within a trajectory. Change of any sort, but especially the more drastic kind, draws attention to process. Families work out adaptations to new settings and individuals join their life histories in marriage. Rapid change makes social contexts more salient by changing them or by pulling people from one setting and placing them into another. To the extent that families and lives are embedded in settings, social change is a major source of their alteration over time.

These concepts define two eras of theoretical and research vitality in the life-course study of families and individual lives: the pre-1940 phase, which is most closely identified with the early Chicago School of Sociology; and the post-1960 decades. The landmark study of the life course in the first era is W.I. Thomas and Florian Znaniecki's *The Polish Peasant in Europe and America* (1918-1920). Among other examples (Elder, 1984), the early work of Ernest Burgess and Willard Waller connected the temporal changes of individual situations to the negotiations, maneuvers, and conflicts of family process, and in some cases placed this family process in a wider social context.

Twenty years later, intellectual currents and problem foci of the 1960s brought a fresh sensitivity to social change and its relation to families and individuals. This occurred in a more sophisticated world of scientific study as contrasted with the pre-1940s. Now analysts could envision ways of studying the interlocking nature of change in people and in environments (Kertzer and Hogan, 1985). Greater recognition of this connection favored a concept of the life course in context, whether of individuals or of families.

The rising variability of family patterns and individual lives during the 1960s also favored adoption of the life course as an approach. The variability of women's lives because of higher rates of divorce and employment (Cherlin, 1981) in particular, required models of individual choice and variation instead of the conventional cycle in which marriage is followed by parenthood and the later years. An expanding number of life-course studies (McLaughlin et al., 1985) have documented the multiple strands of women's lives, their interdependence and cross-pressures. Most American women marry, have children, *and* work for an income, full- or part-time.

The distinctive issues of life-course study include: (1) temporality and order;

(2) the family dynamics of interdependent lives; and (3) unit of analysis.

Temporality and Order in the Life Course

Contemporary perspectives on the life course differ from those of an earlier period by giving greater emphasis to the temporal meanings of age and thus to historical settings. For examples of this shift, we need only compare Thomas and Znaniecki's *The Polish Peasant in Europe and America* with its analysis of generations and lineages in a relatively timeless, abstract realm, to the birth cohort and intergenerational themes in *Family Time and Industrial Time* (Hareven, 1982), a study of successive worker cohorts and their families in a large textile mill with declining economic prospects during the 1920s. Though explicitly historical, *The Polish Peasant* does not locate the immigrants according to birth year and historical setting, nor does it describe their life stage at the time of their migration. Hareven's study provides both of these markers and uses them to assess the implications of industrial change for worker families in the city of Manchester, New Hampshire.

An explicit sense of age grading in lives and family patterns cannot be found in most sociological works on the life course before World War II, but this emphasis is commonplace today (Kertzer and Keith, 1984; Riley, Foner, and Waring, 1987). Three meanings of age are especially noteworthy: (1) individual age or aging, as inferred from chronological age; (2) social age, as expressed in the socially constructed meanings and patterns of life events and roles; and (3) historical age, indexed by birth year and cohort membership (Elder, 1975). The lifetime framework of individual age focuses attention on the course of aging; social time marks off the age differentiated life-span of events and social roles; and historical time locates people in relation to cohorts, places, and events. History and life-course dynamics interact through the medium of cohorts.

Charles Tilly (1987) claims that there is need to "shift analyses from calendar time to sequences," a shift which poses one of the great challenges before family historians. The use of calendar time in life-course analyses means that solar time is used "as the measure of social time," as Tilly puts it. A more accurate way of defining social time is to view it as a social construction based in part on the biological events of age, birth, and death. Social demarcations of the age continuum or of the calendar have special significance when we think of the life course and family. There are, of course, other kinds of social time beyond that based on the calendar (Hagestad, 1986) and Tilly's suggestion that we bring these into the analysis of social change and the family is important. The social markers of historical time represent one example, such as the growth and collapse of the Amoskeag mill in Hareven's study (1982). Cycles of drought and floods provide other illustrations.

The basic flaw in Tilly's recommendation stems from its replacement of one form of social time by another, by sequences or event order. Both forms are needed. Indeed, specific event sequences are likely to have implications that vary by the duration of particular states and by timing, whether early or late in life. Sequences or the ordering of events and activities have been a central feature of life-course research, especially among demographers. Using one-year birth cohorts over much of the twentieth century, Hogan (1981) identified a customary sequence of events among American men in the transition to adulthood—completion of education, entry into full-time em-

ployment, and marriage. The normative meaning of this sequence is undocumented and we generally lack empirical evidence on the normative structuring of life or family patterns (Elder, 1975; Marini, 1984a). However, much of Hogan's analysis explores the implications of event disarrangements, such as marriage before completion of schooling (see also Marini, 1984b). The best example of research on normative violations involves studies of unwed motherhood, including the work of Furstenberg (1976) and Brumberg's (1985) historical study in upstate New York.

The flurry of interest in event sequences has prompted more thoughtful consideration of both customary and unusual sequences. If we can speak of order in the life course, can we also speak of disorder and its implications? Do we know enough about the empirical facts of families and lives to identify types of disorder and the logic of their effects? Hogan's (1981) research generally portrayed "disorder" as costly, but the life context of event disorders clearly matters, as it should. For example, war mobilization is one of the principal causes of disorder for young American men in this century, but an intensive study of this life pattern among Vietnam veterans reports no adverse effects of life-course disarrangements (Laufer, 1986, personal communication). Using data from a nationwide sample of the high school class of 1972, Rindfuss, Swicegood, and Rosenfeld (1986) obtained exceedingly complex results on the relation between event disorder and the transition to parenthood. In a concluding observation of general significance, they point out "that understanding the nature and importance of sequence in the life course requires analyzing what the roles themselves mean and how they are causally linked" (p. 27). This requisite is the missing element in studies of event order and disorder. Moreover, the meaning and logic of role or activity sequences depend in part on additional information regarding the timing and duration of transitions and states.

A sequence of multiple marriages in two cases becomes interesting when we learn that the first marriage lasted 25 years for person A, and only two years for person B. Differences in duration alter the implications of a sequence. In the case of parenting, we know that the childbearing span determines in part the meaning of being a parent and of being a second child. A rapid sequence of births produces a very different family pattern from that of widely dispersed births. In addition, we need to know whether a rapid sequence occurred when the mother was a teenager or ten years older (Furstenberg, Brooks-Gunn, and Morgan, 1987). The handicap of teenage parenthood increases with multiple births in rapid succession. More than ever before, studies of family formation are including the timing, order, and duration of events in multivariate analyses (Hirschmann and Rindfuss, 1982; McLaughlin and Melber, 1986). The neglect of such distinctions is most striking in traditional concepts of the family cycle (Elder, 1978), a sequence of role patterns that generally depict stages of parenthood. Reuben Hill's (1970) nine-stage formulation begins with the newly married childless couple who enters Stage Two with the birth of the first child. The age and status progression of the children moves the parents through the sequence to the postparental and aging family.

This sequential perspective on the family tells us very little about the life course of the mother, father, or children. Couples who eventually have children are marched through the stages without providing information on when they married and had children. Assuming wide differences in mother's age at first birth, from fifteen to

forty years, such timing has profound consequences for the meaning of a family stage or sequence. Likewise, large variations can occur through the variable durations of particular stages, such as childlessness, the launching of children, and the postparental stage. Overall, these deficiencies mean that a sequential model of family stages leaves unclear just how children fit into the life course of their parents.

Temporal distinctions have been made in conjunction with stages of the family or parenthood, as seen in the early studies of Paul Glick (1947) and the more recent historical research of Michael Anderson (1985). Still, the absence of such distinctions in historical work on the family is common (Segalen, 1977). The more central concept of time in the family cycle is that involving relations between two generations and the process by which one generation is replaced by another. Among marriages that result in children the lengthening life span is producing family systems with interlocking cycles. In the four-generation system, they link parent and child, grandparent and parent, and great-grandparent and grandparent. The child will move across four-generational stations in his or her lifetime. As deaths occur, generational turnover (Hagestad, 1982) in the structure of family time changes status and role, self-identity, and behavior. The parenting behavior of adults tends to vary according to whether they have surviving parents and grandparents. Social-emotional distance generally increases between parents and offspring when parents move to the last position on the generational line.

A final observation about the family cycle and the life course concerns the related problems of diverse and interlocking careers and trajectories. The family cycle, as described above, depicts a trajectory in which each marriage is followed by children and survives until the death of one spouse. In an age when American children born in 1980 have a sixty percent chance of experiencing parental divorce or separation by the age of eighteen (Hofferth, 1986), the empirical facts of life-course diversity have made obsolescent the conventional family cycle. In the nineteenth and early twentieth centuries, deaths at all ages also ensured a high level of diversity. The life-course perspective adequately represents such diversity.

The Family Dynamics of Interdependent Lives

Family dynamics of the life course evolve over a relatively long span of time, as represented by the concept of trajectory or pathways, and also over a short span, as in transitions from one state to another. Trajectories of work, marriage, and parenthood are interrelated role paths that structure the life course of individuals, couples, and family units. Transitions refer to a change in state, such as entering and leaving a job, getting married and divorced, giving birth to children and seeing them leave home for non-family living and adult independence. They are always embedded in life trajectories that determine their form and meaning. Indeed, it is now commonplace to investigate the implications of the same transition in different social phases of the life course, such as the early and old-age death of a spouse. A transition which violates age expectations increases both life-course stresses and deprivations (McLanahan and Sørenson, 1985). Such stresses also stem from overlapping transitions, as when the birth of a child coincides with loss of employment.

Trajectories and transitions refer to family processes in the study of careers and events. The conceptual perspective of careers has a distinguished history within the field of occupations and professions,

and it represents one of the few theoretical languages that depict a temporal dimension. In the recent past, however, social scientists studied families as if their careers could be understood in splendid isolation. Indeed, some twenty years ago the individual career represented a standard way of viewing a person's life. Even in the 1970s, Lee Rainwater was able to conclude that studies of socioeconomic and family careers largely proceed "along their narrow ways barely acknowledging the existence of the other" (cited in Young and Wilmott, 1973:xiv). Such narrow preoccupations were shattered by the rising employment of women and correlated problems of managing both family and work careers.

The family dynamics of interdependent lives involves the interlocking nature of trajectories and transitions, both within and across the life stages of family members. These dynamics are rooted in kinship ties which make the events that occur to others personal events of significance. Thus, the greater involvement of women than men in the lives of others markedly increases their vulnerability to stressors in their network, when compared to the experience of men (Kessler and McLeod, 1984). This difference in social ties accounts in part for the higher rank of women than of men in measures of emotional distress. The general premise here is that women respond to the multiple demands placed upon them. An unwillingness to respond could place others in a deprived situation. Consider, for example, young black girls who give birth to a child in early adolescence.

Teenage motherhood occurs among black girls who are typically surrounded by the potential support of a mother and grandmother; yet, the repercussions of young motherhood can diminish this support. Burton (1985; Burton and Bengtson, 1985b) refers to these repercussions as ripple effects in a study of 41 female lineages in black families from Los Angeles; the young daughter becomes a parent, her mother becomes a grandmother, and her grandmother becomes a great-grandmother. This ripple effect has deprivational implications when the birth occurs in early adolescence instead of during the expectable, on-time years of young adulthood.

An early birth to the teenage daughter of a young mother creates a disparity between age and kinship status, in particular, between being young in age and facing the prospects of grandparental status. As a 31-year-old grandmother told Burton: "I'm just too young to be a grandmother. That's something for old folks, not for me." Another mother who was forced into the grandmother role by her daughter's first child explained that "being a grandmother could have waited." By comparison, the women who became grandmothers in their late forties or so were eager for the new role.

Four out of five of the mothers of young mothers refused to accept their new responsibilities as grandmothers. Their refusal shifted the grandmother burden in child care up the generational ladder to the great-grandmother who in many cases was carrying a very heavy load. A great-grandmother in her early fifties complained about the added burden: "I takes care of babies, grown children, and old peoples. I work, too—I get so tired I don't know if I'll ever get to do something for myself."

Age and kinship perspectives on the life course bring complementary insights to important questions concerning individual lives and family relationships (Elder, 1984). Consider the variable age difference between women and their children. The later the age at first birth, the larger the age-gap between mother and child. A large gap magnifies the historical separa-

tion between parent and child in a rapidly changing society, but it also has implications for parental judgment and competence. A small number of studies suggest that older mothers are more effective as parents of young children than are younger mothers (Vanden Heuvel, 1986), other factors being equal. But what happens to the mother-daughter relationship over time? An age difference of 39 years between mother and infant might have positive value through the maturity of the mother and yet become a source of intergenerational estrangement in 25 years. Rossi's (1980) study of mother-daughter pairs found evidence for such estrangement and dispirited aging among the older mothers of teenage daughters.

Births to young adolescents and to women in their late twenties or early thirties are coupled frequently with parental careers of deprivation and privilege, respectively. This is a process by which deprivation and advantage are passed along from one generation to the next. However, studies clearly show that adolescent motherhood does not ensure a life of misfortune or poverty. In a mid-life follow-up of black women who had their first child in adolescence, Furstenberg and his associates (1987) found three important routes to economic security—a continuation of education, control of fertility, and the establishment of a stable marriage with independence from the family of origin. The children of these mothers were more successful with peers and in their academic work than children whose mothers continued to experience a life of welfare dependency and material hardship. Using academic success as the child outcome, they found that maternal welfare status at any point increased the child's risk of academic failure. Women lowered this risk when they made the transition from welfare to independence. The achievement of greater economic security by teenage mothers improved the life chances of the children, but these changes did not completely eliminate the disadvantage of being the child of an adolescent mother.

As applied in this and other research, the concept of interdependent lives is central to the life-course study of families for it represents a concept of reality in which relationships emerge, dissolve, and assume more complex forms. Marital development refers to the emergence of interdependent lives, whereas divorce marks a legal end to the marital obligations and rights of the relationship. Instead of viewing family norms as "givens," we can see them as agreements worked out through family interaction. By taking this process view of interdependence, life-course analysis moves back and forth between the individual and group.

The unit of analysis in such research cannot be both the individual and group (Watkins, 1980), but it can be the individual in a study of the process by which individual actions become family action. The elementary unit in life-course research is the individual, though individuals, the family, and their relation are foci of interest. From this vantage point, the modes of temporal interdependence include (1) the intersection of trajectories and transitions within the individual life course; (2) the relation between the life patterns of family/kin members, such as husband and wife, parent and grandparent; (3) the link between individual development and the corporate life course of the family; and (4) the interplay between all of the above and the larger world of social-historical changes. Examples of the first type of study include research on women's family and work careers (Moen, 1985). The Furstenberg et al. (1987) study illustrates the second type. Hareven's (1982) study of the Amoskeag Mill, its workers and their families, serves as an example of all four modes.

As expressed in the life course, the family dynamics of interdependent lives entail both social supports and constraints, the benefits and costs of social ties. The "givens" of kinship which ensure assistance in time of need also carry obligations to reciprocate in some manner. With some resemblance to the family system of rural Poland in the late nineteenth century (Thomas and Znaniecki, 1918–1920), Hareven (1982) describes the power of the family collective in shaping the family decisions of French Canadians in the mill community of Manchester, New Hampshire, circa 1910–1925.

HOUSEHOLD AND RESIDENCE OVER THE LIFE COURSE

One of the more revealing indications of the shift toward life-course thinking (temporal, contextual, process-oriented) and research comes from work on the household and residence. No approach to family history could be more at odds to that of the life course than views of a domestic household with an average size or composition for specific historical times and places. This method has been used by Peter Laslett and the Cambridge Group for the History of Population and Social Structure to compare the English households of some 100 parishes over two centuries. Excluding boarders and lodgers, Laslett and Wall (1972) found that households across this phase of English history were typically nuclear and relatively constant in size. But by ignoring the kin who lived outside the household, the approach produced a modern version of the isolated nuclear family, a unit divorced from kinship. Also, mean household size failed to represent families in any particular phase of temporal organization. Ironically, this household approach ignored one of the more suggestive contributions from English family studies at the turn of the century, namely, Rowntree's (1901) discovery of compositional change over the course of family life and its powerful socioeconomic consequences.

Ten years ago Maris Vinovskis (1977: 283) identified the more important limitations of the household approach and called for a "more balanced and dynamic analysis of family life in the past. The life-course approach suggests the need as well as the means for linking information about family processes with that of family size and composition within the context of historical change in society as a whole." Some movement in this direction is coming from newly emerging models of the household and from studies of the residential trajectories of individuals.

In a conference on the household, attended by anthropologists and historians (Netting, Wilk, and Arnould, 1984), one of the more noteworthy and widely shared proposals recommended that research investigate the individual decisions of family members and the process by which particular household forms emerge. Individual decisions that generate household patterns offer insight into emergent family forms. They also permit exploration of the process by which households dissolve and undergo reorganization, as through remarriage (Furstenberg and Spanier, 1985). The imputation of any global pattern or mentality to households rests on the problematic assumption that people who live together share ideas and beliefs. Whether empirically true or not, the imputation obscures the process through which "individuals negotiate the relations that give form to households despite different and sometimes conflicting goals, strategies, and notions about what it means 'to live together'" (Yanagisako, 1984:331).

This view of the household is entirely compatible with a life-course approach if one provision is added, namely, that the study focus on the household arrangement of individuals over time instead of on the household unit per se. A record of household composition over a decade or more usually tells a story of change and turnover; people enter through births, care-taking, and the sharing of resources, and some leave through death, care in an institution, military service, and the transition to adult independence. Even over a short period of time, the change is often sufficient to transform the unit under study into a very different social form. This occurs through divorce which is followed by two remarriages.

An empirical example of the problems associated with the longitudinal study of households comes from the Michigan Panel Study of Income Dynamics which has been following more than 5000 American families on an annual basis ever since 1968. Duncan and Morgan (1985:69) observe that "our analysis of family income dynamics began with five years of information and the naive assumption that the same family could easily be compared in the first and fifth years." But the compositional changes were so frequent and substantial that the household proved useless as a unit for cross-time study. The individual became the unit of analysis. "At any point, individuals are assembled into families, can be identified by their relationship to the head of that family, and attain a level of economic well-being that can be measured by the family income or income relative to the needs of that family."

The implications of household change in composition for family income have received much visibility through the Michigan Panel Study (Duncan, 1984). Various estimates of time in poverty have been used, from four to nine years out of ten. Transient members of the poverty category turned out to be indistinguishable from members of the general sample, whereas the chronic cases were usually in one or more of three categories: female, elderly, and black. Change in household composition, in employment status, and in earnings accounted for entry into poverty, duration of stay in poverty, and exit from poverty. Bane and Ellwood (1986) have extended this line of analysis in the Panel study by focusing on the beginnings and endings of spells of poverty.

For the specific household, a spell of poverty begins in the first year that income drops below the poverty line and ends in the year when it rises above the line. All data on poverty spells were included in the analysis if they began between 1970 and 1981, regardless of whether they also ended within this time frame. At the start, a decline in the head's earnings emerged as the single most powerful cause of poverty (38 percent of all spells began this way). This percentage increased to nearly sixty percent for male-headed households with young children, in contrast to only fourteen percent of female-headed households. The formation of a female-headed household accounts for about eleven percent of all beginnings, but about sixty percent of the beginnings for female-headed households. Most important, the authors found that the duration of spells varied according to how they began.

> Poverty spells are longer when the reason that they begin is that the woman has become a female head with a child. The spells that begin for children when their families change from male- to female-headed are longer still, with a mean duration for a new spell of four years and for spells observed at a given time of about eleven years. Spells of poverty that begin with birth are the longest of all, averaging almost eight years for a new spell and nearly 17 years for a spell observed at a point in time...(Bane and Ellwood, 1986:17).

Termination of a poverty spell generally shows a different weighting of factors. More spells ended with a rise in the head's earnings than began with a loss of income by the household head (over fifty percent versus 38). Moreover, an earnings gain among female heads increased their prospects for moving out of poverty. One-third of these households made such a change through the woman's earnings, usually when she entered the job market.

The missing element in this analysis concerns the life-course timing of each spell. Beyond the events of birth and death, we see little recognition that poverty spells have differing consequences when they occur at different points in the life course.

The overall picture shows family structure and life-cycle events as key elements in the transition to poverty, with markedly improved earnings playing a more important role in pulling households out of poverty. Most poverty spells turned out to be very short. Slightly more than forty percent end within a single year. About seventy percent are over within a period of three years. Only twelve percent have the character of a chronic state, lasting ten years or more.

Bane and Ellwood (1986:12) conclude that "those who will be chronically poor are but a small fraction of those entering poverty but a large part of the poor at any time. The long-term poor account for a very large portion of all the person-years of poverty." The heaviest cost of such prolonged deprivation is experienced by black children. They combine the highest risk of poverty status with the poorest chances of leaving this state. Family circumstances (birth out of wedlock, single parent, etc.) increase their chances of being born into poverty and large earnings increases are not likely among adults in the household. As a result, Bane and Ellwood (1986:21) find that "the average poor black child today appears to be in the midst of a poverty spell which will last for almost two decades."

The residential history of such children up to adulthood generally includes episodes of single parenting and other households. Using twelve years of the Michigan Panel data, Hofferth (1985) followed the residential life course of six cohorts of black and white children up to the age of eighteen. By the age of seventeen, approximately one-third of the white children born in the 1960–64 cohort were not in a first-marriage, two-parent family. This compares to three-fourths of the black children in the cohort. If these trends continue, the probability for white children in the 1980–84 cohort will exceed forty percent, a figure which is twice as large for black children. On average, black children are more likely than white children to experience a household in which the parent is single, separated, or divorced; they are likely to spend more time in such households up to their eighteenth birthday; and, most surprisingly, they are less apt to be linked to other families through coresidence and financial assistance. It is the single black parent who is more likely to be isolated, not the single white parent.

Little is known about the effects of different household structures on children who vary in age or about the social meaning of long and short durations in particular household types. The very same appraisal was made in the early 1970s by Michael Katz (1975:299): "We are able to describe with some precision the structural components of households, but what, in fact, do they mean? What consequences for socialization, marital relations, or ego development did various forms of household structure entail?" In response to these questions, Katz suggests that we must have a theory which links social structures to behavior. However, a theory of this kind needs to be informed by empirical descriptions of behavior in particular social structures. Such evidence

is not yet available. However, a relevant study with historical implications has been carried out by Waite, Goldscheider and Wisberger (1986) on residential paths to adult status.

Their question focused on the duration of nonfamily living (living away from home) between age seventeen and first marriage or termination of contact. Does extensive nonfamily living change the attitudes and values of men and women as they approach family roles, in comparison to people who enter family roles directly from the household of their parents? Using a national longitudinal survey with more than 10,000 men and women, the study found that length of independent living made a significant difference in the orientations of women, but not of men. Duration of independent living increased the tendency of women to plan for employment and to accept the prospect of employment for mothers. Women with such experience lowered their expectations on family size and became· more nontraditional in their view of sex roles. The study controlled for orientation before age seventeen. This research brings to mind the work of Michael Katz (1975) on the stage of semi-independence experienced by Hamilton (Canada) youth in the preindustrial era. For a period in adolescence, boys and girls lived and worked as members of a household other than that of their parents. Did this period away from home also foster change in the attitudes and orientations of these Canadian adolescents?

One of the major unknowns in studies of the life-course dynamics of households and income involves the influence of sequences. Does the sequence of household structures matter for children and adults of different ages, and is a particular sequence a determinant of the meaning of specific conditions and their duration? Birth to a single parent may have different consequences depending on what the parent brought to the situation and on the sequence it initiates through marriage, education, or residence with mother. Similar observations can be made about the spells of poverty experienced by people along their career lines. Children who start their life in poverty have relatively poor prospects of leaving this state in the near-term, but what are the more general implications of the timing and duration of poverty for young and old? To answer these questions, we must be more successful in disentangling the effects of income and household change, two highly related events in the life course.

HISTORICAL VARIATIONS AND INFLUENCES: THE CHALLENGE REMAINS

The new post-1960s wave of life-course studies owes much to a growing awareness of the covariation between family and life patterns, on the one hand, and social change on the other. In the vernacular of age stratification (Riley, Johnson, and Foner, 1972), cohorts age in different ways as they respond to an ever-changing environment. Uhlenberg's (1974; 1978) study of American women's trajectories across five cohorts (1890–94 to 1930–34) shows such variation, especially in the rising tendency for white women to survive age fifty with an intact marriage and one child or more.

Prominent among the explanations for this trend are declining mortality among women after age fifteen and among men in childhood, along with a declining risk of spinsterhood and childlessness. Studies of more recent birth cohorts (McLaughlin and Melber, 1986) of American women show a reversal of the trend toward life-course uniformity through trends toward later marriage, delayed childbearing coupled with births outside of marriage in

the pre-adult years, and higher rates of divorce. This pattern of life-course diversity has become one of the central themes of family change among women and men since the 1950s.

Secular trends in mortality and marital instability are underlying processes that shape the life configurations outlined in Uhlenberg's study, but they also demand explanation. Why are the trends occurring? What factors account for rising levels of marital impermanence? Uhlenberg points to a number of potential explanatory factors, but he does not extend analysis to their actual investigation and estimation. At most we end up with a plausible story of how twentieth-century change is linked to women's lives and family patterns. But stories of this kind do not enable us to weigh specific forces, to apportion the variance, and to actually explicate the causal process.

Cohort and Period Effects: What Do They Mean?

A similar limitation appears in studies that have attempted to disentangle the effects of cohort, period, and life stage. For example, the Ann Arbor research team of Rodgers and Thornton (1985) investigated changes in cohort first marriages in the United States from 1900 to 1981. Data came from censuses and sample surveys on both men and women, nonwhite and white. Three major outcomes emerged from the analysis. First, marriage rates changed dramatically with World War I, World War II, and the Great Depression. Both wars preceded an upswing; a large valley occurred in 1930–33 during the Depression and another in 1942–44. Second, a long-term shift toward higher marriage rates occurred in the postwar era up to the 1970s, followed by a sharp decline after 1972. Cohort marriage rates by 1980 closely resemble those observed before World War II. Third, changes in marriage rates were comparable for the most part by age, sex, and race, except for teenagers.

Rodgers and Thornton (1985:21) conclude that "most of the changes in marriage rates observed during this century are the consequences of period characteristics" rather than of differences between cohorts. They draw the same conclusion about rates of marital instability or dissolution: "... the big picture is one of overwhelming historical effects that influenced all subgroups of the population substantially and surprisingly equally" (Rodgers and Thornton, 1985:29). In addition to the rising divorce rate to 1930, they refer especially to the decline in the Depression and the rapid recovery from it, to the extraordinary peak in the mid-1940s, and the upward trend of the 1960s and 1970s. Just what the period influences are remains to be determined empirically. In any case, the challenge is demanding since any satisfactory explanation must account for the generalized trends across cohorts, family stages, and the life course.

Period effects also stand out in studies of what Rindfuss, Morgan, and Swicegood (1984) call the "first-birth process" among white, native-born women in the United States. Using pooled national samples since 1955, they view the process in terms of three sets of influences: (1) aggregate time, as indexed by birth cohort and historical period; (2) social factors, such as education, residence, religion, region, and household composition; and (3) individual time, as indicated by age. The used birth cohorts range from 1915 to 1939. Though mixed with period and cohort estimates, strong historical variations are especially noteworthy in the results.

Social factors affected the first-birth probability in different ways at different points in the life span up to age 35. Thus education had stronger effects among older than among younger women. Another way to interpret this outcome is to note that social factors determined the timing of the first birth. As expected, large effects were observed in the context of aggregate time or history, and social factors tended to interact with historical time to produce variations. For example, better educated women tended to respond more strongly to change in socioeconomic conditions. Both the depressed conditions of the 1930s and increased opportunity during the 1970s are coupled with a strategy of delayed childbearing.

The significance of historical effects in this study is matched by the analysts' frustration over their elusive nature. They could be referring to first marriage or to divorce when they state that "period factors increase or decrease childbearing at all ages and for all subgroups within society" (Rindfuss, Morgan, and Swicegood, 1984:368). A lack of substantial clues to the nature of these effects has much to do, they argue, with the multiple changes that take place in any one period. They point to the women's movement, rising interest rates, and soaring housing prices as factors that could have affected childbearing in the 1970s. To differentiate among such factors, they recommend a longer time series and cross-national analysis. "Given the importance of period factors, such work should be high on the future research agenda" (p. 368). Conceivably this plan of action might provide a clearer picture of historical effects, but there is good reason to assume that such steps will yield little understanding of social history in families and lives.

The basis for this pessimism involves matters of research questions and design. Are we likely to gain essential understanding of historical change when questions are not addressed to this issue? For example, neither the Ann Arbor team nor the Chapel Hill team of Rindfuss and his associates posed questions concerning the influence of specific historical conditions and change on processes of family formation and dissolution. Thornton and Rodgers asked questions regarding secular trends in cohort first-marriages and divorce, while Rindfuss and his colleagues centered their attention on the process of first birth. In both cases, their research branches back to include a wide array of potential factors. The Great Depression is only one set of influences in the Chapel Hill research, and we know that its complexity far exceeds mere economic decline and recovery.

No single study can do justice to the complexities of the full historical record, and yet work should base historical explanations on the best sources available. Otherwise, we are likely to see little more than speculation and broad strokes from a high level of abstraction. Examples of this broad stroke include Easterlin's (1980) thesis about postwar childbearing and its uncertain foundation in Depression family experience.

Linking Social Change to the Family

Instead of beginning with a family outcome and working back to the historical record and other factors, life-course studies have much to gain by following Tilly's charge to family history. The task, as he phrased it, is "to relate the concrete experience of living in families at various points in space and time to large social structures and processes" (1987). This was the objective of Hareven's *Family Time and Industrial Time* (1982), a study of the mill community of Manchester, New Hampshire, circa 1900–1930; and it also represents the objective of *Children of the Great Depression* (Elder, 1974), a longitudinal study which followed a cohort of Oakland, California children (born 1920–21) through the Depression decade and

the World War II to the postwar years of middle age. Other such studies in the United States include Campbell's research (1983) on women in their homefront roles during World War II; and Carol Stack's ongoing study of the return migration of blacks to the South.

Collective biography, Tilly suggests, is the approach family history could employ with profit in linking "individual experience with large structures and processes" (1987). In the form of life-course analysis, such biography might compare household economies across communities on different paths of industrialization. The textile industry favored a household economy in which women and children worked for pay, in contrast to male-oriented mining communities (Elder, 1981). Hareven's study of the Amoskeag mill and its community of workers in Manchester provides a vivid characterization of the reciprocal relation between the family system and industrial capitalism. Mill families and the textile mill were coactors in a change process. We see the rise and fall of the Amoskeag in life chances and family adaptations.

The drama of this trajectory may well have obscured the uneven hand of family misfortune. In any case, we do not see this variation played out in family survival efforts. *Children of the Great Depression* (Elder, 1974) focuses directly on such variation within the Great Depression and traces out its implications through family adaptations for the experience of children and their adult lives. With the deprived households, operations became more labor intensive as children and mother performed more of the tasks by hand. Deprived families became more conflictful and disorganized when compared to more privileged families; and mothers acquired more prominence in matters of affection and authority, when compared to fathers. Each process serves as a micromodel of the relation between family hardship and children's experience. All of the nearly 170 children were members of the Oakland Growth Study at the University of California, Berkeley. Their birth in the early 1920s brought them to adolescence in the Depression and to young adulthood during World War II. Following the notion that social change has different implications for people of dissimilar age, the study assumed that the Oakland children were less subject to the stresses of family hardship than were younger children.

One test of this life-stage principle compared the Oakland cohort of people born in 1920–21 with a cohort of persons who were born in the city of Berkeley in 1928–29 (Elder, 1979). The younger age of the Berkeley children in the Depression placed them at greater risk of psychological impairment from the stresses and disruptions of unemployment and heavy income loss. This risk turned out to be greatest for the younger boys, owing to the effect of adverse change on fathers. For a good many boys, the risk became a reality. Both short-term and long-term disadvantages were most common among the Berkeley males. But even in this group, a Depression legacy of impaired psychological health and limited education was barely evident during the middle years of life.

An unfortunate beginning had been overcome in many cases, but how? This question led to a consideration of turning points in the life course and eventually to the role of military service and war mobilization (Elder, 1986; Elder and Bailey, 1987; Elder and Meguro, 1987). A turning point refers to a social process or mechanism that enables a re-direction of the life trajectory, such as a recasting of life chances from limited opportunity to the promises of a more rewarding, secure life.

War and Military Mobilization: Changing the Life Course

Military service qualifies as a recasting experience of this sort and it also represents one of the most common "male" events. Nine out of ten Oakland males left high school at the end of the 1930s only to be mobilized by the fast-moving events of World War II. Most entered the service in 1942 and 1943. The Berkeley men spent adolescence on the homefront, but seven out of ten ended up in uniform by the end of the Korean War.

For the most part, the war years and military service created a break with a past that was characterized by privation, frustration, and restricted opportunity. When viewed within the transition to adulthood, war mobilization closed some options, created others, and postponed still others. It produced a moratorium for the decision pressures of the age-graded career, a legitimated 'time out' from commitment pressures. Service time rearranged the traditional pathway to adulthood, delaying career progress and obligations.

Early entry into military service in particular could extend the transition to adulthood, postpone family events and responsibilities, and provide a route to future opportunities through separation from home, exposure to new places and people, and access to educational benefits. Historically, this route has been linked to self-improvement and greater opportunity. The data show that perceptions of this kind were most common among young men in both cohorts who had a history of family hardship through the Depression years, a record of school difficulty, and evidence of self-inadequacy in adolescence. They were most likely to join the service at the earliest possible age.

Military service generally entailed a delay in the timing of marriage and first birth among veterans in both cohorts and especially among the early entrants (younger than age 22). By contrast, late entrants more often encountered the costs of leaving an established family and career. As a whole, the early servicemen tended to follow a less conventional path of adult achievement than the late group in both cohorts. They had less education and they did not fare as well in occupational achievement by mid-life. However, they frequently acquired more education after military service and narrowed the gap in life achievement in relation to the late entrants. In both cohorts, the "developmental path" seems to apply most notably to the veterans who entered the armed forces at an early age. From the evidence at hand, these men show the greatest development and career achievement when measured from baseline. Military service was a turning point in many cases.

The disadvantaged origins of men who entered the service at an early age do not favor marital stability or occupational achievement, when compared to the life course of men who entered the service at a later time. But in both cohorts the early veterans were more likely to achieve a stable marriage and their marriages ranked higher on perceived quality, in comparison with the late entrants. Perhaps late mobilization increases marital discord and divorce by separating men from their families. Very few of the early entrants were married when they joined the service. Recent interviews with Oakland and Berkeley veterans who served in World War II and Korea tend to underscore the degree to which late entry fosters marital instability (Elder, 1986). Separation from loved ones and economic problems were cited far more often by late than by early entrants when they were asked about the costs of their term in the service. Time of mobilization within the life course is a matter of some importance in relation to the family.

War mobilization is beginning to receive the attention it deserves as a large, historical process which has profound consequences for the family. Vinovskis (1986) is engaged in a study of Civil War effects in the city population of Newburyport; and Modell and Steffey (1985) show with remarkable clarity how the Second World War both decelerated and accelerated the marriage rate under different circumstances. Something of the complexity of Modell's analysis appears in Campbell's (1983) examination of the diverse ways homefront mobilization in World War II influenced the social worlds of American women. Mayer (1986) is using both demographic data and retrospective life histories in comparative cohort studies of German survivors of the Second World War.

The major challenge is to think more systematically about the properties of war mobilization (Elder, 1986), and then to develop their implications for the family and life course. Time of entry is merely one element of this process. Occupational mobility related to the service and geographic migration represent variable elements of mobilization that have consequences for the individual and family. Service training is another aspect of military service which bears upon lifespan development. A third dimension— combat experience—is perhaps the most visible.

Life-course studies of Vietnam veterans are beginning to document the long arm of war through the lives of surviving veterans and their families. Unstable marriages are one consequence of heavy combat and its legacy in anger, emotional numbing, recurring nightmares and flashbacks (Laufer and Gallops, 1985). The longterm consequences of depression and war are part of a growing body of evidence on the ways biographies can bridge widely separated historical times.

A Design Sequence for Studying Social Change

We began this analytical discussion of social change in the family and life course by noting that cohort studies have tended to leave unspecified the historical sources of observed trends and outcomes. If the life course of women is changing in dramatic ways, as many studies document, we need to know the precise historical influences. What structural and cultural changes have occurred in the marketplace? How are the effects of economic cycles and rising levels of education played out in successive cohorts of women in western industrial societies?

The typical sociological study of family patterns over time has posed questions concerning a family outcome and its sources of variation. The task is to account for variation in the specified outcome. A lengthy historical time-span requires this design, resembling an "in-

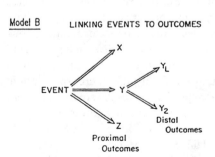

Figure 1. Studying Social Change in the Life Course: Two Models

verted funnel," because it generally produces greater specificity concerning key antecedents and the historical period of significance. As shown by Model A in Figure 1, the design casts a broad net for potent antecedent variables and provides estimates of their relative influence. Thus Hogan's (1981) cohort historical study of the transition to adulthood identified historical periods of special relevance, such as the Great Depression and Second World War. Likewise, Rindfuss and associates (1987) identified the same period as influential for change in family timing.

The design represents a process which has particular significance during the initial stage of research. It is a process of identifying potentially salient antecedent variables, of sorting them out and weighing their relative influence. Some of the important antecedents may tap historical changes of particular significance, as in rising levels of education, economic cycles, and the increasing employment of women. But the process by which such changes make a difference generally remains unclear and an attractive lure for speculation. We are left with a black box, a period or cohort effect.

Unknowns of this sort provide a point of departure for studies that relate macrochange to the micro-level of family behavior. Examples of this line of inquiry, as noted, include Hareven's study of the life course in relation to industrial growth and decline within the textile community of Manchester, 1900–1930; studies of the Great Depression and its influence on the family and life course; and ongoing studies of the aftermath of war in the lives and families of surviving members of cohorts.

The distinctive feature of this work is its explication of historical change, a task which typically generates multiple lines of consequences, each branching off in a different direction. Unlike the design of Model A, this design is focused directly on historical change and its consequences. By seeking to understand the effects of a type of social change, this inquiry pursues the implications of change wherever they may lead. A good many of these implications actually emerge from an explication of the social change itself.

SUMMARY

The decline of abstract macro-theories of the family over the past quarter century has been accompanied by the development of perspectives involving contextual, dynamic, and temporal aspects of family process and structure. The life course is one of these emerging perspectives, though it dates back at least to the early Chicago School of Sociology and the work of W.I. Thomas. This early period and the post-1960s are distinguished by rapid social change that made process, time, and setting especially relevant to an understanding of the family.

Two developments illustrate the shift toward these aspects of contemporary life-course study: (1) a growing interest in family transitions, both normative and non-normative, in relation to social change; and (2) a view of the domestic household which stresses its dynamic and temporal features. The timing of family events, marriage, and children, has received much attention in the research literature, and for good reason. Timing has powerful consequences in the life course, both within the family and across the generations. This area of study also underscores the necessity of placing the life course within the larger context of kinship and generational change. The study of age brings age grading and timing to the life course of people and families, along with historical context, while intergenerational analysis highlights the "given" nature of family ties, the interlocking lives of each generation, and the cross-generational

link by which historical experiences and influences are transmitted.

For a good many years, historical research on the household ignored the contextual nature of kinship, the processual aspects of social relations that give rise to decisions and living arrangements, and temporal features of the household, as in the residential history of members. This practice is best known through reliance on measures of mean household size. Longitudinal studies over the past decade have documented the changing size, composition, and dynamics of households, as well as the intimate relation between household economics and structure. Household change is so pronounced that it severely limits the possibility of following a domestic unit over time. Accordingly, research has turned to the individual and his or her living arrangements, to the probability of entering and leaving certain households, and to residential pathways. This new work places poverty and family structures within the life course and the intergenerational life cycle.

The life-course perspective emerged in part from recognition that individual and historical change are intertwined. Social change occurs in part through change in people and cohorts, whereas both individual and family changes result from transformations of the larger environment. Cohort studies of family variables show the critical role of period influences which extend across all cohorts. Such effects leave much to the imagination, however. What is included under a period effect? Influences of this kind are often interpreted through mere speculation. More productive results are likely to stem from research that actually explicates the effects of historical change on the family and life course. Macro-changes should be traced to household, family, and kin.

This connection involves the family dynamic of interdependent lives, an avenue by which historical change alters the life course. *Children of the Great Depression* (Elder, 1974:15) refers to the outlook that people acquire from their world, "an outlook that reflects lives lived interdependently in a particular historical context." Hard times in the Great Depression influenced the lives of adolescents through the economic hardship and job losses of parents, and also through the lives of grandparents who shared the household. For American youth during World War II, the distinctive feature of adolescence included war-related employment of parents from sunup to sundown, the military service and war trauma of older brothers, and the mobilization of school children for civil defense and the war effort. To understand historical forces and the family, we need research on lives lived interdependently, a concept that is fundamental to a life-course perspective.

ACKNOWLEDGMENTS

Preparation of this article was supported by a NIMH Senior Scientist Fellowship (MH00567) awarded to the author.

REFERENCES

Anderson, Michael. 1985. "The Emergence of the Modern Life Cycle in Britain." *Social History* 10:69–87.

Bane, Mary Jo, and David T. Ellwood. 1986. "Slipping Into and Out of Poverty: The Dynamics of Spells." *Journal of Human Resources* 21:1–23.

Brumberg, Joan Jacobs. 1985. "Ruined Girls: Family and Community Responses to Illegitimacy in Upstate New York, 1890–1920." *Journal of Social History* 18:247–272.

Burton, Linda M. 1985. "Early and On-Time Grandmotherhood in Multigenerational Black Families." Unpublished doctoral dissertation, University of Southern California.

Burton, Linda M., and Vern L. Bengtson. 1985. "Black Grandmothers: Issues of Timing and Continuity of Roles." Pp. 61–77 in *Grandparenthood*, edited by Vern L. Bengtson and Joan F. Robertson. Beverly Hills, CA: Sage.

Campbell, D'Ann. 1983. *Women at War with America*. Cambridge, MA: Harvard University Press.

Cherlin, Andrew J. 1981. *Marriage, Divorce, Remarriage: Marital Formation and Dissolution in the Postwar United States*. Cambridge, MA: Harvard University Press.

Duncan, Greg J. 1984. *Years of Poverty, Years of Plenty*. Ann Arbor, MI: Institute for Social Research.

Duncan, Greg J., & James N. Morgan. 1985. "The Panel Study of Income Dynamics." Pp. 50–74 in *Life Course Dynamics: Trajectories and Transitions, 1968-1980*, edited by Glen H. Elder, Jr. Ithaca, NY: Cornell University Press.

Easterlin, Richard. 1980. *Birth and Fortune: The Impact of Numbers of Personal Welfare*. New York: Basic Books.

Elder, Glen H., Jr. 1986. "War Mobilization and the Life Course: A Cohort of World War II Veterans." Paper presented at the annual meetings of the American Sociological Association, New York City, September.

———. 1985. *Life Course Dynamics: Trajectories and Transitions, 1968-1980*. Ithaca, NY: Cornell University Press.

———. 1984. *Families, Kin, and the Life Course: A Sociological Perspective*. Pp. 80–135 in *The Family*, edited by Ross D. Parke. Chicago: University of Chicago Press.

———. 1981. "History and the Family: The Discovery of Complexity." *Journal of Marriage and the Family* 43:489–519.

———. 1979. "Historical Changes in Life Patterns and Personality." Pp. 117–159 in *Life-Span Development and Behavior*, edited by Paul B. Baltes and Orville G. Brim. New York: Academic Press.

———. 1978. "Family History and the Life Course." Pp. 17–64 in *Transitions: The Family and the Life Course in Historical Perspective*, edited by Tamara K. Hareven. New York: Academic Press.

———. 1977. "Family History and the Life Course." *Journal of Family History* 2:279–304.

———. 1975. "Age Differentiation and the Life Course." *Annual Review of Sociology* 1:165–190. Palo Alto, CA: Annual Reviews.

———. 1974. *Children of the Great Depression*. Chicago: University of Chicago Press.

Elder, Glen H., Jr., and Susan L. Bailey. 1987. "The Timing of Military Service in Men's Lives. In *Social Stress and Family Development*, edited by Joan Aldous and David Klein. New York: Guilford Press.

Elder, Glen H., Jr., and Yoriko Meguro. 1987. "Wartime in Men's Lives: A Comparison of

American and Japanese Cohorts." *International Journal of Behavioral Development*, forthcoming.

Featherman, David L. 1986. "Biography, Society, and History." In *Human Development and the Life Course: Multidisciplinary Perspectives*, edited by Aage B. Sørenson, Franz Weinert, and Lonnie Sherrod. Hillsdale, NJ: Erlbaum.

Furstenberg, Frank F. 1976. *Unplanned Parenthood: The Social Consequences of Teenage Childbearing*. New York: Free Press.

Furstenberg, Frank F., Jeanne Brooks-Gunn, and S. Philip Morgan. 1987. *Adolescent Mothers in Later Life*. New York: Cambridge University Press.

Furstenberg, Frank F., and Spanier Graham. 1985. *Recycling the Family*. Beverly Hills, CA: Sage.

Glick, Paul C. 1947. "The Family Cycle." *American Sociological Review* 12:164–174.

Hagestad, Gunhild O. 1986. "Dimensions of Time and the Family." *American Behavioral Scientist* 29:679–694.

—————. 1982. "Parent and Child: Generations in the Family." Pp. 485–499 in *Review of Human Development*, edited by T.M. Field, H.C. Huston, L.T. Quay, and G.E. Finley. New York: Wiley.

Hareven, Tamara K. 1982. *Family Time and Industrial Time: The Relationship Between the Family and Work in a New England Industrial Community*. New York: Cambridge University Press.

—————. 1978. *Transitions: The Family and the Life Course in Historical Perspective*. New York: Academic Press.

Hernandez, Donald J. 1986. "Childhood in a Sociodemographic Perspective." Pp. 159–180 in *Annual Review of Sociology*, edited by Ralph H. Turner and James F. Short, Jr. Palo Alto, CA: Annual Review Inc.

Hirschman, Charles, and Ronald R. Rindfuss. 1982. "The Sequence and Timing of Family Formation Events in Asia." *American Sociological Review* 47:660–680.

Hill, Reuben. 1970. *Family Development in Three Generations*. Cambridge, MA: Schenkman.

Hofferth, Sandra L. 1985. "Children's Life Course: Family Structure and Living Arrangements in Cohort Perspective." Pp. 75–112 in *Life Course Dynamics: Trajectories and Transitions, 1968-1980*, edited by Glen H. Elder, Jr. Ithaca, NY: Cornell University Press.

—————. 1986. "Response to a Comment by Bumpass on 'Updating Children's Life Course.'" *Journal of Marriage and the Family* 48: 680–682.

Hogan, Dennis P., and Nan Marie Astone. 1986. "The Transition to Adulthood." Pp. 109–130 in *Annual Review of Sociology*, edited by Ralph H. Turner and James F. Short, Jr. Palo Alto, CA: Annual Review Inc.

Hogan, Dennis P. 1981. *Transitions and Social Change*. New York: Academic Press.

Katz, Michael B. 1975. *The People of Hamilton, Canada West: Family and Class in a Mid-Nineteenth-Century City*. Cambridge, MA: Harvard University Press.

Kertzer, David I., and Dennis P. Hogan. 1985. "On the Move: Migration in an Italian Community, 1865–1921." *Social Science History* 9:1–23.

Kertzer, David I., and Jennie Keith (eds.). 1984. *Age and Anthropological Theory*. Ithaca, NY: Cornell University Press.

Kessler, Ronald C., and Jane D. McLeod. 1984. "Sex Differences in Vulnerability to Undesirable Life Events." *American Sociological Review* 49:620–631.

Laslett, Peter, and R. Wall (eds.). 1972. *Household and Family in Past Time*. London: Cambridge University Press.

Laufer, Robert S. 1986. Personal communication.

Laufer, Robert S., and Mark S. Gallops. 1985. "Life-Course Effects of Vietnam Combat and Abusive Violence: Marital Patterns." *Journal of Marriage and the Family* 47:839–853.

Marini, Margaret Mooney. 1984a. "Age and Sequencing Norms in the Transition to Adulthood." *Social Forces* 63:229–244.

—————. 1984b. "The Order of Events in the Transition to Adulthood. *Sociology of Education* 57:63–84.

Mayer, Karl Ulrich. 1986. "German Survivors of the Second World War: The Collective Experience of Birth Cohorts and Impacts on the Life Course." Paper presented at the annual meeting of American Sociological Association, New York City, September.

McLanahan, Sara S., and Aage B. Sørenson. 1985. "Life Events and Psychological Well-Being Over the Live Course." Pp. 217–238 in *Life Course Dynamics: Trajectories and Transitions, 1968-80*, edited by Glen H. Elder, Jr. Ithaca, NY: Cornell University Press.

McLaughlin, Steven D., et al. 1985. *The Cosmopolitan Report on the Changing Life Course of American Women*. Seattle, WA: Battelle Memorial Institute.

McLaughlin, Steven D., and Barbara D. Melber. 1986. *The Changing Life Course of American Women: Life-Style and Attitude Changes*. Seattle, WA: Battelle Memorial Institute.

Modell, John, and Duane Steffey. 1985. "A People's

War to Protect the American Family: Military Service and Family Formation, 1940–1950." Paper presented at the Social Science History Association meeting, Chicago, September.

Moen, Phyllis. 1985. "Continuities and Discontinuities in Women's Labor Force Activity." Pp. 113–155 in *Life Course Dynamics: Trajectories and Transitions, 1968-1980*, edited by Glen H. Elder, Jr. Ithaca, NY: Cornell University Press.

Netting, Robert M.C., Richard R. Wilk, and Eric J. Arnould (eds.). 1984. "Introduction." Pp. xiii–xxxviii in *Households: Comparative and Historical Studies of the Domestic Group*. Berkeley, CA: University of California Press.

Riley, Matilda White, Anne Foner, and Joan Waring. 1987. "Sociology of Age." In *Handbook of Sociology*, edited by Neil Smelser and Ronald Burt. Beverly Hills, CA: Sage Publications.

Riley, Matilda White, Marilyn Johnson, and Anne Foner. 1972. *Aging and Society: A Sociology of Age Stratification*. New York: Russell Sage.

Rindfuss, Ronald R., S. Philip Morgan, and C. Gray Swicegood. 1987. *The Transition to Parenthood*. Berkeley, CA: University of California Press.

Rindfuss, Ronald R., C. Gray Swicegood, and Rachel Rosenfeld. 1986. "Disorder of the Life Course." Unpublished paper. Carolina Population Center, Chapel Hill, NC.

Rindfuss, Ronald R., S. Philip Morgan, and C. Gray Swicegood. 1984. "The Transition to Motherhood: The Intersection of Structure and Temporal Dimension." *American Sociological Review* 49:359–372.

Rodgers, Willard L., and Arland Thornton. 1985. "Changing Patterns of First Marriage in the United States." *Demography* 22(2):265–279.

Rossi, Alice S. 1980. "Aging and Parenthood in the Middle Years." Pp. 137–205 in *Life-Span Development and Behavior*, vol. 3, edited by Paul B. Baltes and Orville G. Brim, Jr. New York: Academic.

Rowntree, B.S. 1901. *Poverty: A Study of Town Life*. London: Macmillan.

Segalen, Martine. 1977. "The Family Cycle and Household Structure: Five Generations in a French Village." *Journal of Family History* 2:223–236.

Thomas, W.I., and F. Znaniecki. 1918–20. *The Polish Peasant in Europe and America*, 2 volumes. Chicago: University of Chicago Press.

Tilly, Charles. 1987. "Family History, Social History, and Social Change." *Journal of Family History* 12 (1–3): 319–330.

Uhlenberg, Peter. 1978. "Configurations of the Life Course." Pp. 65–97 in *Transitions: The Family and the Life Course in Historical Perspective*, edited by Tamara Hareven. New York: Academic Press.

Uhlenberg, Peter. 1974. "Cohort Variations in Family Life Cycle Experience of U.S. Females." *Journal of Marriage and the Family* 36: 284–292.

Vanden Heuvel, Audrey. 1986. "The Timing of Parenthood and Intergenerational Relations." Unpublished master's thesis, University of North Carolina, Chapel Hill.

Vinovskis, Maris A. 1986. "Have Social Historians Lost the Civil War? Some Preliminary Demographic Speculations." Paper presented at the annual meetings of the American Sociological Association, New York City, September.

———. 1977. "From Household Size to the Life Course: Some Observations on Recent Trends in Family History." *American Behavioral Scientist* 21:263–387.

Waite, Linda J., Frances Kobrin Goldscheider, and Christina Wisberger. 1986. "Nonfamily Living and the Erosion of Traditional Family Orientations Among Young Adults." *American Sociological Review* 51:541–554.

Watkins, Susan Cotts. 1980. "On Measuring Transitions and Turning Points." *Historical Methods* 13:181–186.

Yanagisako, S.I. 1984. "Explicating Residence: A Cultural Analysis of Changing Households Among Japanese Americans. Pp. 330–352 in *Households: Comparative and Historical Studies of the Domestic Group*, edited by R. McNetting, R.R. Wilk, and E.J. Arnould. Berkeley, CA: University of California Press.

Young, Michael, and Peter Wilmott. 1973. *The Symmetrical Family*. New York: Macmillan.

THE LIFE COURSE OF SEVENTEENTH-CENTURY IMMIGRANTS TO CANADA

Yves Landry
Jacques Légaré

ABSTRACT: *Using the register of the early French Canadian population, the "Programme de recherche en démographie historique" (Université de Montréal) has set out to identify the demographic parameters behind the individual life course of the cohorts of immigrants which founded the country. The authors selected for their study all the individuals born outside of Canada who settled in Canada before 1680. The analysis covers not only the timing of the marriages and births of children of the immigrants, from their arrival to their death, but also the intensity of the phenomena that characterize their family life. The idea is to identify the proportion of individuals who lived through the main phases of the family life cycle (pre-parental, parental, post-parental) and to measure their timing. So as to avoid hiding the diversity of demographic behaviors behind broad averages, the study takes into account such basic variables as sex, length of life, number of marriages contracted, and number of children born.*

The demographic study of the family in history encompasses the broad areas of nuptiality, fertility, and mortality in past populations. Because of the overlapping

Yves Landry, research assistant at the Programme de recherche en démographie historique of the Université de Montréal, is currently working on the historical demography of New France.

Jacques Légaré, Professor of Demography, Université de Montréal, is Co-Director of the Programme de recherche en démographie historique. His principal research interests are in historical demography, life-course analysis, adult mortality and aging of populations.

of these phenomena, the analyst needs a concept permitting an integrated and comprehensive perspective on individual demographic behavior within the family with respect to the particular development of the family unit. The first empirical studies of the historical demography of the family in the United States and Canada used primarily the concept of family life cycle which emphasizes the evolution of the family unit before, during, and after parenthood, with variables based on the couple rather than the individual (Glick and Parke, 1965; Landry and Légaré, 1984; Lapierre-Adamcyk et al., 1984).[1]

By applying this concept to the study of rural families in Canada before 1700, the timing of changes occurring in the family was established and the means of measuring the intensity of the phenomena were introduced. These indicated that only a minority of families experienced all the stages of the family life cycle. It was thus revealed that, because of high infant mortality and a prolonged period of expansion, very few couples experienced any real period of stability involving responsibility for all children born. The families of the great majority of couples were prematurely reduced, since, according to our estimation, fifty percent lost a child before the sixth year of marriage. Moreover, only in exceptional cases, for less than twenty percent of marriages, do we find both spouses living together after having raised their family. Most marriages had ended by the time the last child had left home (Lapierre-Adamcyk et al., 1984:65–72).

There is a need, however, to expand the concept of family life cycle into the broader one of individual life course which relates individual development to that of the family unit (Hareven, 1978:1–64; Hareven, 1985). The transition to this new concept allows taking into account all the successive marriages of an individual, and to cumulate the children born in each. Thus the historical realities of individuals and families are closely connected. Since the demographic data used in this study were computerized so as to provide information on both individuals and family units (Desjardins, 1985a), this study will use the new approach.

The family life of individuals will be analyzed in its conjugal and parental aspects; each will be examined for the intensity and timing of the demographic phenomena involved. We will calculate not only the mean age of the individual at points such as first marriage, widowhood, remarriage, birth of the first and last children, first and last departure of a child, and death, but also the proportion of individuals who experienced the various events mentioned. In order not to obscure the diversity of behavior with general averages, observations will take into account variables such as sex, longevity, number of marriages contracted, and number of children born. We will thus obtain results which allow us to determine the main parameters of family life during the colonial period. The picture which emerges, although specific to the first inhabitants of Canada, should be a useful point of reference for historians of the modern family. Beyond the analysis of family structure which has been particularly studied so far by American historical demographers (Smith, 1982:10), there is the global presentation of individual demographic behavior within the family. It is to this that we will devote ourselves, for the first time using the empirical observation of a large population.

DATA

A computerized register of the early French Canadian population has been completed by the Programme de recherche en démographie historique (P.R.D.H.) of the Université de Montréal for the period before 1730, covering the first century of the colony's existence. It contains over 100,000 vital records from 86 parish and mission registers. The processing of this great quantity of data has created over 63,000 files on individuals associated with 12,000 families (Desjardins, 1985b). This register corresponds very closely to the ideal historical data base as described by Sundin and Winchester (1982).

Because of the longitudinal perspective emphasized in historical demography, observation of an extensive period of time is necessary. Since most of the files in the population register are currently incomplete, we first selected 3,380 individuals born outside Canada who formed families in the St. Lawrence Valley before 1680. This population represents all the French pioneers who founded the Canadian population, and it is currently the subject of many different analyses by P.R.D.H. researchers (Charbonneau et al., forthcoming). The present study has gained from their efforts a better understanding of all the characteristics involved. The need for complete information on individual life courses for our study nevertheless imposes certain choices. We excluded the 586 individuals who had married outside Canada at least once, the 235 people who emigrated out of Quebec, and the 968 cases for whom one of the family files

does not provide the date of marriage or does not identify the surviving spouse or his/her age upon being widowed. When we also exclude the rare individuals (only ninety cases) who married three or more times (since the individuals excluded for the various reasons overlap in many cases), we are left with 2,236 individuals—1,375 men and 861 women—who will provide the data for our study. They are all immigrants who arrived in Canada single, contracted one or two marriages in Canada to Canadians or other immigrants, and have had their demographic life courses completely documented.[2] We should mention, however, that the choices made restricted the proportion of twice-married individuals. Thus, our calculations of the intensity of remarriage will represent minima.

CONJUGAL LIFE

Table 1 divides the analyzed population according to sex, age at death, and number of marriages. As might be expected, the effect of longevity on the number of marriages is clear. The rarity of women in the colonial environment increased the intensity of remarriage among those living beyond 50 years: almost a fourth of them married twice. The opposite is true for men who died early in life: very few, less than five percent, had the op-

Table 1
Immigrant Marriages by Sex and Age at Death
($N = 2236$)

Number of marriages	Men			Women		
	Dead before the age of 50	*Dead at 50 or over*	*Total*	*Dead before the age of 50*	*Dead at 50 or over*	*Total*
1	96.8	85.5	88.9	86.9	76.3	79.0
2	3.2	14.5	11.1	13.1	23.7	21.0
Total	100	100	100	100	100	100
N =	408	967	1375	221	640	861

Note: The analysis is of immigrants marrying for the first time before 1680 in Canada. See text.

Table 2
Age at Marriage and Order of Marriage
($N = 2236$)

Number of marriages	Men				Women			
	First marriage		Second marriage		First marriage		Second marriage	
	Age	N	Age	N	Age	N	Age	N
1	28.8	1222	—	—	21.1	680	—	—
2	28.0	153	46.4	153	20.3	181	37.8	181
Total	28.7	1375	46.4	153	21.0	861	37.8	181

Note: The analysis is of immigrants marrying for the first time before 1680 in Canada. See text.

portunity of remarrying, especially since male immigrants married relatively late in life.

As shown by Table 2, there is a considerable gap between men and women with respect to age at marriage. For both first and second marriages, the difference is greater than seven years. The contrast at first marriage can be explained by the great difference in age at the time of immigration. Women who arrived in Canada were an average of three or four years younger than male immigrants. However, the difference is related primarily to the great imbalance between the sexes in the marriage market, which encouraged young women to wed soon after arriving while compelling men to become estab-

lished before attempting to marry. Men and women who married twice contracted their first marriage at an earlier age than those who married only once. This is a reflection of the fact that there were greater chances of widowhood and remarriage if one married at an early age. We should also mention the great diversity of ages at second marriage[3], which could take place at any age. Half of first marriages, however, took place between the ages of 24 and 29 for men and between sixteen and 22 for women.

Were men or women more likely to survive their spouses? It appears that women were, given the age gap between spouses (see Table 3). Whatever the number of marriages or age group at

Table 3
Married Persons Surviving Last Spouse
($N = 2236$)

Number of marriages	Men			Women		
	Dead before the age of 50	Dead at 50 or over	Total*	Dead before the age of 50	Dead at 50 or over	Total*
1	2.0%	30.1%	21.0%	12.0%	71.1%	54.4%
2	(7.7%)**	18.6%	17.6%	(17.2%)**	55.9%	49.7%
Total	2.2%	28.4%	20.7%	12.7%	67.5%	53.4%

*The total proportion of widowers and widows does not equal 100% given that marriages were sometimes contracted with people who were not part of the population studied.

**These proportions have been calculated from very small numbers and have to be used with caution.

Note: The analysis is of immigrants marrying for the first time before 1680 in Canada and surviving their last spouse. See text.

Table 4
Widowed Persons and Orphans
($n = 961$)

	Men			Women		
Number of orphans*	Widowed before the age of 50	Widowed at 50 or over	Total	Widowed before the age of 50	Widowed at 50 or over	Total
0	29.6	68.2	53.9	19.9	79.9	50.8
1–3	34.9	17.8	24.1	46.4	19.7	32.7
4+	35.5	14.0	22.0	33.7	0.4	16.5
Total	100	100	100	100	100	100
$n =$	152	258	410	267	284	551
Average number	2.5	1.0	1.6	2.6	0.3	1.4

*Living unmarried children who have not reached the age of 15 are considered orphans living in the family at the time of the spouse's death.

Note: The analysis is of immigrants marrying for the first time before 1680 in Canada and becoming widowed from first marriages. See text.

death, the frequency of widowhood was always higher among women than men: the average ratio is more than two to one. Distribution according to age at death shows, not surprisingly, that the earlier one died, the greater the chance of preceding one's spouse to the grave.

Besides a widow or widower, half of deceased spouses left behind at least one dependent child (see Table 4). The surviving spouse inherited an average of 1.5 children. This figure increases to 3.1 when only the widows and widowers left with at least one dependent child are considered. The number of dependents was particularly high for those under fifty years of age, with several children who had not yet reached the age of marriage. More than a third had at least four young children; some had seven, eight, or even nine.[4] We can speculate that the number of dependent children must have influenced the decision to remarry.

At least a third of surviving spouses from first marriages remarried (see Table 5). However, this frequency varied considerably according to age at the spouse's

death. While the majority of young widows and widowers remarried, remarriage took place in only a minority of older individuals. The number of dependent children does not seem to have hindered the remarriage of young widows and widowers. Among those widowed at the age of fifty or more, a greater proportion of men were left with dependent children (see Table 4). A significant number of these fathers with young children, more than a quarter, remarried (see Table 5). Older widows, however, seldom remarried, whether or not they had dependents.

Figure 1 shows the overall timing of the conjugal life of individuals according to sex and number of marriages. This graph reveals the complexity of individual life courses and the resulting difficulty of accounting for them. However, we can point out certain patterns in the relationships between nuptiality and mortality among immigrants who settled in Canada before 1680. It seems clear that, for those individuals who married in Canada, most of their adult life, considered as the period between the end of celibacy and death, unfolded

Table 5
Widowed Persons, Orphans, and Remarriage
(N = 961)

Number of orphans*	Men									Women								
	Widowed before the age of 50			Widowed at 50 or over			Total			Widowed before the age of 50			Widowed at 50 or over			Total		
	RM	NR	T	RM	NR	T	RM	NR	T	RM	NR	T	RM	NR	T	RM	NR	T
0	78	22	100	13	87	100	26	74	100	45	55	100	8	92	100	15	85	100
1–3	68	32	100	28	72	100	49	51	100	63	37	100	5	95	100	45	55	100
4+	67	33	100	28	72	100	51	49	100	62	38	100	(100)**	(–)**	100	63	37	100
Total	70	30	100	18	82	100	37	63	100	59	41	100	8	92	100	33	67	100

Notes: The analysis is of immigrants marrying for the first time before 1680 in Canada and becoming widowed from first marriages. See text.

RM = Remarriage
NR = No remarriage
T = Total

*Living unmarried children who have not reached the age of fifteen are considered orphans living in the family at the spouse's death.
**These proportions have been calculated from very small numbers and have been used with caution.

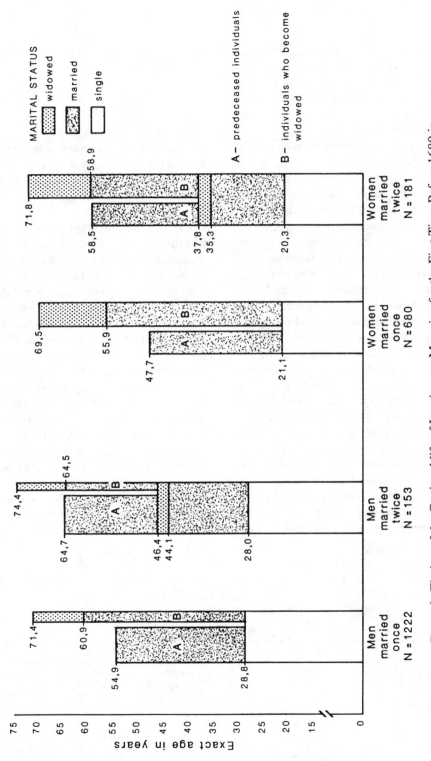

Figure 1. Timing of the Conjugal life of Immigrants Marrying for the First Time Before 1680 in Canada According to Sex and Number of Marriages (1 or 2) (*N* = 2236)

207

within marriage. The proportion of adult life spent with a spouse (see shaded area) was 92 percent for men and 81 percent for women. The significant portion of women's lives spent in widowhood is due not so much to the average length of widowhood between two marriages or at the end of life, but to the frequency of widowhood, which is more than twice as frequent as for men. The length of individuals' lives seems closely related to the number of marriages; longevity encouraged remarriage, as we have seen. Dissolution of the marriage occurred at all ages and was more frequently followed by remarriage of the surviving spouse if it occurred at an early age. When we establish the age at death according to sex by calculating the weighted average or the ages at death (seen in Figure 1) of those people who either survived their spouses of not and married once or twice, we find that, on the average, women died at a slightly higher age than men: 60.7 years compared to 59.3 years for men. However, when they died before their spouses, women generally died earlier than men in the same circumstances, because of the important age gap between spouses. The period of widowhood (see dotted area), when not followed by remarriage, lasted an average of 13.5 years for widows and

ten years for widowers, who then died at a respectable age of over 70.

PARENTAL LIFE

While a study of conjugal life establishes the timing of marriages on an individual basis, a study of parental life deals with the relation between the individual and the timing of increases or reductions in the family.

If all their marriages are considered, we find that nine percent of individuals were infertile. Others had from one to twenty-seven children.[5] Each individual had an average of 7.2 known children (see Table 6). Early mortality occurring within the period of fertility directly affected the number of children; men and women who died before the age of 50 generally had many fewer children than those who died later. Despite the stability of their unions, those who only married once had fewer children than those who married twice. Thus, the period of infertility occurring during widowhood was largely compensated for by earlier age at first marriage (see Figure 1) and by the longer average duration of the reproductive life (for those who died before 50, a difference of two years for men and five years for women).

Table 6
Number of Children
($N = 2236$)

Number of marriages	Men						Women					
	Dead before the age of 50		Dead at 50 or over		Total		Dead before the age of 50		Dead at 50 or over		Total	
	$\bar{n}$	N	$\bar{n}$	N	$\bar{n}$	N	$\bar{n}$	N	$\bar{n}$	N	$\bar{n}$	N
1	4.4	395	8.2	827	6.9	1222	5.5	192	7.7	488	7.1	680
2	4.9	13	8.5	140	8.2	153	7.0	29	8.0	152	7.8	181
Total	4.4	408	8.2	967	7.1	1375	5.7	221	7.8	640	7.3	861

Note: The analysis is of the average number of children of immigrants marrying for the first time before 1680 in Canada and the number of their marriages.

Table 7
Departure of Children
($N = 2032$)

Number of known children	N	Frequency of departure of children by			
		Death	Marriage	"Emancipation"	Total
1–5	579	40.4	39.1	20.5	100
6+	1453	35.9	38.5	25.6	100
Total	2032	37.2	38.7	24.1	100

Note: The analysis is of the children of those immigrants who married for the first time before 1680 in Canada.

All children born within the family inevitably left it. It is possible to calculate the timing of these departures despite the absence of regular censuses by using death and marriage dates for the children and formulating certain hypotheses. Thus, we fixed 25 years, the legal age of majority, as the maximum age for leaving the family. Those who died[6] or married before this age were considered to have left the family, while those survivors who were still unmarried were considered to have left by "emancipation."

Table 7 shows the frequency of the three types of departure for the population studied. Approximately as many departures resulted from marriage as from death, nearly forty percent for each. The percentage of children leaving the family because of death corresponds roughly to the probability of dying before the age of 25, calculated by Hubert Charbonneau (1975) at 41.1 percent for Canadian generations born of seventeenth-century marriages. The differences according to the number of children born are too small to allow any definite conclusions, especially since the unknown fate of some of the children decreases the significance of the distinction between departures due to death and to "emancipation."

Figure 2 shows the average timing of parental life of all the individual studied, for pre-parental, parental, and post-parental stages.[7] The average length of pre-parental stage, or the interval between the date of marriage and the birth of the first child, was relatively long, about two years, and inversely proportional to the number of children born, since fecundability was greater for the parents of large families. Men then experienced a long parental stage, which lasted the rest of their lives, while women, who married earlier, often lived to see the last departure of a child and embarked upon a post-parental stage which lasted on the average almost three years for those with a large family and almost six years for the others.

Detailed analysis of the parental stage according to the size of the family seems to show a significant dichotomy, but one must be careful in interpreting it. The parental stage of those with small families seems similar to that of families today: a period of expansion followed by a period of stabilization and then by reduction (Lapierre-Adamcyk et al., 1985:64–68). In fact, the use of averages is deceptive. Only 24 percent of men and 38 percent of women had their last child before the first departure of a child. In large families, the

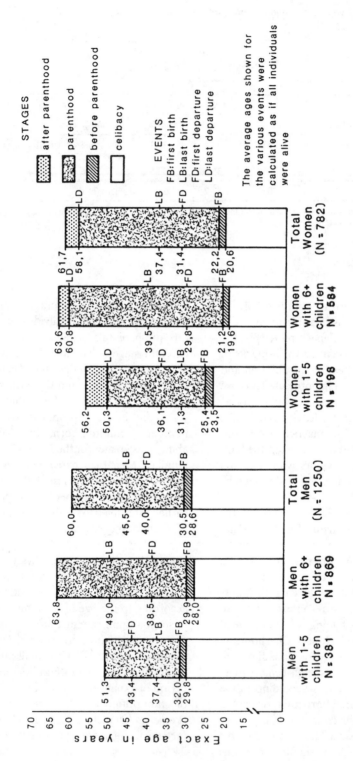

Figure 2. Timing of the Parental Life of Immigrants Marrying For the First Time Before 1680 in Canada According to Sex and Number of Children Born (at least one) ($N = 2032$)

first departure occurred an average of ten years before the last birth. The early appearance of the period of family reduction is not surprising in an era when only six out of ten children reached the average age of marriage. It is particularly evident for individuals who had six or more children: usually, the first child had left the family before the father or mother was halfway through the period of fertility.

Nor can we disregard the significant variation in the percentage of parents surviving at the beginning and end of the period of family reduction. When the first child left the family—three out of four times because of death—only 12 percent of fathers and 4 percent of mothers were deceased. However, when the last child left twenty-five years later, in over 85 percent of cases as a result of marriage or "emancipation," 68 percent of fathers and 39 percent of mothers were dead. Less than a third of men and almost two-thirds of women were left to enjoy a few years of life without dependent children.

Finally, it should be noted that the fertile men and women studied died at an older age than those who experienced no parental stage: Sixty and 62 years for those who had at least one child compared to 52 and 51 for the infertile, respectively.

CONCLUSION

The concept of the individual life course proves to be useful for summarizing the demographic behavior of unmarried immigrants who settled in Canada before 1680. Since analysis is based on the smallest common denominator—the individual—more varied applications are possible, based on variables determined by the researcher.

One of the many avenues of research facilitated by application of this concept is women's history, which tends to be obscured by the family framework that uses

the history of the couple. Some of the results presented here, in our view, help to shed light on the important parameters of the lives of French women who settled in Canada during the seventeenth century. In addition to providing demographic data that add to the basis for our knowledge of the family life of the past, this type of research leads the way to a greater understanding of the relationship between biology and cultural behavior. The practice of nursing and the use of wetnurses, which influences the size of the family, is only one example. This type of material encourages the kind of interdisciplinary cooperation which should provide the history of the family with its most important discoveries in the years to come.

ACKNOWLEDGMENTS

Preparation of this study was made possible by the financial support of the Social Sciences and Humanities Research Council of Canada, the FCAR Fund, and the Université de Montréal. The authors wish to thank Réal Bates for his collaboration.

NOTES

1. The family life cycle can be broken down into three stages. The first is the pre-parental stage, lasting from marriage to the first live birth. The second is the parental stage, lasting from the first live birth to the last departure of a child. This stage includes two parts: expansion, from the first to the last birth; and stabilization, from the last birth to the last departure of a child. The third stage is the post-parental stage, lasting from the last departure of a child to the dissolution of the family. This also has two parts: joint, from the last departure of a child to the dissolution of the union by the death of the first spouse; and isolated, from the dissolution of the union to the dissolution of the family by the death of the second spouse or his/her remarriage.

2. Since burial records were not available for 640 individuals, death dates were attributed to them by statistical methods based on the data last mentioning them as alive and first mentioning them as deceased. We have every reason for trusting in the

value of the averages calculated from these approx-imations even in absence of individual precision.

3. Standard deviations for age at marriage are, at second marriage, 11.4 (men) and 12.9 (women), in comparison with 5.4 (men) and 5.5 (women) at first marriage.

4. At the death of his spouse Marie Vié on May 25, 1682, Hubert Simon, known as Lapointe, was the father of nine children from one to fourteen years old and three others from sixteen to twenty years old, all unmarried.

5. At the head of the list is Jean Poitras who had 17 children from his first marriage of 27 years with Marie-Sainte Vieπ and ten others from his second marriage of 16 years with Marie-Anne Lavoie. He was approximately 70 at the birth of his last child.

6. A hypothetical date of death was determined for the children of unknown fate in the following way: for children whose baptism is the only record in the population register before 1730, since the probability is high that they died soon after baptism, we took the baptismal date as the date of death; for children whose last recorded appearance is not bap-tism, the date of death was fixed midway between the date of the last recorded appearance and the date of "emancipation."

7. See the definition of these stages in Note 1.

REFERENCES

Charbonneau, Hubert. 1975. *Vie et mort de nos ancêtres. Etude deΙImographique.* Montréal: Les Presses de l'Université de Montréal.

Charbonneau, Hubert, Bertrand Desjardins, André Guillemette, Yves Landry, Jacques Légaré, and François Nault, with the collaboration of Réal Bates and Mario Boleda. 1987. *Naissance d'une population: les Francais établis aus Canada au XVIIe siècle,* forthcoming.

Desjardins, Bertrand. 1985a. "The Computerized Register of the Early French Canadian Popula-tion." Paper presented at the annual meeting of the Population Association of America, Boston, Massachusetts, March 28–30. Summarized in *Population Index* 51:383.

———. 1985b. "Quelques éléments de l'expé-rience informatique du Programme de re-cherche en démographie historique." In *Infor-matique et prosopographie.* Paris: Editions du CNRS.

Glick, Paul C., and Robert Parke, Jr. 1965. "New Approaches in Studying the Life Cycle of the Family." *Demography* 2:187–202.

Hareven, Tamara K., ed. 1978. *Transitions: The Family and the Life Course in Historical Per-spective.* New York: Academic Press.

Hareven, Tamara K. 1985. "Les grands thèmes de l'histoire de la famille aux Etats-Unis." *Revue d'histoire de l'Amérique française* 39:185–209.

Landry, Yves, and Jacques Légaré. 1984. "Le cycle de vie familiale en Nouvelle-France: méthodol-ogie et application à un échantillon." *Histoire sociale/Social History* 17:7–20.

Lapierre-Adamcyk, Evelyne, Yves Landry, Jacques Légaré, Denis Morissette, and Yves Péron. 1984. "Le cycle de la vie familiale au Québec: vues comparatives, XVIIe-XXe siècles." *Ca-hiers québécois de démographie* 13:59–77.

Smith, Daniel Blake. 1982. "The Study of the Fam-ily in Early America: Trends, Problems, and Prospects." *The William and Mary Quarterly* 39:3–28.

Sundin, Jan, and Ian Winchester. 1982. "Towards Intelligent Databases: Or the Database as His-torical Archivist." *Archivaria* 14:137–158.

LIFE-COURSE PATTERNS AND PEASANT CULTURE IN FRANCE: A CRITICAL ASSESSMENT

Martine Segalen

ABSTRACT: *French scholars of the family and peasant culture have made little use of the life-course framework of analysis. The present study argues that the concept of life course is not neutral and implies the possibility of free choice for the individual. Postulating such choices conflicts with the social organization of peasant society where individuals' lives are embedded in the family and the group. Examining the various stages of the life cycle, the study gives examples of the collective aspects of social life, and its various economic and cultural facets. It then investigates various factors leading to the break-up of communal life and the rise of individualism, which made the use of the life-course concept relevent to analysis.*

French historians and social anthropologists researching French peasant culture have made little use of the life-course concept, even though the scientific literature on the family has proliferated during the past twenty years (Segalen, 1985a). Specific factors account for this situation. Life-course patterns have to be investigated with the aid of census lists that are mainly from the nineteenth century, but nineteenth-century French historians have been more interested in studying broad patterns of industrialization and changes in mentality than individual careers. At a

Martine Segalen is director of research at the Centre National de la Recherche Scientifique and head of the Centre d'Ethnologie Francaise, a research center devoted to the anthropological study of French society and culture. Author of Love and Power in the Peasant Family: Rural France in the Nineteenth Century *(Chicago, 1983), she is currently investigating the relationship between industrialization, urbanization, and family changes in Nanterre, a suburb of Paris.*

deeper level, this concept has not appealed to students of French peasant family and society because it fails to account for the specific features of peasant culture. The concept of "life course" envisages the study of the various stages an individual passes through in a life career; the concept of "peasant culture," however, points to the "collective consciousness, the common world of experiences, values and knowledge" shared by a group (Löfgren, 1981:30). The two concepts thus entail antagonistic qualities: individuality and collectivity.

Tamara Hareven (1978) has shown that in the examination of critical transitions the life-course concept helps relate individual time, family time and social time; David Kertzer and Andrea Schiaffino (1983:366) assert that it relates "individual-level processes to changing historical conditions." How can we associate a concept focussing on the individual with "peasant culture," which refers mainly to a group structure? The life-course concept raises many questions because it implies an ideological bias. It is not neutral because it suggests that everywhere everyone aims at achieving personal goals by making free choices. This is a very debatable proposition with respect to French peasant society and culture.

A further question raised by the life-course concept is the historical and social differentiation of the so-called traditional culture. Folklorists have always stressed the uniqueness of the culture they report on, because one of their major aims is to describe the "singularities" of the region studied. Noting local differences that can be assigned to language, historical heritage or local invention, their observations all fit within the same framework of *rites de passage*, or symbolic reconstructions, that help us understand the relationships between men, nature and the universe. The "peasant culture" concept implies

that French society was singular and unique throughout time and across space. Yet we know that France is characterized by a great variety of socioeconomic patterns; each region differs from its neighbor with respect to type of agriculture, methods of land cultivation, cultural patterns, language, types of residence, furnishings, and style of clothing.

One way to assess the effects of social change on peasant culture, and to trace the historical differentiation within French peasant society is to look for the period of time when the "life course" concept becomes relevant to the study of social changes, i.e., the period when the rise of individualism begins. The break-up of French communal peasant culture, we must remember, began at different times and proceeded at various speeds.

The purpose of the present study is thus to delineate, within the variety of French peasant societies, the transition from a holistic society to an individualistic one (Dumont, 1977:12). In a holistic society, the individual as such does not exist because he is part of a two-tiered group, the two tiers being the family and the community. In the individualistic society, there is no mediating collectivity other than the family, and the individual has to deal directly with employment and residence, the two concerns necessary for survival in the contemporary world.

CONTROL AND THE COLLECTIVITY

Numerous studies of the French family carried out by French, English and American scholars in recent years have all made plain the control exercised over the individual by close kin and the more widely deployed kin group. Robert Wheaton has stated this fact well by writing: "Until very recent times indeed, the subordination of the individual to the strategy of the kin group has determined the dominant values of French family life and formed the basis of many crucial decisions in the lives of the individuals, sometimes at the expense of these individuals, sometimes at the expense of the larger society outside the kin group" (Wheaton, 1980:21). The control exercised by the community and the dialectic between family and community control have been studied less. This is what the present investigation will devote its attention to, by following the successive stages of an individual's life.

The births of children are female affairs, involving the family and neighborhood; the socialization of the child is predominantly familial, and it starts with the giving of the name. The strict observance of Catholic ritual is due to its symbolic importance; through the chosen name, continuity of the family will be assured, linking past to present generations, dead ancestors to new descendants. During the entire life of the individual the name will be a social marker of a collective identity. Often, the official first name or surname is unknown or, at least, little used. The individual will be addressed with a nickname, the surname of the household he lives in, or the name of the farm his family is working.

The first group taking care of the child are the female members of the household. In addition to the mother, we know that in large households of the past there were always a servant, an older sister, and, outside or within the household, a grandmother to help with the baby and later on to socialize the toddler. The baby did not belong to the parents, but to the household. At the age of seven, when the child starts working on the farm or at the family shop, he will join his age group. In this process, he internalizes his membership in a local community that is perceived as a rival of neighboring communities. Children learn nicknames characterizing the "other"; these are generally disparaging

collective nicknames or short songs that contain the nicknames and help memorize them. In lower Brittany as well as Limousin, for example, studies have described battles between gangs of young children identifying themselves by reference to their residence (upper or lower part of the town) or in terms of the town against the surrounding hamlets. These divisions within the community help mark the boundaries of each group and create a feeling of belonging that will last a lifetime.

The "age class" phenomenon separating boys from girls and each of these by age is found everywhere in France. The "age class" controls the collective socialization of adolescent children but is also significant in community activities. Children have the task of carrying out various calendar rituals linked to Easter and Christmas; as adolescents, they will bear the responsibility of overseeing the respect accorded to cultural norms regarding conjugal behavior, and, more generally, all sex-linked attitudes. This is the specific task of the peasant youth group, as well as of the young in medieval and early modern cities who performed appropriate rituals during carnivals. But carnivals were typically urban events with complex symbolic, social and political meanings, whereas the tasks of the youth group in rural areas were more specifically focused on sexual attitudes and relationships.

A crucial transition in the life course is the formation of the couple. Here again, in traditional peasant culture, the pairing of couples was largely public and took place either during ritualized processes such as *donages* (public pairing of couples) in eastern France, or at fairs or religious events. The famous *maraichinage* of the Vendée marshes exemplifies the practice: young couples *maraichinent* collectively under their umbrellas, or at the cafés.

Very common is the *pose des mais*, between April 30th and May 1st, when young boys go together during the night to the woods and cut branches from various trees; then each boy affixes to the window of his sweetheart a tree branch to declare his love. Spinsters were publicly ridiculed in the same metaphorical way.

One of the critical phases of the life course is marked by the age of leaving the household. In contrast to other European countries such as England (Kussmaul, 1981), French families did not as a rule place their children elsewhere as servants. When they did do so, the practice was not meant to give the child a chance to be exposed to another cultural pattern of education, as for instance, when a boy from the countryside would serve in an urban family. French peasant families kept their children home until they married, or, at least, such was the cultural goal. Poorer families, however, had to place their children as servants, sometimes as early as at the age of ten. Having been placed in a household in the same geographical area as that of their parents, these children continued to share the same values. They were supposed to be treated like one of the family, and often a young servant would have the same work, food, and bed as the child of the house who was of the same age and sex. Placing children as servants therefore had a different meaning and purpose in France than in other countries, where husbandry was meant to develop personality. In France, families would let their younger children go only reluctantly, and starting life as a servant was a sign of poverty.

One of the clearest examples of how the concept of life course creates problems when applied to peasant culture is in the choice of a spouse. Here again, France appears very different from England, where, at least after the seventeenth century (Gillis, 1984:138), the freedom to

choose one's spouse was extensive. This contrasts with the behavior of French families who impose their choices on their children. Of course, this general assertion needs to be modified with respect to time, area, and the social level of the peasant. We must keep in mind that in rural villages, not everybody was a peasant.

Rural France was characterized by protoindustrialization lasting as late as the 1880s, so that village populations had in them craftsmen and women working for industry, earning wages, and not depending solely on their parent's wealth. However, a general endogamous pattern of marriage is obvious, even among workers involved with protoindustry.

Some categories of peasants controlled the marriage of their children very tightly, insuring social reproduction and struggling against the division of their land. This is particularly the case among winegrowers; and in many other types of agricultural activities we find the pattern of "relinking marriages" between familial groups. This was a way of exchanging spouses among allied families and avoiding consanguineous marriages. The process of formation of the couple only infrequently involved the choices of the young, who had to submit themselves to the parental will (Segalen, 1985b).

Marriage rituals in France exemplify the collective nature of the act of marriage. This characteristic of marrying appears to have lingered much later in France than in rural England (Gillis, 1984:155). Until the middle of the twentieth century, some marriage rituals were a time of display and an effort to gain status from costly arrangements. Impressive quantities of food were prepared, served and eaten over a period of two days or more. In an agriculture still very routinized, marriage was also one of the main social events breaking monotonous routine. The number of people invited reflected the social status of families, and the emotions of the young couple did not count for much in comparison with the importance assigned to the creation of new kinship ties.

Additional evidence of the compliance of the individual will, with the collective interests of the household, can be found in the rate of celibacy. Celibacy was particularly high in those areas of France where the system of *ostau* ("house", in Occitan) prevailed. The aim of each household was to pass the farm, its lands, and its collective rights to the next generation untouched, or, if possible, expanded. During the centuries, and in spite of the egalitarian principles of the French Civil Code, property was bequeathed to one heir, the other children receiving only a sum of money for their shares in the family patrimony. Marrying one child—the heir—to a girl who would bring into the household a sum of money, and marrying out a daughter in what was often a cross-sibling marriage was a family strategy designed to avoid dividing the property. The other children would then have the choice of migrating or of staying at home as spinsters and bachelors, to be treated more or less as servants by the brother who had become the head of the household. The portion accruing to these unmarried persons was supposedly their property, but, in practice, they would never sell it because of the felt obligation to keep the family holding whole. Their nephew became their heir, and head of the household in the next generation. A similar system seems to have been prevalent in Northern Finistère, a *départment* of Brittany. There, in each generation, the siblings who became priests and nuns would never sell their share of the property, and also bequeathed it to the nephew who was successor of his father.

This acceptance of bachelorhood appears to be a strong evidence of the way

people's individual desires were subordinated to the needs of the larger community. There seems to have been little resentment about what we could judge as the sacrifice of personal goals. When considering these situations, we must make sure we do not apply our contemporary feelings to a different culture; we need to establish distance to avoid viewing historical persons through our contemporary, middle-class, scholarly lenses. Still, it was true that the development of this collective peasant culture was produced at the expense of large numbers of the unmarried, predominantly female, who left villages for cities in a steady flow during the seventeenth, eighteenth, and nineteenth centuries. For the women, the life course often included spinsterhood, unwanted pregnancies or early death.

When we continue our exploration of life-course events as seen in popular culture, we can find yet other examples of collective control over what we see now as private life. These are the important and perduring cultural events known as charivaris and *asouades*, taking place at special times of the annual calendar.

In these rituals, the community expressed its disapproval of some types of marriages, for instance, those violating the rules of age-group or social endogamy. The community also disapproved of the beating of husbands by wives, women who managed the household in their husband's stead, and women who did not behave as women. What progressively became matters within the realm of privacy, late in the nineteenth century were still matters of collective concern. Prints depicting the *dispute de la culotte* always contain a neighbor, symbolizing the community which has a right to control relationships between the sexes, even after marriage.

Aging is also a critical stage of the life cycle. In French peasant society, again in contrast to England where old people were often in poorhouses, the old were in charge of the group, and especially of the family group. Older, poor, and unemployed laborers were collectively supported, and each community had its "own" beggars. As late as the end of the nineteenth century in lower Brittany, beggars would knock at the doors they were tacitly assigned to, and in exchange for a prayer would receive milk and potatoes. Though the Revolution helped a number of peasants to become owners of their lands, a larger number became poorer because of the disorganization the Revolution entailed. They roamed the countryside until the 1850s. The vast majority eventually migrated to towns, since we know that villages experienced a decline in population after that date.

Speaking more generally, the household which could afford it would support its own old people. Aging and retirement patterns varied in accordance along with different inheritance systems. In the *oustau*, parents did not retire until the end of their lives, often creating strong tension between themselves and the impatient heir. In areas of partible inheritance, a contract would be written when the successor married, providing the old couple with food, furniture, clothes, wood until their death. Depending on the inheritance pattern, the old couple would remain on the farm, or build a small house for themselves. Whatever the solution to the problem of caring for the aged, and whatever tensions arose in the system, the matters were handled collectively by the community, the heir, or the group of siblings.

The foregoing examples, selected from among many elements of French peasant culture, are enough to illustrate the emphasis in that culture on the family, the neighborhood, the community—collectivities which could control each phase of the life course and make the substantive

"individual," someone who thinks about himself only, meaningless. Yet these descriptions are vague, undated, and not specified with regard to social strata. These shortcomings can be blamed partly to the looseness of our vocabulary: integration within the household, the kinship group, and the community differs according to various cultural patterns and differentiates social roles. We are also hindered by the vagueness of the concept of peasant culture. It is necessary to investigate what makes people think as a group before they think as individuals. Even if we do not understand culture as being the outcome of economic and social conditions of production, it appears nevertheless that we have to relate the levels of thought and behavior to each other. This historical materialism is necessary to explore social reproduction and to understand the eventual erosion of the importance of the collectivity and the emergence of individualism.

INTEGRATION WITH HOUSEHOLD, KIN GROUP, AND COMMUNITY

An individual feels bound to a larger unit because all members of this unit share material possessions such as a lease, movable items, land, a name, or collective rights in the soil.

Throughout the centuries at the bottom of the social scale there existed laborers and journeymen. Their household size was generally smaller than that of farmers or landed peasants; they experienced a high degree of mobility, either in familial groupings or as individuals; they were not attached to a community in which they had rights. They had to make decisions for themselves in trying to find employment either in agriculture only or simultaneously in agriculture and village industry. This pattern was evident in many areas of France, notably in such northern areas as Artois, Flanders, Picardy, and the north of the Parisian Basin, where landholding resembled the English estate system.

By contrast, for those peasants who held a lease or land, a household was a collective unit of labor, residence, and social and biological reproduction. In areas where peasants had been landed for centuries, the household bore a name and had a reputation; we now have a good understanding of the phrase *à honneur*, applicable to areas where households were in constant rivalry with one another and each individual had the duty to support the reputation of the collectivity (Castan, 1974). In the eastern part of France, in Franche-Comteπ and Bourgogne, a very complex mixture of Roman and German law prevailed until the end of the nineteenth century, placing a strong emphasis on the community of brothers who were equal heirs and shared property, even when their households were separate. In spite of the individualization of inheritance introduced by the French Civil Code, the emphasis on the fraternal link was still strong until the 1950s, the father always trying to settle property on all his sons. The use of surnames containing the word *chez* (e.g., *chez Martin*), which refers to a family group, exemplifies the collective nature of these units, whose existence can be traced back to Middle Ages and is related to particular conditions of newly developed lands (Salitot-Dion, 1979), The Bigouden system, by comparison, individualizes brothers *and* sisters who had always insisted on getting an equal share of family property (Segalen, 1985b).

The sense of belonging is again different in the *communautés taisibles* of Central France, where a long historical tradition and unchanging conditions of production had kept together married brothers and sisters under the rule of master, somewhat

as in the Yugoslavian zadruga. Until the beginning of the nineteenth century, these communities imposed collective work and collective eating practices upon nuclear families, and the consanguineous marriages common there had the purpose of keeping the lands undivided.

Beyond the household unit, whose contours might differ from area to area, there also existed larger collective units based on the community. In *pays Basque*, the system of the "first neighbor" was prevalent until late in the twentieth century. Each "first neighbor" had a special duty to help a family during crucial stages of life, birth, marriage and death. In the latter two events, the neighbor was in charge of inviting guests to the ceremonies. The "first neighbor" would substitute for the linked household: in case of *asouade*, if a husband was reluctant to ride a donkey publicly, the first neighbor had to replace him.

The collectivities to which individuals and households were attached did not encompass all the parishes and communes. They were generally smaller and coincided with the group involved in the collective work and holding collective rights. These groupings were often rivals, carrying on antagonisms their members had learned as children. The Breton lands are dotted with clusters of two to five farms; each of these hamlets had a *leuquer*, a common collective space shared by all farms where goods could be stored temporarily, or grain threshed. A group of these hamlets—a *quartier*—possessed in common either pastures, or a quarry, or the right to collect seaweed used as fertilizer. Villages were strongly motivated collectively to protect these rights, which were old and had often been defended in the courts throughout the nineteenth century.

We always tend to impose our contemporary classifications on property rights, making clear-cut distinctions between the landed and the landless peasants. But these distinctions are not always so sharp in reality. We find cases of collective familial property with individual use rights, and cases of communal property. In Cantal, Lozère, and Aveyron, a large part of the landed territory was not in private hands; there were pastures, arable fields, woods owned commonly, in addition to collective ovens, places to shoe horses, and mills. The poorer sections of the population could survive by tilling and grazing their animals on land they could not afford to own individually. Collective possession implied collective organization of tasks; for instance, collective use of woodland was organized so that each household of a particular section of the community was entitled to an equal share. Wood was cut and hauled by a collective team comprising a number of families, a team that in the 1960s was still called *bouades* or *bougades*, after the old feudal term designating transportation dues (Parain, 1971: 101). In these instances, collectiveness guarantees equality: in Saint-Véran (Hautes-Alpes), the annual allocation of patches of woodland which families could cut and use for their own needs was made by lot (Delamarre, 1970:141). Examples of collective work are also numerous: collective herding of flocks was the staple practice in Saint-Véran, where each sheepowner would be in turn the common shepherd for the flocks of the village. The number of days he served was in proportion to the number of heads he owned. In different circumstances, in Champagne, the common shepherd was salaried by the assembly of inhabitants to take the flock to the communal pastures (Delamarre, 1970:249–252). In the Jura, an association of milk producers still controls and organizes *fruitières*, where the cheese of Comté is manufactured. Each farmer, however small his production of milk, has a share in the enterprise.

These cases exemplify the importance of the collectivity, however divided for different purposes, in the economic organization of work. When describing the collectivity, folklorists tended to emphasize the festive aspects, giving us a mythical image of the "good old times," when men would help one another and be spontaneously generous. What these descriptions forget is the calculating aspect of this economic cooperation. There was no chance of survival outside the group. Each individual has to be assigned to a household in order to benefit from any help or share in any collective rights.

This does not mean, however, that all had equal rights. Peasant communities had been stratified, as of the seventeenth century at least, in terms of farmers, daily laborers, craftsmen, etc. Were there different patterns of integration within the group that could be linked to social status? Investigating the degree of social integration when the community sets itself at center stage is difficult: everybody participates, but it is also true that the richest hold key positions. For instance, the *bachelleries* of Poitou involve adolescent boys ranging from the sons of daily laborers to the sons of landed peasants, because the financial resources for the activity are provided through collective money-collecting. The *bachellerie* dignitaries, however, belong to the local aristocrats, officers, or wealthy craftsmen or peasants (Pellegrin, 1982:105–211). The celebration of feminine festivals in Northern France (Sainte-Catherine, *filles du voeu*), involve a competition between the richest families of the village in dressing their daughters in white gowns. Even poorer girls participated, but, again, only the wealthiest were honored.

By exploring the various aspects of collective work and property, I do not mean to suggest a mechanical link between material conditions and self-effacement, but to stress that people could hardly think of themselves solely as individuals when all their actions were embedded in the household and the collectivity. There is doubt, therefore, that the holistic peasant society hinders social change. There can be no social mobility within a group whose aim is to reproduce itself without alteration over the generations. Henceforth, though we can observe internal innovation, no true technological revolution can take place unless introduced from the outside. The shattering of peasant culture and its communal sense of belonging, observable in socioeconomic conditions as well as cultural activities, came from a combination of social, economic and cultural changes.

THE EMERGENCE OF INDIVIDUALISTIC THINKING

It is hard to assign priority to the effects of migration, education, urbanization and industrialization in bringing about the changes we want to describe. All these terms are identically deceptive.

Let us consider migration, for instance. Some areas of France have a very long tradition of migration. In the poor, densely populated areas of Cantal, Loze²re, and Aveyron, men left to go south as pit-sawyers during the cold season all during the eighteenth century, but reversed this pattern by migrating north to Paris at the end of the nineteenth. This migration did not break up ties with their families and villages of origin. Although an interesting immigrant subculture did develop in Paris, the so-called traditional culture of Aubrac was prolonged for many years precisely because of the economic support coming from the migrants who had left their villages. Actually, the traditional peasant culture that anthropologists observed in the 1960s in the highland pastures of Aubrac was strongly influenced by Parisian tastes. A new music instrument, the accordion, was adopted, and took its place next to the true old *cabrette*. Music and dances were revived through the Parisian dances of immigrants, who drew on folklore to create their own musical and dancing culture in the urban setting. The *bourrée auvergnate* continued in Aubrac because it was danced in Paris.

Acculturation processes involve complex feedbacks accompanying various migration patterns. In the case of Aubrac, acculturation was a slow process, whereas in Brittany, where migration was sudden and heavy after the First World War, it involved a true conflict between country and city, the former being considered by the migrants themselves as "retarded" and the latter as modern and developed. As a result, the communal values were discarded and kinship ties often severed, resulting not only in individualization but also in isolation.

The educational processes also had very different effects on peasant culture. For a long time, school was seen as the enemy of families, depriving parents of labor in exchange for benefits to the children that could not be perceived. Then, at some point, schooling was integrated into the families' collective strategies. Among the children sent to school, one would be entitled to further his education to become a school teacher. His share of the family property could be disregarded, since the parents had already given him his share in the form of education. In other cases, however, education became disruptive of the whole social system, when all children, educated at a minimum level, left the family family to seek employment elsewhere.

Industrialization and urbanization, both disruptive factors of the peasant culture, are by no means synonymous. In

France industry developed outside cities in the process of protoindustrialization. Also, many cities have a very long history because their development was based on commercial or administrative activities which were not necessarily linked to industry.

The expansion of salaried jobs certainly played a major role in the break-up of traditional rural economic and cultural patterns. Instead of a common, collective income that rarely went to the individual worker, a salary was now given to an individual for performing a specific task. Suddenly, young girls and boys could set aside their own money for later independent life, not having to depend on the good will of their parents. Yet by doing so they lost all control over the means of production.

What is striking in the French case compared to the English is the slow pace of proletarianization, as defined by Charles Tilly (1984:1). In France, wage workers in peasant villages were very common in the eighteenth century, but they were also farmers, or had access to collective lands for cultivation or cattle-grazing. They were always part of the peasant culture whose values and beliefs they shared, and they abided by its collective norms. Besides, they often owned their means of production and thus had some kind of control over capital; through this, they also had control over the younger generation. The strong integration of the worker in the household is revealed by the control the head would exercise over his children's marriages and the high endogamy rate that prevailed in such communities. Besides, wage-work was sometimes abandoned, and we can observe instances when workers involved in protoindustrial activities left their crafts to return to cultivation.

However, the development of salaried jobs did sometimes result in the break-up of peasant communities. This process is exemplified well in those communities where *parsonniers* found salaried jobs as workers for the Thiers cutleries. Not only did the salaries (however meager) permit them to set up independent households, but they also helped promote the idea of individualization.

Many economic, social, and cultural developments combined to break up peasant culture in different places and at different speeds. On the economic side, the agricultural revolution at the beginning of the nineteenth century made necessary the privatization of collective lands. The feeling of privacy emerged together with the development of individuality; youth groups slowly vanished and charivaris increasingly came to be occasions for enjoyment rather than expressions of community control. Their disappearance was supported by the Church, which had long fought these collective expressions of social control. The loosening of communal ties appears to be a consequence of a complex set of factors, and is marked by the disappearance of symbolic language, which was so prominent during rituals. The wealth of symbolic references—meteorological, animal, agricultural, natural—that had nourished peasant culture now vanished. Rituals had often used the metaphor of a plant, whose local name could be used as a pun, to point to deviant behavior. For instance, one could spread *coucous* (the local name of a flower) between the cuckold's and the lover's homes. Within the span of one generation, these references—a true symbolic language in a community sharing the same knowledge of its environment—vanished, together with proverbs that often used metaphorical comparisons.

The break-up of peasant culture took place at different speeds in different areas. The countryside near the expanding cities lost the communal values of peasant culture first. But areas such as Brittany experienced the traditional pattern much longer, for a variety of reasons: unique language, control of society by the Church, separation of the areas of production and commerce.

Birth limitation is at the same time a sign of the development of individualism and a reinforcement of it. Though France was characterized by an early fall in general fertility (Wrigley, 1985:9), regional variations were also important, and the continued general increase of the population meant that in this respect different areas behaved very differently. Brittany did not experience birth limitation until the 1880s, whereas the southwest and Norman peasants were well-known for the small size of their families. It would be interesting to establish if the continuation of high fertility rates correlates with the continuation of traditional peasant culture. But, sooner or later, once the general process was underway, there was no reversal of it, and peasant values and norms were shattered by the intrusion of capitalist relationships within agriculture. We can see this, for example, in the revolt of the *cadets*, bachelors who started using the courts at the beginning of the twentieth century to make sure they were given their equal share of property, in disregard of the heir and the *oustau*.

SUMMARY AND CONCLUSIONS

This study has presented the position that the life-course concept is ill-suited for analysis of French peasant families in the past, because the individual's choices were made by the older generation, and the individual career was embedded in the household and controlled by the community. Besides, this concept does not seem helpful for the investigation of the importance of kin to marriage and inheritance patterns, a new issue recently opened in research on the French family.

This study explored also the various degrees and aspects of integration and the factors that led eventually to the breaking up of communal patterns. Though demographic data are totally lacking to support our position, it might find some help from E.A. Wrigley, who underlines the strong parallels between France and Sweden (Wrigley, 1981:183). The development of the wage economy and the intrusion of capitalistic relationships within agriculture have transformed the peasant culture of former times, mainly by eliminating the pressure of the community and household on the individual's decisions. However, this does not mean that a cultural pattern has been replaced by a kind of generalized middle-class culture and that in the community there is room for only class relationships and antagonisms. Communities still exist, but it is often more difficult now to trace their boundaries because the boundaries are often symbolic or imaginary (Cohen, 1985). Whatever its new forms, the community no longer controls the individual life course, leaving this burden to the contemporary family.

REFERENCES

Castan, Yves. 1974. *Honnêteté et relations sociales en Languedoc, 1715-1780*. Paris: Plon.

Cohen, Anthony P. 1985. *The Symbolic Construction of Community*. London: Tavistock.

Delamarre, Mariel Jean-Brunhes. 1970. *Le berger dans la France des villages. Bergers communes à Saint-Véran en Queyras et à Normée en Champagne*. Paris: CNRS.

Dumont, Louis. 1977. *Homo aequalis. Genèse et épanouissement de l'idéologie économique*. Paris: Gallimard.

Gillis, John R. 1984. "Peasant, Plebian and Proleterian Marriage in Britain 1600–1900." Pp. 129–162 in *Proletarianization and Family History*, edited by David Levine. New York: Academic Press.

Hareven, Tamara. 1978. "Cycles, Course and Cohort: Reflections on the Theoretical and Methodological Approaches to the Historical Study of Family Development." *Journal of Social History* 12:97–109.

Kertzer, David, and Andrea Schiaffino. 1983. "Industrialization and Co-residence: A Life Course Approach." Pp. 359–391 in *Life Span Development and Behavior*, vol. 5, edited by Paul B. Baltes and Orville G. Brim, Jr. New York: Academic Press.

Kussmaul, Ann. 1981. *Servants in Husbandry in Early-Modern England*. Cambridge: Cambridge University Press.

Löfgren, Orvar. 1981. "On the Anatomy of Culture." *Ethnologia Europaea* 12:26–46.

Parain, Charles. 1971. "Fondements d'une ethnologie historique de l'Aubrac." Pp. 23–116 in *L'Aubrac*, Tome 2. Paris: CNRS.

Pellegrin, Nicole. 1982. *Les Bachelleries. Organisations et fêtes de la jeunesse dans le centre ouest, XV-XVIIIe siècles*. Poiters Mémoires de la Société des antiquaires de l'Ouest. 4e série, T. xvi.

Salitot-Dion, Michelle. 1979. "Coutume et systemè d'héritage dans l'ancienne Franche-Comté." *Etudes Rurales* 74:5–22.

Segalen, Martine. 1985a. "Sous les feux croisés de l'histoire et de l'anthropologie: la famille en Europe." *Revue d'histoire de l'Amérique Francaise* 39:163–184.

———. 1985b. *Quinze générations de bas bretons. ParenteΙΙ et société dans le pays bigouden Sud.* Paris: Presses Universitaires de France.

Tilly, Charles. 1984. "Demographic Origins of the European Proletariat." Pp. 1–85 in *Proletarianization and Family History*, edited by David Levine. New York: Academic Press.

Wheaton, Robert. 1980. "Introduction: Recent Trends in the Historical Study of the French Family." Pp. 3–26 in *Family and Sexuality in French History*, edited by Robert Wheaton and Tamara K. Hareven. Philadelphia: University of Pennsylvania Press.

Wrigley, E.A. 1981. "Marriage, Fertility and Population Growth in Eighteenth Century England." Pp. 137–185 in *Marriage and Society: Studies in the Social History of Marriage*, edited by R.B. Outwaithe. London: Europa.

———. 1985. "The Fall in Marital Fertility in Nineteenth Century France." *Historical Social Research* 34:4–21.

INDIVIDUAL AND FAMILY LIFE COURSES IN THE SAGUENAY REGION, QUEBEC, 1842–1911

Gérard Bouchard
Isabelle de Pourbaix

ABSTRACT: *Because it embraces such a long period and a wide area, the computerized reconstruction of families based on a regional population register opens up new perspectives for research into social reproduction, as well as geographic and social mobility. The study makes use of the Saguenay population register to study individual and family life courses over two generations. Focus is mostly upon the demographic and occupational factors that determine social conditions and reproduction of families. More specifically, discussion and findings center upon theoretical and methodological issues raised by the study of social reproduction and family inheritance systems; a description of individual and family histories from a demographic and occupational standpoint; an account of the strategies that families adopt to establish children as farmers in a predominantly rural society.*

INTRODUCTION

As part of its Research Project on Regional Societies, our research group (SOREP) has recently begun an inquiry into what we call, for the moment, "the family cycle": the history of families and their individual members in relation to demography, socio-occupational and geographic mobility, transmission of land, and other factors.[1] The geographic and historical context of this study is the Saguenay region (see map) from 1842 to 1911. At the end of this period, the region numbered forty parishes and had a population of 50,000.

Gérard Bouchard is director of SOREP (Université du Québec à Chicoutimi), an inter-university research center specializing in social history and human genetics. Isabelle de Pourbaix is currently doing Ph.D. research in social and historical demography in the Department of Demography, University of Montreal.

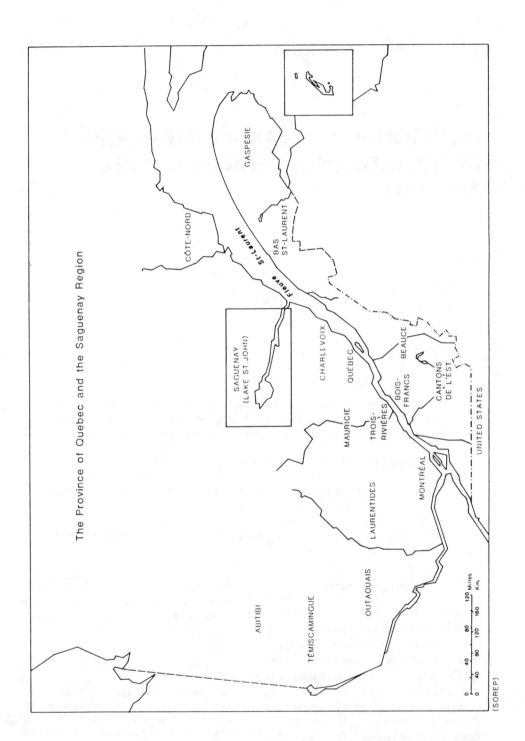

The Province of Quebec and the Saguenay Region

(SOREP)

The computerized reconstitution of families for this period has been completed; the 125,000 baptism, marriage, and burial records has resulted in the creation of 22,000 family records which are now available for analysis. It should be remembered that each family record reproduces, as it were, the history of a married couple, since it brings together all the information relating to it under a single heading. Each record contains as many mentions of a couple as appear in the parish registers, an average of 5.6 mentions for the period 1842-1911. To each of these entries is attached information about residence, occupation, ability to sign, the family names and first names of both spouses, the type of event (birth, marriage or death) creating the certificate, and so on. In a great number of cases, these records constitute almost complete biographies; for instance, 52 percent of the record used for the purposes of this study contain at least thirteen entries, and fifty percent contain eleven or more statements of occupation. In this article, we shall present the first findings of our study. These results are concerned with individual and family characteristics, with socio-occupational courses or itineraries (within and between generations) and with the setting up of children in life. First, however, a number of points concerning methodology need to be clarified.

METHODS AND CONCEPTS

This clarification is necessary for two reasons. First, the family cycle model poses difficulties as great as those involved in the analysis of systems of land transmission. Second, the reconstitution of families gives the researcher access to a wealth of information to deal with problems which have hitherto been somewhat badly perceived, as in the case of the organiza-

tion of socio-occupational data used in constructing individual life courses.

Family history or family cycle?

The family cycle model has been the subject of considerable criticism in recent years (see, among others, Hareven, 1978a; Vinovskis, 1977; Trost, 1977). In particular, it has been charged with limiting life courses to a series of steps and stages which too easily gives rise to anachronism, and an unacceptably high degree of uniformity. It is also said that the model is insufficiently flexible for the incorporation of data about individual biographies. In addition, it does not take sufficiently into account the great diversity exhibited by family histories, even when considered in one particular place and over a short period of time (Uhlenberg, 1974). These criticisms do not all arise from similar grounds, and it would indeed be possible, at least in part, to obviate them by making a few simple adjustments. Be this as it may, the family cycle model is primarily aimed at phenomena of a repetitive nature, and tends to produce interepretations expressed in terms of a relatively fixed sequence of steps. Such interpretation however, is not our main objective. We want to observe modes of social reproduction from the standpoint of the family: to establish to what degree, and by what means, a couple succeeds in setting up its children in life.[2] The family cycle model seems inherently too limited a device through which to view the complexity of family life. We do not see, in particular, how to incorporate into this model all of the various dynamics that relate to demography (biological reproduction), economy (material reproduction), relationships which develop within the family and through kinship, and geographic mobility and types of household, unless we proceed on the assumption of an extremely hypothetical synchronicity among these various processes.

Our aim prevents and exempts us from being hampered by these assumptions or constraints. The study of social reproduction calls, first of all, for a recognition of the objective facts[3] that characterize the situation of each family, and, second, for the most precise possible description of the complex strategies and mechanisms that shape the social destinies of the rising generation. What follows from this is the need for an exploratory approach toward the nature of family life, based on the utilization of empirical models of reproduction. In addition, it is obviously preferable to leave room for a twofold approach, concentrating, on the one hand, on strictly family processes (couple formation, procreation, accumulation of property, transmission of wealth, intra-family relations, etc.) and on the other, on those factors which primarily relate to the individuals themselves (demographic history, socio-occupational and geographic courses, etc.).

For the reasons stated above, we reject in our study the notion of family cycle, which appears to create more problems than it helps to solve. We shall refer simply to individual and family histories when we wish to designate the complex courses woven by economy, demography, social relationships, and culture, as seen from the vantage point of the family. It is clear, then, that these courses and histories will have to be examined as interacting factors to be analyzed at the micro-diachronic level made possible by the family records.[4] We believe this approach to be best suited both to the reproduction of the experience of social actors in a collective context, and to the understanding of structural changes through an examination of individual life courses (e.g., the identification of discontinuities within and between cohorts).

The Transmission of Family Property: An Open or Closed System?

With regard to the setting-up of children in life, and in particular to the Saguenay system of transmitting the family estate, we carried out an inquiry based on traditional sources such as notarial archives, assessment registers, and interviews recorded on questionnaires. The disappointments of this preliminary inquiry were nonetheless extremely instructive from a methodological point of view.[5]

Unlike the European systems we know about, the Saguenay system of property transmission does not have closed boundaries; as a consequence, it does not display that kind of defensive reflex whose overriding concern is the preservation of the patrimonial estate. At first sight, it might appear that demographic conditions would tend to push it in this direction. An exceptionally high level of fertility in the region (Pouyez et al., 1983, ch. 6) heightens the dilemma faced by every generation in every society: how is a single household to provide for the establishment of several others? Actually, in Saguenay this dilemma is resolved by the abundance of new, cheap land. In an isolated setting where job opportunities are very scarce, couples endeavor to set up as many children as possible on the land. This end is often reached by adopting strategies that result in their moving from the old homestead to acquire larger tracts of land farther afield. Once there, the family itself provides the manpower needed to clear the land. In this, and in many other ways (purchases, inheritance, illegal occupation), the patrimonial estate increases in size. Very soon however, pieces begin to break away from it, as children marry. In the course of one generation the family estate is subjected to a series of expansions and contractions. As for the setting-up of the children on the land, this too is arrived at by very diverse routes: land may be sold or given to the children; and they may receive money in the form of a gift or a loan, either through inheritance or in other ways. Thus not only the accumulation but also the transmission of property are processes that may extend over a few decades, and entail several episodes. The transmission of property in particular is accomplished in three distinct phases: (a) assigning to married sons recently acquired and partially cleared lots; daughters do not receive land; parents try to marry them off to sons already set up by their own families; (b) assigning to a son (who is almost never the eldest) some of the "old" property or paternal land when the head of the family decides to retire; (c) assigning property left over at the death of the last surviving spouse; this usually takes the forms of chattels whose distribution often redresses imbalances brought about by previous bequests, notably to the detriment of the daughters.

We can see how this system or set of practices is in many respects markedly different from those found in old rural societies grappling with the problems of overpopulation and tied to land that can no longer be expanded. It appears, by the way, that this observation could have far-reaching applications, since the particular set of circumstances reported here are far from exclusive to the Saguenay. On the contrary, the same features are to be found in most of the regions of Quebec in the period when the land was being

Table 1. Transmission of Family Possessions: Models of Open and Closed Systems

Variables	"Pyrenean" closed system	Open system
Arable land	Completely occupied; quite rigidly bounded by natural obstacles.	Expanding; no fixed borders for variable periods.
Population dynamics	Stationary; significant emigration in every generation.	Increasing; little or no emigration.
Orientation of the system	To preserve the estate and to exclude non-heirs.	To assure the expansion of the estate; to set up as many children as possible.
Spatialisation	Rootedness and continuity of the family; stability of the estate.	Individual and family mobility; instability of the estate.
Patrimonial estate	Well-designated, fixed entity; represents family identity.	Dispersed, moving, polymorphous entity (lands or goods).
Rules of inheritance	Imperative, durable; fixed by law or custom.	Little or badly defined; leave room for strategies, improvisation, and paternal or parental "about-faces."
Transmission	One-shot, dramatic event, premeditated meticulously for a long time.	Process spread out in three phases, each of which may comprise several episodes.
Household structure	Variable, perhaps predictable, according to the prevailing inheritance system.	Predominantly nuclear.

opened up, and are equally present not only throughout Canada, but elsewhere in North America (Bouchard, 1983:44ff.). All this suggests an opposition between two models, one applicable to new territory still undergoing expansion, and the other to old lands that have long ago reached saturation point. The most striking example of the latter is provided by the Pyrenean populations. The fact, moreover, that so many studies of families and inheritance systems have chosen these populations as their subject, is remarkable in itself.[6]

We have sketched out the contours of these two models (Table 1). The reader will understand that these are "ideal types": an open system, still expanding, whose primary concern is not with preventing the disintegration of the estate; a "shut-in" system in which a fixed number of spaces are constantly threatened and coveted. We should remember that each of these systems does incorporate certain features of the other. For example, it is obvious that in open systems tensions may occur between the desire to set up children and the desire to preserve the estate, particularly when the saturation point of the arable land is being approached. In the same way, closed systems may nonetheless allow for some internal leeway, which could itself give rise to some instability, as has been shown in the case of Pyrenean societies (Mendras and Jollivet, 1971). Beyond these reservations, there are important methodological lessons to be drawn from the study of new lands that are still undergoing expansion.[7] In the first place, it is expedient to free ourselves from the "Pyrenean syndrome" and reintroduce the factors of improvisation, of long- and short-term strategies, of diversity and movement, into the study of "inheritance" systems. It is also necessary to enlarge the scope of the study sufficiently to allow the process of transmis-

sion to unfurl as it should. This extension must be carried out in two directions: first, in time, since transmissions may take place over several decades; and, second, in space, since setting-up strategies relate to much wider areas than that of the village, to which for obvious reasons most researchers have confined themselves. In order to investigate the process of transmission in its entirety, the inquiry must also be carried out on the micro-diachronic scale, which permits for the observation of important aspects that would otherwise escape notice (e.g., the phenomenon of provisional settings-up that end in failure). Another point is that every kind of transmission (donation, bequest, loan, etc.) should be taken into account, and we should be capable as well of tracing the individual destinies of children who were neither set up by their parents, nor received an inheritance. Finally, in order to assess the effectiveness of accumulation and transmission strategies, it would seem necessary to evaluate the exact demographic burden on each family (its adult offspring) and its distribution in terms of sex and age differences between the children.

But mere agreement on these methodological suggestions is not enough. They cannot be put into practice without confronting the major problem posed by sources of information. The reconstitution of all land transactions carried out in one village over several generations, although representing a great deal of work, can be accomplished. At the regional level, this task becomes totally impracticable; other strategies need to be adopted. The computerized population registers, based on the reconstitution of families and genealogies, hold the promise of providing a workable alternative.[8] These registers permit the reconstruction of individual and family histories over a relatively long period—more than a century—

and on a much greater scale than that of the village.

As for the measurement of data relating to the setting-up of sons on land to the effectiveness of inheritance strategies, we have decided to confine ourselves exclusively to socio-occupational courses. Our assumption is simply that each established son in one way or another and for some period of time, however short, declares himself to be a farmer. This declaration of occupation thus becomes a kind of indicator of his being set up as a farmer in a region where practically all agricultural workers own the land they work on. Admittedly, this tactic does not provide a detailed account of all the subtleties involved in the transmission system, but it at least provides a very exact measure of its results.

Finally, it is in order to mention very briefly the problems raised by the occupational data with regard to the study of mobility. These problems are twofold. On the one hand, a large number of declarations do not refer to occupations as such. In a pilot study, we have established that only 63 percent of the titles declared really corresponded to a real change of work (Bouchard, 1984, 1985). On the other hand, we were faced, as usual, with the necessity of classifying these titles into categories, a well-known painful task. The categories used have been developed in the course of a extensive research, the results of which have been published elsewhere (Bouchard, 1984; Bouchard and Pouyez, 1985).

PRELIMINARY FINDINGS

Our research into historical demography and social history draws exclusively on the Saguenay population register. Thanks to the new perspectives opened up by the register, we are now able to control the major constraints encountered in the selection of basic data. For example, we did not have to take into consideration such factors as the persistence of families, that studies carried out on the parish level usually have to deal with.

As we have already stated, our aim is above all to examine individual life courses as they interact with the family histories they are part of. The life course of an individual, as we have already defined it, corresponds to the period that lies between first marriage and death; but it obviously touches on other questions relating to preceding and succeeding generations. Actually, the particular form taken by an individual's life course is rooted in his family of origin, and in turn determines, to a large degree, the fate of his descendants. In practical terms, an individual's life course is traced by means of information contained in the register that marks off the progress of his family life. In accordance with these demographic events, we see the individual's family expand, contract, break up, another family being created and so on. Some elements however, refer only to the father of the family, as with the statement of the father's occupation on each entry in the family record. The father's declarations of occupation thus serve to describe his work history, just as declarations of place of residence may serve to describe his and the family's geographic course.

In this exploratory essay, we will present a number of aspects relating to the individual and family lives of Saguenayans, while limiting ourselves for the moment to demographic and occupational characteristics. Particular attention will however be given to methodological considerations pertaining to the study of life courses.

Selection of data

In choosing the individuals and families whose life courses are to be studied, we

Table 2. Selected Cases for the Exploratory Study of Saguenay:
Socio-Occupational Life Courses (1942-1911)

Identification	Fathers	Sons	Sons-in-Law
The father of the first generation is married in the Saguenay	307	820	735
The father of the first generation is married outside the Saguenay	217	633	593
TOTALS:	524	1453	1328

have adopted two criteria that we consider essential to the intergenerational
perspective within which we wish to develop our study on social reproduction:
(a) the families selected had to have at
least one son who was married in the Saguenay region (we leave aside, for the
moment, the study of families having
married daughters only, as transmission
takes a particular form in these cases); (b)
their records had to have sufficient genealogical depth to allow for comparison between fathers and sons from the point of
view of their respective life courses within
the specified chronological framework
(1842-1911). A considerable number of
the families that took part in the massive
immigration at the beginning of this period, however, were already constituted
before their arrival in the Saguenay (people married outside the region). It was
important to treat these families as if they
had only just been constituted, so as to
allow the life courses of the fathers and the
sons to be compared as fully as possible.

Two types of families were taken into
account, and they need to be distinguished, since we have no information
pertaining to the history of couples prior
to emigration:[9] the first type consists of
families formed in the Saguenay before
1856, having at least one son subsequently
married in the region; the second consists
of families who emigrated to the Saguenay before 1856 who were still in the first
phases of constitution (couples recently
married), and having at least one son who

married later on in the region; these families must also have had at least three baptisms registered in the Saguenay before
the marriage of one of the children.[10] In
the following text the term "father" will
refer to heads of families selected from the
first generation (see Table 2).

On the whole, the fathers married off
roughly five of their children in the Saguenay, about as many boys as girls. This
figure is slightly higher for immigrant
families, which can easily be explained:
the fathers who married outside the region may have done so well before 1842
(when the settlement began in the Saguenay), thus giving their children the chance
of reaching age of marriage before the
children of parents married in the Saguenay. In fact, we observe that children of
immigrant families started to marry approximately ten years before the others
(the former commencing in 1849 and the
latter 1859). We thus deal with a total of
1453 father-son and 1328 father-son-in-
law relationships.

Elements of Individual and
Family Biographies

Before we begin the study of socio-
occupational characteristics and the establishment of children, it is in order to
provide a brief description of the data
relating to demographic individual and
family histories.

Figure 1 illustrates how the deaths of
the fathers are situated relative to the time

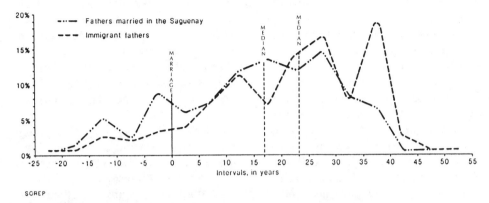

Figure 1. Distribution of Fathers According to Time Elapsed Between
the First Marriage of a Child and their Death (Saguenay, 1842-1911)

of marriage of a first son. According to whether or not they were married in the Saguenay, fathers were present at the first of their children's marriages in the respective proportion of 81.4 percent and 89.3 percent. In fact, because of the particular nature of the Saguenay demographic system (see note 5), most of them were present at the marriage of several of their children. The shape of the two curves of the graph draws attention to two funda-

mental parameters: (a) the age at marriage and the rank of the first married child in the family; (b) the age at marriage and at death of the father. Figure 2 shows to what degree the fathers survived the marriages of all their children.[11] While almost nine-tenths of them were present at the first marriage, about half were still able to attend the last. Furthermore, these data also underline the heterogeneity of the life courses.

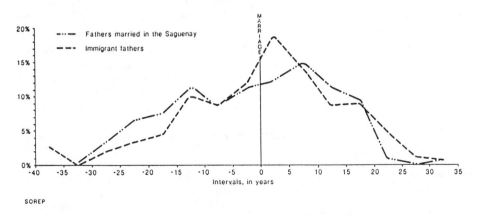

Figure 2. Distribution of Fathers According to Time Elapsed Between the Marriage of
the Last Child to be Married and their Death (Saguenay, 1842-1911)

Before entering into a detailed description of the life courses, it is important to know how much information we have at our disposal. A great number of entries relating to couples—each entry corresponding to the recording of an event—are involved in the reconstruction of family histories: an average of nineteen for the father's families, and between eleven and twelve for the families of the children, keeping in mind that in the latter case the histories are incomplete at the end of the observation period. Standard error of the means is not negligible, however (at approximately six and nine), which should once more remind us that we are dealing with family histories whose nature, and above all duration, is diversified. However, for ninety percent of the families, records in the register cover a period of at least twenty years, and for half of this number the period is forty years or more. The observation of individual life courses, i.e., from the beginning of the observation[12] to the death of the father, covers a period of almost the same length: eighty percent of the life courses are followed for at least five years, and fifty percent for at least forty years.

The duration of the life courses of the fathers chosen for our study is a result of two factors: age at marriage and age at death—assuming, of course, that they do not emigrate to another region. This does not apply to sons and sons-in-law, since their life courses are far from complete in

1911. Age at marriage and at death therefore represent essential data, since they determine the duration of a life course, and thus allow us to situate the context in which children are set up. Our data reveal that the age at marriage was relatively low, oscillating between 22 and 25 years of age (Table 3). This should not be surprising, as it matches very closely the figures for other rural regions of Quebec during the same period (Pouyez, Lavoie, Bouchard et al., 1983: Table 6.10). There is, however, a noticeable tendency for sons to get married at a younger age than their fathers, while at the same time the average marrying age, in the Saguenay as well as elsewhere in Quebec, was increasing. We will see later how this tendency can be associated with the settlement context.

The average age at death is high in the case of the fathers: 66.4 for those married in the Saguenay and 71.1 for immigrant fathers. This discrepancy is easily explained. Since they were born later, the fathers married in the Saguenay had not yet all died in 1911. Those who died at an advanced age are not included in the calculations, and their absence reduces the real value of the average age at death for fathers. The long life courses of the fathers are obviously due to the longevity: 65 percent of them, in fact, lived past the age of 65—but again, we have to remember that those values do not hold for the whole population. The number of fathers who married more than once is quite

Table 3. Mean Age at Marriage

Subgroup I	Subgroup II	Subgroup III	Subgroup IV	Subgroup V	Subgroup VI
Fathers married in the Saguenay	Sons of I	Daughters of I	Fathers married outside the Saguenay	Sons of IV	Daughters of IV
(N = 185)	(N = 619)	(N = 516)	(N = 217)	(N = 428)	(N = 396)
25.5 years	24.5 years	21.9 years	—	24 years	22.8 years

small. First marriages represent close to nine-tenths of the total, both for immigrants and those already residing in the region. This finding will obviously assume its full significance only when all the ages at death of their wives, ages at remarriage and the intervals between widowhood and remarriage are compiled. In any case, the succession of conjugal histories will have to be considered as an important variable in the study of family inheritance systems.

The analysis of individual histories cannot dispense, however, with an in-depth study of the family situation. What kind of milieu did the fathers grow up in? What real demographic weight should we assign to their children, i.e., how many of these survived into adulthood? What are the conditions for the setting-up of sons and daughters? A preliminary sketch of family histories should serve to answer the questions, at least partially.

As Table 2 already suggests, Saguenay families in the nineteenth century were characterized by an exceptionally high level of fertility. In the case of the fathers married in the Saguenay, the average number of births is fixed at between nine and ten. We should stress that these figures apply to both complete families (in which both partners survive the wife's period of fecundity) and incomplete families. Taking into account factors such as the reliability of the data and the types of families under consideration, everything suggests that Saguenay women were still subject to a "natural fertility" quite to the same degree as the Hutterites, the Anabaptist sect which rejects any form of contraception. This hypothesis is confirmed by results published by Pouyez et al. (1983: ch. 6). Using the Coale method to compare the marital fertility level of Saguenayans with that of Hutterites, the authors arrive at an index-rating higher than 1.00, which is already considered the highest level of fertility.

In order to emphasize the specificity of these results, we have made comparisons with eight other so-called "natural fertility" systems. This operation admittedly needs to be refined by carefully controlling the bases of comparison, but we may already conclude that the level of fertility in the Saguenay during the nineteenth century was exceptionally high.

Few prenuptial conceptions (two percent) are recorded[13] whereas more than half of the first children are born in the twelve months following marriage. Let us recall however that, by definition, every father sampled has generated at least one birth. Two years after being formed, 83.6 percent of the families saw the birth of their first child, and in almost every other case, this first birth took place before the end of the first three years of marriage.

Figure 3 illustrates in more comprehensive fashion the rate at which certain events occurred in the families of the fathers who married in the Saguenay. We have taken the liberty here of incorporating part of the terminology developed by Lapierre-Adamcyk et al. (1984) in their recent works on the family life cycle in Quebec. Since their research was conducted on complete families, our data are unfortunately not comparable to theirs. On the average, births in families are spread out over a period of almost twenty years, starting from the time of marriage. This figure also includes incomplete, and therefore smaller, families. The standard deviation is high (7.5), and the mode is set at 24 years of age. To arrive at a truly rigorous analysis of the stages that mark off the evolution of the family, it would be necessary to restrict ourselves to the study of complete families.

Nonetheless, by virtue of our selection criteria, all the fathers chosen married off at least one (male) child. We are therefore able to measure the interval separating the marriage of the parents and that of the

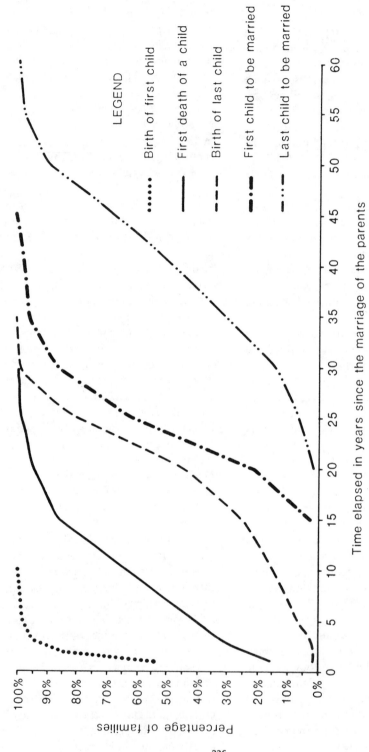

SOREP

Figure 3. Calendar of Demographic Events in the History of the Family
(Saguenay, 1842-1911)

236

first child. The children get married quite quickly. A fifth of the first marriages take place roughly twenty years after those of their parents, and fully half of them take place after 23 years. Most marriages of children are concentrated in the period between the parent's twentieth and thirtieth years of married life. Moreover, a substantial number of children get married even before the growth of the family is completed, giving rise to the situation, rarely seen nowadays, in which uncles and aunts are younger than their nephews and nieces.

Some families experience the first death of a child very early. In half of the families, this event occurs in the first eight years of marriage. We should add to this that almost every family has to deal with the loss of a child even before the last child in that family is born. Although births are spread out over approximately twenty years, marriages are more concentrated. If we compare median differences, we discover an interval of twenty years for births and sixteen years for marriages. It is easy to see why so many fathers were able to attend all of their children's weddings: a high proportion of fathers survived into relatively old age, and 75 percent of families married off their children in 46 years of married life.

The preceding facts combine to produce a picture of fathers who live a long time as the heads of very large and rapidly growing families, in which a high proportion of the children get married. But the measures of central tendency should also alert us to the diversity of family situations that our analysis will have to take into account.

Socio-Occupational Courses

Among the elements which shape an individual biography, the socio-occupational life course occupies a central position.

With respect to social reproduction, this life course needs to be approached from both the inter- and intra-generational perspectives; the relationships between fathers and children, and more especially their sons, will thus receive particular attention.

A simple glance at the occupations held by one individual already tells much about his social position; a key element in our investigation, however, is the interaction between the life courses of the fathers and those of their children. This interaction is expressed both in terms of the factors determining how the children are established (transmission of land, setting-up strategies, etc.), and in terms of intergenerational social mobility (position of the children compared to that of the father). In addition, it is essential that these interactions be measured for each of the children, since their rank and sex constitute indispensable differentiation factors. The Saguenay population register allows us to submit these variables to close scrutiny. Research such as this obviously requires a good prior knowledge of the socio-occupational structure of the population as a whole, but we chose first of all to evaluate just those facts that pertain to the very formation of individual life courses. It will be remembered that we are working here on individual histories reconstructed from entries in the civil register linked together into family records. This poses, from the very outset, a problem with regard to under-registration of occupations, the extent of which we have been able to measure. On the whole, the proportion of mentions of couples (or entries) carrying statements of occupation varies between 72 percent and ninety percent. Moreover, we know that for 92 percent of the families studied, more than half of the mentions contain such declarations. This means, for instance, that for the fathers of the first generation, we have an average of fourteen declarations of an occupation at different points in time.

In the course of his lifetime an individual may hold several different occupations. For reasons discussed in the first part of this article, we shall restrict ourselves here to the level of categories of occupations. Whatever movements we discern will consequently refer to wider mobility than to changes of occupation in the more limited sense. The extent of this mobility is presented in the Table 4.

In the case of the fathers, almost sixty percent always belonged to the same socio-occupational category for the duration of our observation period; this figure is somewhat lower in the case of the children (around 52 percent for the sons and sons-in-law of fathers married in the Saguenay, and 58.5 percent for those of immigrant fathers). We shall refer to these as homogeneous life courses, as opposed to heterogeneous life courses which include two or more occupational categories. The discrepancies observed in this respect between individuals of the first and second generations are obviously due to the primitive state of development of the regional economy. During the first stages of settlement, most fathers were farmers exclusively. A certain degree of division of labor subsequently appeared, giving rise to a diversification of professional categories.

That said, we see that Table 4 brings out highly contrasting situations, among which it would be useful to identify different types or patterns. Statistical criteria need to be established to allow for discrimination between non-mobile, mobile, and unstable types (e.g., four, five, or more category changes). Beyond these considerations, close attention must be given to some very specific factors, such as the numerous shifts between the same categories, the affinities between and compartmentalization of different occupations, the categories most associated with instability, and periodization in life courses which could involve an alternation of mobile and stable phases. Finally, it would be equally useful, while taking all the necessary precautions, to attempt a foray into the area of the occupations themselves. It is at this point that we perceive all the interest as well as the methodological

Table 4. Numbers and Percentages of Declarations of Occupation in Individual Life Courses (Saguenay, 1842-1911)

	Subgroup I	*Subgroup II*	*Subgroup III*	*Subgroup IV*	*Subgroup V*	*Subgroup VI*
	Fathers married in the Saguenay (N = 307)	Sons of I (N = 820)	Sons-in-law of I (N = 735)	Immigrant fathers (N = 217)	Sons of IV (N = 633)	Sons-in-law of IV (N = 593)
Average number of mentions in the family records	19.8	11.1	11.4	18.3	12.0	11.9
Average number of declarations of occupation	14.3 (72.2%)	9.9 (89.2%)	10.1 (88.6%)	13.1 (71.6%)	10.7 (89.2%)	10.7 (89.9%)
Standard deviation	6.3	6.5	6.8	5.8	7.2	7.6
Median	14.9	9.4	9.8	12.9	10.1	9.8

difficulties that a longitudinal analysis of occupational courses can generate.

Since the classification work is still underway, we shall limit ourselves here to a study of homogeneous life courses. Table 5 shows the socio-occupational categories of which these life courses are made up. The occupational structure that existed at the beginning of the colonization period demonstrates the vital importance being established on the land. Within the category of farmers are assembled almost all the fathers, and a very large proportion of their descendants. In fact, this category refers more to a condition than to a single occupation. The farmer is perhaps not restricted to working on his farm, but the fact that he owns one permits him to provide for the basic needs of his family in this isolated region where the requirements of day-to-day survival dominate every other consideration (Bouchard, 1977, 1981). Our study of transmission based on setting up children on the land takes on its full significance when seen within this context: we can understand how much importance a father will attach to assuring his children a future as farmers, at a time when the other careers offered almost no viable alternatives.

As pointed out earlier, the occupational structure seems to become more diversified in the second generation. Although farmers are still in the majority, a few sons

Table 5. Measures of Socio-Occupational Mobility By Subgroups
(Saguenay, 1842-1911)

Number of different categories in the lifecourse	Subgroup I Fathers married in the Saguenay	Subgroup II Sons of I	Subgroup III Sons-in-law of I	Subgroup IV Fathers married outside the Saguenay	Subgroup V Sons of IV	Subgroup VI Sons-in-law of IV
	(N = 307)	(N = 820)	(N = 735)	(N = 217)	(N = 633)	(N = 593)
1	59.9%	51.3%	53.9%	60.8%	58.6%	58.5%
2	30.9%	34.3%	32.1%	28.1%	29.4%	29.0%
3	8.8%	10.6%	8.7%	9.2%	7.7%	8.8%
4	0.4%	0.4%	1.9%	1.9%	1.1%	0.8%
5	0.0%	0.6%	0.4%	0.0%	0.5%	0.3%
6+	0.0%	0.1%	0.1%	0.0%	0.0%	0.0%
Unidentified categories*	0.0%	2.7%	2.9%	0.0%	2.7%	2.6%
Number of changes of categories						
0	59.9%	51.3%	53.9%	60.8%	58.6%	58.5%
1	12.0%	16.8%	15.1%	13.8%	14.2%	13.3%
2	12.4%	14.1%	12.8%	9.2%	10.3%	10.6%
3	5.9%	5.5%	6.1%	5.1%	3.5%	5.1%
4	5.2%	3.8%	3.4%	5.1%	5.2%	5.2%
5	1.6%	2.7%	2.6%	2.8%	3.0%	1.8%
6+	3.0%	3.1%	3.2%	3.2%	2.5%	2.9%
Unidentified categories*	0.0%	2.7%	2.9%	0.0%	2.7%	2.6%

*Cases in which occupation is unknown.

have managed to set themselves up as tradesmen or craftsmen. A large number of them, however, find themselves in the uncertain position of being non-specialized workers. The variable duration of the observation periods obscures the interpretation we can give to these results, but we already know that the condition of farmer predominates among the homogeneous occupational courses that we were able to observe over the longest periods.

As for the heterogeneous courses, we wish to find out which categories the individuals belonged to before changing occupations. At this stage in the inquiry, it is important to note that our findings are not intended as indicators of social mobility, but simply of those categories that are most likely to be abandoned. Out of all the fathers who married in the region, and subsequently changed to another category, 24 percent had begun as farmers and eleven percent as day laborers (the rest are divided among very diverse categories). The fate of the former could well be associated with a failure, and of the latter with a success. In the case of the children, assuring their future as farmers never seems certain: 57 percent of sons attempt to make a living as farmers before having to give up this occupation, which is also the case of fifty percent of the sons-in-law. However, whether they are homogeneous or not, we can see that life courses are closely associated with the establishment of farms and the condition of farmer.

Turning to another set of problems, we ask to what degree, and in how many different ways did parents succeed in setting up their sons and daughters? This question is admittedly too vast to allow an answer within the scope of this article. For the moment, we shall simply indicate the main components of the problem (difficulties of measurement, variables of differentiation, etc.). The question of setting up children is different from that of social

reproduction. In the latter case, we draw on comparisons between the life courses of fathers and sons at the same stages in their development (e.g., occupation at times of marriage of the father and son). On the other hand, a father establishes each of his children at a different stage of his own life course, and, therefore, at different moments in his own career. We have reason to think, then, that the nature, extent, and value of the patrimonial estate will vary accordingly. The marriages of the children will have to be considered in relation to the progress of the life history of the father, and consequently, all the marriages occurring within a single family cannot be treated in the same fashion. In order to judge that an individual has been successfully established, it is necessary to observe his life course over a sufficiently long period. It is not enough to note that a son declares himself to be a farmer at the time of his marriage. His persistence in this undertaking revealed by subsequent declarations of occupations is the indicator we employ in the absence of precise knowledge on the extent and composition of his property. In this way, we have calculated that among the sons of the second generation, 72 percent were successfully established as farmers. From now on, numerous questions remain to be answered: what effect do different types of paternal life course have on the career of the children? What effect does the size of the family have on setting-up strategies? To what degree do these strategies influence geographical mobility?

CONCLUSION

The study of the interaction between the individual and family life, carried out at the micro-level and considered from the point of view of social reproduction, provides a useful approach to the problem of social change and continuity. The first (though still experimental) attempt was meant to demonstrate the interest of the approach, and at the same time, its theoretical and methodological difficulties, which are sometimes traceable to the fluidity of the concepts, and sometimes to the very nature of phenomena.

Our preliminary findings encourage us to continue this research in certain important areas. First, on the demographic level, our approach allows us to overcome the anonymity of aggregate measurement and bring out the particularities of people and situations. From now on we shall give preference to probabilistic notions of behavior and to multivalued analysis, rather than to the usual demometric tools. Then, on the social level, the utilization of the Saguenay family biographies promises a detailed survey of occupational courses and the factors which condition them. More particularly, the richness of our data will permit a very precise analysis of the establishment and the transmission of land.

NOTES

1. We should point out that this inquiry is also the topic of a doctoral thesis currently being prepared by I. de Pourbaix of the Department of Demography at the University of Montreal.

2. This obviously does not exclude the application of the model in other contexts, as, for example, in demography and anthropology, where it could be used to establish phases of family evolution. This was shown recently (September, 1984) at a colloquium on the demography of the last phases of the family cycle, organized by the U.I.E.S.P. in Berlin, West Germany.

3. These data are primarily demographic in nature: the number of children who reach adult age, marital patterns, etc.

4. Let us note that our methodological stance is substantially similar to the positions taken by such authors as Elder (1978, 1981), Bertaux (1982), Hareven (1978b), and Reuband (1980).

5. The results and a methodological discussion of this inquiry have been presented in detail in

Bouchard (1981, 1983). Also, for a presentation of the Saguenay region in historical and demographic perspective, see Bouchard (1977), Pouyez, Lavoie, Bouchard and Roy (1983).

6. Commencing with what is undoubtedly the most famous: that of Frédéric Le Play (1884) on the Méluga family, close to the village Les Cauterets (now ville d'eaux).

7. It should not be overlooked that these same lessons apply to the study of the most ancient contexts, which are usually treated as closed systems.

8. We are referring here to registers such as those constructed for the Saguenay region (SOREP), Nouvelle-France (group of H. Charbonneau and J. Légaré) and Utah (group of M. Skolnick).

9. This distinction is admittedly not yet warranted by any specific research hypothesis. We are employing it for the moment as a simple methodological precaution, which may prove unnecessary.

10. This requirement ensures that families of the second type were still in their expansion phase when they emigrated to the Saguenay.

11. Note that the phrase "last child to be married," both in the text and in the Figures, designates the last marriage that took place before 1911—the end of our time period. This obviously excludes a few marriages that may have taken place after this date.

12. Observation begins at marriage for the fathers married in the Saguenay, and from the date of the first entry in the register for the fathers who emigrated to the Saguenay.

13. Births occurring less than eight months after marriage.

REFERENCES

Bertaux, Daniel. 1982. "The Life Course Approach as a Challenge to the Social Sciences." Pp. 281–296 in *Aging and Life Course Transitions: An Interdisciplinary Perspective*, edited by T.K. Hareven and K.J. Adams. New York: Guilford Press.

Bouchard, Gérard. 1977. "Family Structures and Geographic Mobility at Laterrière, 1851-1935." *The Journal of Family History* 11:350-369.

————. 1981. "L'étude des structures familiales pré-industrielles. Pour un renversement de perspectives." *Revue d'Histoire Moderne et Contemporaine* 28:545-571.

————. 1983. "Les systèmes de transmission des avoirs familiaux et le cycle de la société rurale au Québec, du XVII au XXe siècle." *Histoire sociale/Social History* No. 31:35-60.

————. 1984. "The Saguenay Population Register and the Processing of Occupational Data: An Overview of the Methodology." *Historical Social Research/Historiche Sozialforschung* No. 32: 37–58.

————. 1985. "The study of occupational mobility in the Saguenay region through computerized family reconstitution"(unpublished paper).

Bouchard, Gérard, and Christian Pouyez. 1985. "Les catégories socio-professionnelles: une nouvelle grille de classement." *Labour/ Le Travailleur* No. 15:145–164.

Elder, G.H. Jr. 1978. "Family History and the Life Course." Pp. 17–64 in *Transitions: The Family and the Life Course in Historical Perspective*, edited by T.K. Hareven. New York: Academic Press.

————. 1981. "History and the Family: The Discovery of Complexity." *Journal of Marriage and the Family* No. 43:489–518.

Hareven, Tamara K. 1978a. "Cycles, Courses and Cohorts: Reflections on Theoretical and Methodological Approaches to the Historical Study of Family Development." *Journal of Social History* 12:97–109.

Hareven, Tamara K. (ed.) 1978b. *Transitions: The Family and the Life Course in Historical Perspitive*. New York: Academic Press.

Lapierre-Adamcyk, E., Y. Landry, J. Legare, D. Morissette, and Y. Peron. 1984. "Le cycle de la vie familiale au Québec: vues comparatives, XVIIe-XXe siècles." *Cahiers québécois de démographie* 13:No.1.

Le Play, P.G. Frédéric. 1884. *L'organisation de la famille selon le vrai modèle signalé par l'histoire de toutes les races et de tous le temps*. Tours: Mame.

Mendras, Henri, and Marcel Jollivet. 1971. *Les collectivités rurales françaises. Etude comparative de changement social*. Paris: A. Colin.

Pouyez, C., Y. Lavoie, G. Bouchard, R. Roy, et al. 1983. *Les Saguenayens. Introduction à l'histoire des populations du Saguenay, XVIe-XXe siècles*. Québec: Presses de l'Université du Québec.

Reuband, Karl-Heinz. 1980. "Life Histories: Problems and Prospects of Longitudinal Designs." Pp. 135–232 in *Historical Social Research. The Use of Historical and Process Data* (Historische Sozialwissenschaftliche Forschungen, Vol. 6), edited by Jerome M. Clubb and Erwin K. Scheu. Stuttgart: Klett-Cota.

Trost, Jean. 1977. "The Family Life Cycle. A Problematic Concept." Pp. 468–481 in *Le cycle de la vie familiale dans les sociétés européennes*, edited by Jean Cruisenier. Paris: Mouton.

Uhlenberg, Peter. 1974. "Cohort Variations in Family Life Cycle Experiences of U.S. Females." *Journal of Marriage and the Family* 34:284–292.

Vinovskis, M.A. 1977. "From Household Size to the Life Course. Some Observations on Recent Trends in Family History." *American Behavioral Scientist* 21:263–287.

A JAPANESE PERSPECTIVE ON THE LIFE COURSE: EMERGING AND DIMINISHING PATTERNS

Kiyomi Morioka

ABSTRACT: *The period after World War II has witnessed in Japan the emergence of new family characteristics, including a life-course pattern that includes substantial periods of extrafamilial existence. Affecting at this time only a minority of contemporary Japanese, the new pattern is particularly noticeable among young adults and among the old, especially among old women; and appears to be related to the widespread acceptance of the conjugal family system among the younger generations and the development of welfare policies aimed toward the old. Available sources permit an examination of the new pattern through contrasts with the pre-World War II period (when the ie system dominated) and through the study of familial settings of relevant cohorts in the past two decades.*

INTRODUCTION

The present investigation is an attempt to clarify the major features of the family career of present-day Japanese from data derived from national censuses.[1] By "family career" (or "family-setting career") I mean the pathway which an individual, rather than a family unit, follows through a series of varied family settings as people move through adult life. My analysis of the family-setting career of the Japanese will reveal that in the pre-World War II period people followed the life course in line with the *ie* system, and that, in contemporary Japan, though involving only a minority of persons, a new life-course pattern has emerged which results in an extrafamilial existence instead of a stem-family setting.

Kiyomi Morioka is Professor of Sociology, Faculty of Literature and Arts, Seijo University, Tokyo, Japan. His research interests include the sociology of contemporary Japanese family life as well as the comparative study of the historical development of familial structures and values.

Japanese census reports do not allow us to do cohort analysis covering the whole process of aging from birth to death. The best we can do, by employing special tabulation results and ordinary census tables, is to cover fifteen years by connecting three points in time, i.e., 1965, 1975, and 1980. In order to reconstruct the shift that would have taken place during a longer time span, we have to make use of cross-sectional data (especially from the pre-World War II period) as supplementary to longitudinal materials.

The family-setting career of an individual can be conceived of, first, as a shift between an intra-familial and an extra-familial existence. Accordingly, a relevant question is to ask in which age class one is prone to be leading an intra-familial or an extra-familial existence. In other words, we have to investigate a variation by age in which one tends to remain within or to secede from one's families of orientation and procreation. I will approach this problem first by focusing on individuals who live outside the familial context. I will then make an inquiry into those living in the familial context and examine the pattern of the shift between family forms by cohort as well as the age-group variation of the family forms. These analyses are expected to reveal the significant family-setting careers of present-day Japanese. At the same time, I want to shed light on historical change, the factors conducive to change as well as the implications of change, by comparing the post-World War II data with cross-sectional data from 1920.

PEOPLE LIVING IN AN EXTRA-FAMILIAL CONTEXT: THE CHANGE OF THEIR RATIOS

Teizo Toda (1887-1955), a pioneer of family sociology in Japan, clearly recognized the significance for family studies of people living outside a domestic group, and undertook to study the subject for the first time in the materials of Japan's first national census of 1920 (1926: 279-330, 1937: 165-208). It is Toda's 1920 data that I will rely upon in the present investigation.

In line with the definition used in the national census that is the major source of my data, I shall adopt an operational definition of the family as a group of co-residential close kin. Unmarried young children living separately in large cities may remain within the family circle of the parents back in the country. The national censuses which make the household the unit of survey, however, invariably fail to identify as family members those who live outside of the household of their close kin. Consequently, censuses treat non-coresidential unmarried children, even when they actually remain members of parental homes, as people outside of the family. In this way, the family as defined operationally is not necessarily identical with and tends to be smaller than the family as manifested in mutual recognition of close relatives. Still, I assume that information about the number of those living separately from close kin is valuable, for it suggests variations and changes of actual non-family population.

Japan's national censuses separate 'household' into 'ordinary household' and 'quasi-household,' and 'ordinary household' into 'kin household,' 'non-kin household' and '(independent) one-person household.' A 'kin household' contains at least one member who is a relative of the head, while a 'non-kin household' does not include any member who has a kinship tie to the head. The family as defined above is to be found in the 'kin household' category and relatives living there form an intra-family population. The remaining non-family population consists of people of the following four categories: (1) non-

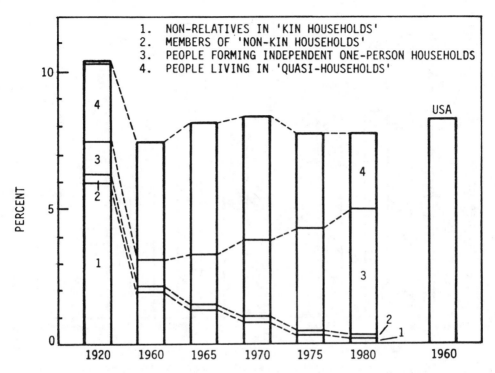

Figure 1. Shifting Ratios of People Living Apart From Relatives, by Category

Source: See text.

relatives in 'kin household'; (2) members of 'non-kin household'; (3) people forming an (independent) 'one-person household'; and (4) people living in a 'quasi-household' (dependent one-person household and institutional household).

We can secure data about these four categories of non-family population in 1920, 1960, 1965, 1970, 1975 and 1980 from census reports and special tabulation results published separately (Naikaku Tokeikyoku 1928, 1929; Sorifu Tokeikyoku 1962, 1969, 1970, 1974, 1978, 1984). Figure 1 shows the shift of ratios of non-family population to the total population in these six census years.

The oldest data to which we have access come from 1920 when Japan was still pre-

dominantly a rural and agricultural society. The ratio of workers in primary industry was then as high as 54 percent although industrialization had advanced considerably under the impact of World War I in Europe. Toda predicted that the ratio of non-family population would increase with the progress of urbanization, paying special attention to the higher ratios found in large cities. Contrary to the prediction, however, the ratios have remained steady at a level as low as eight percent in the post-World War II period. Even in recent years, when the ratio of workers in primary industry has decreased to the level of eleven percent, the ratio of non-family population has not shown any noticeable increase. This persistence of

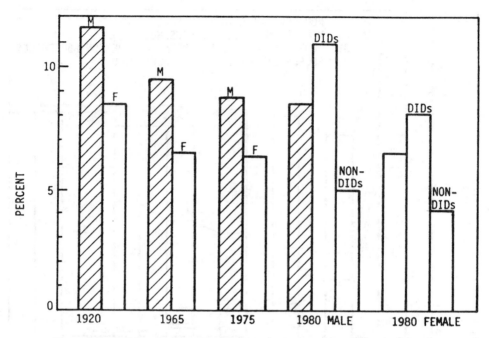

Figure 2.   Shifting Ratios of People Living Apart from Relatives, by Sex
(and by District, 1980)

Source and abbreviations: See text and p. 253.

the non-family ratio is attributable to the change in the age structure of the total population. If we divide Japan into densely inhabited urban centers and remaining rural areas, the ratio is obviously higher for the former than for the latter, as seen in Figure 2.

Although the ratios of non-family population have remained largely unchanged for the twenty years from 1960 through 1980, Figure 1 shows that the dominant category has changed remarkably. In 1920, about sixty percent of the non-family population was non-relatives in kin households, but this ratio has decreased consistently to the recent level of less than three percent. The category which has risen to a dominant position is people in quasi-households: they reached about

sixty percent of the total non-family population during 1960-65. But their ratio, too, has decreased since, and the ratio of persons in independent one-person households has increased recently to the level of about sixty percent of the total. The replacement of non-relatives in kin households first by those in quasi-households and then by those forming independent one-person households reflects the process of dissolution of self-employed businesses based on the labor of adult members in the households, including servants. It was self-employed businesses that had buttressed Japan's economy in the early phase of industrialization.

Some comparative evidence can be brought to bear for understanding this phenomenon in Japan. Turner (1973) notes that about thirty percent of the households in late nineteenth-century England contained servants whose services made up for the labor shortage in the family business. Laslett (1977) refers to the same historical trend when he points to the disappearance of domestic servants as the most marked family change that took place during the industrialization of England. Based on the demographic data on Providence, Rhode Island, in the latter part of the nineteenth century, and in the United States in 1970, Chudacoff and Hareven (1979) concluded that about one hundred years ago a considerable number of families contained non-relatives in their

households, and that the decrease of non-kin population in family households since then was accompanied by the increase of people in one-person or institutional households. Hareven (1978) mentions that one of the most significant historical developments in American society was the disappearance of non-kin in family households, a process largely completed around the end of the 1930s. The same trend as observed in England and the United States took place in Japan also, but about half a century later, that is, during the period from the early to the latter part of the twentieth century, specifically from the post-World War I period until the 1950s.

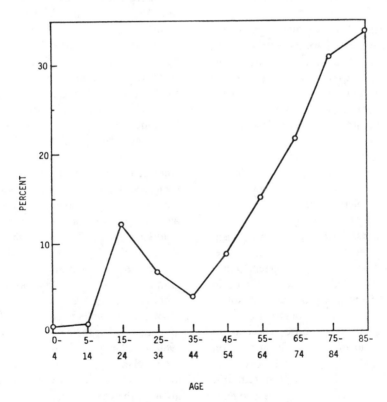

Figure 3.   Ratios of People Living Apart from Relatives, by Age
(USA: 1960)

Source: Belcher (1967).

Figure 2 shows the shift of ratios by sex. In each of the four census years, i.e., 1920, 1965, 1975 and 1980 (the only ones for which relevant data are available), the ratio for males was higher than that for females: the latter is about seventy percent of the former. Men have tended to live outside the family more often, experiencing fewer obstacles in this than women. For 1980, the available information also reveals variations by district. The ratios of non-family population were about two times higher in densely inhabited urban centers than in the remaining rural parts of Japan. Rural-urban discrepancies were more remarkable for men than for women. The variations are due partly to sex- and district differential migration, including movements from rural areas into urban centers.

One can ask in which age-grades are people more prone to live outside of the family. Figure 3 indicates that in the United States, as of 1960, the ratios of the non-family population were high in the young age strata (15-24 years), and in the middle-aged and aged strata (55 years old and over), especially the very old strata (75 years of age and over). The age category of 15-24 covers the period of transition to adulthood and includes the events of school completion, first-job entry, and marriage. In other words, it marks the membership shift from the family of orientation to that of procreation. Therefore, young people in this age group tend to live outside of the family. On the other hand, in old age the family of procreation dissolves because of the departure of grown children and the death of a spouse. The reasons why the ratio of non-family population increases in these two age brackets are quite obvious. The question remains, however, whether these reasons also hold true for the Japanese, who maintain family formation norms greatly different from their American counterparts.

Figures 4 and 5 demonstrate the variation of ratios of the non-family population in Japan by age class in 1965, 1975 and 1980, by connecting ratios in these three census years for each cohort. The dot shows the ratios in 1920. The figures reveal the recent shift of ratios for each cohort as well as the post-war change which manifests itself in the comparison with the 1920 data.

The ratio is extremely low for young boys and girls, but increases suddenly for adolescents. It then declines rapidly for the middle-aged and finally rises again for the old people. In spite of similar features shared by both sexes, the substantial differences that exist between men and women cannot escape our attention.

Figure 4 shows the men's variation by age. Very astonishing is the increase of ratios for young men, especially for young adults 20-24 years of age. The ratio for this age group is as high as 36 percent, a peak reached after sudden successive rises from the level of less than one percent for low teens (10-14 years) and of eighteen percent for older teens (15-19 years). The ages with a sudden rise of the ratios of non-family population are precisely the period when men experience consecutively events such as admission to college, school completion, and first job entry. Since 1977, 94 percent or more of junior high school graduates attended senior high schools. While senior high school students remained in their parental homes, most graduates who got their first job after high school completion left home. A majority of graduates who entered colleges located in cities also left their parental homes. In 1980, about 45 percent of men in the 20-24 age bracket were students or graduates of junior colleges or universities. Consequently, the ratio of non-family population increases suddenly in the 15-19 age bracket, which coincides with the events of high school completion, and it reaches

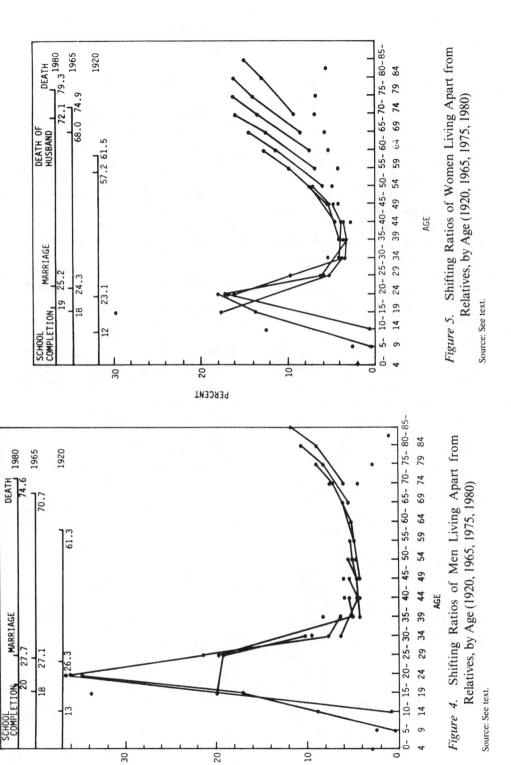

Figure 4. Shifting Ratios of Men Living Apart from Relatives, by Age (1920, 1965, 1975, 1980)

Source: See text.

Figure 5. Shifting Ratios of Women Living Apart from Relatives, by Age (1920, 1965, 1975, 1980)

Source: See text.

its apex in the 20-24 age bracket, coinciding with the timing of graduation from college.

The ratio decreases sharply in the 25-29 and 30-34 age brackets. The average age at first marriage for men (about 27 years) suggests that the sudden decreases are due largely to the formation of the family of procreation by these young men. Then, during the thirty-year period from 35 to 64, the ratio remains stable at the lowest level of about five percent. In these age brackets almost all men live in a family life. A recent tendency for the ratios in these ages to increase slightly may be attributable to the recent increase of divorce rates for middle-aged men. Following that, in the age brackets of 65 years old and over, the ratio of non-family population increases because of children's departure from parental homes and the death of a spouse. The recent increase which has become remarkable requires the exploration of additional causal factors.

The above observation by age and cohort reveals a relatively constant age variation of ratios for the recent fifteen years from 1965 to 1980, with the exception of old age when the ratio has increased remarkably.

During the two decades from 1960 to 1980, Japan experienced unusually high levels of economic growth, accompanied by large-scale changes in various sectors of life. Among major changes are the modernization of family structure as seen in the sudden shrinkage of average household size and the increased prevalence of nuclear forms, the remarkable improvement of quality of life as exemplified by a greater size of housing space per person and the widespread use of durable consumer goods, the changing conjugal relations as seen in the predominance of love matches vis-à-vis arranged marriages, an increasing divorce rate, and advances in family welfare policies especially for old

people. These tremendous changes have facilitated the acceptance of new, conjugal-dyad-centered, family norms as defined legally in the revised Civil Code in 1947, and these in turn have promoted changes in family life and related areas of activities. How are these post-war historical changes reflected in the age variation of the ratios of non-family population? I have attempted to probe this problem by comparing data from 1965-1980 with those from 1920.

The first thing to note in the 1920 ratios of non-family men is the considerably higher ratio for young boys, but no materials at my disposal provide a clue to explain it. The second is that the ratio for the 15-19 age bracket was as high as 34 percent, suggesting an earlier start of departure from parental homes (by about five years) than in the post-war pattern. The younger age at departure can be explained by the earlier age at school completion, which is estimated about thirteen years, four years earlier than for the post-war boys. Those who left parental homes to receive a higher education contributed to an increase of the ratio in the 10-14 age bracket, though only one out of four primary school graduates attended middle schools in those days. On the other hand, the sudden rise in the 15-19 age class is thought to be attributable to the departure due to a job entry, because the primary school graduates left home, when employed by a promising enterprise, after a few years' stay at home, working as a family hand for the business their parents owned and operated. If primary school completion had been followed directly by first job entry, the ratio in the 10-14 age class would have been much greater.

The third point to note is the relatively high ratios for the 30-39 age brackets. This will be explained by referring to the 'current population' policy of registration in the 1920 national census, that is, the policy of gathering information from people in the place where they happened to be at the time of census, not necessarily the place of settled residence. This policy tends to magnify a ratio of non-family population in the most mobile age brackets such as the thirties.

The fourth point is a decrease of the ratio in old age. After World War II, however, the tendency has been reversed. The discrepancy between the 1920 and the post-war data has expanded because of a great increase of the ratio in recent years. In 1920, the old people were taken care of by and within the family. The older the people, the smaller ratio of them left outside of the family. Today the reverse is true. The family which took care of the aged parents was a stem family household composed ideally of at least two couples in successive generations in the same family line. The stem family had the institutional prop of the *ie* system. Under the *ie* system of the pre-war days, the heir to the headship of the household lived together with his parents even after marriage, and formed a stem family. Upon the death of his aged parents, the stem family was transformed into a nuclear family which was to last for ten years or more until the marriage of the next heir. Upon the next heir's marriage, the family restored the stem family, in which the aged head and his wife were to spend the final stage of their lives. Thus, it is obvious that the low ratio of non-family population in the old age brackets in 1920 reflects the major pattern of the family-setting career of the Japanese men in those days. The pattern was revealed quite clearly by aged men who were least mobile. On the other hand, the recently rising ratio of non-family population in the old age brackets suggests a decline in the pattern of family-setting career under the *ie* system, and also the erosion of the *ie* system itself. In this sense, the ratio in the old age bracket is an

indicator of the family change brought about by the post-war socio-economic changes.

In the case of women (Figure 5), the peak in young age brackets is much lower than in the case of men. The increase of the ratio in the 15-19 bracket follows in the footsteps of men of the same age, while in the 20-24 age class it lags much behind the men's. The remarkable increase in the younger bracket reflects a rising level of education completed by women. On the other hand, the slow increase in the older bracket is the result of a presumably sharp increase in the entry into the first job following school completion and a decrease due to the first marriage which takes place at younger ages than for men. Parental preference of colleges and/or jobs, which their daughters can attend or enter without moving away from the parental home, is also conducive to a lower peak than for men in the same age bracket.

The women's ratio declines more rapidly after its peak than the men's because the average age at first marriage for women is earlier than for men. The age bracket where the ratio is lowest is the thirties, five years younger than for men. While the lowest stage covers thirty years of men's lives from 35 to 64 years of age, it encompasses only ten years or so of women's lives from 30 to 39, and starts to rise again after forty. Recent increases particularly for women aged sixty years old and over are marked. The same tendency is observed for men, but the increase for women starts earlier and is much more remarkable than for men. As a result, the rising second peak in old age today is as high as the first peak around twenty years. In this respect, a sharp contrast has emerged between the sexes. As I stated earlier, an increasing proportion of old people is left outside of the family, and is isolated from daily care and protection provided by coresiding close relatives. This old age alienation is far more marked for women who, when young, tend to remain under the parental authority and protection to a greater extent than men.

The age variation for women in 1920, represented on Figure 5 with a dot, indicates a sharp peak in the young age brackets, though not so high as for men. The peak stands out in the 15-19 age class, five years earlier than the present-day peak in the young stage. In addition, the ratio in the 10-14 age bracket was a little over twelve percent, greater than that for boys of the same age, while it is less than one percent for contemporary girls. In the early period of the twentieth century, the average age at school completion for girls was about twelve years. This means that many of them took jobs sooner or later after finishing primary school education. Consequently, girls living outside of the family comprised a considerable number already in the 10-14 age bracket, and the

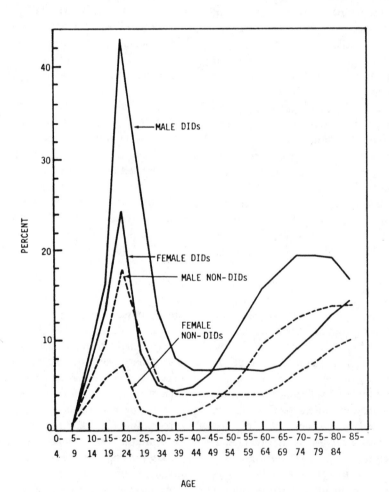

Figure 6.   Ratios of People Living Apart from Relatives,
By Sex, District of Residence, and Age (1980)

Source: See text.

age variation of the ratios was highest in the 15-19 age class. That the ratio declined sharply in the next 20-24 age bracket is due to the relatively young age at first marriage. In those days, only about twenty percent of primary school graduates attended middle schools. Therefore, the major reason for leaving parental homes is deemed to have been an entry into jobs distant from home towns.

Another significant historical change for women is suggested by the fact that the increase of the ratios in old age was small in 1920. In those days, women, also, lived the final stage of their lives by and large in a stem family household. If compared with old men, however, the ratios of the non-family population of women were still slightly greater. One reason for this was that the cases where women survived their husbands occurred more often than the reverse. Women who, while young, remained in the parental homes more often than men, tended to be deprived of family life in their old age more frequently than men. This sex difference has remained consistent and has become greater today.

It is assumed that the ratio of non-family population varies according to the kind of community where people live. Since no longitudinal data relevant to rural-urban variation are available, I constructed Figure 6 on the basis of the cross-section data in 1980, using the distinction between Densely Inhabited Districts (DIDs) and the non-DIDs. The ratios of non-family men are 11.2 percent for the former, and 5.1 percent for the latter; those of women 8.3 percent for the former, and 4.3 percent for the latter. The ratios for the DIDs are about twice as great as for the non-DIDs among both men and women. In every age bracket of the two sexes, the ratios are greater for the DIDs than for the non-DIDs. Consequently, the peaks in young and old ages are higher for the DIDs. Especially high

peaks are evident for young men and old women in the DIDs. The high peak for urban young people and the corresponding low peak for rural youth are the results largely of rural-urban migration and the concomitant differential mobility in the two areas. On the other hand, the height for urban old people cannot fully be explained by the reference to migration and mobility issue; it reflects the disintegration of the *ie* household in urban centers and its general persistence in rural communities.

THE RATIOS OF NON-FAMILY POPULATION BY HOUSEHOLD CATEGORY

Materials elucidating the changing ratios of non-family population by category are available in the three census years of 1965, 1975, and 1980. First, among young men (Figure 7), the ratios of non-relatives in kin households, which had been the major category in 1920, have decreased remarkably during the recent fifteen years. The ratios of people in quasi-households who replaced non-relatives in kin households in creating the peak have declined and have tended to be replaced by the rising ratios of people in independent one-person households. While the decrease of the ratios of non-relatives in kin households was brought about by the decay of self-employed businesses, the increase of the ratios of people in independent one-person households is due largely to the improved living standards, especially to improved housing facilities. Next, among middle-aged and aged men, the ratios of non-relatives in kin households have been quite small and have continued to decline recently. By contrast, the ratios of people in independent one-person households have been rising. On the other hand, the ratios of those in quasi-households have decreased, suggesting a complementary relation with the ratios of those in inde-

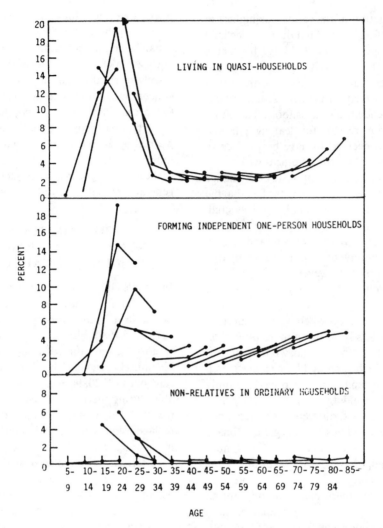

Figure 7.   Men Living Apart from Relatives, by Household Category
(1965, 1975, 1980)

Source: See text.

pendent one-person households which have been rising. The marked increase of the ratios in old ages of persons in quasi-households, however, reflects the fact that a majority of old people in this category consist of those in institutional households such as sanatoria and old-age homes rather than those in dependent one-person households, which tend to be replaced by independent one-person households. An analysis of the increasing ratios of the non-family population among old people reveals the significant contribution made by improved welfare policies aimed at them, as well as an erosion or change of the *ie* system which has weakened its protective function toward them.

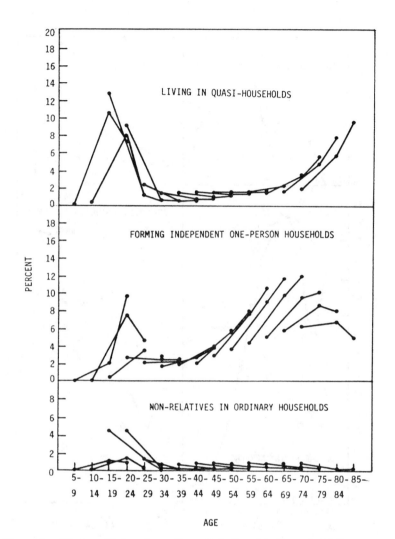

Figure 8. Women Living Apart from Relatives, by Household Category
(1965, 1975, 1980)

Source: See text.

Basically, the same trends are evident among women (Figure 8), except for their lower peak in young age and higher one in old age. One point worthy of special mention is that the increase in the 60-74 and the 75 and over age brackets is represented by the rise of ratios of women in independent one-person households and in quasi-households respectively.

THE SHIFT OF RATIOS OF PEOPLE LIVING IN A FAMILIAL CONTEXT

More than ninety percent of the total population of Japan lives in family households. In what forms of the household do they live? Census data relevant to this question are available in the 1975 and 1980 tabulation results. Figures 9 (men) and 10 (women) have been constructed by

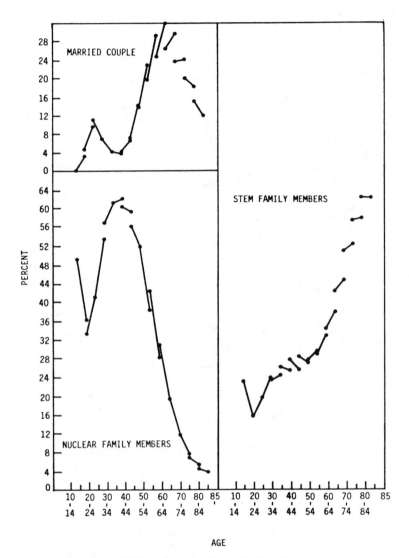

Figure 9.   Shifting Ratios of Men Living with Relatives
(1975, 1980)

Source: See text.

connecting ratios of the same cohorts at
two points in time. They show age variations among three major household
forms: 'married couple,' 'nuclear family,'
and 'stem family.' 'One-parent family' and
'others' are omitted here as insignificant
because of negligible ratios.

Since sex differences are negligible with
regard to the pattern of age variation of
ratios, I do not adopt a separate treatment
by sexes, but treat them in a combined
manner. At very young ages when the
ratios of non-family population are quite
low, people live mostly in nuclear family

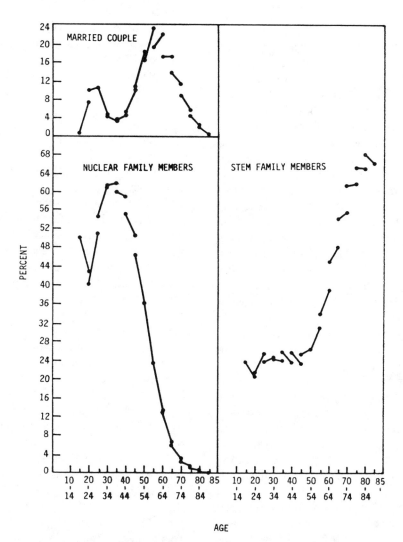

Figure 10.   Shifting Ratios of Women Living with Relatives
(1975, 1980)

Source: See text.

or stem family households. But the ratios of people living in these household forms decline sharply in adolescence or young adult ages when the ratios of non-family population reach a peak. After the peak of the ratios of non-family population in the 20-24 age bracket, the ratios of people living first with spouse only and then in

nuclear family households rise sharply. After the 40-49 age brackets, however, the ratios of people living in nuclear family households drops suddenly, while those with spouse only and in stem family households increase in proportion. In the 65 and over age brackets, the ratio of people living with spouse only is on the decline, and that of stem family house-holds continues to rise in parallel with the ratio of non-family population.

Behind the ups and downs by house-hold form, we can discern two distinctive family-setting careers. In one, the individ-ual moves from a nuclear family house-hold in the 30-49 age bracket to a stem family household with a coresiding mar-ried son or daughter. In the other, the movement is from a nuclear household in the same ages to a married couple house-hold with all married or unmarried chil-dren living apart, and finally to an extra-familial existence after the death of a spouse. The latter represents the life course that corresponds to the conjugal family system, the former the life course prevalent under the *ie* system, which is regarded as the Japanese variant of the stem family system. The recent parallel trends consisting of the increase of the ratio of old people living outside of the family or only with a spouse, on the one hand, and the decrease of the ratio of those living in stem family households on the other, suggest the increase of the number and ratio of people who have accepted or have to accept the life course corresponding to the conjugal family system.[2]

The life course under the *ie* system pre-supposed and was formed by the collec-tive life course of *ie* members. One accepted a particular alternative at a turn-ing point selected by significant members of the *ie* household, rather than choosing it by oneself. In this way, an intercontin-gency and an interlocking were guaran-teed among the life courses of different family members. The emerging conjugal family system in Japan which tends to produce a married couple household and an extra-familial existence in old age has the effect of isolating the life course of individuals from the great life course of the *ie* household. An increase of the

number of the people who adopt a life course pattern in accord with the conjugal family system will bring about a change in the view of life course. What change will take place is open to future investigation.

CONCLUSIONS

In summary, our findings regarding the non-family population indicate that the ratio of this population has remained sta-tionary at the level of eight percent in contemporary Japan. But the major cate-gory forming the non-family population has changed from non-relatives in kin-households to quasi-household residents and, finally, to those in independent one-person households, during the past sixty years or so. The latter change reflects, first, the diminishing importance of self-employed business enterprises in the pro-cess of Japan's industrialization and, second, the recent improvement of the quality of life especially in housing facilities.

There are also differences by sex and by district as well as age variation to be noted in the non-family population. The ratio of non-family population is greater for males than for females, and for the DIDs than for the non-DIDs. Moreover the ratio of non-family population is great for young people, particularly for young men. Among the major reasons why the ratio for young women is not so great as that for young men are the ten-dency of unmarried female students and workers to stay in their parental homes, and their average age at first marriage, which is lower than men's by three or four years. The earlier the age at first marriage, the lower is the peak of the ratio in the young age brackets. The rela-tively low peak for the American youth in 1960 (Figure 3) can be explained in terms of the much younger average age at their first marriages.

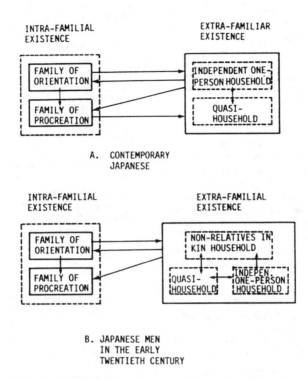

Figure 11. Model Family-Setting Careers: A Comparison.

The ratio of non-family population is low for middle-aged people. They are the most prone to lead an intra-familial existence. Interestingly, for the aged, the ratio of the non-family population used to be the lowest for old men. After World War II, however, it has risen especially for aged women who tend to survive their husbands. While young, women remain under parental authority and protection to a greater extent than men but, when aged, it is they who tend to be removed from family life far more than men.

Several concluding observations are also in order about the historical changes in the life course among the Japanese. While people in the prewar period followed the life course in accordance with the *ie* system, a new life-course pattern has emerged in contemporary Japan. The new pattern, though affecting only a minority of the population at this time, ends in extra-familial existence rather than in a stem family setting. A widespread acceptance of the conjugal family system within the younger generations and the development of welfare policies for old people have been conducive to the emergence of this new pattern. Figure 11, comparing the modal family-setting careers of Japanese (men) at the present time and in the early twentieth century, helps us understand the historical change during the past half century or so. The post-war increase of the ratio of nuclear family households has produced a great number of young people with no experience of the three-generation household. When they get married, it is most likely that even an heir to the household headship will prefer a

neo-local residence apart from his parents, and a wider circle of Japanese will
accept the new life-course pattern.

NOTES

1. An earlier version of this article was presented
as a paper in the session "The Life Course and
Generations: U.S.-Japanese Comparisons," at the
80th Annual Meeting of the American Sociological
Association in August, 1985, in Washington D.C.
That paper, and the present article, are based on
Morioka (1981), which has been expanded and revised to include the census materials of 1980 and the
life-course perspective. The aim is to deepen the
understanding of the life-course materials of middle-
age married men residing in Shizuoka City. The
Shizuoka materials, produced by a team of Japanese investigators, encompass research on several
significant careers, including residential, occupational, economic, problem-solving, health, and intergenerational. In the present article I have confined my observations to the family-setting career.
2. Kobrin (1976) reports on the expanding population of 'primary individuals' (as defined by the
U.S. Bureau of the Census in 1947), which has
become evident in the U.S. since 1950, and was
especially marked in the 1960s. Young people
(males) 18-24 years old and old persons (females) 65
years of age and over have recorded a remarkable
increase in the ratio of 'primary individuals' during
the above decade. As a result, three stages of living
arrangements have emerged in the life cycle of a
modal adult: (1) premarital independence among
young people (one-person household, non-kin
household, group quarters); (2) marriage; (3) post-
family independence among the old people. Economic prosperity and an expanded range of personal choice and freedom may be the explanation
for the increasing proportion of 'primary individuals,' and Kobrin's observations will find parallel
evidence in Japan.

REFERENCES

Belcher, John C. 1967. "The One-Person Household: A Consequence of the Isolated Nuclear
Family?" *Journal of Marriage and the Family*
29:534–540.
Chudacoff, Howard P., and Tamara K. Hareven.
1979. "From the Empty Nest to Family Dissolution: Life Course Transitions into Old Age."
Journal of Family History 4:69–83.

Hareven, Tamara K. 1978. "Historical Changes in
the Life Course and the Family: Policy Implica-
cations." Pp. 338–345 in *Major Social Issues: A
Multidisciplinary View*, edited by J. Milton
Yinger and Stephen J. Cutler. New York: The
Free Press.
Kobrin, Frances E. 1976. "The Primary Individual
and the Family: Changes in Living Arrangements in the United States Since 1940." *Journal
of Marriage and the Family* 38:233–239.
Laslett, Peter. 1977. "Le cycle familial et le proces-
sus de socialisation: caracteristiques du schema
occidental considere dans le temps." Pp. 317–
378 in *The Family Cycle in European Societies*,
edited by Jean Cuisenier. The Hague: Mouton.
Morioka, Kiyomi. 1981. "Hi-kazokuteki seikatsu-
sha no suii." ("Shifts of Non-family population"). *Kikan Shakai Hosho Kenkyu* (The Quarterly of Social Security Research) 16(3):
82–93.
Naikaku Tokeikyoku (Census Bureau, Prime Min-
ister's Office, Government of Japan). 1928.
Taisho 9 Nen Kokusei Chosa Hokoku (1920
Population Census of Japan), Zenkoku (Japan),
Vol. 1.
———. 1929. Taisho 9 Nen Kokusei Chosa
Hokoku (1920 Population Census of Japan),
Zenkoku (Japan), Vol. 3.
Sorifu Tokeikyoku (Census Bureau, Prime Minis-
ter's Office, Government of Japan). 1962.
Showa 35 Nen Kokusei Chosa Hokoku (1960
Population Census of Japan), Vol. 2, Part 5.
———. 1969. Showa 40 Nen Kokusei Chosa
Hokoku (1965 Population Census of Japan),
Vol. 5, Part 1.
———. 1970. Kukusei Chosa Tokubetsu Shukei
Kekka - Setai oyobi Kazoku (Population Cen-
sus of Japan, Special Tabulation Results:
Household and Family).
———. 1974. Showa 45 Nen Kokusei Chosa
Hokoku (1970 Population Census of Japan),
Vol. 5, Part 1, Division 2.
———. 1978. Showa 50 Nen Kokusei Chosa
Hokoku (1975 Population Census of Japan),
Vol. 5, Part 1, Division 2.
———. 1984. Showa 55 Nen Kokusei Chosa
Hokoku (1980 Population Census of Japan),
Vol. 4, Part 1, Division 2.
Toda, Teizo. 1926. *Kazoku no Kenkyu* (A Study of
the Family). Tokyo: Kobundo.a
———. 1937. *Kazoku Kozei* (Family Composi-
tion). Tokyo: Kobundo.
Turner, Christopher. 1973. "Developmental Cycles
and Transformations in Social Structure."
Paper presented at the 13th ISFR, Paris.

The Craft
of Family History

THE CHARACTER OF FAMILIAL HISTORY, ITS LIMITATIONS AND THE CONDITIONS FOR ITS PROPER PURSUIT

Peter Laslett

ABSTRACT: *This is a deliberately controversial piece, deriving the duties of the historian of the family from the ethical philosophy of Immanuel Kant. It criticizes the following tendencies in the treatment of the subject: the tendency to read history backwards (the Whig interpretation of history), to see it in terms of the doctrine of modernization (disastrous for the history of the family), to fail to recognize that familial change goes forward at the pace of social structural change, the slowest of all paces of change. The notion of approaches (a demographic approach, a feminist approach and so on) is rejected and the subject is defined as one of those within historical sociology, the type of all social science. An appendix deals with misinterpretations of the introduction to* Household and family in past time.

I shall argue that the historian of the family, like all investigators of society and of its history, must recognize three distinguishable duties. The first is a duty to his own generation, and the second to people in the past. The third is shared not only with other historians and social scientists but with all scholars and scientists. This is the duty to search after the truth to the utmost of his capacity, or of hers, recognizing that it may be impossible to avoid some degree of bias but doing all that can be done to reduce it.

Especially under our third head, the recital of these duties may seem a somewhat pedantic and heavy-handed way of celebrating the completion of some twenty years of work on the history of the family, and the tenth anniversary of the founding of *The Journal of Family History*. But there are times when it is useful to reflect at large on the task in which we

Peter Laslett, Trinity College, Cambridge, is co-founder and now Advisory Director of the Cambridge Group for the History of Population and Social Structure, and Director of the Rank Xerox Unit at the Cambridge Group.

have been engaged, and when this happens we should not shrink from asking ourselves why we ought to be doing this thing and not others, and what are our responsibilities in undertaking it. There is no better way, in my view, of compelling us to recognize the character of our subject, its problems and its limitations, than by asking questions of an ethical type.

I shall maintain that history in all its forms is to be thought of as historical sociology, and that historical sociology is the proper general description of the study of society as a whole, whatever particular title has been adopted for a part of that study—economics, social anthropology, social psychology and so on. Family history is to be looked on as a particular area within historical sociology, demarcated by its subject matter, and also to some extent by its methods. In an appendix I shall venture to speak out in defense of an admittedly controversial work of my own, the introduction to *Household and Family in Past Time* (1972), against what seems to me to be a persistent, pervasive and corrosive misunderstanding.

OBLIGATIONS OF FAMILY HISTORIANS TO THEIR OWN CONTEMPORARIES

It has not been usual to mention the duty of historians to the present generation before their duty to the people of the past, or even to maintain that they have a duty to their contemporaries at all. Nevertheless the case is quite easy to make out for the historian of the family, even though it must not be supposed that the historical sociologist's obligations to contemporaries should ever be allowed to lead to neglect of those which are owed to the people of the past. The three obligations named at the outset differ, somewhat, in their character. Our duty to the present is more personal than the other two. It is a

citizen's responsibility to our own generation in familial matters, particularly urgent because of the widespread conviction that the family is in decline, or is in process of being replaced by other institutions, perhaps several of them, which may or may not fulfil its traditional functions. It is for familial historians to decide how far these essentially historical statements are correct, whether for example the functions of the family have indeed been such as to justify such deep disquiet if they are being weakened.

This gives us a citizen's role as accredited experts, to whom those concerned with welfare, with social solidarity and with mutual support, can turn for information on an institution which they believe to be threatened. Under these circumstances it behoves us to get things right. But the importance of that role is not only social, political or administrative. Our own contemporaries care deeply about their families—their children and grandchildren, their spouses, their parents, their brothers and sisters. Abundant evidence exists to show that they care about these ties more than anything else and are often quite involved with relatives of other kinds. They have a right to know where they are in these respects, and the way to show them is to find out where they would have been in the past, and to make the comparison. In responding to their need for information we have to shoulder a responsibility which arises from our common humanity, and one which we share with all social scientists.

We might say that this first of our obligations demands that we do our best to understand ourselves in our own time, along with our contemporaries, to understand ourselves in our own terms. Common humanity requires of us as people who have undertaken to study the past a corresponding attitude towards earlier generations of mothers and fathers, children, grandchildren, servants and kinsfolk.

OBLIGATIONS TO THE PAST AND TO SCHOLARSHIP

The familial sentiments which now affect us and our coevals so profoundly, cannot but be supposed to have affected our predecessors too. How far their familial feelings were the same as our own is an intricate question, a historical question which we have to try to answer. Nevertheless there can be no doubt that birth and courtship, marriage and death were of salient importance to them, and that their family relationships bulked large in their emotional world, and in their world of work as well. This implies that we are bound to try to understand their situation, attitudes and actions in their own terms as well as in our own, understand them in their time and understand their purposes for themselves as well. Such an obligation cannot be quite the same as the obligation to our own contemporaries. Because those vanished individuals are not in a position to ask questions of us and because we cannot inform them of anything, it is more a question of scholarly integrity than of citizenship. But there is an obligation all the same.

In a scholarly journal dealing with scientific matters our third duty, to seek for the truth, to respect the facts and to eschew ideological bias, needs neither justification, exposition nor defense. If we neglect it we condemn ourselves as cheats or propagandists, or as both. We should go about our work bearing in mind Isaac Newton's self-reproachful judgment on his own intellectual career. "I seem like a boy playing on a seashore, and diverting myself now and then finding a smoother pebble or a prettier shell than the ordinary while the great ocean of truth lay all undiscovered before me" (Brewster, 1860: ch.27).

It is satisfactory to be able to claim that the mark of our own generation of students of the past is that we are concerned with the whole body of former societies, with the experiences, attitudes and aims of every single person which those societies comprised, of whatever religion, race or gender. We are no longer prepared to acquaint ourselves and our readers only with the outlook, attitudes and actions of an elite, exclusively with those masculine wielders of political power and owners of property, those purveyors of opinions and ideologies, those military and economic overlords and actors, whose doings filled the history books written for our parents.

The almost entire absence of women and children and of family relations in the accounts of the past which were created and circulated before our own activity began is the clearest illustration of how that history failed to be a history of all people all the time. It was not, and did not recognize that it ought to have been, concerned with females as well as with males, with infants as well as with adults, with servants and workers as well as with masters, mistresses and employers. Once we acknowledge, however, that our obligation as historians is to the interests and aims of everyone who lived before our day and in our day as well, we find ourselves faced with Immanuel Kant's well-known principle of behavior to our fellow humans, alive or no longer alive. We are to treat them as ends in themselves, to respect their purposes, their familial purposes along with the rest. The everyday emotions and customary desires of the ordinary persons of former generations, every single one of them, have an urgent claim on our attention.

CONTRADICTIONS BETWEEN
OUR OBLIGATIONS AND
FOUR PRINCIPLES OF PROCEDURE

Written out in full, the task to be undertaken in response to such a challenge must seem overwhelming, so multifarious and intricate as to be beyond our capacity. It could be said that since no one can undertake the impossible, the impossible cannot be our duty. We must say in response that we are perfectly aware that to do everything we could be required to do would be far beyond our powers. Our task has to be abbreviated; we have to seek ways of reducing its daunting complexity under convenient heads of discussion; we have to specialize, sample and select as students of society always have to do when faced with the full complication of their study. We recognize furthermore that in order to abbreviate in this way we have to have a theory or a series of theories, and that these may be hard to work out, and to establish objectively. The whole task is made more exacting because of the peculiar problems of defining the family, or families, and of understanding them adequately, especially as they change in accordance with the laws of their development. The difficulties do not end even here, however.

For one thing there is bound to be tension between the necessity of generalizing and abbreviating on the one hand and the requirement that we see individuals as individuals on the other, in the past and the present. Moreover our responsibility to our own generation, and to ourselves as members of it, may or even must conflict in the long run with our responsibilities to each and every one of our predecessors, even though the two sets of duties are of a somewhat different character. Nevertheless, no one expects that a subject such as ours can be entirely free of incoherence, any more than mathematics is finally free

of contradiction.[1] Ethical theorists are quite reconciled to the ultimate necessity of making choices, and when our duties conflict we too shall have to choose between our own time and its infinite number of predecessors. But we shall do so in full recognition of our obligations, to the one side and to the other. Our obligation to the truth, as has been stated, can never be in question.

The argument which follows sets out the implications of what has been said about the reasons why we should pursue familial history by putting four principles forward, and adding some observations and consequences. The first principle has to do with the knowledge which we have about the situation of the family in the present, together with what is often called the state of the art of social investigation. The second principle lays it down that familial history has always to be pursued from the past looking forwards, and never from the present looking backwards. The third insists on the inevitably limited and inferential character of all familial history, and the fourth declares that familial change must be recognized as proceeding at its own peculiar pace in what will be called social structural time.

Principle 1:
Knowledge of the Present
and of Technique

The first principle needs little further explication. We must have this obligation if we are to respond to the issues raised by family life in our own day and in our own countries and cultures. My point is a quite literal one. I believe that American family historians should read official reports on the contemporary American family and its condition, on divorce, illegitimacy, demographic trends and so on, just as their British counterparts should conscientiously study such publications of the

Office of Population Censuses and Surveys. Likewise with French familial scholars and the rest. We should feel obliged to get to know the contents of publications like *The Journal of Marriage and the Family* as well as *The Journal of Family History*, as many as we can manage. A casual, intuitive, journalistic knowledge of these circumstances of our own day is insufficient, as is a willingness to be content to inform ourselves about our own country and no other.

With this goes the rather more exacting duty of doing all we can to familiarize ourselves with the techniques requisite to the analysis of social behavior, the family along with everything else. This means all relevant methods and knowledge, those used by psychologists, economists, anthropologists, political scientists and sociologists. The numerical practices of demography and statistics are obviously salient here, if only because we will have to abbreviate, to deal in means, variances, probabilities. Like our companions in the other social sciences, but in our case particularly because of the traditions of historical study, we have to disregard the objections which were so often met with when the subject began, and which are still being repeated, at least in British universities, objections as to the inhumane character of techniques of this kind, especially of automatic computation.

It is open to us to insist that these techniques are scholarly requirements for work such as ours. In acquiring and practising them we are being faithful to the enlightenment of our own generation; the great humane figures of the past certainly did not disdain the technical advances of their own times, especially those which extended social knowledge.

All that can be at issue here is sufficient expertise to understand the results obtained by these techniques, and enough of their workings to be able to master them when required. Those who become possessed by methodology, maniacal significance testers or computer buffs, have to be regarded as a liability. Victims of such error do our job badly. Indeed they frequently fail to get as far as making contributions of a substantive kind. But what they do cannot affect those who do the job well.

An important part of the contemporary knowledge which we have to acquire in order to keep faith with our own generation consists in a close acquaintance with the ideological prepossessions of the contemporary world. Whatever our personal sympathies and convictions we must be aware of what Marxism makes of the family, or feminism, or religious systems, or political conservatism. This we have to do in any case if we are to know what our contemporaries think. But there is another reason.

Rival schools of social analysis often have fresh and interesting suggestions to make even if biases in results and recommendations are to be allowed for. Feminist scholarship in my view has shown itself to be the most powerful and revealing intellectual activity in respect to the study of the family in the social structure, past and present, especially when feminism is combined with neo-Marxist critical theory. But we also have to pay attention to a miscellaneous variety of other doctrines and theories. The teachings of the Church, or French literary theorists of deconstruction, could be as important on particular occasions as multiple decrement life tables or the computer simulation of kin numbers using Monte Carlo methods.

Principle 2:
Proceeding Forwards in Time and Avoiding the Use of 'Modernization'

So much for our first principle as to knowledge of the contemporary social world and the means of social analysis. The second principle, that of pursuing familial history forwards and never backwards in time, may seem rather less familiar, though its references turn out on examination to be historians' common-places. The obligation to our own genera-tion which we have so strongly insisted on encourages us to look selectively on what happened in the past, having ourselves and our generation uppermost or exclu-sively in mind. The interest tends to be in those elements or events which antici-pated, led up to and therefore help to explain ourselves, and especially our fam-ily situation, our demographic and other particularities. In such a mood it is under-standable that we should be strongly im-pelled to work backwards in time and concentrate our attention solely on those items in the past which contrast most con-spicuously with what we experience now, or which appear to do so, or those which seem in other ways to have been particu-larly significant for us in our own day. The rest may get left out, and our other set of duties, that to previous generations as per-sons, come to be completely overlooked.

Traditional historians have a phrase for this habit. They call it *Whig* history in ref-erence to a famous book by Sir Herbert Butterfield, which anatomized the phe-nomenon, *The Whig Interpretation of His-tory* (Butterfield, 1963). If historians are liable to fall into this way of thinking, social scientists using evidence from the past seem never to escape it. How firmly attached they are to the practice can be witnessed by the concept and term "mod-ernization," which invevitably selects those elements only from former states of our society which enabled it to become the society we now inhabit. Such an attitude must tend to imply that the whole past historical process is to be taken to culmi-nate in ourselves, our institutions and our doings. Not only is the contemporary

world assumed to be the aim and end of all that happened in our past, it is also looked on as the inevitable object and final state of developing or "moderniz-ing" societies elsewhere. A whole set of sociological theories have been based on these assumptions. Grouped under the general heading of convergence, these theories have laid it down that all coun-tries and cultures must be expected to pursue, and to have pursued, a similar path to an identical future. Family and kinship are important constituents of this overall change towards a universal condi-tion of modernity.[2]

Instances of this backward looking way of thinking are not far to seek among his-torians of the family. We may take, as an example, *The Making of the Modern Fam-ily* by Edward Shorter (Shorter, 1976) pub-lished in 1976 and accorded a very wide circulation in several countries. Its object seems to be to focus attention on every anticipation of our own contemporary familial life, on each first appearance of any of its elements. Little attempt seems to be made to understand and accept the familial purposes of our ancestors in the way described above. Indeed past ac-tresses and actors on the familial stage tend to have their motives questioned and their humanity slighted. Shorter blandly announces, for example, his assumption that in the past, in what he and many others call the pre-modern period, parents cannot have loved their children.

The really remarkable thing, however, is that Shorter decides in the course of his exposition that our contemporary family life, i.e., what nearly all of his readership would think of as the "modern" family, is not modern at all, but "post-modern." "Pre-modern" and "post-modern," these nonsensical expressions have become quite widely used in the later 1980s. They betray the incapacity of the Whig outlook to grasp the very nature of the historical process, which can have no moment of culmination in the *now* of any generation. Since the present is perpetually travelling through time with us, and all things modern along with it, everything in the past is necessarily "pre-modern" which thus becomes a roundabout way of saying "historical." Moreover, there can in logic be nothing existent in the present (or in the past) which is "post-modern," for "post-modern" can only mean the future.

We cannot go to any length into the discussion of the concept of modernization.[3] However, modernization and the family is a recurrent theme in the discussion of the family and its history, and has been so in a sense for well over a century. What is more, modernization has preoccupied those concerned with highly important topics allied to the family, past and present, such as aging.[4] We shall have to consider modernization and the family in a little more detail.

What seems to have happened is this. The verb "to modernize," literally to bring up to date, in its gerundival form "modernization," has acquired a second meaning, denoting the bringing into being of a pattern of social attributes. These intellectual, cultural, even technical and economic characteristics, had been judged to be the crucial features distinguishing "developed," "advanced," or "industrial" societies from all other societies. By taking up a stance in an "advanced," notionally the most "advanced" country, that is the U.S.A. as it was in the 1940s and 1950s, and by reading history backwards in the way we have set out in the case of Shorter, it has been possible to present in outline a total integrated process of change which all "advanced" societies have already experienced, and which all other societies will spontaneously experience, or can be cajoled into experiencing, even commanded to undertake. We need not here enter into a list or a description of the

characteristics themselves,[5] except to note that "modern" in the case of the family always denotes family groups of the simple, nuclear kind such as were quite accurately observed to have been almost universal in the United States of the 1940s and 1950s, together with independence of that nuclear family from its kin network and freedom of the individual from kinship control.

Once this concept of modernization had gained currency, it seems to have become progressively disengaged from any connotation of literal contemporaneity. It could consist in any social structure anywhere in the world at any time approximating to any degree to the chosen attributes of the U.S.A. in the 1940s and 1950s. Because the society of the United States has changed since that period, however, and because indeed industrialization, wherever it is found, is itself a process of continued, intensifying, irreversible[6] transformation, the attributes which had been grouped together as modernization no longer describe the present situation of advanced societies. It is presumably this which has persuaded people into coining and using the absurd phrases "post-modern" or "post-industrial." Thus it has come to pass that historical sociologists, those concerned with the family along with the rest, have lost control of an indispensable term of their discussions — modern meaning what is now — and all their usages for change over time have become uncertain.

People studying social structure and its changes are not alone in the dilemma thus created. Architects, architectural critics and architectural historians, for example, are now also faced with the loss of "modern" as a word and as a concept, since the adjective is being retained by them to describe a style which was until yesterday contemporary, accepted, approved. At the present moment, however, this style is coming to be regarded as out-of-date, and accordingly to be rejected. For architects "modern" now denotes "antiquated": its meaning has been reversed.

As might be expected, some architects are also adopting the nonsensical expression "post-modern" to describe the up-to-the-minute style of building which they now approve. Others presumably adopt a solution to the problem which seems to be favored by some historians of the family, which is to accept the two distinct meanings for "modern" (and presumably for "modernization"), where it is usually to be taken in its ordinary sense of what is now (or being brought into that state), but sometimes is to be understood in its special bundle-of-attributes meaning, where contemporaneity is not necessary.[7] Whatever the architects may feel, this expedient has to be judged unsatisfactory to the historical sociologist, since there appears to be no way of knowing which use is intended, except only from the context, sometimes explicit but usually not. "Modern" remains equivocal in its meaning, but worst of all from our present point of view its identification with the disposition to read history backwards is encouraged. This in turn serves to perpetuate the tendency to overlook the aims of our predecessors in time and to write in contempt of their integrity and their humanity.

Reading History Backwards and Changes in Family Composition Over Time

The necessity of reading forwards in time must not be taken to imply that hindsight is to be rejected. We need not lose our temporal advantage as historians, but we must not allow it to override our duties to past people. For the consequence of looking in the backward direction over time, must bring with it, as has been hinted already, a breach of faith with our prede-cessors. In so doing, we thrust our own preoccupations perpetually in front of theirs, in disregard of the ethical imperatives set out earlier. But we are also led into serious omissions and misunderstandings, not only in respect of the past, but in respect of the present, that is in respect ourselves and our situation. We distort or even falsify the present because by reading backwards we get the things wrong which we need to get right if we are to see ourselves in contrast with and growing out of what went before. It so happens that the history of the family contains a particularly conspicuous example of such a misapprehension.

It was because Frédéric Le Play, perhaps the most influential and in some ways the most fruitful, but certainly in this respect the worst of familial historians, looked back on the former state of the family in Europe exclusively with his own preoccupations about his own present in mind, that he made his notorious error of order about the original universality of large and extended households. Talcott Parsons and others, who uncritically followed his authoritative example, replicated his mistake. They did so, however, while applying a highly misleading theory, the theory that the familial condition of "primitive," undeveloped societies, as to kinship as well as to familial structure, could be used as a proxy for the former condition of Western, developed societies. So strong it would seem was the habit of reading history backwards that little attempt was made to check this unpersuasive theory against such evidence as was then available concerning the actual character of European familial life in the preindustrial past, as to kinship or as to the structure of the domestic group. Apparently it was just assumed that the situation must have been as the theory required, and that it changed towards that of the isolated, nuclear family in Europe in the way it was to do everywhere else as "modernization" proceeded.

The responsibility for this monumental confusion, especially for the complete absence of evidence, rested of course with historians as well as with sociologists and anthropologists. Until the family came to be recognized as fit and proper, a necessary object of historical analysis, almost nothing had been done by historians to seek out information on familial subjects, or to include familial questions and familial change when "social," as opposed to political, economic, religious or intellectual, histories were being composed.[8] It has proved a relatively straightforward task to expose the misconceptions, a task which was indeed carried out in the approved historical way, that is by establishing the largest possible body of comprehensive evidence, comparative in time and space, taking up a position in a particular country as far back as that evidence extended, and working forwards towards the present day. Nevertheless serious misinformation had been spread about for a century or more with consequent misapprehension about the position and character of the family as it is today as well as it had been in former times. Hard as we have worked on these points in the last fifteen or twenty years, some of the final consequences of Le Play's having taken the wrong turning in the 1850s still remain.

A limiting condition for reading history forwards is that there should be enough reliable data. The decade of the 1540s was chosen as the starting point for the study of the family by the Cambridge Group because this is the earliest point for which in the case of England, our chosen vantage point, complete parish register evidence existed. Complete here means including all three series, baptisms, marriages and burials, which are found recorded from that exceptionally distant date in our country. Such data enabled us, by the method known as family reconstitution for certain individual parishes and later by backward projection for the total population, to reconstruct the demographic record, and, using other documents and techniques, to bring to light the English familial record as a whole. We were thus enabled to work forwards in time for as much as 450 years, nearly half a millenium, time enough we hoped for us to grasp the pace and character of familial change in the long term and the short. The significance for historical sociology of the familial evidence from one country only became fully apparent because from the outset we acquainted ourselves with such information as we could find from other countries, other cultures, other periods and modes of production. Our duty under the present head in its complete version is to proceed forwards in time, comparing backwards for interpretative purposes when necessary, and comparing horizontally in the way just laid down.

We had an additional motive for starting at the very furthest backward reach of our reliable English information. Since so much of our knowledge of previous periods would have to remain so uncertain, it was important to get as close as we could to what might be called the threshold of informational darkness. We could then use our estimates of the pace of familial change to judge of the likelihood of certain hypotheses about what happened at the turn of the fifteenth and sixteenth centuries, as to a rise in the age of marriage for example, or a transformation in the whole character of familial life when the "feudal" epoch faded.[9] For the most part however we were, and are, forced to recognize that familial knowledge for the England of centuries previous to the sixteenth would have to rely on inference to an increasing extent as temporal distance receded. Hindsight would have to be liberally used, though never to the extent of reversing the direction of our study from forwards to backwards. We could at least proceed with our eyes open to the dangers, make what allowances we could, and try to estimate the degree of uncertainty of our conclusions. For other cultural areas, for central Italy for example, the threshold of informational darkness lies further back, in certain respects though not in all. But occlusion must occur for human societies everywhere, at periods very recent as social structural time is reckoned.

Principle 3:
Inferential Character of
Familial History

The third of our principles asserts in fact the inferential character of all familial history, and not only of that which deals with epochs earlier than 1500. There is a sense in which this assertion is a truism. Only an old-fashioned positivist would claim that such recordings as we find in parish registers which are only available after that date represent real, true, knowledge, observational knowledge, observational knowledge about the family because baptisms, marriages and deaths are eminently familial events. In reality of course the familial historian can only infer information about the family and kinship from demographic data. He or she has to do the same from the data of listings of inhabitants which have been used so extensively in revising the legacy of Le Play. The more informed, imaginative and judicious the familial historian is and the more fruitful a theorist—the more, I suppose I should have to add, the principles we are here examining are shown forth—the more likely it will be that familial descriptions will ring true. But they will be inferential still.

Our study is marked unfortunately with examples of unconvincing, indeed untenable inferences from demographic knowledge, perhaps because that knowledge appears to be so clear and unequivocal as compared with other sources. A conspicuous instance is the claim that since babies died so easily in the past, parents invested little of their love in a new-born child, an inference which helps to account for Edward Shorter's assurance on the point. This particular deduction from figures, figures which have incidentally been exaggerated and carelessly handled by those who have used them for the purpose, have been shown to be untenable. They are inconsistent with the anthropological evidence, with the conclusions of psychologists on parenting and the development of children, with a great deal of the literary and epistolary evidence left behind by the very persons who are supposed to have displayed the attitude. Demographic "fact" is not familial "fact." But neither should these other, more literary sources be taken for evidence of a straightforward "reflective" kind.

In reality we have no direct, unequivocal insight into families and familial life in the past. Few would doubt that argument from literary and other attitudinal data as we call it has to be inferential to an even greater extent than argument from demographic data, in spite of the richness and suggestiveness of literary and other materials. With literary evidence, especially with what I have called "high" literary evidence in an essay on this topic, elaborate theories have to be used to make inferences, just as they have to be used in abbreviating the bewildering variety of social facts as a whole. Our activity, as was also claimed in that context, is a theory-laden activity (Laslett, 1976). No one, for example, who supposed that the word *reflection* even approximately describes what we find in our sources, a direct, one-to-one image, that is to say, of the family as it really was there and then, can be said properly to understand our activity as familial historians.

There are numbers of consequences of this discussion of inference and of the strictly limited character of what family historians can do and say which are of importance to us, but only two can be touched on here. The first is that the theories which we use for each inferential purpose should always be explicit, never left to be filled in by the reader. An example might be the series of implications evidently intended when expressions such as "bourgeois," or "work ethic" are used in relation to a policy of a family, or the outlook on labor of a master. The writings of family historians seem to be replete with such suggestive allusions to class determination of attitudes and actions, without the process of inference from these suggestions ever being adequately specified: a sort of inferential impressionism in fact.

The second consequence is even more discouraging for easy generalization. It is that a great deal of what we find ourselves doing consists in the discovery of our ignorance, ignorance which is finally due to the highly particular conditions required for evidence of the past of the family to survive into our present. An example might be the age at marriage, a circumstance as we now recognize, of the first importance of the familial life of any society, the age at marriage in, shall we say, Anglo-Saxon England. All we seem to know on that topic, which might turn out to be crucial for the study of English household forms and of the Western family generally, comes from a few scattered, unrelated literary references. In such a situation it is clearly preferable for us to accept the nescience, to resist any attempt to guess, any disposition to invent theories of Anglo-Saxon family life and social structure based on what could or might have been. The recognition of what

we shall never know might be called the beginning of wisdom for the historian of the family.

Principle 4:
Familial Change in
Social Structural Time

I have left myself too little space to discuss inference and uncertainty at all effectively, and I shall have to deal with the fourth principle, that familial change proceeds in social structural time, in an entirely summary fashion. By social structural time is meant pace of change, or tempo, rather than time itself, and the propositions are as follows. Political change, literary and aesthetic change, economic change, demographic change, ideological change, religious change, legal and constitutional change (where the constitution is the political framework) and finally social structural change, all have their characteristic paces. Some of these are fast relative to others, some are slow, and there is a spectrum from the fastest to the slowest. Political change goes on at the greatest speed, though rivalled by literary and aesthetic change, by fashion in fact, and social structural change goes on at the most deliberate pace of all.

The issue of importance to family history is that it is a mistake, an ordinal error once again, to put the family into the wrong category of pace of change. There is obvious uncertainty about the constituents and the boundaries of the divisions I have hastily named, and about the nature of the relationships between them.[10] Family and kinship in all their connotations are quite evidently affected by fluctuations in the economy, and by alterations in class relations and in productive methods. Demographic variations, ideological, religious, legal and even political vicissitudes likewise have their impact. But these and all other elements are certainly influenced in their turn by modifications in familial composition or behavior, and there can be no doubt that the family as an institution has to be placed under the heading of the social structure, so that its rate of change is very slow.

There are two circumstances which combine to ensure that familial change should be leisurely, almost as gradual perhaps as social change in any other direction. The family consists in a systematic normative structure, and normative change is usually a deliberate, inch-by-inch operation. It belongs, as the French would say, to *l'histoire immobile* rather than to *l'histoire conjoncturel*. We are all aware that some norms, and among them familial norms, can stay virtually the same in their content over many centuries, and we can imagine them persisting from far back into prehistory. Moreover the familial normative structure is container-like, since one of its purposes is to outlast demographic emergencies and vicissitudes, economic ups and downs, ideological turnabouts and religious transformations.

The initial training of nearly all historians is still in political history, and the political pace seems to continue to determine the historical outlook as a whole. The fondness of historians for the concept, the flavor, the word *revolution*, could be said to demonstrate this fact—a political expression for a political type of occurrence, swift, dramatic but only very rarely associated with a structural shift. It is to be expected that family history should be seen by many of those who have taken it up to change with political periods (centuries, reigns, regimes, even ministries) and at a political pace. It is also to be expected that sooner or later the word *revolution* will be used in relation to it, if indeed that has not already occurred.

It is for the reader to decide whether the habit of mind giving rise to such statements is indeed widespread among historians of the family. Nothing would be gained by exaggerating the prevalence of such failures of judgment, such lack of realism, such naivete, as it might be called. Nevertheless this obliquity of outlook is certainly to be found. There is no need to go any further for an illustration than the familial changes, not simply oscillations or vagaries, but deep-seated modifications of form, which are claimed to have occurred in Lawrence Stone's rich and informative book *The Family, Sex and Marriage in England, 1500-1800* (Stone, 1977). As long as we find such accounts of breakneck familial transformation—first in one direction for a reign or two, then in another, now a reversion, then a collapse—to be persuasive to ourselves and to our readers, we shall continue to be at the mercy of almighty politics in the analysis of the familial past. *L'histoire conjoncturel* will retain its influence over us, and we shall misunderstand the character of familial change, proceeding as it does in social structural time.

SCHOLARSHIP AND FAMILIAL HISTORY

This brings us finally to some observations on the four principles which have been laid down. Obvious and even jejune as some of them may seem, they may be thought controversial in their way, and they are certainly in contrast with the actual practice of many familial historians as shown forth in their publications. The markedly "Whig" tendencies of the social scientists writing in this field, and of some of the historians, the ignorance of appropriate techniques, even hostility to their use, on the part of those with a background in the humanities, have already been remarked upon. It is only just, however, to refer to the disregard of the traditions of established scholarship in humane subjects which can be observed from time to time among ourselves.

If it is permissible to make a personal comment or two on this, I should like to draw attention to the original intentions of the Cambridge Group for the History of Population and Social Structure as to scholarly practice in relation to the documents recording the families of the past. The principle we set out to maintain was that every exercise on such documents should specify the name of the settlement concerned, the date of its description by an observer of the past, and its population size. No proportion was to be recorded without specifying the standard error. In the ideographic system which had been evolved for the exhaustive representation of domestic groups, care had been taken to distinguish as precisely as possible between the primary family (the conjugal family unit as it was called), the household and a unity which was denominated as the houseful. Boundary lines had been specified to demarcate these unities, and it was imperative to insert them into every set of representations. Without these indications it could not be unequivocally determined quite where, in the researcher's opinion, one domestic group ended and another began.[11] The further use of the system was to have been to enable researchers wherever they were to interchange descriptions of domestic groups in ideographic form, particularly when the originals appeared in the language of the country or region concerned, especially languages using non-European scripts, like Russian or Arabic, or written in characters, like Chinese and Japanese. Without such a universal mode of intercommunicating independently of translation it was difficult to see how the comparative exercises essential to the development of the study could be initiated and sustained.

It has not worked out like this, even at the Cambridge Group itself. The published works of historians of the family do not go to such scholarly lengths: sizes of populations at risk are not always specified, even dates of observation are sometimes omitted and standard errors are scarcely ever met with. When family groups are represented graphically, the boundaries demarcating the unities which, in the researcher's opinion, are to be discerned within them, are seldom indicated, and the denotation of the houseful by such indicators has virtually disappeared. Not only have the precedents described been largely disregarded, but little attempt has been made to work out improved conventions of this kind. In the case of the scheme for the analysis of household composition, which is discussed in the appendix to this article, alternative, more revealing sets of classification have been repeatedly suggested, but never in sufficient detail to cover every familial possibility. What is more, each researcher has tended to invent a new system in disregard of those of his predecessors, except, it should be admitted, occasionally that of the Cambridge Group itself.

These may seem to be points of final, fussy detail, but the persistent neglect of them has had the expected effect. It has become extremely difficult to make clear, unequivocal comparisons between the results presented by different researchers. It seems likely, moreover, that this failure to develop common categories, conventions, standards of accuracy has given rise to misunderstandings and controversies which need never have occurred.

To leave these minutiae and to come to substantive matters, there has been a particular unwillingness to face problems of systematic familial change as distinct from economic and demographic vicissitude affecting familial strategies and individual familial behavior. There is a conspicuous example here in the extensive discussion of changes in the family cycle which may have occurred over time. It has been re-peatedly implied that changes in the fam-ily cycle have taken place, and that they have sometimes been changes of norms or of practice and not simply responses to varying economic conditions, or accom-modation to new demographic regimes. But, as several authorities have pointed out, the actual definition of a family cycle for purposes of this kind, let alone the working out of a whole series of instances belonging to different time points, pre-sents excessively difficult problems. Easily made assertions represent what turn out to be virtually unrealizable scholarly pro-jects. In introducing from the work of Glen Elder the concept of transitions in the life course into familial historical stud-ies, and asserting that these have also changed over time, Tamara Hareven added to our subject in a most interesting and important way. But the question re-mains whether such differences in transi-tions, which are again multiple and complex concepts, can indeed be said to be normative changes or responses within an established familial system which lie within their established tolerances. This question as far as I can see has been left unanswered.

In the volume called *Statistical Studies and Historical Social Structure* published by K.W. Wachter, E.A. Hammel and my-self in 1978, it was insisted that to demon-strate differences over time or between places with anything like certainty would require very much larger differences in relevant statistics describing families than had at that time been realized. What was true of the exercise there in question, to do with stem-families, must be true of other familial characteristics. We nevertheless find, however, that even very small differ-ences, in the timing by age of transitions, to return to our example, are published as suggesting or even demonstrating system-atic familial change. And this often with-out any reference to estimates of statistical significance, which in the case of life course transitions would perhaps present very awkward problems. This is only a single example of the neglect of our duty to put into practice the ever-improving analytic techniques of our fellow scientists in our own generation. Once more it is the failure to make progress which I find discouraging.

POINTLESSNESS OF THE DISCUSSION OF FAMILY HISTORY IN RELATION TO THE SOCIAL SCIENCES

Our subject, like all others, contains a number of overdiscussed topics. I suppose it is generally recognized that I feel the question of the stem-family to be one of these topics. But more depressing in view of what has been asserted above is the perennial discussion of relations between historical and social scientific knowledge. If what has been asserted so far is correct such discussion is largely devoid of signif-icance or of interest. There is no sociolog-ical outlook which can in logic be *op-posed* to the historical, a point brought out with great force and clarity by Philip Abrams (1982) in his book on historical sociology. Historians cannot *borrow* from the demographers, the economists, the anthropologists, the psychologists. All that can happen is internal redistribution, and modifications in the division of labor.

It follows from this that we must avoid seemingly useful but finally illogical and misleading categorization in describing and reviewing our subject. There can be no demographic as *opposed* in any logical fashion to other types of "approach" to the family history, as Michael Anderson (1980) in an otherwise illuminating and useful analytic essay seems to have sup-posed. People may overemphasize demo-graphic fact in analyzing the past of the family and so lack balance, but they are not by so doing employing a demographic approach. In any case, it was not exaggerating the importance of demography which, it seems to me, faulted the account which Anderson criticizes—rather the overconcentration on a single source, namely, listings. Nor, it should be obvious, can there be feminist historians, or socialist historians all with their particular and characteristic types of family history. A person can have feminist convictions and also be a historical sociologist working on the family, a more interesting one in my view for that reason, but cannot be termed a feminist as a scholar of the subject pursued. "Feminist" and "socialist" history, "quantitative history," "cliometrics," and "social science history" are all alike inconsistent in their titles anyway with the principles laid out here. They imply a fundamental misconception of the enterprise to which familial history belongs.

The history of the family must be regarded as a topic in historical sociology. It is an important topic, just as important but only just as important as the family in general can be said to be in contemporary social structures and in the social structures of our predecessors in time. There is nothing particularly special about familial history, except that the recognition of the necessity and indeed the duty of undertaking it is fairly recent. The principles which have been laid down, it must surely have been recognized, are those which apply to all pursuits in historical sociology, and familial history is one among the others. It must be apparent also that, for me at any rate, history inevitably informs social investigation of every conceivable kind. Historical sociology is both the proper description of what all those who call themselves historians are in fact engaged in, and the type of every social science.[12]

APPENDIX

The *Introduction to Household and Family in Past Time, 1972*

"A collection of individual listings is a collection of still photographs and they cannot be used as if they were movie strips. We find ourselves for the most part forced to discuss a process as if it were a state." This passage appears on page 34 of the *Introduction* to *Household and Family in Past Time*, which I shall refer to as HFPT. On page 67 of that book it was announced that simulation might transcend this limitation. It was the expedient most likely to resolve the problem of processing from the cross-sectional evidence of census-type documents to the cohort-type, processual analysis which the proper study of families and familial life required.[13] The third chapter in HFPT was written by Jack Goody, usually recognized as the codifier of the concept of the domestic cycle (see Goody, 1958). Eugene A. Hammel was also a contributor (Ch. 14: 'The Zadruga as Process'), while he, Goody, and the late Meyer Fortes, all three leading anthropologists and exponents of the processual character of familial life, guided and advised throughout the whole series of episodes which led to the Cambridge meeting of September 1969 and the publication of its proceedings as HFPT in 1972.

In spite of all this, that book, and especially its *Introduction*, became identified with a static approach to the analysis of the family and seem to have remained so. HFPT appears now to represent a "medieval" stage of the study of family history, when the developmental cycle had not been recognized, a stage which the "modern" researcher has outgrown and must castigate. Although the concept of the developmental cycle is at least as old as Seebohm Rowntree's *Poverty* (Rowntree, 1900), and can be traced as far back as Gregory King's research of the 1690's (see Laslett, 1985), the writer still finds himself being introduced to audiences as someone who was unaware of its importance to family studies when his first works were written, or as if he had "come to terms with it" only in more recent publications (Mendels, 1986:83).[14] The effect has been to give something of a reprieve to the earlier view which the *Introduction* had set out to attack, the mistaken belief that in "premodern," precapitalist times the family group had everywhere and always been large and extended. Attention has tended to be reserved to those areas, cultures, places and periods which it could indeed be shown that large-scale, complex households had been important, or even, occasionally, dominant in the ordinary experiences of ordinary people.

Such an unfortunate outcome could be said to be a breach of faith with our ancestors, certainly our ancestors in the Western and Northwestern European areas, most of whom lived on the plains and in the river valleys, in the towns or in the cities, or in England, on all of which sites simple family households were entirely predominant, and hence in a commanding position among Western populations as a whole. But this is decidedly not the impression left by books like that of Flandrin, *Families in Former Times*,[15] or even by the numerous articles on family groups which have appeared in the *Journal of Family History*. In 1985 two eminent experts on Asian family systems seem to have been so much impressed with the discussion of evidence from these exceptional areas in Central and Southern France, Germany and elsewhere in Europe that they could actually declare as an established truth that "Western Europe was dominated by the stem family system."[16] No doubt this could be a source of reassurance to the spirit of Le Play,

ensconced as we may imagine it to be in that solid, complacent memorial bust which graces the Jardin de Luxembourg in Paris. But it is to the despair of the collector and analyzer of the whole body of evidence on the history of family systems over the European continent, because it seems to demonstrate that we shall never succeed in communicating the true situation to those looking at our continent from the outside.

The *Introduction* to *Household and Family* was intentionally challenging and controversial, aimed at arousing interest in a new subject. In this it could immodestly be claimed to have been successful, since so much has been published on family history which makes direct reference to it. But there was a price to be paid in overemphases, inaccuracies and errors, scarcely avoidable in any case in an attempt to generalize on so large a scale in undeveloped intellectual territory. Numbers of scholars have pointed these out to the chastened but grateful author, of whom Lutz Berkner (1975) was perhaps the most effective and illuminating.[17] But the most damaging mistake in that book, the one which has perhaps contributed more than anything else to subsequent misapprehension about the family and its composition, especially in the European past, was neither one of fact nor of analysis, and was scarcely open to correction. It was a serious miscalculation as to the stock of knowledge of the book's intended readership, especially their acquaintance with statistics and statistical thinking, entirely elementary statistical thinking though it was. I refer here to the now notorious null hypothesis.

A null hypothesis, let me venture to remind the reader,[18] is one which all good research practice advises a researcher to set up to test the significance of the findings made. Let us proceed, it states, by discovering if the difference between A and B is large enough under the circumstances to be significant, and to what degree. If no significance can be shown, the null hypothesis that there is no difference cannot in fact be refuted. To the entire innocent this may seem an awfully roundabout way of doing things, but the reader of the *Introduction* was not assumed to be an entire innocent. What an entire innocent was likely to suppose, was that the null hypothesis about families, that they must be assumed to be nuclear unless it could be proved otherwise, asserted something completely different, that all families were in fact always and everywhere nuclear in form. An entirely uncomprehending, absolutely unjustifiable conclusion of course, but one which is undoubtedly accepted, especially in non-English-speaking countries. With hindsight it is obvious that it was culpable, a crass mistake of the author to put it in this way, to use the null hypothesis or statistical expressions at all. Family historians were not up to it in the 1970s, and this still unfortunately seems to be the case.

This expository disaster, as it must be called, did much therefore to account for what has been named a persistent, pervasive, and corrosive misunderstanding of HFPT, and consequent continued misapprehensions about the familial past of Europe. Some of the uses of the confused apprehension of that *Introduction*, however, look almost wilful to its author, wilful on the part of those who must have known what a null hypothesis was but perhaps had reasons to take advantage of the misinterpretation described. Even Franklin Mendels (1986:82, 85) writes about the null hypothesis as if it were something against which blows could be struck, or something which could appear amongst phenomena which had to be saved if a doomed proposition was to prolong its life.[19] To recommend a particular form of hypothesis to test in a particular

situation is surely to give a piece of advice, the advice that it is on the whole preferable to suppose families simple than complex if nothing is known about them, rather than to advocate a proposition or to put forward a hypothesis. Let me assure him and all others who have taken HFPT in this sense that I never supposed in the early 1960s, or at any time since, that nuclear families were always and everywhere dominant or prevalent. In the preface to the original volume it was hoped "that no open-minded reader of the *Introduction* could come away with such a stereotype in his head."

The last element which can be discussed in this survey of the misunderstandings of HFPT and their consequences concerns the household structure or household composition table (p. 31 of the *Introduction*). This table and the classificatory system on which it is based, now go under the title of Hammel/Laslett or more simply Laslett, though it is made clear on page 33 that it was adopted with only one modification from Louis Henry's *Manuel de dèmographie historique* (1967). The table, its classes and subclasses have been very extensively used for analyzing communities or larger populations in respect of the kinship composition of households, and sometimes for comparing one to another. This last practice has no doubt been encouraged by the title which was given to an article elaborating and refining the system: "Comparing Household Structure Over Time and Between Cultures," (Hammel and Laslett, 1974). It was probably unwise to have used this phrase, or to have given the impression that such comparisons at large, and for numbers of analytic purposes, had been the object for which the system was originally adopted.

The classification belongs strictly with the limited purposes originally envisaged for the relevant part of the *Introduction* to HFPT. This was to find some way of comparing communities and populations in order to be able to determine whether or not it had been true in the past that they were usually characterized by family households which were non-nuclear, non-simple in form. We wanted to go a little further than this, that is, to be able to get some ordinal scale, showing how much more or how much less, prevalent complex households had been in the past than they are now. Therefore, the system had to be developed to the point where all possible relationships within domestic group could be covered, otherwise some households would have had to be omitted as unclassifiable and comparisons blunted. Such details were also useful for many other purposes, when married to the ideographs, like determining how many people lived alone, or how many in one-parent families, or how many households there were with a resident married son which might fit the definition of the stem family household at its crucial developmental stage. We wanted clear and quasi-numerical outcomes, if not on the ratio scale, as to the proportions of nuclear households in relation to households of other types, and we found ourselves able to get them.

In developing our categories and sub-categories, therefore, we were not concerned with the development cycle of households as such, articulating successive forms so as to follow that cycle. This cannot in fact be done with the Hammel/Laslett classification, and I know of no system which allows for it and also satisfies that other essential criterion, providing for all relationship possibilities.[20] Nor were we much exercised with comparisons to which the nuclear form was irrelevant, as for example between areas of stem family households and of joint family households, though our table could be used to cover such eventualities in some detail. All of which meant that the Hammel/Laslett table could not be used for all the classifi-

cations and comparisons which historians of the family want to make and should make. The plain fact is that when the classificatory system was being developed, I myself had never seen any examples of communities where complex households were of much numerical importance, apart from the one or two contained in the chapters of HFPT itself. Subtler, more inclusive, comparisons require development of more advanced classificatory systems, and so of course do comparisons made for purposes other than kin composition, the vitally important purpose for example of comparing households as work groups.[21] Numerous criticisms have been made of the system because of its weaknesses in the respects which we have discussed, and numerous other classifications proposed, though none that I know of which satisfies the condition of covering all rational possibilities, and none which seems to have established itself as more useful than the Hammel/Laslett original. In recent years it might be said that its handiness has been a disadvantage. It may have stood in the way of more searching comparisons, better modeling, more penetrating analysis.

Michael Anderson in characterizing HFPT and the work of the Cambridge Group generally as evincing what he insists on calling the *demographic* approach (Anderson, 1980), also describes our classificatory system as enclosing families within vacuum flasks, thus cutting each off from all the others, and severing kin links between individuals in different households. It has already been insisted that such was not our object with our ideographs, nor was it in the classificatory table. Insofar as this was the outcome, it was an unintended, incidental effect of devising a set of conventions to distinguish families of a nuclear form from all others. To analyze you have to compare; to compare you have to classify; classification entails drawing boundaries, and we could not escape this ineluctable succession.

It is not the intention of this note to deny that HFPT was imperfect, obtuse to some degree, and occasionally misleading. An originator is understandably anxious, however, to do all he can not to get in the way of those who come after. In this respect, alas, the *Introduction* to *Household and Family* seems not to have done its job all that effectively.

NOTES

1. Nor needs anyone sensitive to the issues suppose that the object is a value-free social science. However hard we strive towards impartiality we cannot transcend our situation in the professional classes of our countries, our membership of the caste of *universitaires*. We may be bound to try to understand our contemporaries and predecessors as fully as we can, but this gives us no rights of judgment over them.

2. The literature on modernization is bewilderingly large. The best guide to the concept for the historian is E.A. Wrigley, 1972.

3. A study is in preparation by Jack A. Goldstone and Peter Laslett with the provisional title "Four Forbidden Historical Expressions." One will be "modernization."

4. See, e.g., the collection edited by Donald O. Cowgill and Lowell D. Holmes *Aging and Modernization* (1972) and compare Peter Laslett (1987). Aging could be said to be an area where the responsibilities of the family historian to his contemporaries is at its greatest, since if he goes wrong there is serious misinformation on an entirely crucial topic. Some social gerontologists are well aware of this, and Jill Quadagno (1982) argues a systematic and documented case against modernization theory (pp. 22–25).

5. See Wrigley's article referred to in note 2.

6. There is a complication here because, especially in England, a process of de-industrialization is now often referred to, implying a reversion to a state before industrialization occurred. In fact what seems to be meant is a decline of manufacture, or even a tendency towards its disappearance, from

areas where industrial progress has made established manufactures inefficient or obsolete. But society in these areas is still industrial society, and the otiose expression *de-industrialization* implies an unjustifiable identification of industrialization with the production of goods in factories.

7. This seems to be the position of Daniel Scott Smith in Smith (1983), the latest of the series of valuable studies on this theme.

8. Social history had previously tended to be written about as one of the sections of general textbooks given over to political and other subjects, with an emphasis on the quaint and the interesting and little attempt at systematic investigation. Even when whole treatises were devoted to the subject, as distinct from popular outlines, specific statements about such topics as the real character of the family were usually lacking, as for example in G.M. Trevelyan's *English Social History* (Trevelyan, 1942). It is therefore difficult to find examples of historians coming out with the statement that families were large and kin-complicated, that kinship dominated everyday life, and that there was change towards smaller families and weakened kinship influence as the present time approached. This lack of a target was a disadvantage when family history first launched its critical enquiry. We were accused of attacking straw men.

9. For the view that over these centuries marriage age did rise for women in Europe and that there was a familial transformation (see, e.g., Hajnal, 1965; Burgiére, 1972; and Lawrence Stone, 1975). Hajnal subsequently modified his opinion and the whole question is reviewed, with the conclusion that regional rather than temporal variation is at issue, by R.M. Smith (1981); and more recently by Smith in his contribution to his own book *Land, Kinship and the Life-Cycle* (1984).

10. There are also leading questions as to the extent to which change is cyclical or linear between types of social entity or activity, or the extent to which types of change entrain each other. Further issues concern the differences in rate of change at different times, and the possibility that our own day change of all kinds has been quickened, particularly change in the family. The position as a whole will be set out in a contribution to a collective volume to be edited by Michael Young and Tom Schuller, on the sociology of time.

11. Such notational demarcation was decidedly not intended to imply the existence of impassable barriers between individuals located in different domestic groups, or between those domestic groups themselves. See *Appendix* of *Household and Family In Past Time*.

12. This is not the context to discuss historical

sociology as such, which will be reserved to a future occasion. Some desultory remarks will be found in the introduction, sub-titled 'The necessity of a historical sociology,' to Laslett (1977).

13. This decision had been taken before the *Introduction* was written and simulation exercises were already in progress: see note 85 on page 67 of HFPT. These exercises gave rise to the volume *Statistical Studies of Historical Social Structure*, by K.W. Wachter, E.A. Hammel and Peter Laslett (1978), though largely ignored by those who have insisted that HFPT and subsequent work by the Cambridge Group were essentially static. The book succeeded in simulating families over time and so in relating cross-sectional with cohort analysis, though its major outcome in this direction was to show that demographic restraints cannot have been the reason for the absence of the stem family form from the English records. The really important conclusion, however, was a sobering one: to demonstrate that literal imitation of such social process as the developmental cycle of the family was a chimaera (see the chapter by Wachter and Hammel in Bonfield, Smith, and Wrightson, 1986). There is in fact no straightforward way to compare families as dynamic entities between cultures and over time.

14. In France and Italy especially, studies analyzing family groups have tended to consist in a rote recital of the alleged defects of HFPT followed by the use of its household composition table and often not much more. This is the more understandable in these countries, since only a few passages of the *Introduction* have been translated into French (*Annales ESC*, 1972:847-872) and from the French into Italian (Barbagli, 1977). Recently there has been a marked change in Italy (Viazzo, 1984; Barbagli, 1984) but attempts to put more of HFPT into French, or further methodological and household analysis, have miscarried.

15. Appearing in French in 1976, and in English in 1979, and widely used as if applicable to all pre-industrial family structures. Simple or nuclear families seem to have little interest for French researchers, though it must be said that Dupâquier's study of the Paris basin (1973) does ample justice to them, and that Mitterauer and Sieder (1982) is quite clear about their predominance in the West.

16. Hanley and Wolf (1985: Introduction). An attempt to estimate the frequency of the stem family form, not in the Western and Northwestern area of Europe where it is a negligible presence, but in what is called the West/Central or Middle region of Europe is made in Laslett (1983). Even the most enthusiastic defender of the privileged position of the stem family in all discussions of this tangled subject would find it difficult to demonstrate that stem

families were experienced in this region by anything like a majority of all the people.

17. Among the more senior scholars, Pierre Goubert was the most formidable (see Goubert 1977). Although HFPT was reprinted in paperback shortly after publication, there has been no opportunity as yet to revise the text and correct the numerical errors, pointed out by John Hajnal and several others.

18. If a full account is wanted, the best known is in Siegel (1956).

19. Mendels (1986) reviewing Wall, Robin and Laslett (1983), the successor volume to HFPT. In this otherwise interesting and appreciative piece Mendels seems to suppose that it was Berkner himself who introduced the family cycle to historians, which cannot be true. But Mendels is quite right to appreciate Berkner's work very highly and to deplore his departure from historical scholarship. In raising some questions about Berkner's work in Wachter, Hammel, and Laslett (1978), there was no intention of trying to limit the damage it did to the null hypothesis (how could that have made sense?) but to raise some queries about his use of evidence in his discussion of the stem family, and to show that it can have been operative in only a very weak form indeed in the area where Berkner claimed that impartible inheritance brought about its presence. It is very unfortunate that Berkner had left academic life before he had time to respond.

20. Households are occasionally found in the data which cannot be classified in the Hammel/ Laslett table and which therefore have to be placed after all in an indeterminate category, thus reducing the usefulness of the system. We have had to reconcile ourselves to this, and to the circumstance that no classification could cover all possible occurrences, quite apart from indeterminacies due to defects in the data. In a recent article in the new journal *Continuity and Change*, Lee and Gjerde, (1986) have now modified the Hammell/Laslett system to provide a reconstruction of the stem family and simple family household cycles.

21. See Laslett (1983) where work characteristics are brought alongside kin relations, in a rather clumsy and unsatisfactory fashion.

REFERENCES

Abrams, Philip. 1982. *Historical Sociology*. Shepton Mallet: Open Books.

Anderson, Michael. 1980. *Approaches to the History of the Western Family 1500-1914*. London: Macmillan.

Barbagli, Marzio. 1977. *Famigliae mutamenti sociale*. Bologna: Il Mulino.

————. 1984. *Sotto lo stesso tetto; mutamenti della famiglia in Italia dal XV al XX secolo.* Bologna: Il Mulino.

Berkner, Lutz. 1975. "The Use and Misuse of Census Data for the Historical Analysis of Family Structure." *Journal of Interdisciplinary History* 5:721–738.

Binstock, Robert A., and Ethel Shanas, eds. 1985. *Handbook of Aging and the Social Sciences.* 2nd ed. New York: Van Nostrand Reinhold.

Bonfield, Lloyd, Richard Smith, and Keith Wrightson, eds. 1986. *The World We Have Gained.* New York: Basil Blackwell.

Brewster, Sir David. 1860. *Memoirs of the Life, Writings, and Discoveries of Sir Isaac Newton.* 2nd edition. London.

Burgière, André. 1972. "De Malthus à Weber: le mariage tardif et l'esprit de l'entreprise." *Annales E.S.C.* 27:1128–1138.

Butterfield, Herbert. 1963. *The Whig Interpretation of History.* London: G. Bell and Sons.

Cowgill, Donald D., and Lowell D. Holmes, eds. 1972. *Aging and Modernization.* New York: Appleton-Century-Crofts.

Dupaquier, Jacques. 1973. "Croissance démographique régionale dans le Bassin parisien au XVIIIᵉ siècle." Pp. 231-250 in *Sur le population française au XVIIIᵉ et au XIXᵉ siècles: hommage à Marcel Reinhard.* Paris.

Goody, Jack, ed. 1958. *The Developmental Cycle in Domestic Groups.* Cambridge: Cambridge University Press.

Goubert, Pierre. 1977. "Family and Province: A Contribution to the Knowledge of Family Structures in Early Modern France." *Journal of Family History* 2:179–197.

Hajnal, John. 1965. "European Marriage Patterns in Perspective." Pp. 101–143 in *Population in History,* edited by D.V. Glass and D.E.C. Eversley. Chicago: Aldine.

————. 1983. "Two Kinds of Pre-Industrial Household Formation System." Pp. 65–104 in *Family Forms in Historic Europe,* edited by Richard Wall, Jean Robin, and Peter Laslett. Cambridge: Cambridge University Press.

Hammel, Eugene, and Peter Laslett. 1974. "Comparing Household Structure Over Time and Between Cultures." *Comparative Studies in Society and History* 16:73–109.

Hanley, Susan, and A. Wolf, eds. 1985. *Family and Population in East Asian History.* Stanford: Stanford University Press.

Henry, Louis. 1967. *Manuel de dé²mographie historique.* Paris. Oroz.

Laslett, Peter. 1972. "Introduction: The History of the Family." Pp. 159–204 in *Household and Family in Past Time,* edited by Peter Laslett and Richard Wall. Cambridge: Cambridge University Press.

————. 1976. "The Wrong Way Through the Telescope: A Note on Literary Evidence in Sociology and Historical Sociology." *British Journal of Sociology* 26:319–342.

————. 1977. *Family Life and Illicit Love in Earlier Generations.* Cambridge: Cambridge University Press.

————. 1983. "Family and Household as Work Group and King Group." Pp. 513–563 in *Family Forms in Historic Europe,* edited by Richard Wall, Jean Robin, and Peter Laslett. Cambridge: Cambridge University Press.

————. 1985. "Gregory King, T.R. Malthus and the Origins of English Social Realism." *Population Studies* 39:351–362.

————. 1987. "The Emergence of the Third Age: An Essay in the History of Population and Social Structure in the 20th Century." *Aging and Society.*

Lee, James, and John Gjerde. 1986. "Comparative Household Morphology of Stem, Joint, and Nuclear Household Systems: Norway, China, and the United States." *Continuity and Change* 1:89–111.

Mendels, Franklin. 1986. "Family Forms in Historic Europe." *Social History* 11:81–87.

Mitterauer, Michael, and Reinhard Sieder. 1982. *The European Family.* Chicago: The University of Chicago Press.

Quadagno, Jill. 1982. *Aging in Early Industrial Society: Work, Family, and Social Policy in Nineteenth-Century England.* New York: Academic Press.

Rowntree, Seebohm. 1901. *Poverty: A Study of Town Life.* London.

Siegel, Sidney. 1956. *Non-Parametric Statistics for the Behavioral Sciences.* New York: McGraw-Hill.

Shorter, Edward. 1976. *The Making of the Modern Family.* New York: Basic Books.

Smith, Daniel Scott. 1983. "Modernization and the Family Structure of the Elderly in the United States." *Zeitschrift für Gerontologie* 17:251–269.

Smith, Richard M. 1981. "The People of Tuscany and their Families in the Fifteenth Century." *Journal of Family History* 6:107–128.

Smith, Richard M. (ed.). 1984. *Land, Kinship and the Life Cycle.* Cambridge: Cambridge University Press.

Stone, Lawrence. 1975. "The Rise of the Nuclear Family in Early Modern England." Pp. 13–57 in

The Family in History, edited by Charles E. Rosenberg. Philadelphia: University of Pennsylvania Press.

————. 1977. *The Family, Sex and Marriage in England, 1500-1800*. London: Harper and Row.

Trevelyan, G.M. 1942. *English Social History*. London: Longmans, Green, and Co.

Viazzo, Per Paolo. 1984. *Forme di famiglia nella storia Europea*. Bologna: Il Mulino.

Wachter, Kenneth, Eugene Hammel, and Peter Laslett. 1978. *Statistical Studies in Historical Social Structure*. New York: Academic Press.

Wall, R.W., Jean Robin, and Peter Laslett, eds. 1983. *Family Forms in Historic Europe*. Cambridge: Cambridge University Press.

Wrigley, E.A. 1972. "The Process of modernization and the Industrial Revolution in England." *Journal of Interdisciplinary History* 3:225–260.

OBSERVATIONS ON THE DEVELOPMENT OF KINSHIP HISTORY, 1942–1985

Robert Wheaton

ABSTRACT: *The post-World War II development of kinship history was initiated by the emergence of methods for the analysis of quantitative historical-demographic sources: in France by means of the Family Reconstitution Method based on genealogical records and parish registers; in England by the analysis of nominative household censuses. The essay discusses five areas of subsequent development in the field: (1) the search for an investigation of large-scale kinship structures, and their influence on society as a whole; (2) life-course analysis, which integrates both events in individual life histories and larger historical events with the household developmental cycle; (3) interactions between kinship and economic relations, and particularly the roles played by women in the economic life of the family; (4) the effects of kinship on social relations at the community level; and (5) the relationships between kinship and social structures more generally. In this last respect, the essay emphasizes the influence of the particularly French intellectual institutions and traditions, and of the alliance theory of marriage on the distinctive direction taken by French social historians. Finally, the essay considers the study of mentalités, as it has influenced kinship history.*

HISTORICAL KINSHIP STUDIES BEFORE THE 1970s

The revival of historical interest in kinship, starting in the 1940s and 1950s, is, in a sense, only one aspect of the general revival of social history following the Second World War. The sub-field is now sufficiently distinct however, and its success, measured by any standard of intellectual achievement, is sufficiently marked to justify separate attention.

The history of kinship[1] did not, of course, originate in the 1940s and 50s. We

Robert Wheaton, Concord, Massachusetts, is sometime Associate Editor of the Journal of Family History *and a student of the social history of France in the seventeenth century.*

should acknowledge our debt to the generally maligned nineteenth-century pioneers of family history: Morgan, Tyler, Engels, Maine, and Le Play, to mention several of the principal figures. Because they forced their insufficient empirical information into a variety of evolutionary schemes, and because they largely subscribed to the theories of racial hierarchy then current, we judge their conclusions to be incorrect and morally unacceptable. This should not blind us to the fact that they formulated a way of thinking about kinship as an object of scholarly research, seeing it as one component of the system of social relations, changing over time and differing across space. These are the terms in which we still approach the subject. These writers were the first to describe and analyze kinship terminologies and systems, household structures, familial economic functions, sex roles, and legal and religious norms as parts of the total social fabric of any society, tasks not so different from those we are still grappling with (Harris, 1968; on Morgan, see Fortes, 1969:3–18).

These early works of family history appeared and remained largely outside the confines of academic family history. Consequently, when anthropology and sociology turned away from grand evolutionary schemes around 1900, the systematic study of family history ceased until after the Second World War. The kin group as a form of social organization subject to change over time was generally not studied by historians because it was not recognized as relevant to the questions that occupied them. Genealogical study concerned only particular kin groups and the descent of power and property within them. Legal historians wrote extensively on family law but studied norms with scant regard for practice. Had the European family been characterized by large-scale kin groups with political and eco-

nomic power or with evident social presence—comparable, say, to the Chinese clans—presumably kinship would have been studied along with other social and political institutions. The notable exceptions to this neglect of kinship were in writings about the medieval period, when large kin groups did occasionally figure in the historical records. Phillpotts devoted a book to *Kindred and Clan in the Middle Ages and After: A Study in the Sociology of the Teutonic Races* (1913). Bloch's chapters on kinship in *Feudal Society* (1961:123–142; originally published just before the Second World War) approached the contemporary conception of kinship history. Homans' *English Villagers of the Thirteenth Century* (1960; originally published in 1941) grew out of the rare combinations of talents of a scholar who was a professional sociologist with historical skills, training, and imagination. Duby's *Société aux XIe et XIIe siècles dans la région mâconnaise* (1953) represents the high point of this prequantitative development of kinship history.

In the 1940s and 1950s professional historians, increasingly influenced by the work of sociologists, anthropologists, and demographers, began to regard kinship as an institution which was significant to the investigation of historical questions in all times and places, and new methods were developed to deal with it. The roots of recent kinship history are to be found in demography, and specifically in historical demography. Perhaps because of the dislocation of populations and the establishment of new states at the close of World War II, as well as concerns over rapid population growth in the Third World, there was intense activity in demography, much of it sponsored by the United Nations. In France the Institut National des Études Démographiques (INED) was established in 1945. By the early 1950s a demographer, Louis Henry, and a historian, Pierre Goubert, apparently working independently, developed the family reconstitution method (FRM) for analyzing historical records of vital events.[2] The FRM, first using genealogical records (Henrepin, 1954; Henry, 1956) and soon thereafter parish registers (Gautier and Henry, 1958), enabled researchers to establish the vital statistics for historical populations. In 1956 Fleury and Henry published *Des Registres paroissiaux à l'histoire de la population. Manuel de dépoillement et d'exploitation de l'état civil ancien* (Fleury and Henry, 1956). Has any other book so small in size (12 x 19 cm, 84 pages) guided so much subsequent historical research?[3]

The FRM produced aggregate statistics bearing on age at marriage, duration of marriages, the number of children born to a "completed" marriage, socially differentiated mortality rates, the seasonality of vital events, and the net reproduction rate, all of which raised questions about life within the conjugal family unit and the relationships among its members. Henry discovered the altogether unanticipated fact that some couples among the bourgeoisie of Geneva had exercised some measure of control over the number and spacing of children born during a completed marriage by the beginning of the eighteenth century (Henry, 1956:180).

The immediate goal of the FRM had been aggregate statistics pertaining to population size and the factors bearing on its fluctuations. From the very beginning, however, the founders of historical demography realized that the type of information just referred to threw new and unexpected light on kinship and in particular on the conjugal family unit. In the preface to the very first monograph to appear, Henrepin's *La Population canadienne au début du XVIIe siècle*, Gemaehling had written: "Instead of limiting himself to describing from without an en-

semble of demographic phenomena, as one ordinarily does, [Henrepin] has been able, thanks to the facts at his disposition, to penetrate into the intimate life of the families studied . . . " (Henrepin, 1954, xvi). The first systematic presentation of such data appeared in Goubert's *Beauvais and the Beauvasis* (Goubert, 1960: text, 25–84, and graphs, 40–67).[4]

The development of the FRM became known to a group of English scholars who undertook to apply it to English parish registers. At the same time Peter Laslett recognized the demographic potential of a seventeenth-century nominative household census book compiled by the rector of Clayworth. All this work eventuated in an article published jointly by Laslett and Harrison (Laslett and Harrison, 1964, reprinted in Laslett, 1977) and in essays by Wrigley on the Colyton registers (Wrigley, 1966, 1968). Laslett had drawn on the Clayworth, Cogenhoe, and Colyton material in *The World We Have Lost* (Laslett, 1965a). The Cambridge Group for the History of Population and Social Structure was established in 1964 and its first publication was *An Introduction to English Historical Demography from the Sixteenth to the Nineteenth Century* (Eversley, Laslett, and Wrigley, eds., 1966).[5]

Analysis of nominative household censuses posed problems and raised questions which were different from those resulting from the FRM, and to a certain extent suggested a different approach toward kinship. These were explored in *Household and Family in Past Time* (Laslett and Wall, 1972), which developed out of a conference sponsored by the Cambridge Group in 1969. In the "Introduction" Laslett proposed a scheme, worked out in collaboration with Eugene Hammel, for the definition of household types, the classification of households by structural characteristics, and an ideographic system for representing households (Laslett, 1972). This "Introduction" drew sharp criticism from, among others, Berkner in an essay review, "The Use and Misuse of Census Data for the Historical Analysis of Family Structure" (Berkner, 1975). Berkner pointed out that a single census represents cross-sectional data collected during a single time period; and that, since any given household is likely to change its structure over time, no conclusions about the relative incidence of the different household structural types could be validly inferred. Laslett had concluded from the various analyses in *Household and Family in Past Time* that the incidence of stem family households was in all likelihood a very uncommon cultural feature. Berkner's analysis of household structure of a 1763 census in the northern Austrian village of Heidenreichstein (Berkner, 1972) demonstrated that the stem household structure occurred there frequently. Berkner's census had included information on the age and status of household residents, and by applying the concept of the developmental cycle, Berkner showed that many households would at one time or another pass through a stem stage. Berkner's criticism was pertinent, for in the "Introduction" Laslett had overstated his case—in spite of the fact that the volume, which he himself had edited, included an essay describing the developmental cycle of domestic groups among the LoWiili and LoDagaba of Ghana (Goody, 1972) using the concept by then well established in English anthropology by Fortes. Fortes had described the developmental cycle of the joint family in *The Web of Kinship among the Tallensi* (Fortes, 1949a:63–77), and had written in the same year that "... ties of kinship, marriage and affinity regulate the structure of domestic and family groups, which have no permanent existence in time. Each domestic group comes into being, grows and expands,

and finally dissolves" (Fortes, 1949b:60). *Household and Family in Past Time* also included an essay by Hammel with its powerful argument for regarding "the zadruga as process" (Hammel, 1972). The use of the nominative household census, informed and modified by the concept of the household developmental cycle, has joined the Family Reconstitution Method as one of the twin foundation piers of kinship history.

Czap's discovery of "the perennial multiple family household" in Russia represents a significant alteration to the concept of the household developmental cycle (Czap, 1982). In many instances the Mishino serf households maintained their size and structure through complex organization, internal renewal, and recruitment from without. "Complex households structured in this way frequently survived for generations insulated from the effects of the developmental cycle of individual conjugal family units" (Czap, 1982:24).

RECENT INVESTIGATIONS: STRUCTURES

The product of the FRM is a record of the primary kin relations between husband and wife, parent and child, and siblings. The household described in nominative censuses is a unit limited (by definition) by coresidence. Yet the concept of kinship subsumes far more than primary relationships and coresidence, and in the last two decades the development of the field has been in the exploration of the wider dimensions of kinship. This expansion can here be discussed only superficially under a few rubrics, and I regret that references to historians and works of major consequence must often be entirely omitted. In particular, the present essay disproportionately reflects the author's own concerns with French and English social history. Each historian would, I am sure, come up with a different set of rubrics and a different bibliography.

Kinship Over Time:
Genealogical Studies and the
Existence of Larger Structures

The application of electronic data processing to the rare instances where long-term genealogical records have survived or can be reconstituted now permits the historian to reconstruct genealogical tables for large populations. Such reconstructions enable the researcher to determine whether there exist patterns of marital exchange between large-scale kin groups—lineages, for example—or between geographical regions, such as villages. One such effort traces kinship among fifteen generations of Bretons inhabiting the southern Pays Bigoudin (1720-1980) (Segalen, 1985). The author does indeed detect a pattern of marriage between persons affinally related, which permits the linking of lineages without violating ecclesiastical incest taboos (i.e., marriage within the degrees prohibited by the Roman Catholic Church). Plakans, in *Kinship in the Past* (1984), has proposed methods for establishing whether evidence for the existence of lineages modelled on those described by Fortes (1945) can be found to exist in a group of villages in the Schwalm region of West Germany, using the *Stammtafeln*. These are genealogical records assembled by German genealogists from parish registers. Will systematic analysis of them reveal any behavioral patterns, such as a pattern of marital exchange between certain descent groups?

The work of both Plakans and Segalen raises the interesting distinction between kinship relations of which, at least on the surface, only the researcher is aware, and those of which the actors can be shown to

be or to have been conscious; and the further question of whether, in fact, Lévi-Strauss' unconscious models can influence social behavior (Lévi-Strauss, 1963: 276; Charbonnier, 1961:43). Netting has observed the loosely structured functioning of patrilines over several centuries in the Swiss village of Törbel (Netting, 1984: cited in Plakans, 1984:202-204). The Chicoutimi project described by Bouchard in the present collection utilizes a very large genealogical data base to trace the descent of genetic characteristics through a historical human population. In this case, of course, the question of consciousness is irrelevant (Bouchard and de Pourbaix, 1987).

Kinship History:
Life-Course Analysis

Demographers from the beginning have recognized the impact of historical events on populations, since these events are reflected by changes in long-term curves. This is more difficult for the historian of kinship to do, since the historian is rarely able to follow a large number of households in sufficient detail over a long period of time to observe their reactions to historical events. By refining and expanding the concepts of the family developmental cycle and the individual life course, a group of American historians and sociologists have elaborated the necessary techniques. Elder's classic monograph, *Children of the Great Depression* (1974) follows the impact of the 1930s on successive age cohorts of persons growing up in those years. Hareven in *Family Time and Industrial Time: The Relationships between the Family and Work in an Industrial New England Community* (1982) follows mill workers in the Amoskeag Mills of Manchester, New Hampshire, through the period 1900 to 1936 both in terms of their lives as individuals and as family members. Life-course analysis goes beyond the question of household structure to examine the timing of crucial events in the life course of the individual, establishing distinctive "cohort life patterns."

> ... Three general modes of temporal interdependence are important aspects of life course analysis: the intersection between life or family history and social history, between the life course of the family unit and that of individual members, and between the events in the family and other institutional sectors—the the economy, polity (Elder, 1978:55).

We have also come to better appreciate the flexibility of household forms in preserving a cultural preference for certain "kinship ideologies" over time. Halpern and Wagner have studied the tendency of the South Slavs of Orašac to emphasize the father-son tie under rapidly changing demographic and economic circumstances (Halpern and Wagner, 1984). The most comprehensive survey of recent developments in household studies is Netting, Wilk, and Arnould (1984).

Kinship and the Economy

Berkner, in his 1975 critique of Laslett referred to above, criticized the focus on household composition for ignoring or at least distorting the relationship of the household to the economy. Laslett had argued in *The World We Have Lost* that for most people in the seventeenth century the household was both a unit of consumption and production, and that production moved into the factory only at the time of the industrial revolution (Laslett, 1965a:1–21). Subsequently, however, analysis of agricultural economies has indicated that recruitment of a workforce composed of members of the same kin group might draw on several different households (Goode, 1970:241–242), and in the seventeenth-century Bordelais of

southwestern France parcels of inherited land held undivided were sometimes farmed by the heirs, although they lived under separate roofs (Archives Départementale de la Gironde, Series 3E). Conversely, a labor force might be recruited in part from non-resident paid laborers (Smith, 1984:36–37). We know of one extraordinary instance where "marriage without co-residence" was common: in some parts of eighteenth-century Austria, female servants and male farm laborers formed valid marriages while still residing in the households of their respective employers (Mitterauer, 1981:177–181).

The relationships between systems of inheritance and household structure, and kinship relations has been explored in considerable detail (Goody, Thirsk, and Thompson, 1976; Greven, 1970; Wheaton, 1980; Yver, 1966; Goody, 1983, and Smith, 1984). The study of the impact of industrialization on kin relationships in Lancashire by Anderson (1971) indicated that the immigration of laborers from the countryside to industrial towns resulted in urban households which were larger and more complex than their rural counterparts.

The rapid growth of women's studies has acted as a marked stimulus to the study of kinship. In particular, the previously neglected contributions of women to the household economy has been given close attention (Tilly and Scott, 1978; Tilly, 1979; Segalen, 1980, *inter alii*).

Kinship and the Local Community

Laslett's early essay on "The Gentry of Kent in 1640" (Laslett, 1948) stressed the importance of kinship ties between county families in unifying the governing class of the county, in creating links with the urban wealth of London, and in fostering immigration to Virginia, where, according to Laslett, the kin networks tended to reproduce themselves. The role played by kinship in migration has subsequently been studied extensively (Hareven, 1982; Yans-McLaughlin, 1982, *et alios*). The political role of the ruling social strata has been examined in *Family, Lineage and Civil Society. A Study of Society, Politics and Mentality in the Durham Region 1500-1640* (James, 1974). Of great methodological interest is Smith's application of network theory in evaluating the relative importance of relationships between an individual and his kin as opposed to persons not-kin in a thirteenth-century Suffolk community (Smith, 1979). His conclusion is that in those respects reflected by the documentation (the manorial court records) links of kinship played a relatively restricted role. The particular importance of Smith's essay lies in the fact that it demonstrates one method for untangling the complex web of kin and non-kin social relationships which surround an individual member of a community.

Kinship and Social Structure

Anthropologists often assume that the component elements of social structure are kin-based groups. Murdock's *Social Structure* (1949) is in fact a study of kin groups; and this is the unstated assumption in Fortes' "Time and Social Structure: An Ashanti Case Study" (Fortes, 1949:54–84). The historian is likely to find that the populations of more complex societies are divided into non-kin based groups—groups such as the Orders in pre-revolutionary Western Europe, into which the society divides itself, or groups such as Weber's status groups created by the historian for analytical purposes. The relations between these elements of the social structure compose the system of social relations at the highest level of historical-sociological analysis. One of the principal challenges to historical kinship

studies has been to examine how the institutions of kinship relate to these high-level aggregations.

The greatest progress, both theoretical and empirical, in studying this question has been made in France, where a series of monographic studies of regions or of individual cities in the early modern period have appeared in the wake, as it were, of Goubert's *Beauvais et les Beauvaisis* (1960): Deyon's *Amiens, capitale provinciale. Étude sur la société urbaine au 17e siècle* (1968), Couturier's *Recherches sur les structures sociales de Châteaudun* (1969), Robin's *La Société française en 1789: Semur-en-Auxois* (1970), Fréche's *Toulouse et la région Midi-Pyrénées au Siècle des lumières vers 1670-1789*, Mousnier's *La Stratification sociale à Paris aux XVIIe et XVIIIe siècles* (1976), and Bardet's *Rouen au XVIIe et XVIIIe siècles: Les mutations d'un espace social* (1983), to mention the most notable works only.

This astonishing list of works is the result not only of the industry of their authors, but of the peculiar French intellectual and institutional traditions in which they developed and of the political issues being debated in French academic circles after the Second World War. In an effort to improve the French system of higher education, the École Pratique des Hautes Études (EPHE) had been established in 1868 by the then Minister of Education, Victor Dury. In the last decades of the nineteenth century, Durkheimian sociology became a strong influence in French university life (Clark, 1973:162–195), and, in 1901 Durkheim's nephew, Marcel Mauss, became a *maître de conférences* in the Fifth Section, devoted to "religious sciences." Mauss became co-director until 1941, and that position was taken over by Lévi-Strauss in 1951. The celebrated Sixth Section, specializing in the study of economic and social science, was established under the direction of Febvre in 1947 (Clark, 1973:42–51). Both the line of descent and the institutional connections are relevant here, for Mauss, working within the framework of Durkheim's theories of social solidarity, published in 1925 *Essai sur le don, forme archaique de l'échange* (Mauss, 1967) which emphasized the importance of exchanges in creating cohesion. This theory Lévi-Strauss was to generalize further in his conception of communication within a social structure.

> In any society, communication operates on three different levels: communication of women, communication of goods and services, communication of messages. Therefore kinship studies, economics, and linguistics approach the same kinds of problems on different strategic levels and really pertain to the same field (Lévi-Strauss, 1963:289).

Elsewhere, Lévi-Strauss writes:

> Kinship systems and marriage rules embody the rule of that very special kind of game which consists, for consanguineous groups of men, in exchanging women among themselves, that is, building up new families with the pieces of earlier ones, which should be shattered for that purpose (Lévi-Strauss, 1960:283).

In this manner the conception of marriage as a system of exchange within society established itself among French sociologists and anthropologists. The disciplines of sociology and anthropology were not isolated from French historical thought. In this connection, another pedigree obtains: Berr, like Durkheim a disciple of the philosopher Boutroux, had devoted his life to synthesis in the social sciences, founding, with others, the International Center for Synthesis and the *Revue de Synthèse historique* in 1900 (Keylor, 1975:128). Burguière has described the direct but subtle influence

which Berr had on Febvre and Bloch in the founding of the *Annales*, which was intended from the beginning to encourage interdisciplinary history (Burguière, 1979: 1347–1359). This interdisciplinary ideal was further embodied in the celebrated Sixth Section of the EPHS, established through Febvre's influence and under his direction in 1947, and closely linked to the *Annales* (Coutau-Bégarie, 1983:260).

Following the publication of *Les Structures élémentaires de la parenté* (Lévi-Strauss, 1949), which was built upon the exchange concept of marriage, and the publication of *Anthropologie structurale* in 1958 (Engl. trans. Lévi-Strauss, 1963), Lévi-Strauss' structuralism became a powerful force in French intellectual life. His conception of social structure, outlined in the latter volume, is both rigorously formal and dynamic: social *structures* are *models* either entertained by the actors in the society or constructed by observers of it—models of social *relations* between groups in the society. The definition of the individual elements of the social structure is at least in part dependent on their relations with the other elements (Lévi-Strauss, 1963:269–319). Regarding the place of kin groups within this structure, Lévi-Strauss writes:

> ...The relation between the social group as a whole and the restricted families which seem to constitute it is not a static one, like that of a wall to the bricks it is built with. It is rather a dynamic process of tension and opposition with an equilibrium point extremely difficult to find, its exact position being submitted to endless variations from time to time and from society to society (Lévi-Strauss, 1960:284).[6]

For the historian to apply these theories, there are two prerequisites: he or she must identify the analytical elements of the social structure and must have documentary sources of marital exchanges within them. We shall return to the first point shortly. The documentary sources in France were available in the form of marriage contracts, which had been widely used there from the re-introduction of Roman law in the Middle Ages and early modern period; these contracts had survived, moreover, in vast numbers in the notarial archives. They had been used for some time by both legal and social historians to describe familial arrangements (e.g., Boutrouche, 1947; Hillaire, 1957). In 1955 Labrousse proposed the systematic (i.e., quantified) analysis of notarial documents as a source for social history (Labrousse, 1955). At the Sixth Section of the EPHE Daumard and Furet, using electronic data processing, undertook an analysis of all the 2,597 surviving marriage contracts for Paris for the year 1749 in the Minutier centrale, the notarial archives of Paris at the Archives nationales (Daumard and Furet, 1959, 1961). They produced a cross tabulation linking groom's and bride's fathers, classified according to seventeen socio-professional categories, which were described in terms of the settlements brought to the marriages. Such cross-tabulations were to become the basic tool for subsequent social-structural research.[7]

We can now turn to the question of the unit of analysis in social structure. In 1948 a Russian historian published a Marxian analysis of popular revolts in France between 1623 and 1648, based on a cache of documents from the archives of Chancellor Sèguier which had fetched up in the Saltykov Shchedrin Library in Leningrad. The book was translated into German in 1954, and appeared in French in 1963 (Porschnev, 1963). Mousnier responded to both Daumard and Furet and to Porschnev by re-examining French social structure of the early modern period. Rejecting Marxian class analysis, Mousnier argued that all developed societies are divided according to one of three principles: caste, order, or class. This typology

Mousnier appears to have taken from Weber (who had been made accessible to the French by Aron), although Mousnier may have become acquainted with his work through the English translation in Gerth and Mills (1958; see also Mousnier, Labatut, and Durand, 1965; Mousnier, ed., 1968; Mousnier, 1969; on Aron, see Clark, 1973:230). According to Mousnier, French historians had erred by misapplying the concept of class (a social division based on the relation of individuals to the means of production) to prerevolutionary society, which was in fact a society of orders, as was clearly set forth by seventeenth-century contemporaries, most coherently by Loyseau (Mousnier, Labatut, and Durand, 1965; now further developed in Mousnier, 1974:1–23). In criticizing Daumard's and Furet's analysis of Paris marriage contracts, Mousnier took a similar tack, arguing that they had failed to classify their subjects according to status, i.e., "the esteem, honor, or dignity attached by the society to social function which may have had no connection at all with the production of material goods" (Mousnier, Labatut, and Druand, 1965: 15; and Mousnier, ed., 1968). The application of Mousnier's conceptions of seventeenth-century social structure resulted in an extremely elaborate stratification system producing large numbers of small groups of people constituting hierarchies within hierarchies (for an example, see Mousnier, 1976). In terms of studies of kin relations, Mousnier insisted that social position could be determined only by examining both an individual's ancestry and his contemporary relationships resulting from both consanguinity and affinity. This was illustrated in his study of Sèguier's own kin group and of representative officials with whom he corresponded (Mousnier, ed., 1964:t. I, 26–38, and 48–184). The combination of the two principles, i.e., stratification by status group and genealogical history, is best illustrated in Couturier's analysis of Châteaudun, which reconstituted genealogies by computer program (Couturier, 1969). Mousnier and the Centre de recherches sur la Civilisation de l'Europe moderne, which he directs at the Sorbonne, lie outside the charmed circle of the "Nouvelle Histoire," or "*Annales* School," but nevertheless the influence of the theories just outlined can be perceived in the work of its members (Couteau-Bégarie, 1983:302–308), even those of a neo-Marxist persuasion (e.g., Robin, 1970). As an alternative to genealogical reconstruction, Wheaton has applied network theory to re-create the bilateral kindreds brought into existence by marriage alliances; the relative frequency of links between occupational categories within kindreds can then be used to construct the analytical elements and the relationships between them which represent a model of the social structure (Wheaton, 1985).

Recently McCaa, also using network theory, has described the patterns of marital alliance between the extremely complex social groups of Parral, Mexico, in 1788–1790, groups which are constituted on the basis of both economic and racial criteria (McCaa and Swann, 1982; McCaa, 1984). The reoccurrence of references to network theory in the present essay indicates that a growing number of kinship historians—and of social historians in general—have found it a useful methodology for analyzing complex relationships between both individuals and groups of individuals (see Plakans, 1984: 217–240; Foster, 1984; and Rutman and Rutman, 1984).

A comparison of the various cross-tabulations which appear in the monographs cited above lead to several conclusions. First, the division of society by reference to the three orders is not heuristically particularly useful. The boundaries

between the three orders are indistinct. An analytical division of these societies into (1) the propertied classes, (2) those of marginal economic resources, and (3) the propertyless creates far more distinct classifications. Second, the classic Marxian classes do not appear; in particular no cluster corresponding to the "bourgeoisie" can be elicited from the data. Third, while a larger number of analytical sub-groups based on clusters of similar occupations and status within occupations emerges clearly from these analyses, the boundaries between clusters are in all classes permeable. While the number and constitution of clusters are generally similar in all the monographs, the distinctive character of each region, town, or city is reflected in its social structure. Particularism prevails.

Like Mousnier, Laslett in *The World We Have Lost* argued that Weberian distinctions between status groups were applicable to seventeenth-century English society, whereas Marxian class analysis was not; but this did not lead him, as it did Mousnier, to an integrated conception of the place of kinship in social structure. Peter Laslett had begun his academic career as a political scientist with an interest in seventeenth-century English political theory and its relationship to the Civil War, in particular Filmer's *Patriarcha* (Filmer, 1949) and John Locke's *Two Treatises on Government* (Locke, 1960), the latter written in part as a refutation of Filmer's Royalist defense. Filmer had based his defense of royal absolutism on its purported derivation from Adam as patriarch of the first family. Filmer argued that this authority had been inherited not only by every male head of household but preeminently by the king as the patriarch of all patriarchs, so to speak. Laslett was fascinated by the fact that a theory which is to the twentieth-century reader so much balderdash could have called forth refutations from numerous contemporary theorists, including the formidable John Locke. Laslett concluded that Filmer's argument found a receptive audience in an England which in the seventeenth century was steeped in the everyday experiences of familial patriarchal authoritarianism.

Laslett also became taken up by the debate over the nature of the English Civil War, a controversy which, in the 1950s, had ideological overtones. Christopher Hill and other leading historians followed Marx and Engels in interpreting the Civil War as a class struggle between the remnants of the medieval feudal class and a bourgeoisie enriched by its mercantile and nascent industrial prosperity. Laslett adapted Weber's theoretical distinction between class, status, and power [as interpreted by W.R. Runciman, Laslett's colleague at Trinity College (Runciman, 1963)] to argue that England was "a one class society," by which he meant that the elite four percent of the population monopolized wealth, the highest status positions, and political power. The elite also was the only social group with a consciousness of itself as a nation-wide class. The remaining ninety-six percent of the population Laslett divided into status groups described by occupation. The Civil War, he argued, was a struggle for political power between factions of the elite; it could not have been based on class struggle reflecting conflicting economic interests because no opposing *class* existed.[8]

For descriptions of early modern English social structure Laslett turned to Sir Thomas Smith's *The Commonwealth of England*, written in the 1560s, and, in greater detail, Gregory King's "Scheme of the Income and Expense of the Several Families of England Calculated for the Year 1688," which distributes the total number of families (1,349,586) into twenty-six status groups (Laslett, 1965a:30–37). At the most general level, a parallel exists between the way Laslett views the structure of

the kinship system and that of the social system: both are additive, the sum, that is, of their individual clearly demarcated constituent units. The *relationships* between the elements do not, in the last analysis, contribute to the conception of the total structure. The most elaborate attempt to apply Weber's model to English social structure was that by Stone (1966), but, like Laslett, Stone in his subsequent massive study of *Family, Sex and Marriage in England 1500 to 1800* (1977) did not undertake systematically to link kinship and the larger social structure.

English scholars generally have not attempted to construct detailed analyses comparable to those of the French. The marriage contract seems to have been used much less widely, and English archives have no equivalent of the notarial resources that are available in France. The structure of English higher education does not encourage the production of the massive *these* required in France for the Doctorat d'État. There is in England no equivalent of the Sixth Section of the École Pratique des Hautes Études, since 1975 independently established as the École des Hautes Etudes en Sciences Sociales, with its auxiliary facilities of cartographers and computer programmers and access to subsidized publications (Coutau-Bègarie, 1983). Perhaps even more important, however, is the fact that English historians were far less influenced by alliance theory and Lévi-Strauss formulation of structuralism.[9] The desire to extend the study of kin group beyond the conjugal family unit has led social historians everywhere to draw on both the theory and practice of kinship in anthropology (see Farber, 1981; Kertzer, 1984).

RECENT INVESTIGATIONS: MENTALITIES

Thus far I have completely ignored what one might call the alternate tradition in kinship history present from the very beginning, namely, the study of *mentalités*. From 1944 on Philippe Ariès pursued the independent research which resulted in a remarkable book, *Histoire des populations françaises et de leurs attitudes devant la vie depuis le dix-huitième siècle* (1948). In retrospect, the importance of this book lies in the fact that it revealed the subjects, the theses, the sources, and the methods which Ariès developed during the next four decades. The book itself had little impact at the time on academic history; its successor, *L'Enfant et la vie familiale sous l'ancien régime*, which appeared in France in 1960 and in English translation two years later, has had immense influence.[10]

Ariès tells us in his autobiographical *Historien du dimanche* that his initial forays into historical demography were a response to his awareness of the divergence in France between the norms and the actualities of sexual comportment, and, in particular, by the widespread practice of fertility limitation and birth control. Ariès sensed that demographic statistics might reveal patterns in sexual behavior and provide explanations for them (Ariès, 1980:80–92). At the same time he characteristically made impressionistic use of literary sources to complement his demographic data and to support hypotheses about periods for which there were, then, no statistics. From our present vantage point Ariès' demographic and statistical methods seem grossly inadequate, but his themes emerge clearly. The ability to regulate to a large extent the biological facts of birth and death has altered our cultural attitudes towards the forces of nature and, more particularly, has changed the nature of the family, the relations among its members, and their relationships with the larger society. Ariès acknowledges the influence of Febvre and Bloch in arousing his interest in popular mental attitudes

(Ariès, 1980: 53), and he is in this respect the heir of one current in the *Annales* School, while the historical demography practiced by Henry and Goubert continued the quantitative current. As Febvre had concluded that there was no place for atheism in the modern sense of the term in Rabelais' intellectual *Gestalt* (Febvre, 1968), Ariès argued that the peasant of early modern France could not conceive manipulating natural forces in such a way as to limit conception (Ariès, 1949; 1953).

Unlike quantitative family history, the study of *mentalité* has never succeeded in finding a unified coherent empirical methodology. Two approaches have predominated. The first is the scrutiny of the language and the provisions of a single type of document, such as court interrogations (e.g., Castan, 1974:162–251). Macfarlane's *The Family Life of Ralph Josselin, A Seventeenth-Century Clergyman* brilliantly reconstructs Josselin's conceptions of kinship from the close analysis of his diary (Macfarlane, 1970). The second method has come to be called 'thick description' (after Geertz, 1973:3–30). 'Thick description' is an impressionist, almost *pointiliste* method in which a general statement or generalized description is supported by marshalling disparate kinds of evidence—see, for example, Davis' "Ghosts, Kin, and Progeny: Some Features of Family Life in Early Modern France" (1977). The main limitation of the first approach is that while it tells us how people thought, it leaves us ignorant of how they acted. The problem with 'thick description' is quite simply that there is no way of evaluating the extent to which contrary evidence has been filtered out either from the historical record or (consciously or unconsciously) by the historian's interpretation of the record.

The core of contemporary kinship history rests on quantitative structural analysis. Examination of the conceptions which people held, individually and collectively, about kinship, and the representations which they made of these conceptions[11] can immensely enrich this core and suggest new avenues of inquiry and analysis. But until it is linked to the quantitative core, it remains conjectural.

ACKNOWLEDGMENTS

I would like to thank my fellow participants in the 1985 Clark Conference for their comments and criticisms of an earlier and very different version of this paper. David Gaunt and Andre Burguirè in particular brought to my attention the fact that the original intentions of the early French historical demographers were oriented towards purely demographic questions. My thanks to Tamara K. Hareven for encouraging me to write this essay, and for her encouragement and collaboration in family history research over many years. Andrejs Plakans, my successor as Associate Editor of the *Journal of Family History*, has helped for many years to keep me in touch with developments in the field and has been a constant source of intellectual stimulation.

NOTES

1. The term 'kinship' is deliberately used in preference to 'family' in this context, although 'family history' is the more common expression. The meanings of 'family' in English are several and differ significantly; the meaning of 'kinship' is inclusive and relatively clear—except perhaps to those who use it most frequently, cultural anthropologists. In this essay the word is used here to refer to a social relationship arising from a tie based on either descent or alliance or both, and to the groups created by such ties. Unless otherwise specified, the term will be used to refer to ties and groups of which the actors in the society are themselves aware, although, as we shall discuss later, they may sometimes be recognized only by the researcher.

2. For an excellent recent précis see Dupâquier, 1984.

3. These works were all published by the INED.

Henry had first announced the development of his method in an article, "Une richesse demographique en friche: les registres paroissiaux" (Henry, 1953); in the following year Goubert described his own work already in progress in "Une richesse historique en cours d'exploitation: les registres paroissiaux" (Goubert, 1954). Subsequent research has shown that the method has already been independently developed in Germany in the 1930s by Deimleitner and Roth, and by the Swedish demographer, Hyrenius, who published his results in 1943. The work of these *devanciers* was not noticed by other historians at the time, nor was it known by Henry and Goubert when they developed the FRM (Dupâquier, 1984:27–28; Imhof, 1976).

4. With characteristic precocity Ariès had already raised the question of deliberate fertility control in his *Histoire des populations françaises et leurs attitudes devant la vie dupuis le XVIIIe siècle* (Ariès, 1948:471–487) and in an article the following year in *Population* (Ariès, 1949).

5. See Laslett 1965a, and 1965b for outlines of these events. An important collection of essays in European historical demography, *Population in History*, also appeared in 1965 (ed. Glass and Eversley, 1965). Hajnal's (1965) influential thesis concerning the "uniqueness of the European marriage pattern," and its possible economic consequences appeared in this collection. Hajnal has recently revised the theory in the light of subsequent findings (see Hajnal, 1983).

6. For a fuller discussion of the application of Lévi-Strauss' structuralism to historical analysis, see Wheaton, 1973:1, 13–28.

7. This is the earliest instance which I have located of such a cross-tabulation of marriage alliances. Tilly (1964:81–99) presented his material on the Vendée similarly. To the best of his recollection, Tilly worked out this format independently, on the analogy of the sociological research by contemporary scholars on similar social subjects (Personal communication, 28 Sept., 1986).

8. The concept of a non-egalitarian one-class society is, so far as I know, unique to Laslett, who arrived at it by adding to the Marxian criterion of economic situation and self-consciousness that of a sense of national identity. It has been argued that the concept of class, as used by the social historian, implies the coexistence of more than one class, since the definition of class depends as much on exclusion and contrast with other, comparable groups within the society. Laslett does, in fact, suggest that his one class implies the existence at least *in potentia* of a second class, "everyone else" (Laslett, 1965a : 23).

9. Charles Tilly has brought to my attention the use by Foster in *Class Struggle in the Industrial*

Revolution of the analysis of the marital alliance concept. Apparently this approach was widely criticized in England (Foster, 1974).

10. Ariès was regarded as an outsider by the French academic world, first, because of his extreme right-wing political and religious sentiments and openly avowed adherence to the Action française, and, second, because he was not *universitaire*. Initial recognition of the importance of *L'Enfant et la vie familiale* came in the United States when the English translation was published in 1962 (Coutau-Bégarie, 1983:312–315).

11. See the recent effort to interpret pictorial representation of the early modern Italian family by Hughes (1986).

REFERENCES

Anderson, Michael. 1971. *Family Structure in Nineteenth Century Lancashire.* Cambridge: Cambridge University Press.

Archives départementales de la Gironde, Serie 3E. Archives notariales.

Ariès, Philippe. 1948. *Histoire des populations françaises et leurs attitudes devant la vie dupuis le XVIIIe siècle.* Paris: Éditions Self.

———. 1949. "Attitudes devant la vie et devant la mort du XVIIe au XIXe siècles." *Population* 4:463–470.

———. 1953. "Sur les origines de la contraception en France." *Population* 8:465–472.

———. 1960. *L'enfant et la vie familiale sous l'ancien règime.* Paris: Plon.

———. 1980. *Un historien du dimanche.* Paris: Éditions du Seuil.

Bardet, Jean-Pierre. 1983. *Rouen aux XVIIe et XVIIIe siècles. Les mutations d'un espace social.* 2 vols. Paris: SEDES.

Berkner, Lutz K. 1972. "The Stem Family and the Developmental Cycle of the Peasant Household: An Eighteenth-Century Austrian Example." *American Historical Review* 77:398–418.

———. 1975. "The Use and Misuse of Census Data for the Historical Analysis of Family Structure." *Journal of Interdisciplinary History* 5:721–38.

Bloch, Marc. 1961. *Feudal Society.* Chicago: The University of Chicago Press.

Boutruche, Robert. 1947. *La Crise d'une société. Seigneurs et paysans du Bordelais pendant la Guerre de Cent Ans.* Paris: Les Belles Lettres.

Bouchard, Gerard, and Isabelle de Pourbaix. 1987. "Individual and Family Life Courses in the Saguenay Region, Quebec, 1842–1911." *Journal of Family History* 12:225–242.

Burguière, Andreπ. 1979. "Histoire d'une histoire: La naissance des *Annales.*" *Annales* 1979:1347–1359.

Castan, Yves. 1974. *Honnêteté et relations sociales en Languedoc 1715-1780.* Paris: Plon.

Charbonnier, G. 1961. "Entretiens avec Claude Lévi-Strauss." *Les Lettres Nouvelles* 10:43–56.

Clark, Terry Nichols. 1972. *Prophets and Patrons: The French University and the Emergence of the Social Sciences.* Cambridge: Harvard University Press.

Coutau-Bégarie, Herveπ. 1983. *Le Phénomène "Nouvelle Histoire." Strategie et idéologie des nouveaux historiens.* Paris: Economica.

Couturier, Marcel. 1969. *Recherches sur les structures sociales de Châteaudun 1525-1725.* Paris: S.E.V.P.E.N.

Czap, Peter, Jr. 1982. "The Perennial Multiple Family Household, Mishino Russia, 1782–1858," *Journal of Family History* 7:5–26.

Daumard, A., and F. Furet. 1959. "Méthodes de l'histoire sociale. Les archives notariales et la meπcanographie." *Annales* 1959:676–693.

———. 1961. *Structures et relations sociales à Paris au milieu du XVIIIe siècle.* Paris: Librairie Armand Colin.

Davis, Natalie Zemon. 1977. "Ghosts, Kin, and Progeny: Some Features of Family Life in Early Modern France." *Daedalus* 106:87–114.

Deyon, Pierre. 1967. *Amiens, capitale provinciale. Étude sur la société urbaine au 17e siècle.* Paris: Mouton.

Duby, Georges. 1953. *La Société au Xie et XIIe siècles dans la région mâconnaise.* Paris: Presses Universitaires de France.

Dupâquier, Jacques. 1984. *Pour la démographie historique.* Paris: Presses Universitaires de France.

Elder, Glen H., Jr. 1974. *Children of the Great Depression.* Chicago: University of Chicago Press.

———. 1978. "Family History and the Life Course." Pp. 16–64 in T.K. Hareven, ed., *Transitions: The Family and the Life Course in Historical Perspective.* New York: Academic Press.

Eversley, D.E.C., Peter Laslett, E.A. Wrigley, W.A. Armstrong, and Lynda Ovenall. 1966. *An Introduction to English Historical Demography.* London: Weidenfeld and Nicolson.

Farber, Bernard. 1981. *Conceptions of Kinship.* New York Elsevier.

Febvre, Lucien. 1968. *Le problème d'incroyance au XVIe siècle: la religion de Rebelais.* Paris.

Filmer, Sir Robert. 1949. *Patriarcha and Other Political Works.* Oxford: Basil Blackwell.

Fleury, Michel, and Louis Henry. 1956. *Des Registres paroissiaux à l'histoire de la population. Manuel de dépouillement et d'exploitation de l'état civil ancien.* Paris: INED.

Fortes, Meyer. 1945. *The Dynamics of Clanship Among the Talensi.* Oxford: Oxford University Press.

————. 1949a. *The Web of Kinship Among the Talensi.* Oxford: Oxford University Press.

————. 1949b. "Time and Social Structure: An Ashanti Case Study." Pp. 54–84 in Fortes (1949).

————. 1969. *Kinship and the Social Order. The Legacy of Lewis Henry Morgan.* London: Routledge and Kegan Paul.

————. 1971. "Introduction." Pp. 1–14 in Goody (1971).

Fortes, Meyer, ed. 1949. *Social Structure. Studies Presented to A.R. Radcliffe-Brown.* London: Oxford University Press.

Foster, Brian L. 1984. "Family Structure and the Generation of Thai Social Exchange Networks." Pp. 84–105 in Netting, Wilk, and Arnould, 1984.

Foster, John. 1974. *Class Struggle in the Industrial Revolution; Early Industrial Capitalism in Three English Towns.* London: Wiedenfeld and Nicolson.

Frêche, Georges. 1974. *Toulouse et la région Midi-Pyrénées au Siècle des Lumières vers 1670-1789.* N.p.: Editions Cujas.

Gautier, Étienne, and Louis Henry. 1958. *La population de Crulai, paroisse normande. Étude historique.* Paris: INED.

Geertz, Clifford. 1973. *The Interpretation of Cultures.* New York: Basic Books.

Gerth, H.H., and C. Wright Mills, eds. 1958. *From Max Weber: Essays in Sociology.* New York: Oxford University Press.

Glass, D.V., and D.E.C. Eversley. 1965. *Population in History. Essays in Historical Demography.* Chicago: Aldine Publishing Co.

Goode, William J. 1970. *World Revolution and Family Patterns.* New York: The Free Press.

Goody, Jack. 1972. "The Evolution of the Family." Pp. 103–124 in Laslett and Wall, eds., *Household and Family in Past Time.* Cambridge: Cambridge University Press.

————. 1983. *The Development of the Family and Marriage in Europe.* Cambridge: Cambridge University Press.

Goody, Jack, ed. 1971. *The Developmental Cycle in Domestic Groups.* Cambridge: Cambridge University Press.

Goody, Jack, Joan Thirsk, and E.P. Thompson, eds. 1976. *Family and Inheritance. Rural Society in Western Europe 1200-1800.* Cambridge: Cambridge University Press.

Goubert, Pierre. 1954. "Une richesse historique en cour d'exploitation. Les registres paroissiaux." *Annales ESC* 1954:83–93.

————. 1960. *Beauvais et le Beauvaisis de 1600 à 1730. Contribution à l'histoire sociale de la France du XVIIe siècle.* 2 vols. Paris: S.E.V.P.E.N.

Greven, Philip J., Jr. 1970. *Four Generations: Population, Land, and Family in Colonial Andover, Massachusetts.* Ithaca: Cornell University Press.

Hajnal, J. 1965. "European Marriage Patterns in Perspective." Pp. 101–143 in D.V. Glass and D.E.C. Eversley, eds., *Population In History.* Chicago: Aldine.

————. 1983. "Two Kinds of Pre-Industrial Household Formation System." Pp. 65–104 in Wall, Robin, and Laslett, eds., *Family Forms in Historic Europe.* Cambridge: Cambridge University Press.

Halpern, Joel M., and Richard A. Wagner. 1984. "Time and Social Structure: A Yugoslav Case Study." *Journal of Family History* 9:229–244.

Hammel, E.A. 1972. "The Zadruga as Process." Pp. 335–373 in Laslett and Wall, eds., *Household and Family in Past Time.* Cambridge: Cambridge University Press.

Hareven, Tamara K. 1982. *Family Time and Industrial Time: The Relationship Between the Family and Work in a New England Industrial Community.* Cambridge: Cambridge University Press.

Hareven, Tamara K., ed. 1978. *Transitions. The Family and the Life Course in Historical Perspective.* New York: Academic Press.

Harris, Marvin. 1968. *The Rise of Anthropological Theory. A History of Theories of Culture.* New York: Thomas Y. Crowell Co.

Henrepin, Jacques. 1954. *La Population canadienne au début du XVIIIe siècle. Nuptialité, Fecondité. Mortalité infantile.* Paris: INED.

Henry, Louis. 1953. "Une richesse démographique en fiche. Les registres paroissiaux." *Population* 8:281–290.

————. 1956. *Anciennes Familles Genevoises. Étude démographique: XVIe-XX siècle.* Paris: INED.

Hillaire, Jean. 1956. *Le re^{1}gime des biens entre e^{1}poux dans la re^{1}gion de Montpellier du de^{1}but du XIIIe sie^{2}cle a^2 la fin du XVIe sie^{2}cle.* Montpiellier.

Homans, George Caspar. 1960. *English Villagers of the Thirteenth Century.* New York: Russell and Russell.

Hughes, Diane Owen. 1986. "Representing the

Family: Portraits and Purposes in Early Modern Italy." *The Journal of Interdisciplinary History* 17:7–38.

Imhof, Arthur E. 1976. "Généalogie et démographie historique en Allemagne." *Annales de démographie historique* 1976:77–107.

James. Mervyn. 1974. *Family, Lineage and Civil Society. A Study of Society, Politics, and Mentality in the Durham Region, 1500-1640*. London: Oxford University Press.

Kertzer, David I. 1984. "Anthropology and Family History." *Journal of Family History* 9:201–206.

Keylor, William R. 1975. *Academy and Community. The Foundation of the French Historical Profession*. Cambridge: Harvard University Press.

Labrousse, Ernest. 1955. "Voies nouvelles vers une histoire de la bourgeoisie occidentale aux XVIIIe et XIXe siècles." Pp. 514–530 in *Decimo Congresso internazionale di Scienze Storiche*, Relazioni, IV, Storia moderna.

Laslett, Peter. 1948. "The Gentry of Kent in 1640." *Cambridge Historical Journal* 1948:148–164.

————. 1965a. *The World We Have Lost. England Before the Industrial Age*. New York: Scribners.

————. 1965b. "The History of Population and Social Structure." *International Social Science Journal* 17:582–593.

————. 1972. "Introduction: The History of the Family." Pp. 1–89 in Laslett and Wall, eds., *Household and Family in Past Time*. Cambridge: Cambridge University Press.

————. 1977. *Family Life and Illicit Love in Earlier Generations. Essays in Historical Sociology*. Cambridge: Cambridge University Press.

Laslett, Peter, and John Harrison. 1963. "Clayworth and Cogenhoe." Pp. 157–184 in H.E. Bell and R.L. Ollard, eds, *Historical Essays 1600-1750 Presented to David Ogg*. London: Adam and Charles Black.

Laslett, Peter, and Richard Wall, eds. 1972. *Household and Family in Past Time*. Cambridge: Cambridge University Press.

Le Roy Ladurie, Emanuel. 1976. "Family Structures and Inheritance Customs in Sixteenth-Century France." Pp. 37–70 in J. Goody, J. Thirsk, and E. P. Thompson, eds. *Family and Inheritance. Rural Society in Western Europe 1200-1800*. Cambridge: Cambridge University Press.

Lévi-Strauss, Claude. 1949. *Les Structure élémentaires de la parenté*. Paris.

————. 1960. "The Family." Pp. 261–285 in H.L. Shapiro, ed., *Man, Culture, and Society*.

New York: Oxford University Press.

————. 1963. *Structural Anthropology*. Garden City, NY: Doubleday.

Locke, John. 1960. *Two Treatises on Government*. Cambridge: Cambridge University Press.

Macfarlane, Alan. 1970. *The Family Life of Ralph Josselin, A Seventeenth Century Clergyman. An Essay in Historical Anthropology*. Cambridge: Cambridge University Press.

Mauss, Marcel. 1967. *The Gift. Forms and Functions of Exchange in Archaic Societies*. New York: W.W. Norton and Co.

McCaa, Robert. 1984. "*Calidad, lase*, and Endogamy in Colonial Mexico: The Case of Parral, 1788–1790." *Hispanic American Historical Review* 64:477–502.

McCaa, Robert, and Michael Swann. 1982. "Social Theory and the Log-Linear Approach: The Question of Race and Class in Colonial Spanish America." Discussion Paper No. 76, Department of Geography, Syracuse University.

Mitterauer, Michael. 1981. "Marriage without Co-residence: A Special Type of Historic Family Form in Rural Carinthia." *Journal of Family History* 7:177–181.

Mousnier, Roland. 1969. *Les hiérarchies sociales de 1450 à nos jours*. Paris: Presses universitaires de France.

————. 1970. *La Plume, la faucille, et le marteau. Institutions et Société en France du Moyen Age à la Révolution*. Paris: Presses Universitaires de France.

————. 1974. *Les Institutions de la France sous la monarchie absolue*. Tome I. Paris: Presses Universitaires de France.

————. 1976. *La Stratification sociale à Paris aux XVIIe et XVIIIe siècles. L'échantillon de 1634, 1635, 1636*. Paris: Editions A. Pedone.

Mousnier, Roland, ed. 1964. *Lettres et mémoires adressés au Chancellier Seguier (1633-1649)*. 2 tomes. Paris: Presses Universitaires de France.

————. 1968. *Problèmes de stratification sociale. Actes du Colloque International (1966)*. Paris: Presses Universitaires de France.

Mousnier, R., J.-P. Labatut, and Y. Durand. 1965. *Problèmes de stratification sociale. Deux cahiers de la noblesse pour les États Généraux de 1649-1651*. Paris: Presses Universitaires de France.

Murdock, George Peter. 1949. *Social Structure*. New York: The Free Press.

Netting, Robert McC., Richard R. Wilk, and Eric J. Arnould, eds. 1984. *Households. Comparative and Historical Studies of the Domestic Group*. Berkeley: University of California Press.

Phillpotts, Bertha Surtees. 1913. *Kindred and Clan in the Middle Ages and After: A Study of the Sociology of the Teutonic Races.* Cambridge: Cambridge University Press.

Plakans, Andrejs. 1984. *Kinship in the Past. An Anthropology of European Family Life 1500-1900.* Oxford: Basil Blackwell.

Porschnev, Boris. 1963. *Les Soulevements populaires en France de 1623 à 1648.* Paris: S.E.V.P.E.N.

Robin, Régine. 1970. *La Société française en 1789: Semur-en-Auxois.* Paris: Plon.

Runciman, W.G. 1963. *Social Science and Political Theory.* Cambridge: Cambridge University Press.

Rutman, Darrett B., and Anita H. Rutman. 1984. *A Place in Time: Middlesex, Virginia, 1650-1750.* New York: W.W. Norton.

Segalen, Martine. 1980. *Mari et femme dans la société paysanne.* Paris: Flammarion.

―――. 1985. *Quinze générations de Bas-Bretons. Parenté et société dans la pays bigouden Sud 1720-1980.* Paris: Presses Universitaires de France.

Shapiro, Harry L., ed. 1960. *Man, Culture, and Society.* New York: Oxford University Press.

Smith, Richard M. 1979. "Kin and Neighbors in a Thirteenth-Century Suffolk Community." *Journal of Family History* 4:219–256.

―――. 1984. "Some Issues Concerning Families and their Property in Rural England 1250-1800." Pp. 1–86 in R.M. Smith, ed., *Land, Kinship and Life-cycle.* Cambridge: Cambridge University Press.

Smith, Richard M., ed. 1984. *Land, Kinship and Life-cycle.* Cambridge: Cambridge University Press.

Stone, Lawrence. 1966. "Social Mobility in England, 1500–1700." *Past and Present* 33:16–55.

―――. 1977. *The Family, Sex and Marriage in England 1500-1800.* New York: Harper and Row.

Tilly, Charles. 1964. *The Vendée. A Sociological Analysis of the Counterrevolution of 1793.* Cambridge: Harvard University Press.

Tilly, Louise A. 1979. "The Family Wage Economy of a French Textile City: Roubaix, 1872–1906." *Journal of Family History* 4:381–394.

Tilly, Louise A., and Joan W. Scott. 1978. *Women, Work, and Family.* New York: Holt, Rinehart and Winston.

Wall, Richard, Jean Robin, and Peter Laslett, eds. 1983. *Family Forms in Historic Europe.* Cambridge: Cambridge University Press.

Wheaton, Robert. 1973. "Bordeaux before the Fronde." Ph.D.. dissertation, Harvard University, Cambridge.

―――. 1980. "Affinity and Descent in Seventeenth-Century Bordeaux" Pp. 111–134 in Wheaton and Hareven, eds., *Family and Sexuality in French History.* Philadelphia: University of Pennsylvania Press.

―――. 1985. "The Application of Network Theory to the Analysis of the Social Structure of Bordeaux in the Seventeenth Century." Paper delivered at the Annual Meeting of the American Historical Association.

Wheaton, Robert, and Tamara K. Hareven, eds. 1980. *Family and Sexuality in French History.* Philadelphia: University of Pennsylvania Press.

Wrigley, E.A. 1966. "Family Limitation in Pre-Industrial England." *Economic History Review* 19:82–109.

―――. 1968. "Mortality in Pre-Industrial England: The Example of Colyton, Devon, over Three Centuries." *Daedalus* 97:546–580.

Yans-McLaughlin, Virginia. 1982. *Family and Community. Italian Immigrants in Buffalo 1800-1930.* Urbana: University of Illinois Press.

Yver, Jean. 1966. *Egalité entre héritiers et exclusion des enfants dotés. Essai de géographie coutumière.* Paris: Editions Sirey.

WOMEN'S HISTORY AND FAMILY HISTORY: FRUITFUL COLLABORATION OR MISSED CONNECTION?

Louise A. Tilly

ABSTRACT: *Although the intellectual projects of women's history and family history have been diverse, there have been some fruitful interrelationships as well as continuing disagreements about conceptualization and method. A systematic examination was carried out of the content of articles published in the period 1976-1985 in the* Journal of Family History, *in three self-defined feminist or women's studies journals, and in four general historical journals. Definitions of the two fields were derived from this exercise. These show that women's history, unlike family history, is movement history; it is closer to more central historical fields in the kinds of questions it asks and in method. Because of its role in placing women as a group into a context of family relationships, family history has an important contribution to make to women's history. To the extent that diversity among women, institutions and informal politics become more central to women's history, it will come closer to family history.*

The relationship of women's history and family history has been problematic since their contemporaneous emergence as newly-defined, energetic fields of the early 1970s. In her introduction to a set of articles from the Second Berkshire Conference on Women's History (held at Radcliffe, October, 1974), for example, Gerda Lerner wrote, "historians working on family ask a great many questions pertaining to women, but family history is not in itself women's history" (Lerner,

1975: 8). In the same journal issue, Ellen DuBois was emphatically negative in opening her essay: "The major theoretical contribution of contemporary feminism

Louise A. Tilly is Professor of History and Sociology in the Graduate Faculty of the New School for Social Research, New York. She is completing a book on workers and the state in nineteenth-century Milan and preparing a new edition of Women, Work and Family *with her co-author, Joan W. Scott.*

has been the identification of the family as a central institution of women's oppression" (DuBois, 1975: 63). She went on to argue that the chief value of the nineteenth-century suffrage movement was that it "by-passed women's oppression within the family, or private sphere, and demanded instead her admission to citizenship, and through it, admission to the public arena. By focusing on the public sphere, and particularly on citizenship, suffragists demanded for women a kind of power and a connection with the social order not based on the institution of the family and their subordination within it" (DuBois, 1975: 63).

Observers could well assume from these remarks that the "twain"—family history and women's history—could never meet. Although the paths of these two fields of history have indeed often been separate, there have been some fruitful interrelationships as well as continuing disagreements about conceptualization and method. The present study argues that family history and women's history differ in three basic ways: (1) women's history, unlike family history, is movement history; (2) women's history is closer to more central historical fields in the kinds of questions it asks; and (3) it is also closer methodologically. The study examines the history of relations between the fields and concludes by asking what the future holds: greater integration or continuing autonomy of both women's history and family history?

The method followed here involves interrogation of the documents produced in these two fields. New areas in a discipline tend to develop first, and more rapidly, through the publication of articles rather than books, and women's history and family history are no exception to this rule. The sources for this study, consequently, are all the articles published since its inception to the present in the *Journal*

of Family History (first published in autumn, 1976), and for the same period in two sets of other journals: (1) self-defined feminist or women's studies journals—*Feminist Studies* (first published in 1972; although not specializing in women's history, this journal has published the largest number of articles in the field of any of the journals I examined, including selected papers from the several Berkshire Conferences of Women's History);[1] *History Workshop* (first published in 1976, this journal declared its feminist outlook in its first issue, and changed its subtitle with Issue 13, 1982, from *Journal of Socialist Historians* to *Journal of Socialist and Feminist Historians*);[2] and *Signs: Journal of Women in Culture and Society* (first published 1975); and (2) four general historical journals—the *American Historical Review*, *Journal of American History*, *Journal of Interdisciplinary History*, and *Journal of Social History*.

We first examine the contributions to the *Journal of Family History*, deriving from this a definition of family history practice and then comparing the family history content of both general and feminist journals to that in the specialized one. Following this examination, the article then discusses the theoretical contribution of family history to women's history, examines the content of women's history articles in the feminist journals, and constructs a definition of women's history. As a conclusion, the article discusses the trends in the subject matter and methodology of family history and women's history that suggest little possibility of any merger but a continued—perhaps greater than in the past—opportunity for fruitful interrelationships.

Neither women's history nor family history is a monolithic, clearly bounded field of study. Both of these histories have their own history, even though they are both recent arrivals to the discipline. Emphases have changed, and new foci have emerged. Both fields have been very dynamic; their practitioners have stretched and probed the fields' boundaries, sought out new sources and methods, posed new concepts and developed explanations. It is impossible to do justice to either field in this essay. Nevertheless, using the strategy of deriving definitions based on the assumption that articles published in the specialized journals qualify, it is clear that both fields have central problems and methods that make them distinctive.

The "Statement of Purpose" in the first (Autumn, 1976) issue of The *Journal of Family History* declared:

> We define "family" broadly to encompass the study of the internal structure and processes of family and kinship, as well as their interaction with the larger society and with community, economic, legal, religious and educational institutions (*Journal of Family History*, 1:3).

In his 1980 overview of family history, Michael Anderson (1980) addressed the topic through a taxonomy of "approaches": demographic, household economics, and sentiments or attitudes. Following Tilly and Cohen (1982), and adding a fourth approach, the political/institutional, which emphasizes connections between family and other processes and institutions, Table I classifies 159 articles on family history that appeared in the *Journal of Family History* from its first issue through 1985 and compares them to articles in the other journals.[3]

Table 1
Family History Articles Classified by Journal and Approach
1976 - 1985

Name of Journal		Demography, Kinship	Household Economics	Sentiments, Attitudes	Politics/ Institutions	Other	Total
Journal of Family	N	70	26	30	1	32	159
History	%	44	16	18	.6	20	
Feminist	N	—	—	—	—	2	2
Studies	%						
History	N	—	4	—	—	—	4
Workshop	%						
Signs	N	—	—	—	—	1	1
	%						
American	N	—	2	1	—	—	3
Historical Review	%		67	33			
Journal of	N	2	5	1	—	1	9
American History	%	22	56	11		11	
Journal of	N	20	4	1	1	4	30
Interdisciplinary	%	67	13	3	3	13	
History							
Journal of	N	9	7	5	—	4	25
Social History		36	28	20		16	
Total	N	101	48	38	1	45	233
(Row)	%	43	21	16	.4	19	

Of course, all the articles concerning demographic and household structure, and those about household economic dynamics, deal with women as well as men, at least implicitly. Nevertheless, discussions in which these approaches are adopted tend to address households and demographic *rates* rather than men and women as actors or subjects. Marriage, for example, is discussed as an institution, or as a measurable occurrence within a population, with little reference to sex-specific experience or individual meaning. The modal article in The *Journal of Family History* approaches its questions through some form of collective biography: "the assembly of standardized descriptions of individual units—persons, households, firms, places, events, or something else—into portraits of the entire sets, and into means for studying variation among the individual units" (C. Tilly, 1985: 1). Fifty-four percent of the articles published on family history in its own journal in the last ten years have taken the demographic and household economics approaches; the demographic approach alone accounts for 44 percent of them. The family household is most often the unit of analysis in the household economics approach, and the individuals or households in the demographic approach. In both cases, however, the method is to aggregate units and examine distributions of events or behaviors in the population and patterns of variation in time and space, and among groups. Discussions of sentiments or attitudes were about equally common in the diverse "other" category, and there was only one article that discussed family relationships with institutions.

The four approaches entail characteristic clusters of questions or problems. The demographic approach, for example, asks questions about temporal changes in demographic rates or processes and how these vary among groups or across space.

Life-course analysis puts these outcomes into historic, life-cycle and cohort context. The household economics approach asks about household decision-making strategies and who gains or loses from them. Family historians focusing on sentiments and attitudes try to uncover information about what people believed or how they subjectively experienced family life or population processes.

To what extent do the nonspecialized journals publish family history of a similar sort? Seventy-five percent of the family history articles found in this review of periodical literature appeared in the *Journal of Family History*. The other twenty-five percent were distributed very unevenly in the non-specialized journals involved, whether general or feminist.

The *Journal of Social History* and *Journal of Interdisciplinary History* were much more likely to publish articles on family history than were the more conventional historical journals. This tendency was constant over the entire period, and there were no temporal trends in the numbers of articles published annually by nonspecialized journals. The distribution of articles by approach in the two social history journals resembled that in the *Journal of Family History*: in both of them, demographic and household economics approaches prevailed by a substantial majority. The *American Historical Review* and the *Journal of American History*, however, included no articles of these types. The presence of the *Journal of Family History*, then, seems to have encouraged or at least not discouraged the publication of family history articles in other journals, but these journals are not equally interested in all types of family history. A division of labor has developed in which social history journals continue to publish family history articles similar in method and content to those in the specialized journal, while the more conventional journals neglect the topic.

With respect to theory, there are many areas in which family history in its various approaches contributes to women's history. Demographic family history, for example, describes and analyzes the demographic underpinning for studying women's lives. How many women lived, of what age, where, in what kind of residential arrangement, of what marital status? Understanding the structure of the female population, its characteristic patterns, and how it changes with time, is an essential starting place for women's history. Through demographics, it is possible to discover variation along class or ethnic lines, life cycle or life course, and geographic location, and how these matters changed historically.

The workings of the family as a unit in which various economic and social processes have been embodied is the central problem of the household economics type of family history. Here are found such matters as reproduction and child rearing, the distribution of resources among individual family members, and others in which decision-making processes are central. The family household as residential unit and the place where economic decisions—which may affect its individual members very differently—are made, is the critical concept here. Household analysis based on census or census-type listings or family reconstitution makes it possible to observe structural relationships and patterns of behavior among ordinary women whose lives are not well-documented by more individual-level or literary sources. Family strategies about socialization and education, who shall work outside the home and within, when children may or must leave home or marry are implicit principles which family historians derive from observing actual patterns of behavior in family households,

"as if" the patterns expressed rules. The household economics type of family history is a tool for comparing women and men—wives and husbands, brothers and sisters, parents and children, or non-kin—in family households as they relate to each other and to institutions such as labor markets or schools; and for evaluating their relationships, whether oppressive, collaborative or contentious.

Ideas, norms, and systems of representation of family are surveyed and analyzed in the sentiments or attitudes approach to family history. Here behavior is less salient than in the other approaches, and sources are likely to include the statements of observers outside families as well as family members' writings or recorded speech. Here, as in the other approaches, *comparison* is the key, most often of concepts concerning gender—social constructions of relationships between the sexes.

Nevertheless, in the feminist journals, family history in the manners just described above is almost completely eschewed. The only exception is Chaytor's (1980) attack on practitioners of the household economics approach. There she briskly criticizes family history for having neglected the social and economic segregation of the sexes, the subordination of women to men, and the content of social relations. She castigates demographic family historians for detaching kinship from family/household relations and for writing about families as though the interests of the sexes and generations were identical and their interaction harmonious. Her own study, a demographic one, demonstrates considerable fluidity in household structure and family-kin relations. Harris's (1982) comment on Chaytor's article both supports Chaytor's feminist perspective and upholds the importance of studying variation in household boundaries, and both writers accept the method and problematic of demographic family history. Both call for more sensitivity to sexual inequality and power questions in interpretation; both agree, moreover, that knowledge about family is a necessary, but not sufficient arena for the study of women. Chaytor's piece, and three responses to it (the other two being highly critical of her position), appeared in *History Workshop*. Two critiques of family history appearing in *Feminist Studies* (Breines, Cerullo and Stacey, 1978; Rapp, Ross and Bridenthal, 1979) argue that it is too accepting of modernization theory, Whiggish, tends towards functionalism, "naturalizes" or "normalizes" the family as a unit, and ignores inequalities within the family and class divisions outside. Finally, Hareven (1976) published in *Signs* a defense of the usefulness of the concept of modernization in understanding family historically.

Clearly, family history in its demographic, household economics and sentiments/ attitudes approaches is an uncongenial partner for most women's historians whose work is published in feminist journals. Why? Here we must examine the concept of "feminist," as applied to themselves by these journals.

The authors of a recent study of feminist scholarship are very forthright on this question. They first demonstrate historically that "feminist scholarship was born of a social movement and received into the pre-established structure of academic disciplines" (DuBois et al., 1985: 2). Nevertheless, they conclude that in order to facilitate analysis, they must accept a broad definition of feminism:

The problem with translating a set of political injunctions into a set of scholarly criteria is that the result is a definition of feminism as an ideal type, in comparison to which almost all scholarship falls short, if only because of limitations of subject matter. Eventually we came to understand that there were many feminist perspectives among scholars, none of which we wished to exclude and that at this stage in the growth of the field, even work "just on women," if it tells us something we did not know before, can be seen as feminist, if that term is broadly conceived (DuBois et al., 1985: 8).

They later point out, nevertheless, that the way that some social historians have addressed the family had contradictory implications for women's history. "While their focus on domesticity, children, and sexuality suggested a much greater openness to women's traditional concerns, women themselves were identified with the family in a way that totally ignored their independent existence and hid the conflicts they had in and with the family institution" (DuBois et al., 1985: 21). And they conclude, finally: "At the heart of feminist scholarship in all fields of study is an awareness of the problem of women's oppression and of the ways in which academic inquiry has subtly subsidized it, a sense of the possibilities for liberation, and a commitment to make scholarship work on women's behalf" (DuBois et al., 1985: 197).

Similar ambivalence and eventual political commitment has marked the several declarations of purpose in *Feminist Studies*. The first issues declared in the journal committed to "encouraging analytic responses to feminist issues and analyses that open new areas of feminist research and criticism" (1974); a revised statement (1975) mentions feminism not at all simply "scholarly and other analytic treatments of issues related to the status of women." The present statement is an explicit declaration not only of commitment to "responses to feminist issues . . . feminist issues . . . feminist analysis . . ." but also to a close relationship to a feminist movement and its goals: "We wish not just to interpret women's experiences but to change women's condition. For us, feminist thought represents a transformation of consciousness, social forms, and modes of action" (1979).

History Workshop's first issue (1976) contained a separate editorial on "Feminist History" which noted that "women's history is not an inevitable extension either of social or of socialist history." Sally Alexander and Anna Davin wrote further (1976: 5) that their purpose was "to contribute to the development of feminist history in the broader sense . . . " and to reappraise family history "because this has often been the only place for historical mention of women." In the first issue of *Signs* (1975: VIII), its editors were more sparing in their use of the word feminism: "We want *Signs* to represent the originality and rigor of the new thinking about women, sexuality, sex roles, the social institutions in which the sexes have participated, the culture men and women have inherited, inhabited, and created." Nevertheless, they firmly acknowledge their links to the women's movement: "Nor would the journal have appeared if it were not for intellectual movements congruent with the new scholarship about women, such as studies of the family, and for great social movements, particularly the New Feminism."

Most feminist scholarship, then, by definition and political commitment, wishes to go beyond family to individual women and, especially, women who are autonomous actors or struggling to expand their horizons. The questions and problems of women's history in its feminist form focus on oppression and subordination on the one hand, and agency and autonomy on the other.

Nevertheless, even though the approaches that are common in family history are seldom found in the feminist journals, family history with a different emphasis does appear. Carroll Smith-Rosenberg (1975), in the first article of the

first issue of *Signs*, discussed women's affective and erotic relations in the "female world" (within the family and between families) that went along with the "rigid gender role differentiation" in nineteenth-century families and society. She argues that the absence of men—busy with their careers—from middle-class family life allowed women to build affective relationships and rituals with kin and friends. Ellen DuBois later criticized Smith-Rosenberg for overemphasizing the private sphere and women's culture, and called for a greater focus in women's history on feminism as a political movement. In response, Smith-Rosenberg made more explicit her concern with women's expression of their sexuality in their "sphere," which she differentiated sharply from male constructs of women's sphere. For her it is sexuality, not women's culture, both within and outside family or marriage, that ought to be one of the central concerns of women's history, for it offers a vitally important key to understanding ordinary women's lives. Here she seems to be calling for something similar to Gayle Rubin's notion of a sex/gender system, a set of psycho-social relationships that goes beyond kinship (DuBois, Buhle, Lerner, Kaplan, and Smith-Rosenberg, 1980; Rubin, 1975).

In other discussions of sexuality, Joan Kelly [-Gadol] (1976) also described it and the quality of family relations as important indicators of women's status; Nancy Cott (1978) saw "passionlessness" in the antebellum United States as serviceable to women "in gaining social and familial power." The feminist journals' approach to family, then, is often through sexuality, especially women's ability to express it in autonomous ways. The discussion over whether sexuality or politics should be central in women's history is the scholarly version of the current debate in the women's movement over difference and equality. That debate divides those who argue that equality pure and simple, on all levels but particularly in economics and politics, must continue to be the primary goal of the women's movement and those who believe that the emphasis on equality has prevented a social solution of exclusively female problems such as childbirth and de facto ones like child care. Proponents of equality argue that any emphasis on female difference reopens the door to discrimination and may actually prevent women from being able to benefit from expanding opportunities.

Sexual politics, or struggle within or outside families about inequality of the sexes has also been a common focus in women's history (for examples, see Farragher and Stansel, 1975; Lebsock, 1982; Ross, 1982; Weisberg, 1975). Not all sexual politics works to women's disadvantage; articles classified here include a family household analysis (Jones, 1982) that identifies possible forms of female power and strength within family under certain conditions, and an examination of wives' political action based on "organizing within their own workplace" (Frank, 1985). If one stretches sexual politics to include division of labor in families, it approaches household economics; women's historians most often emphasize inequality of access to resources and power along gender lines in families as suggested by Chaytor (1980) and Harris (1982), Tilly and Scott (1978), Moch (1983), Ryan (1981), Hareven (1982), Lebsock (1984), Hewitt (1984), and Jones (1985).[4] In these studies, household patterns are derived from census analysis, as in demographic family history, but at the same time the family is seen as a support to its members; unequal outcomes for its members based on sex are recognized. Jones (1985), Ryan (1981) and Hewitt (1984) emphasize also the varying relationships of family and women of differing class and race, while

Moch (1983) shows the way family sponsorship of migration can differ greatly for men and women and between places with different economic characteristics. Finally, an argument that family issues can carry women into the public arena has been made by Louise Tilly (1981) and Temma Kaplan (1982) who examine, in quite different ways, the effect of social and household divisions of labor on women's collective action. The emphasis on sexuality as an arena for autonomy, family as an arena for struggle, and family as one of the possible launching platforms for politics all signal feminist approaches, which vary in their attribution of centrality to family and public spheres. All share a tension between seeing women as independent actors and understanding them as victims of forces outside their control.

"Family," then, is not one of the categories in which history is conceptualized in the feminist journals. For most of their authors, family is contingent, relational to women as individuals, in politics, in work, in marriage, as spinsters, or within female networks, friendships, or love affairs. Family appears as an interest that may facilitate women's entry into politics, an institution shaping their relationship to labor markets and housework, the consequence of marriage, the locus of most heterosexual relations and something to be evaded or confronted in sexual politics. In feminist history articles, "family" is distributed across other concerns rather than being an independent category.

What is an appropriate classification for the subject matter of, or approaches to, women's history? Table 2 displays the women's history articles first published in *Feminist Studies*, *History Workshop*, and *Signs* crudely classified under three substantive rubrics that account for more than two-thirds of the articles: politics, work (including housework), and sexuality (including marriage and sexual poli-

Table 2
Women's History Articles Classified by Journal and Subject
1976 - 1985

Name of Journal		Politics	Work (including housework)	Sexuality (including marriage, sexual politics)	Other	Total
Feminist	N	15	7	18	16	56
Studies	%	27	13	32	29	
History	N	6	8	8	2	24
Workshop	%	25	33	33	9	
Signs	N	8	1	9	14	22
	%	25	3	28	44	
Journal of	N	—	9	11	7	27
Family History	%		33	41	26	
American Historical	N	2	1	—	2	5
Review	%	40	20		2	
Journal of	N	6	4	2	4	16
American History	%	38	25	13	25	
Journal of	N	2	6	4		12
Interdisciplinary History	%	17	50	33		
Journal of	N	3	11	9	8	31
Social History	%	10	36	29	26	
Total feminist journals		29	16	35	32	112
Total nonspecialized journals		13	31	26	21	91
Grand Total		42	47	61	63	203

tics). The "other" category includes theoretical, methodological, or bibliographic essays (review articles, however, are excluded), and topics such as education, religion, high culture, and biography. Sexuality is the largest substantive category in all three of the journals, averaging 31 percent across them. In both *Feminist Studies* and *History Workshop*, the sexuality category is larger than "other"; *Signs* has a more eclectic set of history articles, with 44 percent classified as "other", thus outweighing sexuality at 28 percent. *Signs* and *Feminist Studies* have given less space to articles on work than *History Workshop*, a difference perhaps linked to its dual socialist and feminist approach.

There were also fewer articles to be classified as "other" in *History Workshop*.

The classification rules were of necessity subjective and arbitrary. The dividing line between politics and work led to classification of workplace struggle (including housewives' protest against high prices) as "work" rather than "politics." Sexual politics, as long as it was between individuals (as in prostitution) or located in families was classified under "sexuality." To the extent that sexuality was an element in public and collective struggle over resources and the distribution of power in formal or informal politics, it was classified under politics. Articles concerning women's voluntarism (Sklar, 1985) and collective strategies such as network formation in reform movements (Ryan, 1979) or separate female institutions (Freedman, 1979) were classified as politics. The tabular classification can demonstrate the distribution of the articles in exclusive categories, but it is no help in trying to understand overlapping relationships. In the feminist journals alone, it is clear that all three women's history categories contain elements of family history, particularly the economics of household and work, but also marriage and sexuality. What women's history journals leave out almost completely is the demographic type of family history. In this respect, they resemble the conventional historical journals.

Methodological and interpretive differences reinforce the differences in substantive emphasis. Compared to family history, women's history is less likely to draw on formal analysis, whether quantitative or not. Women's historians have written more often about individuals, one event, a singular institution, than about groups of these. They are less likely to compare than family historians and their explanations are more often constructed by example. Consciousness is more central in women's history, partly because of the greater degree of emphasis on individuals, and individual-level evidence, but also because so much of women's history is an effort to understand political and discriminatory outcomes whether in the arena of politics, work, or sexuality. Where family history is an integral part of social history, women's history has no overall commitment in this direction. Its methods and conceptualizations are usually more conventional even though its subject matter is not new.

Overall, Table 2 shows that articles on women's history are more likely to appear in nonspecialized journals than are family history articles. In family history only

32 percent of the articles reviewed appeared in journals other than *Family History*; in women's history the proportion that appeared in general journals was 45 percent. How do the articles in the non-feminist journals compare with those in *Feminist Studies*, *History Workshop* and *Signs*? In terms of quantity, the social history journals—except for the *Journal of Interdisciplinary History*—and the *Journal of American History* published the greater number of women's history articles. *Interdisciplinary History* published fewer and the *American Historical Review* published the least. The *Journal of American History*, with about twice as many articles per issue than the *American Historical Review*, published three times as many articles in women's history. The *Journal of Interdisciplinary History* was much more open to family than to women's history. Indeed, *The Journal of Interdisciplinary History*'s two-issue review of "The New History in the 1980's" included an essay on family history, but none on women's history. Lawrence Stone noted in that issue that "the changing position of women in the family has been intensely studied in recent years in America . . . The central issues are the facts, the causes, and the consequences of change: change in women's power over general family decision-making, over property, and over birth control and child-rearing; and change in women's participation in productive economic activity inside or outside the home, involving change in the concept of the double sphere, the male as the bread winner"(Stone, 1981: 85). Stone thus subsumed women's history to his concept of family history, the feminist anathema! The *Journal of Family History* and the *Journal of Social History* approached the feminist journals in sheer numbers of articles in women's history.

In content, the *Journal of Family History* articles about women were highly unlikely to discuss politics. The *Journal of American History* focused more heavily on politics and work than did the feminist journals or the social history journals. Articles in the latter, in fact, were equally likely to be concerned with sexuality as were those in feminist journals, and to balance this tendency with a strong proportion of articles on work. Twenty-two articles were impossible to classify as *either* women's history or family history: five in the *Journal of Interdisciplinary History*, eleven in the *Journal of Social History*, four in *Feminist Studies*, two in *Signs*. Most of these articles discussed women's work and family, family and women's politics, and a few, demography and sexuality. Table 2 reveals more common ground than Table 1, which reported a resounding absence of articles on family in the feminist journals. By the weak definition of feminist scholarship discussed above, the articles on women's history in the nonspecialized journals, because they provide new information on women, are feminist. They seldom declared any political commitment to feminism as a movement, however, and their perspective was less often explicitly feminist than were the articles the journals so designated.

Has there been any change over time in the journals likely to publish women's history or the content of articles? No publication trends appear in the general or feminist journals. Women's history articles in the *Journal of Family History* have tended to be clustered in special issues (Women, Work and Family, 1979; Widowhood, 1982; Spinsters and Spinsterhood, 1984). Nevertheless, since 1979, that journal has greatly increased its coverage of women's history.

To the extent that women's history has been movement history, it has tended to skirt family history. So far, women's history has been more conventional in method and subject matter (in that it has studied individuals, and unique events, rather than groups and patterns of behavior) than has family history. Although the classification of women's history articles does not show any evolution of subject matter, the impression emerges that social historical approaches seem to be becoming more common among the younger women's historians. Lebsock (1984) and Hewitt (1984) are examples here; they emphasize variation among different groups of women. Such a rapprochement with social historical methods in women's history will bring it closer to family history.

Further, although women's historians are agreed that the field not be subsumed in family history, and indeed conceive their problems in ways that preclude this, they are currently faced with a set of problems that will lead them to acknowledge family as the kind of intermediary among their concerns that family historians believe it to be. What is needed are comparisons among women that take seriously their interests and position in institutions, such as labor markets, schools, churches, and voluntary associations; and how these vary by class, ethnicity, region and so on. Such analysis requires attention to family as a primary group of which all women (and men) are members at some time in their lives. Increased focus on informal, in addition to formal, politics will have the same effect. The continued exploration by women's historians of women's lives in the past needs to move beyond the politics of suffrage to voluntary associations and their politics. It should focus on ordinary women and not heroines; it must examine relationships among women and institutions. To the extent that women's historians accept this challenge they will move closer to family history.

NOTES

1. Because *Feminist Studies* did not publish regularly between 1976 and the present, I included 1974 and 1975 (which together with 1976 comprise four issues) in my sample to make the number of issues more equal. There were no issues in 1977; the journal resumed publication in 1978.

2. *History Workshop* has published only twenty issues, two a year, during its existence.

3. Excluded are 27 articles classified as women's history, as explained more fully below. The inconsistency between this number and the seventeen indexed under the heading "Women and Women's Roles" in the *Journal's* "Cumulative Index to Volumes One to Ten," (1985:No. 4) is due to different classification rules. The index assigns each article to a single major topical category only, with the result that several articles primarily about women appear under other headings.

4. Although no exhaustive survey was done of books, some that are more social historical in method than most women's history have explicitly addressed families as institutions in which women of the past lived at different points in their lives.

REFERENCES

Alexander, Sally, and Anna Davin. 1976. "Feminist History." *History Workshop* 1:4–6.

Anderson, Michael. 1980. *Approaches to the History of the Western Family, 1500-1914.* London MacMillan.

Breines, Wini, Margaret Cerullo, and Judith Stacey. 1978. "Socio-biology, Family Studies and Antifeminist Backlash." *Feminist Studies* 4:43–67.

Chaytor, Miranda. 1980. "Household and Kinship: Ryton in the Late Sixteenth and Early Seventeenth Centuries." *History Workshop* 10:25–60.

Cott, Nancy F. 1978. "Passionlessness: An Interpretation of Victorian Sexual Ideology, 1790–1850." *Signs* 4:219–236.

DuBois, Ellen. 1975. "The Radicalism of the Woman Suffrage Movement: Notes toward the Reconstruction of Nineteenth-Century Feminism." *Feminist Studies* 3:63–71.

DuBois, Ellen, Mari Jo Buhle, Gerda Lerner, Temma Kaplan and Carroll Smith-Rosenberg. 1980. "Politics and Culture in Women's History." *Feminist Studies* 6:28–63.

DuBois, Ellen Carl, Gail Paradise Kelly, Elizabeth Lapovsky Kennedy, Carolyn W. Korsmeyer, Lillian S. Robinson. 1985. *Feminist Scholarship: Kindling in the Groves of Academe.* Urbana: University of Illinois Press.

Faragher, Johnny and Christine Stansell. 1975. "Women and Their Families on the Overland Trail, 1842–1867." *Feminist Studies* 2:150–166.

Frank, Dana. 1985. "Housewives, Socialists and the Politics of Food: The 1917 New York Cost-of-Living Protests." *Feminist Studies* 11:255–286.

Freedman, Estelle. 1979. "Separatism as Strategy: Female Institution Building and American Feminism, 1870–1930." *Feminist Studies* 5:512–529.

Hareven, Tamara. 1976. "Modernization and Family History: Perspectives on Social Change." *Signs* 2:190–206.

————. 1982. *Family Time and Industrial Time: The Relationship between the Family and Work in a New England Industrial Community.* Cambridge and New York: Cambridge University Press.

Harris, Olivia. 1982. "Households and their Boundaries." *History Workshop* 13:143–152.

Hewitt, Nancy A. 1984. *Women's Activism and Social Change: Rochester, N.Y., 1822-1872.* Ithaca, NY: Cornell University Press.

Jones, Jacqueline. 1982. " 'My Mother Was Much of a Woman': Black Women, Work, and the Family Under Slavery." *Feminist Studies* 8:235–270.

————. 1985. *Labor of Love, Labor of Sorrow: Black Women, Work and the Family from Slavery to the Present.* New York: Basic Books.

Kaplan, Temma. 1982. "Female Consciousness and Collective Action: The Case of Barcelona, 1910–1918." *Signs* 7:545–565.

Kelly [-Gadol], Joan. 1976. "The Social Relations of the Sexes: Methodological Implications of Women's History." *Signs* 1:809–824.

Lebsock, Suzanne. 1982. "Free Black Women and the Question of Matriarchy: Petersburg, Virginia, 1784–1820." *Feminist Studies* 8:271–292.

————. 1984. *The Free Women of Petersburg: Status and Culture in a Southern Town, 1784-1860.* New York: Norton.

Lerner, Gerda. 1975. "Placing Women in History: Definitions and Challenges." *Feminist Studies* 3:5–14.

Moch, Leslie Page. 1983. *Paths to the City: Regional Migration in Nineteenth-Century France.* Beverly Hills: Sage Publications.

Rapp, Rayna, Ellen Ross, and Renate Bridenthal. 1979. "Examining Family History." *Feminist Studies* 5:174–200.

Ross, Ellen. 1982. "'Fierce Questions and Taunts': Married Life in Working-Class London, 1870–1914." *Feminist Studies* 8:575–602.

Rubin, Gayle. 1975. "The Traffic in Women: Notes on the 'Political Economy' of Sex." Pp. 157–210 in *Toward an Anthropology of Women*, edited by Rayna R. Reiter. New York: Monthly Review Press.

Ryan, Mary P. 1979. "The Power of Women's Networks: A Case Study of Female Moral Reform in Antebellum America." *Feminist Studies* 5:66–86.

──────. 1981. *Cradle of the Middle Class: The Family in Oneida County, New York, 1780-1865.* New York: Cambridge University Press.

Sklar, Kathryn Kish. 1985. "Hull House in the 1890s: A Community of Women Reformers." *Signs* 10:658–677.

Smith-Rosenberg, Carroll. 1975. "The Female World of Love and Ritual: Relations Between Women in Nineteenth Century America." *Signs* 1:1–30.

Stone, Lawrence. 1981. "Family History in the 1980's: Past Achievements and Future Trends." *Journal of Interdisciplinary History* 12:51–87.

Tilly, Charles. 1985. "Neat Analyses of Untidy Processes." Working Paper No. 5, Center for Studies of Social Change, New School for Social Research.

Tilly, Louise A. 1981. "Paths of Proletarianization: The Sex Division of Labor and Women's Collective Action in Nineteenth Century France." *Signs* 7:400–417.

Tilly, Louise A., and Miriam Cohen. 1982. "Does the Family Have a History? A Review of Theory and Practice in Family History." *Social Science History* 6:131–180.

Tilly, Louise A., and Joan W. Scott. 1978. *Women, Work, and Family*. New York: Holt, Rinehart and Winston.

Weisberg, D. Kelly. 1975. "'Under Great Temptation Here': Women and Divorce in Puritan Massachusetts." *Feminist Studies* 2:183–194.

Family History
and Social Change

FAMILY HISTORY, SOCIAL HISTORY, AND SOCIAL CHANGE

Charles Tilly

ABSTRACT: *The renewal of social history in the 1960s and thereafter challenged the standard historical emphasis on explanation by motive, validation by motive-revealing texts, and explication by narrative. Social historians divided, however, in their relative emphasis on reconstitution of lives as people lived them and on the establishment of connections between ordinary people's behavior and large social processes such as industrialization. The standard method of social history—collective biography—aids the study of connections more than it aids reconstitution, although its uncritical use often suggests false connections, and many borrowings from the social sciences lead to erroneous analogies. Family history illustrates these points as an exemplar for the study of large-scale social change, as a direct contribution to that study, and as a challenge to its improvement. Among the challenges faced by family history and by social history as a whole are (a) the shift of analyses from calendar time sequences, (b) the identification of coherent social units, (c) the specification of regularities in the behavior of those units. The article presents several examples of each point.*

DISCIPLINES

Where does family history fit into the various missions of history as a whole? What contributions does it make to our understanding of large-scale social change? As an interested outsider, let me speculate on these questions without taking the responsibility—or the blame!—for a comprehensive survey of the field. My speculations will lead through general reflections on history as a discipline to the placement of social history within history as a whole and then to a discussion of

Charles Tilly teaches sociology and history, and directs the Center for Studies of Social Change, at the New School for Social Research. His most recent books are Big Structures, Large Processes, Huge Comparisons *(1985),* The Contentious French *(1986) and* La France conteste *(1986).*

family history as an important special form of social history, and the identification of actual and potential contributions of family history to the analysis of large-scale social change.

Any intellectual discipline worth mentioning unites four elements: (1) a set of self-identified practitioners, (2) a series of questions the practitioners single out as important and answerable, (3) a body of evidence they certify as relevant to answering the questions, and (4) an ensemble of legitimated practices that presumably extract answers from the evidence. As practiced in western countries today, history stands out from most other disciplines by virtue of the time-place subdivision of its practitioners; the vagueness of its distinction between professionals and amateurs; the anchoring of most of its dominant questions in national politics; a heavy reliance on documentary evidence; and an emphasis on practices that involve the identification of crucial actors, the imputation of attitudes and motives to those actors, the validation of those imputations by means of texts, and the presentation of the outcome as narrative.

Obviously, this characterization applies unequally to different fields of history. At the edge of ancient history, artifacts start counting more than texts; historians of science organize themselves somewhat less in terms of time-space divisions than do political historians; demographic history includes fewer amateurs than military history; and so on. Seen from outside the discipline, nevertheless, history coheres around an identifiable set of specialized professionals, an established series of pressing questions, a concentration on documentary evidence, and an ensemble of approved practices that lead to the preparation of credible narratives.

Within such a discipline, the sorts of social and economic history that have grown up since World War II occupy a peculiar position. On the one hand, they grew up as auxiliaries to the pursuit of standard big questions such as: what accounts for the rise and fall of ancient empires? To what extent did the growth of large-scale industry mark off a new stage of world history? What caused the great revolutions of our era? On the other hand, their practitioners soon began to identify actors who did not appear in the standard playbill, turned away from the construction of motivated narratives, borrowed extensively from the adjacent social sciences, and started to ask eccentric questions such as: under what conditions have sustained declines in fertility occurred? Have family forms and sentiments changed fundamentally in the era of capitalism? When and how do industrial economies stagnate? These deviations generated plenty of excitement, but made it more difficult to integrate the analyses of social and economic history into attempts to answer the grand old questions.

COMPETING GOALS OF SOCIAL HISTORY

Although social history gathers the miscellanies of many other kinds of history, through all their varieties social historians pursue two main goals. We might call the two objectives *reconstitution* and *connection*. To some degree, the goals compete with each other—at least in the short run. On one side, social historians seek to reconstitute a round of life as people lived it (see, e.g., Lüdtke, 1982, 1985). On the other, they try to connect life on the small scale with large social structures and processes (for a review, see Tilly, 1985). Despite appearances, the distinction has nothing to do with the oppositions particularization-generalization and description-analysis. Reconstitution sometimes generalizes and analyzes, as when Philippe Ariès organizes his knowledge about the iconography of death (Ariès, 1985). Connection sometimes particularizes and describes, as when Myron Gutmann examines local death rates in the Low Countries during the Thirty Years War (Gutmann, 1980).

The distinction between reconstitution and connection comes closer to anthropologists' *emic* and *etic*, which calls attention to the difference between studying speech phonemically, in terms of the standard sounds a native speaker tries to form, and phonetically, in terms of the sounds a trained observer hears; by extension, anthropologists can carry out emic or etic analyses of kinship, of religion, or agriculture, and of most other clumps of social practice (see Davis, 1980; Ortner, 1984). Similarly, social historians sometimes try to recapture the very meanings that past populations saw in their own worlds, but at other times try to apply external categories—modes of production, kinship systems, demographic regimes, and the like—to the experience of living in those same worlds.

Nevertheless, the correspondence between reconstitution and emic analysis, between connection and etic analysis is statistical rather than logical; practitioners of reconstitution are much more likely to search for the categories by means of which the people they study grappled with life, practitioners of connection much more likely to seek externally valid categories for their small-scale observations, but in principle the choices remain independent. Indeed, a secondary but significant stream of demographic history consists of attempts to reconstitute local rounds of life by means of the standardized observations made possible by conventional demography; as in David Levine's or Alan Macfarlane's studies of English villages, reconstitution proceeds mainly by etic means (Levine, 1977, 1984, forthcoming; Macfarlane, 1977).

In actual practice, the relative value and prevalence of reconstitution and connection within social history vary from field to field, problem to problem, and phase to phase of research. In the well-trodden field of European social history, attempts to make connections between small-scale social life and large-scale transformations predominate. In the unmarked zones of African social history, on the other hand, specialists remain properly suspicious of attempts to force local experiences into the frames of world systems, modernization, capitalism, or other purported general structures and processes (see Cohen, 1985; Cooper, 1981, 1983). Similarly, most scholars who construct dense social histories of particular places over substantial periods alternate between reconstitution and connection; Emmanuel Le Roy Ladurie's masterly synthesis of Languedoc's economic and social history sets a model for the sort of dialectic (Le Roy Ladurie, 1966). Thus while the two procedures compete in the short run, they complement each other in the long run.

Over that long run, however, connection must ultimately take priority. If social historians devote themselves chiefly to reconstitution, they will produce many bright fragments of dubious comparability and uncertain relationship. If they concentrate on reconstructing rounds of life as people lived them, they will miss the opportunity to address, criticize, and modify general conceptions of historical development. If they deal with *le vécu* for itself alone, they will misunderstand it and lose their power to explain it (see L. Tilly, 1983). The ultimate contribution of social history to historical understanding as a whole is to connect small-scale social life with great structures and transformations. Or so I believe.

Let me single out European social history, the field I know best, for special attention. Some of postwar history's greatest achievements occurred in European social history: the revision of our ideas concerning population change, the discovery of human faces in revolutionary crowds, the charting of historical variants in family life. Consequently, some of the discipline's sharper controversies have also broken out of the terrain of European social history: whether the typical concerns of European social historians actually blind them to politics, whether classes form in direct response to changes in the organization of production, whether the old extended family is a myth, whether protoindustrialization marked the (or a) standard path to capital-concentrated production, and so on. The controversies have drawn even more attention to the difficulties of integrating the conclusions of European social history into general histories of Europe.

On the whole, modern European social history, as practiced since 1945, has centered on one enterprise: reconstructing ordinary people's experience of large structural changes (for bibliography, see C. Tilly, 1985). In general—but here the choice and the controversy begin—that has meant tracing the impact of capitalism (however defined) and changes in the character of national states on day-to-day behavior. Studies of migration, urbanization, family life, standards of living, social movements, and most other reliables of European social history fit the description. Disputes within the field, by and large, concern (1) the means of detecting ordinary people's experience and describing large structural changes, (2) the actual assessment of that experience, and (3) the identity, character, and causal priority of the relevant structural changes. Social historians contend rather little about whether they ought to be linking big changes and small-scale experiences. They contend instead about how to establish the links.

Much of recent European social history

emits a populist tone. Its writers rail against the history of kings and generals, insist on the intrinsic value of knowing how relatively powerless people lived in the past, claim that synthetic histories commonly misconstrue the character of the masses, and argue for a significant cumulative effect of ordinary people's action on national events such as revolutions and onsets of economic growth.

COLLECTIVE BIOGRAPHY

Populism complements the central method of social history: collective biography. The painstaking accumulation of uniformly described individual events or lives into collective portraits, as in political prosopography, family reconstitution, and analyses of social mobility, takes its justification from the belief that the aggregates so constructed will provide a more telling portrayal of popular experience than the recapitulation of general impressions, observers' commentaries, or convenient examples. It also establishes much of the common ground between social history and sociology, political science, and economics. In those disciplines researchers likewise often build up evidence about aggregates from uniform observations of many individual units.

Collective biography does not exhaust the methods of social historians; many of them use to great effect exemplary individual biographies, glosses on the writings of contemporary observers, inferences from artifacts, and other procedures. Yet social history's heavy reliance on collective biography sets it off from all other branches of history. Within social history, demographic history constitutes an extreme case; almost its entire methodological armamentarium consists of procedures for aggregating individual observations on births, deaths, marriages, and other small events into measures of population characteristics and changes. Other subdivisions of social history complement their collective biographies with distinctly different sorts of evidence; urban historians, for example, commonly couple their analyses of population distribution and change with treatments of economic alterations that rely on a good deal of anecdotal material. Again, many collective biographers play the results of their small-scale studies against serial data on prices, wages, or urban growth for an entire region or country; the series frequently come from administrators' estimates, fiscal records, and other sources that have little or nothing to do with collective biography.

Social historians draw some clear advantages from collective biography. For one thing, the method makes it possible to look simultaneously at the individual and the collective without sacrificing the connection between the two. By means of collective biography, for example, a family historian can place a particular household, with all its individuality, in relation to the distribution of all households in its surroundings. For another, aggregation and disaggregation of the evidence can move in many directions. Households disaggregate into individuals, compound into neighborhoods, cohorts, periods, communities, or social classes, and regroup into sets of kin. Finally, collective biography opens the way to the study of variation: rather than a typical or exemplary household, a distribution of households whose characters may well vary systematically by community, class, period, or age of members. Such works as Wrightson and Levine's collective-biographical study of a single English village over two centuries display the possibility of combining rigor and sensitivity, collective and individual, formulization and interpretation (Wrightson and Levine, 1981).

All of these uses of collective biography

become richer and more rewarding when the researcher can discover and record each unit's peculiar developmental path: rather than age, sex, and occupation for each person, a set of occupational histories; rather than date, form, size, and duration for each strike, distinctive accounts of individual strikes' development. At that point, collective biography becomes life-course analysis. In its weak version, life-course analysis amounts to a technique for arraying evidence about individuals without forcing them into identical categories; it represents a life as a variable sequence within a fixed array of events, events typically referring both to the individual and to the individual's environment. In its strong version, life-course analysis becomes a theory of change in the characteristics and experiences of individual social units. Ordinarily such a theory involves a combination of exigencies, prescriptions, and choices: exigencies that become more or less likely, more or less pressing, at different points in life, prescribed ways of responding to exigencies, choices that entail further exigencies, prescriptions, and choices.

When it comes to using collective biography to link individual experience with large structures and processes, however, we face an interesting difficulty. The records from which an investigator draws evidence on individual experience commonly result from the large structures and processes whose influence the investigator wants to examine: traces of individuals in tax records result from the expansion of a state's fiscal machinery, the recording of births and deaths expands as churches bureaucratize, and so on. As a consequence, uncovering the process in which the state or church intervened becomes a delicate matter, similar in principle to establishing the true number of crimes of various sorts by means of the official record of offenses known to the police.

It is possible, for example, that the records available to use provide a misleading picture of the pace at which different groups adopted permanent family names, simply because the agencies producing our records commonly assigned family names to those people who had to deal with them. Laurel Cornell's analysis of kinship structure in Japan raises the intriguing possibility that the kinship "rules" reported by nineteenth-century jurists and statesmen who provide much of the evidence for the period before 1900 were artifacts of occasional encounters between households and legal authorities rather than operating principles in daily life, much as contemporary American welfare laws encourage elderly or chronically ill couples to divorce or sue each other when one spouse needs publicly supported medical care and they both want the other to retain some of their common property.

Again, comparisons over long periods of time or between different countries run the risk of confounding variable features of the recording process with "true" differences in the behavior an analyst wants to deduce from the records laid down by the recording process. If recorded infanticide increases, how much of the rise results from expanded reporting, and how much from more frequent murders of babies? If Sweden has a higher suicide rate than Great Britain, how much of the difference results from a greater readiness of British officials to label self-destruction as accidental? Perennial problems, more highly visible in collective biography than in many other kinds of historical research.

The answer to such difficulties does not consist of turning away from collective biography. It lies in three old reliables: (1) entering any analysis of biographies, as much as possible, with clear, falsifiable, and modifiable theories of the process in question; (2) complementing those theories with equally clear, falsifiable, and modifiable hypotheses concerning the processes that produced the available evidence; (3) testing the theories, wherever practicable, on more than one source and by more than one method, observing closely how the results of the crucial tests differ as a function of the sources and methods in question.

Within the area occupied by collective biography, social historians are the most likely of all historians to adopt formal methods of measurement and analysis: fragmentation of individual characteristics into variables, quantification of those variables, formal modeling of the processes and structures under study, rigorous comparison of observations with the models, frequently by means of statistical procedures. Where observations are uniform, instances numerous, models complex but explicit, and characteristics of the instances meaningfully quantifiable, formal methods permit social historians to wring more reliable information from their evidence than they could possibly manage by informal means.

There, to be sure, acute controversy begins. Despite the readily available example of survey research, historians have not been nearly as assiduous and successful at measuring attitudes, orientations, and mentalities as they have at quantifying births, deaths, and marriages. Measurement of mentalities remains ill-developed for three main reasons: (1) the sources historians most often have at their disposal rarely provide much direct information on attitudes, orientations, and mentalities; (2) historians' conceptions of such phenomena are typically imprecise; (3) the kinds of historians that emphasize attitudes, orientations, and mentalities commonly doubt that human affairs lend themselves to precise measurement, and therefore invest little or no effort in that presumably futile endeavor. A major object of study and a major mode of explanation in history therefore remain relatively inaccessible for formalization.

Here is another source of controversy: Historians tend to ground their pressing questions in times and places, social scientists to root them in structures and processes; to the extent that social historians adopt social–scientific approaches to their material, they separate themselves from the questions that animate other historical work. What questions should take priority?

Finally, the models and arguments that social historians borrow from adjacent social sciences often fit their historical applications badly—assuming the independence of observations, being indifferent to the order in which events occur, calling for the recurrence of identical sequences, and so on. For all these reasons, and more, historians continue to battle over the value of formal methods in making sense of the past.

FAMILY HISTORY AS AN EXEMPLAR AND A CONTRIBUTION

My serman applies to family history just as much as to other branches of social history (for bibliography and synthesis, see Tilly and Cohen, 1982). It echoes Peter Laslett's own homily on family history in calling for analytically informed histories that move forward rather than backward in time. But it demurs from Laslett's argument that family structure changes in its own autonomous time, and from Laslett's assertion that such specialties as demographic history have no validity independent of family history. The synthetic task at hand, in my view, is to relate the concrete experiences of living in families at various points in space and time to large social structures and processes.

What structures and processes? In the case of Europe, the ebb and flow of em-

pires, the appearance and transformation of Christian churches, the encounter with Islam, the great migrations and conquests, the movement of the cultural and commercial center of gravity from the Mediterranean toward the Atlantic, the rise of national states, and the development of capitalist economies all belong among the changes to which we must relate the history of families. David Herlihy's discussion of the Catholic Church and medieval family history illustrates the value of connecting the intimate experiences of family life—choice of spouses, sexual activity, child care, and so on—to very large structures and processes. In other eras and parts of the world, obviously, we must attend to quite different structures and processes: vast movements of population and depopulation, competing empires, struggling religions.

Properly pursued, family history based on collective biography can greatly strengthen our analyses of large-scale social change. It can serve as an *exemplar* for the study of large-scale social change, as a direct *contribution* to that study, and as a *challenge* to its improvement.

As an *exemplar*, family history faces a number of problems that appear quite generally in the analysis of social change. One is the tracing of direct and indirect effects of large structural alterations, such as the growth of a powerful, bureaucratized church. David Herlihy concentrates on direct effects, features of medieval family life promoted deliberately by churchmen. André Burguière, on the other hand, stresses indirect effects—for example, the way in which the Catholic Church's effort to impose religious control on marriage helped undermine competing local institutions and thereby gave young people more scope for themselves to decide how and when they would pair. The two sorts of changes together constitute the impact of the Church's expansion on family life.

David Gaunt takes up another general problem: the relationship between milieu and social organization. Instead of seeing the family as a stereotyped cultural production, he sees the actual arrangements of coresidence, marriage, and inheritance as variable responses to human problems. The famous stem family, in his analysis, begins to look like an adaptation to by-employment for children where land is scarce, as well as a device for avoiding governmental pressure to divide farmland equally among sons. The Karelian large family (*suurperhe*), on the other hand, appears to thrive on swidden agriculture in regions of abundant land, especially when household members have opportunities for gainful activity outside of cultivation. (David Kertzer and Caroline Brettell apply similar arguments to the variety of households in Mediterranean Europe, and Andrejs Plakans takes a parallel path in dealing with Eastern Europe.) These and other variations that Gaunt examines make a strong case for the plasticity of family forms within the "same" national culture. More precisely, people following similar rules and strategies in different environments create strikingly different varieties of households and kin groups.

Peter Laslett provides a third instance of family history as an exemplar for the study of social change in general. He insists on our verifying, rather than assuming, the uniqueness of the present. Just as many students of war assert, but do not verify, that nuclear weapons have made all analogies with previous forms of war irrelevant, many observers of the contemporary family see it as transformed beyond recognition, or even on its way to elimination. Laslett agrees that we have entered a new age of family life, but demands that we specify its character by means of sustained, meticulous comparison with the past. More generally, Laslett brings out the

value of family history as a way of deciding exactly what features of our present plight represent genuine changes, and therefore require explanation.

In all these regards, and more, family history serves as an *exemplar* by providing models of analysis that ought to be emulated in dealing with a wide range of large-scale processes. Family history also makes a direct *contribution* to the study of particular social changes. Its contribution takes two main forms: directly establishing the overall rhythms of change, and controlling the explanations people offer for massive social changes.

In the first regard, the best examples come from European demographic history. There, the timing of the onset of long-term fertility decline—end of the eighteenth century for France, late in the nineteenth century for many other regions of Europe—immediately identifies a massive fact and an explanatory problem. Likewise, the clear location of rising natural increase in the eighteenth century (not to mention its association with increasing fertility, driven by increasing nuptiality, in England) provides students of proletarianization and industrialization with a benchmark for their analyses.

Family history likewise sets limits on the plausibility of the explanations we may offer for massive social changes. Maris Vinovskis points out that American research has made dubious the ideas that (1) American families moved from the large, extended, patriarchial type transplanted from England to small, nuclear, and relatively egalitarian households; and 2) that as the transition occurred, schools increasingly took over the socialization of children from families. The results of the research challenge any linear explanation—secularization, modernization, or social disintegration of American changes in family and schooling. They add plausibility to explanations stressing the partly contradictory interests of parents in their children's labor and in their children's futures.

FAMILY HISTORY AS A CHALLENGE

Finally, family history faces a series of *challenges* that likewise challenge the study of social change in general. If family historians can meet these challenges, they will again provide models for the analysis of other sorts of social change. Let me mention only three of them:

a. the shift of analyses from calendar time to sequences;
b. the identification of coherent social units;
c. the specifications of regularities in the behavior of those units.

All students of social change face these problems. Family historians have dealt with them in interesting ways, and have thereby challenged their colleagues to do likewise.

From Calendar Time to Sequences

Students of social change have customarily used the calendar and the clock as their standards for the passage of time. That means they have used solar time as the measure of social time. "The use of calendar time to describe social processes," remarks Pierre Allan, "forces the researcher to use the duration units and thus the rhythms prescribed by physical clocks instead of focusing on the interrelationships of social processes in time" (Allan, 1985:2). Clock-watching, Allan points out, obscures regular sequences and covariations in social processes as it encourages observers to treat them as anomalies. Now, clock and calendar times do sometimes provide the bases of social sequences; employers set the workday and the vacation schedule by clocks and calendars, and festivals linked to the solar cycle often mark pauses and transitions in social life. But many social units and processes run on other times; social movements rise and fall on rhythms that correlate with national politics but not with solar calendars, proletarianization involves recurrent sequences that do not appear as temporal regularities, and so on (see Smith, 1984).

As it happens, students of family history encountered the problem of nonclock time early in their specialty's formation, and started to develop methods for dealing with it. The idea of a family cycle, with a mean or median age at which different crucial events occur, represented a partial break with clock and calendar. When Gerard Bouchard and Isabelle de Pourbaix present their "calendar of demographic events in the history of the family" for Saguenay, they adopt the parents' marriage as a reference point, and provide distributions of time elapsed to birth of first child, first death of a child, and other milestones along a family's path. That procedure moves farther away from strict dependence on the clock; if the axis changed from years elapsed since parents' marriage to, say, cumulative number of conceptions to the couple since marriage, the break would be more complete. The notion of life course, for all its current uncertainty, moves somewhat closer to placing individual and household on their own systems of time.

To the extent that family-cycle and life-course analyses still use chronological age of an individual or a household as their metrics, they still rely on the calendar. The next great step: tear up the solar calendar and adopt either an individual clock, a household clock, or a clock based on some other social structure or process. Instead of using calendar age as an indicator of "aging," for example, family historians dealing with married women might try adopting number of progeny (children, grandchildren, and beyond) ever born as their base. Students of mining families might relate household composition to the cycle of a coalfield's opening and exhaustion. And sequencing itself—the order of which crucial events occur in the experience of an individual, a household, or a kin group—might become a direct object of study (see Abbott, 1983, 1984; Abbott and Forrest, 1986). Family historians could thereby confront questions of biological causation more effectively, without falling prey to biological determinism. Because historians of the family have already become aware of the inconvenience of clock and calendar, they have an opportunity to open a new path for many analyses of social change outside of their own area.

Coherent Social Units

Similarly, family historians have learned to be suspicious of conventional definitions for the social units they study: families, households, housefuls, kin groups, and others. Governments and churches frequently enumerate as households sets of people who do not live together, and exclude from those households people who live in the same dwellings. No one knows what "a family"—much less "the family"—is.

On the whole, family historians seem to be heading for two very different solutions: (1) an emic approach in which the analyst identifies the categories and relationships within which a given population organizes sexual relations, cohabitation, child care, and inheritance, then reconstructs the ways those categories and relationships actually operated; (2) an etic approach in which the analyst identifies kinship as those personal networks defined by sexual relations, child care and inheritance, and treats "family" as a precipitate of the interaction between kinship

and coresidence. Among our authors, Martine Segalen leans toward the first solution, Andrejs Plakans toward the second. The viability of the first approach depends on the access of analysts to evidence concerning the substance of everyday social interaction. The viability of the second depends, among other things, on the objectivity of the social networks in question; to the extent that kinship consists not of complete social networks but of procedures for making claims on other people, the object of study will shift with the ebb and flow of interpersonal politics.

Neither approach is obviously correct or superior. Both are very difficult. But success in pinning down the coherent social units in their own domain will make family historians models for students of many other kinds of social change.

Regularities

Conventionally, family historians have identified a population and then attempted to describe the distinctive regularities in its family system: e.g., seventeenth-century English people commonly married late or not at all, while seventeenth-century Russians usually married young and rarely remained unmarried. On so broad a scale, the comparison makes sense and provides important information. But increasing uncertainty about the coherent social units involved has engendered doubt about the status of any generalization a historian may offer concerning a "family system." And the careful application of collective biography has brought about awareness that such labels as "early marriage" and "late marriage" refer to distributions of events rather than to characteristics that can somehow attribute to each individual family in a system, or even to a modal family. Similarly, the terms "stem family" and "polygyny" turn out not to characterize entire family systems, but rather to describe arrangements of co-residence and marriage that appear with greater or lesser frequency in different populations and vary with the household cycle.

Granting the existence of some basic social units, what is the nature of any regularities we can identify in their operation? Do they reside in cultural traits? Recurrent social relationships? Rules that individuals follow in social interaction? Organizational principles? Shared models? To what extent does kinship resemble generative grammar, in which almost everyone uses highly restrictive rules with considerable success, very few people have any self-conscious knowledge of the rules, and no one can map all the possible applications of the rules? On the whole, these questions divide historians of the family into two camps: (1) those who assume that each coherent group of people creates a model of social structures, including family structures, which it then attempts to implement, and (2) those who assume that people adopt operating rules for social relations which precipitate the arrangements we think of as social structure, including family structure.

My own sympathies lie with the second group rather than the first. But the contest remains open. The challenge is to make these contrasting views explicit and empirically problematic, then to do the theorizing and research required to resolve their differences. If family historians can do so, they will again set a model for all students of social change.

ACKNOWLEDGMENT

I am grateful to Louise Tilly, who gave an earlier draft of this paper the benefit of her vastly greater knowledge—theoretical and practical—of family history.

REFERENCES

Abbott, Andrew. 1983. "Sequences of Social Events: Concepts and Methods for the Analysis of Order in Social Processes." *Historical Methods* 16: 129–147.

_____. 1984. "Event Sequence and Event Duration: Colligation and Measurement." *Historical Methods* 17: 192–205.

Abbott, Andrew, and John Forrest. 1986. "Optimal Matching Methods for Historical Sequences." *Journal of Interdisciplinary History* 16: 471–494.

Allan, Pierre. 1985. "Towards Building Social Clocks." Unpublished paper, University of Geneva.

Ariès, Philippe. 1985. *Images of Man and Death*. Cambridge, MA: Harvard University Press.

Cohen, David William. 1985. "Doing Social History from Pim's Doorway." Pp. 191–235 in *Reliving the Past. The Worlds of Social History*, edited by Olivier Zunz. Chapel Hill: University of North Carolina Press.

Cooper, Frederick. 1981. "Africa and the World Economy." *African Studies Review* 24: 1–86.

Cooper, Frederick, ed. 1983. *Struggle for the City*. Beverly Hills: Sage.

Davis, John. 1980. "Social Anthropology and the Consumption of History." *Theory and Society* 9: 519–537.

Gutmann, Myron. 1980. *War and Rural Life in the Early Modern Low Countries*. Princeton: Princeton University Press.

Leasure, J. William. 1983. "United States Demographic and Family History: A Review Essay." *Historical Methods* 16: 163–168.

Le Roy Ladurie, Emmanuel. 1966. *Les Paysans de Languedoc*. Paris: SEVPEN. 2 vols.

Levine, David. 1977. *Family Formation in an Age of Nascent Capitalism*. New York: Academic Press.

Levine, David, ed. 1984. *Proletarianization and Family Life*. New York: Academic Press.

_____. Forthcoming. *Reproducing Families*. Cambridge: Cambridge University Press.

Lüdtke, Alf. 1982. "The Historiography of Everyday Life: The Personal and the Political." Pp. 38–54 in *Culture, Ideology and Politics*, edited by Raphael Samuel and Gareth Stedman Jones. London: Routledge & Kegan Paul.

_____. 1985. "Organizational Order or *Eigensinn*? Workers' Privacy and Workers' Politics in Imperial Germany." Pp. 303–333 in *Rites of Power: Symbolism, Ritual, and Politics Since the Middle Ages*, edited by Sean Wilentz. Philadelphia: University of Pennsylvania Press.

Macfarlane, Alan. 1977. *Reconstructing Historical Communities*. Cambridge: Cambridge University Press.

Ortner, Sherry. 1984. "Theory in Anthropology Since the Sixties." *Comparative Studies in Society and History* 26: 126–166.

Smith, Peter H. 1984. "Time as a Historical Construct." *Historical Methods* 17: 182–191.

Tilly, Charles. 1985. "Retrieving European Lives." Pp. 11–51 in *Reliving the Past. The Worlds of Social History*, edited by Olivier Zunz. Chapel Hill: University of North Carolina Press.

Tilly, Louise A. 1983. "People's History and Social Science History." *Social Science History* 7: 457–474.

—————. "Family, Gender, and Occupation in Industrial France, Past and Present." Pp. 193–212 in *Gender and the Life Course*, edited by Alice S. Rossi. Chicago: Aldine.

Tilly, Louise A., and Miriam Cohen. 1982. "Does the Family Have a History? A Review of Theory and Practice in Family History." *Social Science History* 6: 131–180.

Wrightson, Keith, and David Levine. 1981. *Poverty and Piety in an English Village: Terling, 1525-1700*. New York: Academic Press.

Author Index

A

Abbot, A., 328, 329; with Forrest, 328, 329

Abelson, A., 115

Abrams, P., 276, 282

Achenbaum, A., 281, 282

Alexander, S., with Davin, 309, 314

Allan, P., 327, 329

Allen, D.G., 21, 22

Amorim, M., 90, 91, 103, 115

Anderson, M., 183, 197, 280, 283, 290, 298, 305, 314

Androka, R., with Farago, 167, 174; with Balazs-Kovacs, 165, 174

Anelli, A., 90, 91, 93, 103, 115

Angeli, A., 93, 115; with Bellettini, 90, 92, 103, 115

Angus, D.L., 30, 32, 33; with Mirel, 29, 33

Arensberg, C., with Kimball, 97, 103, 115

Ariès, P., 22, 33, 51, 52, 296, 297, 298, 321, 329

Arnould, E.J., 161, 174

Astrom, S-E., 124, 140

Auwers, L., 22, 23, 33

Axtell, J., 22, 23, 33

Aymard, M., with Delille, 89, 103, 115

B

Bachnik, J., 147, 149, 150, 161

Bailyn, B., 19, 20, 21, 24, 32, 33

Balle-Petersen, P., 133, 139

Baltes, P., xiii, xxii

Balugani, A., with Fronzoni, 89, 103, 115

Bane, M.J., with Ellwood, 188, 197

Barbagli, M., 91, 92, 95, 100, 103, 104, 115, 282, 283

Bardet, J-P., 51, 291, 297, 298

Baric, L., 169, 174

Barron, H.S., 77, 83

Bauer, R., 97, 103, 115

Beauchet, L., 122, 139

Beales, R., 24, 33

Beardsley, R-K., with Hall and Ward, 145, 149, 161

Befu, H., 147, 154, 155, 161

Belcher, J., 244, 260

Bell, H., with Ollard, 297

Bell, R., 108, 115

Belletini, A., 90, 103, 105, 115

Belmartino, S., 89, 102, 115

Bennassar, B., 90, 91, 103, 115

Berkner, L., 21, 33, 97, 115, 278, 283, 287, 288, 297, 298; with Mendels, 114, 115

Bernard, R.M., with Vinovskis, 26, 33

Bertaux, D., 241

Binstock, R., with Shanas, 281, 283

Birkeli, E., 122, 140

Bishop, J., 8, 16

Bloch, M., 286, 292, 297, 298

Blum, J., 173, 174

Bohac, R., 166, 174

Boissevain, J., 107, 108, 116

Bonfield, L., with Smith and Wrightson, 282, 283

Bongaarts, J., with Potter, 146, 161

Bonney, F., 15, 16

Bouchard, G., 225, 231, 239, 241, 325; with de Pourbaix, 289, 297, 298; with Pouyez, 230, 231, 242

Boutruche, R., 293, 297, 298

Subject Index

A

Action-groups
  and US fertility decline, 80–83
Affective relations
  in French families, 38–52
  in the Middle Ages, 11–14
Age at marriage
  in Japan, 57–71
  in Quebec, 233–233
Age classes, 190–192
  in rural France, 215
  in Japanese households, 248–253
Aging
  in rural France, 217

B

Birth control
  in rural France, 223

C

Cambridge Group for the History of Population and Social Structure, 275, 277–281
Childhood
  in rural France, 215
Child-woman ratio
  in the United States, 74–77
Charivaris
  in rural France, 41
Church
  rules of family life, 40–41
Collective biography, 322–324
Community control
  in rural France, 214–218, 290–291
Conjugal relations
  in France, 42

D

Divorce
  in the Middle Ages, 4

E

Economic determinants, 80, 193–194, 219, 290
Education
  and family life, 19–32

F

Family composition
  change over time, 270–272
Family cycle
  in Quebec, 227–228
Family history (as a field), 267–270, 272–273
  and collective biography, 325
  and contemporary history, 266–267
  and feminist scholarship, 308–310
  nature of, 263–281
  obligations of practitioners, 264–265
  regularities in, 329
  in scholarly journals, 305 ff
  and social history, 319–329
  and the social sciences, 276–277
  and social structural change, 273–274
  and time, 327–328
  units of analysis in, 328
  and women's history, 303–313
Family reconstitution
  in Quebec, 225–227, 231–232
Family structure, 151–154, 184–186, 270–272
  and the Cambridge Group, 277–281
  in colonial America, 20–21